SCHAUM'S
OUTLINE OF

DATA
STRUCTURES
WITH JAVA

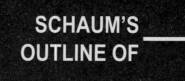

SCHAUM'S
OUTLINE OF

DATA STRUCTURES WITH JAVA

Second Edition

JOHN R. HUBBARD, Ph.D.

Professor of Mathematics and Computer Science
University of Richmond

Schaum's Outline Series

McGRAW-HILL
New York Chicago San Francisco
Lisbon London Madrid Mexico City
Milan New Delhi San Juan
Singapore Sydney Toronto

The McGraw·Hill Companies

JOHN R. HUBBARD is professor of mathematics and computer science at the University of Richmond. He received his Ph.D. from The University of Michigan in 1973 and has been a member of the Richmond faculty since 1983. His primary interests are in database systems and data mining. Dr. Hubbard is the author of several other books, including *Schaum's Outline of Programming with C++*, *Schaum's Outline of Fundamentals of Computing with C++*, *Schaum's Outline of Data Structures with C++*, and *Schaum's Outline of Programming with Java*.

1 2 3 4 5 6 7 8 9 10 11 12 13 14 15 16 17 18 19 20   CUS   CUS   0 9 8 7

ISBN-13: 978-0-07-147698-0

ISBN: 0-07-147698-9

To Anita

PREFACE

Like other Schaum's Outlines, this book is intended to be used primarily for self study. It is suitable as a study guide in a course on data structures using the Java programming language. In American universities, this is typically the second course in the computer science major. The book is also serves well as a reference on data structures and the Java Collections Framework.

The book includes more than 200 detailed examples and over 260 solved problems. The author firmly believes that programming is learned best by practice, following a well-constructed collection of examples with complete explanations. This book is designed to provide that support.

This second edition is a major improvement over the original 2001 edition. Most of the chapters have been completely rewritten. Three entirely new chapters have been added, on object-oriented programming, linked structures, and the Java Collections Framework.

Java 6.0 is used throughout the book, with special attention to these new features of the language:

- The `Scanner` class.
- The `StringBuilder` class.
- Formatted output, including the `printf()` method.
- The enhanced `for` loop (also called the for-each loop).
- Static imports.
- `enum` types.
- Variable length parameter lists.
- Autoboxing.
- Generic classes
- The `Deque`, `ArrayDeque`, `EnumSet`, and `EnumMap` classes, and the `Queue` interface in the Java Collections Framework.

Source code for all the examples, solved problems, and supplementary programming problems may be downloaded from the author's Web site

    http://www.mathcs.richmond.edu/~hubbard/books/

I wish to thank all my friends, colleagues, students, and the McGraw-Hill staff who have helped me with the critical review of this manuscript, including Stephan Chipilov and Sheena Walker. Special thanks to my colleague Anita Huray Hubbard for her advice, encouragement, and supply of creative problems for this book.

JOHN R. HUBBARD
Richmond, Virginia

CONTENTS

SCHAUM'S
OUTLINE OF

DATA STRUCTURES WITH JAVA

Object-Oriented Programming

SOFTWARE DESIGN AND DEVELOPMENT

Successful computer software is produced in a sequence of stages that are typically managed by separate teams of developers. These stages are illustrated in Figure 1.1.

The first stage is a recognition of the problem to be solved. In a corporate setting, this determination could come from market research.

The second stage, which might be omitted as a formal process, is a study of whether the project is feasible. For example, do the development tools exist to produce the software?

In the third stage, a document is typically produced that specifies precisely what the software should do. This requirements document should have enough detail to be used as a standard when the completed software is tested.

In the fourth stage, a thorough analysis is done before any effort or resources are spent designing and implementing the project. This could include a survey of comparable software already available and a cost-benefit analysis of the value of spending the anticipated resources.

Once a decision has been made to proceed, the software design team works from the requirements document to design the software. This includes the specification of all the software components and their interrelationships. It may also require the specification of specialized algorithms that would be implemented in the software.

The implementation consists of programmers coding the design to produce the software.

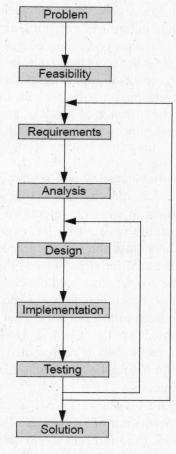

Figure 1.1 Software life cycle

The testing team attempts to ensure that the resulting software satisfies the requirements document. Failure at this point may require a redesign or even some fine-tuning of the requirements. Those eventualities are represented by the two feedback loops shown in Figure 1.1.

1

Testing occurs at several levels. Individual classes and methods have to be tested separately, and then their success at working together must be verified. Finally, the product as a whole is tested against the requirements document.

One final aspect of software development that is not shown in the figure is the maintenance process. After the software has been delivered, its developers remain obliged to maintain it with corrected versions, service packages, and even major revisions. Any major revision itself would follow the same life cycle steps.

OBJECT-ORIENTED DESIGN

One common approach to software design is a *top-down design* strategy that gradually breaks the problem down into smaller parts. This is also called *step-wise refinement*. It focuses on the functional aspects of the problem and the implementation of algorithms. This procedure-oriented design is common in scientific programming.

In contrast, *object-oriented design* focuses on the data components of the software, organizing the design around their representatives. For example, an air traffic control system might be designed in terms of airplanes, airports, pilots, controllers, and other "objects."

The Java programming language is particularly well-suited for implementing object-oriented designs. All executable code in Java is organized into classes that represent objects. For this reason, Java is regarded as an *object-oriented programming language*.

An *object* is a software unit that is produced according to a unique class specification. It is called an *instance* of its class, and the process of creating it is called *instantiating the class*. For example, this code instantiates the `java.util.Date` class:

```
java.util.Date today = new
java.util.Date();
```

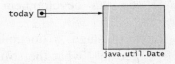

today ▣

java.util.Date

Figure 1.2 A Java object

The variable `today` is a reference to the object, as shown in Figure 1.2. Ignoring the distinction between a reference and the object to which it refers, we would also say `today` is the name of the `java.util.Date` object.

A Java class consists of three kinds of members: *fields*, *methods*, and *constructors*. The fields hold the data for class objects, the methods hold the statements that are executed by the objects, and the constructors hold the code that initializes the objects' fields.

An object-oriented design specifies the classes that will be instantiated in the software. That design can be facilitated and illustrated by the *Unified Modeling Language* (UML). In UML, each class is represented by a rectangle with separate parts for listing the class's name, its fields, and its methods and constructors.

Figure 1.3 shows a UML diagram for a `Person` class with four fields (`name`, `id`, `sex`, and `dob`), a constructor, and three methods (`isAnAdult()`, `setDob()`, and `toString()`). Each of the eight class members is prefaced with a *visibility symbol*:

```
Person
# name: String
# id: int
# sex: char
# dob: java.util.Date

+ Person(String, int, char)
+ isAnAdult(): boolean
+ setDob(java.util.Date)
+ toString(): String
```

Figure 1.3 A UML diagram

```
+ means public
# for protected
- for private
```

(Package visibility has no UML symbol.)

UML diagrams are independent of any implementing programming language. They are used in object-oriented design to specify objects. They should be easy to implement in Java, C++, or any other object-oriented programming language. They provide a kind of pseudo-code for classes. They specify the *state* (i.e., fields) and the *behavior* (i.e., methods) of an object without specifying how that behavior is accomplished. UML diagrams include no executable code.

Specifying what an object can do without specifying how it does it is an abstraction. It allows the design stage to be separated from the implementation stage of the software development. It also facilitates modification of the software by allowing an implementation to be changed without affecting dependent modules. As long as a method's behavior is unchanged, any invoking modules will be unaffected by a change in that method's implementation.

For example, suppose that an airline reservation system uses the Person class specified by the UML diagram in Figure 1.3. Presumably, that software will invoke that class's isAnAdult() method in various modules of the system. The "contract" specified by the software design only requires that the method return the right answer: x.isAnAdult() should be true if and only if x is an adult. How it computes that result is irrelevant. The implementation probably computes the chronological difference between the value of the private field x.dob and the value of the current date. But there is nothing in the contract that specifies that. Moreover, if the implementation is changed, none of the other code in the reservation system would be affected by that change. Such a change might be warranted by the preference of a different algorithm for computing chronological differences, or possibly by a redefinition of the meaning of "adult."

Concealing the implementation of a method from the clients who use the method is called *information hiding*. It is the software designer's version of the spy's principle that says, "If you don't need to know it, then you're are not allowed to know it." It makes software easier to design, implement, and modify.

ABSTRACT DATA TYPES

Abstractions are used to help understand complex systems. Even though they are different, rocks and tennis balls fall at the same rate. The physicist uses the abstraction of imagining a single imaginary point mass to understand the physics of falling bodies. By ignoring the irrelevancies (diameter, weight), the abstraction allows the analyst to focus on the relevancies (height).

Abstractions are widely used in software development. UML diagrams provide abstractions by focusing on the fields (the state) and methods (the behavior) of a class. But at some levels, even the fields of a class may be irrelevant.

An *abstract data type* (ADT) is a specification of only the behavior of instances of that type. Such a specification may be all that is needed to design a module that uses the type.

Primitive types are like ADTs. We know what the int type can do (add, subtract, multiply, etc.). But we need not know how it does these operations. And we need not even know how an int is actually stored. As clients, we can use the int operations without having to know how they are implemented. In fact, if we had to think about how they are implemented, it would probably be a distraction from designing the software that will use them. Likewise, if you had to think about how your car manages to turn its front wheels when you turn the steering wheel, it would probably be more difficult to drive!

EXAMPLE 1.1 An ADT for Fractions

Most programming languages have types for integers and real (decimal) numbers, but not for fractions. Such numbers can be implemented as objects. Here is a design for a fraction type:

```
ADT: Fraction
plus(Fraction): Fraction
times(Integer): Fraction
times(Fraction): Fraction
reciprocal(): Fraction
value(): Real
```

This ADT specifies five operations. Note that the `times()` operation is overloaded.

Note that the ADT uses generic terms for types: `Integer` instead of `int`, and `Real` instead of `double`. That is because it is supposed to be independent of any specific programming language.

In general, a complete ADT would also include documentation that explains exactly how each operation should behave. For example,

```
x.plus(y) returns the Fraction that represents x + y
x.times(n) returns the Fraction that represents n*x
x.times(y) returns the Fraction that represents x*y
x.reciprocal() returns the Fraction that represents 1/x
x.value() returns the numerical value of x
```

UML diagrams can be used to specify ADTs simply by omitting the state information. The Fraction ADT defined in Example 1.1 is shown as a UML diagram in Figure 1.4.

ADTs can be used in pseudocode to implement algorithms independently of any specific programming language. This is illustrated in Example 1.2.

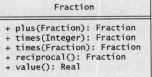

Figure 1.4 An ADT in UML

EXAMPLE 1.2 Using an ADT in an Algorithm

The harmonic mean of two numbers x and y is the number h defined by the formula $h = 2/(1/x + 1/y)$. In pseudocode for `Fraction` types, this could be expressed as:

```
harmonicMean(x: Fraction, y: Fraction) returns Fraction
    return x.reciprocal().plus(y.reciprocal()).reciprocal().times(2);
```

JAVA INTERFACES

In Java, an ADT can be represented by an interface. Recall that a Java interface is just like a Java class, except that it contains no executable code.

EXAMPLE 1.3 A Fraction Interface

```
1    public interface Fraction {
2        Fraction plus(Fraction x);
3        Fraction times(int n);
4        Fraction times(Fraction x);
5        Fraction reciprocal();
6        double value();
7    }
```

This is a direct translation into Java of the ADT specified in Example 1.1.

If an ADT is translated into Java as an interface, then we can implement algorithms that use it as Java methods.

EXAMPLE 1.4 A `harmonicMean()` Method

```
1       public Fraction harmonicMean(Fraction x, Fraction y) {
2          return x.reciprocal().plus(y.reciprocal()).reciprocal().times(2);
3       }
```

Although the Java code in Example 1.4 cannot be executed, we can compile it.

In Java, an interface is a type. Reference variables may be declared to have an interface type, even if the interface has no implementation. For example, the parameters x and y at line 1 of Example 1.4 are declared to have type `Fraction`.

An interface may represent an ADT, as in Example 1.3. More generally, a Java interface is meant to identify a capability. For example, the `Comparable` interface requires the implementation of this method:

```
int compareTo(T type)
```

This means that any variable declared to have type `Comparable` can invoke this method, meaning that it is capable of being compared to other objects.

CLASSES AND OBJECTS

Java is a *strongly typed language:* Every variable must be declared to have a data type. The various Java types are shown in Figure 1.5. These are categorized as either *primitive types* or *reference types*. The eight built-in primitive types are for integers, characters, decimal numbers, and boolean values. Reference types are user-defined, and their variables must be instantiated to hold data. Arrays are reviewed in Chapter 2; interfaces are types that cannot be instantiated; `enum` types are defined by listing all the values that a variable of that type may have.

Classes are concrete data types that specify how their state is stored (the class fields) and how their instances behave (the instance methods). A class is defined in a declaration statement with this syntax:

```
modifers class class-name associations {
   declarations
}
```

where *modifers* are keywords such as `public` and `abstract`, *class-name* is an identifier such as `Person` that names the class, *associations* are clauses such as `extends Object`, and *declarations* are declarations of the class's members.

A class can have six kinds of *members*:
1. *Fields* that specify the kind of data that the objects hold.
2. *Constructors* that specify how the objects are to be created.
3. *Methods* that specify the operations that the objects can perform.
4. *Nested classes*.
5. *Interfaces*.
6. *Enum* type definitions.

Each member of a class must be specified in its own *declaration* statement. The purpose of a declaration is to introduce an identifier to the compiler. It provides all the information that the compiler needs in order to compile statements that use that identifier.

A *field* is a variable that holds data for the object. The simplest kind of *field declaration* has this syntax:

```
modifers type name = initializer;
```

where *modifers* and the *initializer* are optional. For example, the Point class in Example 1.5 declares two fields at lines 2–3. Each has the modifier protected, which means that they are accessible only from within the class itself and from its extensions.

A *constructor* is a subprogram that creates an object. It's like a method with these distinctions:

- Its name is the same as its class name.
- It has no return type.
- It is invoked by the new operator.

The simplest kind of *constructor declaration* has this syntax:

```
modifiers name(param-decls) {
    statements
}
```

Note that a class need not have a main() method. If it does, it is then an executable program. Otherwise, it merely defines a new type that can be used elsewhere.

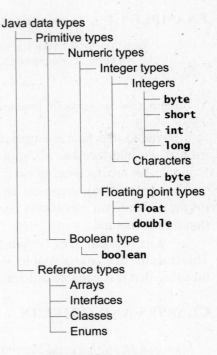

Figure 1.5 Java types

EXAMPLE 1.5 A Ratio Class

```
1   public class Ratio {
2      protected int num;
3      protected int den;
4      public static final Ratio ZERO = new Ratio();
5
6      private Ratio() {
7        this(0, 1);
8      }
9
10     public Ratio(int num, int den) {
11       this.num = num;
12       this.den = den;
13     }
14
15     public boolean equals(Object object) {
16       if (object==this) {
17         return true;
18       } else if (!(object instanceof Ratio)) {
19         return false;
20       }
21       Ratio that = (Ratio)object;
22       return (this.num*that.den == that.num*this.den);
23     }
24
25     public int getNum() {
26       return num;
27     }
28
```

```
29        public int getDen() {
30          return den;
31        }
32
33        public String toString() {
34          return String.format("%d/%d", num, den);
35        }
36
37        public double value() {
38          return (double)num/den;
39        }
40    }
```

Instances of this class represent fractions, with numerator (num) and denominator (den). The static final field ZERO represents the fraction 0/1. It is defined to be static because it is unique to the class itself — there shouldn't be more than one ZERO object.

In addition to its three fields, this class has two constructors and four methods. The *no-arg constructor* (it has no arguments) defined at line 6 is declared private so that it cannot be invoked from outside of its class. It is invoked at line 4 to initialize the ZERO object. This constructor uses the this keyword at line 7 to invoke the two-arg constructor, passing 0 to num and 1 to den.

The two-arg constructor at line 10 is provided to the public for constructing Ratio objects with specific num and den values. Note that, to prevent the ZERO object from being duplicated, we could have included this at line11:

```
if (num == 0) {
   throw new IllegalArgumentException("Use Ratio.ZERO");
}
```

But then we would have to replace line 7 with explicit initializations:

```
num = 0;
den = 1;
```

instead of invoking the two-arg constructor there.

The equals() method at line 15 overrides the default equals() method that is defined in the Object class (which all other classes extend). Its purpose is to return true if and only if its *explicit argument* (object) represents the same thing as its implicit argument (this). It returns true immediately (at line 17) if the two objects are merely different names for the same object. On the other hand, it returns false (at line 19) if the explicit argument is not even the right type. These tests for the two extremes are canonical and should be done first in every equals() method. If they both are passed, then we can recast the explicit argument as an object of the same type as the implicit argument (Ratio) so we can access its fields (num and den). The test for equality of two ratios $a/b = c/d$ is whether $a*d = b*c$, which is done at line 22.

The methods defined at lines 25 and 29 are *accessor methods* (also called "getter methods") providing public access to the class's private fields.

The toString() method at line 33 also overrides the corresponding method that is defined in the Object class. Its purpose is to return a String representation of its implicit argument. It is invoked automatically whenever a reference to an instance of the class appears in an expression where a String object is expected. For example, at line 6 in the test program below, the expression "x = " + x concatenates the string "x = " with the reference x. That reference is replaced by the string "22/7" that is returned by an implicit invocation of the toString() method.

Finally, the value() method at line 37 returns a decimal approximation of the numerical value of the ratio. For example, at line 7 in the test program below, x.value() returns the double value 3.142857142857143.

The program tests the Ratio class:

```
1   public class TestRatio {
2     public static void main(String[] args) {
3       System.out.println("Ratio.ZERO = " + Ratio.ZERO);
4       System.out.println("Ratio.ZERO.value() = " + Ratio.ZERO.value());
5       Ratio x = new Ratio(22, 7);
6       System.out.println("x = " + x);
7       System.out.println("x.value() = " + x.value());
8       System.out.println("x.equals(Ratio.ZERO): " + x.equals(Ratio.ZERO));
9       Ratio xx = new Ratio(44, 14);
10      System.out.println("xx = " + xx);
11      System.out.println("xx.value() = " + xx.value());
12      System.out.println("x.equals(xx): " + x.equals(xx));
13    }
14  }
```

The output is:

```
Ratio.ZERO = 0/1
Ratio.ZERO.value() = 0.0
x = 22/7
x.value() = 3.142857142857143
x.equals(Ratio.ZERO): false
xx = 44/14
xx.value() = 3.142857142857143
x.equals(xx): true
```

The Ratio class in Example 1.5 is *immutable*: its fields cannot be changed.

MODIFIERS

Modifiers are used in the declaration of class members and local variables. These are summarized in the following tables.

Modifier	Meaning
abstract	The class cannot be instantiated.
final	The class cannot be extended.
public	Its members can be accessed from any other class.
strictfp	Floating-point results will be platform-independent.

Table 1.1 Modifiers for classes, interfaces, and enums

Modifier	Meaning
private	It is accessible only from within its own class.
protected	It is accessible only from within its own class and its extensions.
public	It is accessible from all classes.

Table 1.2 Constructor modifiers

Modifier	Meaning
final	It must be initialized and cannot be changed.
private	It is accessible only from within its own class.
protected	It is accessible only from within its own class and its extensions.
public	It is accessible from all classes.
static	The same storage is used for all instances of the class.
transient	It is not part of the persistent state of an object.
volatile	It may be modified by asynchronous threads.

Table 1.3 Field modifiers

Modifier	Meaning
abstract	Its body is absent; to be defined in a subclass.
final	It cannot be overridden in class extensions.
native	Its body is implemented in another programming language.
private	It is accessible only from within its own class.
protected	It is accessible only from within its own class and its extensions.
public	It is accessible from all classes.
static	It has no implicit argument.
strictfp	Its floating-point results will be platform-independent.
synchronized	It must be locked before it can be invoked by a thread.
volatile	It may be modified by asynchronous threads.

Table 1.4 Method modifiers

Modifier	Meaning
final	It must be initialized and cannot be changed.

Table 1.5 Local variable modifier

The three access modifiers, public, protected, and private, are used to specify where the declared member (class, field, constructor, or method) can be used. If none of these is specified, then the entity has *package access*, which means that it can be accessed from any class in the same package.

The modifier final has three different meanings, depending upon which kind of entity it modifies. If it modifies a class, final means that the class cannot be extended to a subclass. (See Chapter 9.) If it modifies a field or a local variable, it means that the variable must be initialized and cannot be changed, that is, it is a constant. If it modifies a method, it means that the method cannot be overridden in any subclass.

The modifier static means that the member can be accessed only as an agent of the class itself, as opposed to being bound to a specific object instantiated from the class. For example, the format() method, invoked at line 34 in the Line class in Example 1.5 on page 6 is a static method:

```
return String.format("%d/%d", num, den);
```

It is bound to the String class itself, accessed as String.format(). On the other hand, the value() method, invoked at line 7 in the test program is a nonstatic method. It is bound to the object x, an instance of the Ratio class, and is accessed x.value().

A static method is also called a *class method*; a nonstatic method is also called an *instance method*. The object to which an instance method is bound in an invocation is called its *implicit argument* for that invocation. For example, the implicit argument in the invocation x.equals(xx) is the object x. (xx is the explicit argument.) Note that every program's main() method is a static method.

COMPOSITION, AGGREGATION, AND INHERITANCE

There are several different ways to associate one class with another: composition, aggregation, and inheritance.

When a class A contains references to instances of a class B and controls all access to those instances, we say that A is a *composition* of B. For example, a University class would be a composition of Department objects. Each Department object belongs to a unique University object, which controls access to its department. If A is a composition of B, we say that an A object "owns a" B object. For example, a university owns a department.

When a class A contains references to a class B whose instances exist and are accessible outside of A, we say that A is an *aggregation* of B. For example, in a university software system, a Department class would contain references to Professor objects who are members of the department, but who also exist outside the department. In fact, a professor could be a member of two different departments. If A is an aggregation of B, we say that an A object "has a" B object. For example, a department has a professor.

When a class A includes all the members of a class B, we say that A is an *extension* of B, and that it *inherits* all the properties of B. For example, a Professor class would be an extension of a Person objects. If A is an extension of B, we say that an A object "is a" B object. For example, a professor is a person.

Figure 1.6 illustrates how these three class associations are represented in UML. Composition is indicated by a filled diamond head adjacent to the composing class, aggregation is indicated by an empty diamond head adjacent to the aggregating class, and inheritance is indicated by an empty arrow head adjacent to the extended class.

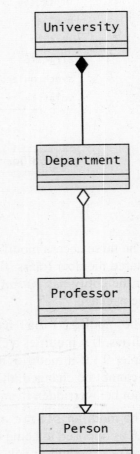

Figure 1.6 Class associations

EXAMPLE 1.6 Implementing Associations

```
1   public class Person {
2     private final String name;
3
4     public Person(String name) {
5       this.name = new String(name);
6     }
```

```
7
8      public String getName() {
9        return new String(name);
10     }
11   }
```

Instances of the Person class represent people.

```
1    public class Professor extends Person {
2      public static enum Rank {INSTR, ASST, ASSOC, PROF}
3
4      private Rank rank;
5
6      public Professor(String name, Rank rank) {
7        super(name);
8        this.rank = rank;
9      }
10
11     public Rank getRank() {
12       return rank;
13     }
14
15     public void setRank(Rank rank) {
16       this.rank = rank;
17     }
18   }
```

The Professor class extends the Person class, inheriting its name field and its getName method. It defines at line 2 an enum field named Rank that specifies the four values INSTR, ASST, ASSOC, and PROF. Its constructor at line 6 requires the professor's name and rank. Note how the Professor constructor uses the super keyword to invoke the Person constructor at line 7.

```
1    public class University {
2      private static class Department {
3        final String name;
4        Set<Professor> members;
5
6        public Department(String name) {
7          this.name = new String(name);
8          this.members = new HashSet<Professor>();
9        }
10
11       public void add(Professor professor) {
12         members.add(professor);
13       }
14     }
15
16     private final String name;
17     private Map<String, Department> departments;
18
19     public University(String name) {
20       this.name = new String(name);
21       this.departments = new TreeMap<String, Department>();
22     }
23
24     public String getName() {
25       return new String(name);
26     }
27
```

```
28    public void addDepartment(String name, Set<Professor> members) {
29      Department dept = new Department(name);
30      departments.put(name, dept);
31      for (Professor prof : members) {
32        dept.add(prof);
33      }
34    }
35
36    public void add(Professor prof, String deptName) {
37      Department dept = departments.get(deptName);
38      if (dept == null) {
39        throw new RuntimeException(deptName + " does not exist.");
40      } else {
41        dept.add(prof);
42      }
43    }
44
45    public Set<String> departments() {
46      return departments.keySet();
47    }
48  }
```

The University class is a *composite* of Department objects. The existence of a department is dependent upon the existence of its university. Therefore, the Department class should be completely controlled and insulated by the University class. This is done by defining it to be a nested private static class at line 2.

The University.Department class has two fields: name (a String), and members (a Set of Professors). It includes an add() method at line 11 for adding professors to the department.

The University class has two fields: name (a String), and departments (a Map of Department objects, indexed by their names). It includes two add() methods (at lines 28 and 36) and an accessor method that returns the Set of department names (at line 45).

Note that the University.Department class is an *aggregate* of Professor objects. The existence of a professor is independent of his or her department's existence. Therefore, the Professor class is defined separately from the University.Department class.

```
1   public class TestUniversity {
2     public static void main(String[] args) {
3       University jsu = new University("JavaStateUniversity");
4       Professor adams = new Professor("Adams", Professor.Rank.ASSOC);
5       Professor baker = new Professor("Baker", Professor.Rank.ASST);
6       Professor cohen = new Professor("Cohen", Professor.Rank.PROF);
7       Set<Professor> profs = new HashSet<Professor>();
8       Collections.addAll(profs, adams, baker, cohen);
9       jsu.addDepartment("Computer Science", profs);
10      Professor davis = new Professor("Davis", Professor.Rank.ASST);
11      Professor evans = new Professor("Evans", Professor.Rank.INSTR);
12      profs.clear();
13      Collections.addAll(profs, davis, evans, baker);
14      jsu.addDepartment("Biology", profs);
15      adams.setRank(Professor.Rank.PROF);
16    }
17  }
```

This test program creates the university with two departments, each containing three professors. Note that Prof. Baker is a member of both departments.

The departments' aggregation of professors is evidenced by two features of this program: A professor may belong to more than one department, and a professor's attributes may be changed independently of his or her department: Prof. Adams is promoted to Professor.Rank.PROF at line 15.

Example 1.6 uses several classes that are defined in the Java Collections Framework (JCF). This library is part of the java.util package. The JCF is outlined in Chapter 4.

Example 1.6 also uses two new Java features, introduced with Java 5.0: *enum types*, and the *for-each construct*.

THE UNIFIED MODELING LANGUAGE

The Unified Modeling Language (UML) is illustrated in Figure 1.6 on page 10 and shows the symbols representing three kinds of association between classes. These are summarized in Table 1.6.

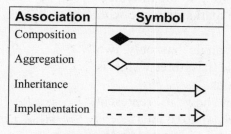

Association	Symbol
Composition	
Aggregation	
Inheritance	
Implementation	

Table 1.6 UML symbols

The implementation symbol is used to show that a class implements an interface.

EXAMPLE 1.7 Implementing the Comparable Interface

Change line 1 of Example 1.5 on page 6 to:

```
1     public class Ratio implements Comparable {
```

and then add these two methods:

```
2     public int compareTo(Object object) {
3       if (object==this) {
4         return 0;
5       } else if (!(object instanceof Ratio)) {
6         throw new IllegalArgumentException("Ratio type expected");
7       }
8       Ratio that = (Ratio)object;
9       normalize(this);
10      normalize(that);
11      return (this.num*that.den - that.num*this.den);
12    }
13
14    private static void normalize(Ratio x) {
15      if (x.num == 0) {  // x == Ratio.ZERO
16        x.den = 1;
17      } else if (x.den < 0) {  // change sign of num and den:
18        x.num *= -1;
19        x.den *= -1;
20      }
21    }
```

The Comparable interface requires the compareTo() method, as specified at line 2. The purpose of the method is to indicate whether the implicit argument is less than, equal to, or greater than the explicit argument. The indicator is the sign of the returned integer: Negative indicates that this < object, zero indicates that this = object, and positive indicates that this > object.

In the case of ratios a/b and c/d, we can tell whether $a/b < c/d$ by cross-multiplying and checking whether $ad < bc$. Since that case should be indicated by returning a negative number, we can simply return $ad - bc$. Indeed, the value of that expression will be negative, zero, or positive, when $a/b < c/d$, $a/b = c/d$, or $a/b > c/d$, respectively. However, that arithmetic trick works only if $b > 0$ and $d > 0$.

To ensure that the denominators are not negative, we employ the static utility method defined at line 14. It ensures that the denominator of its argument is not negative.

Figure 1.7 illustrates how the implementation of an interface is represented in UML. The association symbol is a dashed arrow pointing to the interface. The diagram for the interface marks its name with the stereotype «interface».

Note that an interface rectangle has only two parts, while a class rectangle has three. This is because interfaces have no fields.

Figure 1.7 also illustrates how to represent package membership. The Comparable interface is part of the java.lang package, as indicated by the tab above the interface symbol.

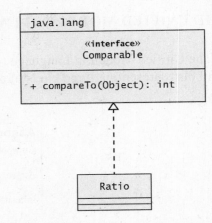

Figure 1.7 Interface implementation in UML

POLYMORPHISM

Java is a strongly typed language, which means that every variable must be declared to have a type which determines how that variable can be used. A char cannot be used where a boolean is expected, and a Ratio object cannot be used where a Person object is expected. But there are some situations where a variable of one type can be used where another type is expected. This is called *polymorphism* (literally, "many forms") because the object appears to have more than one type.

There are several kinds of polymorphism. The simplest kind is called *inclusion polymorphism*. Illustrated in Example 1.8, it refers to the ability of an object to invoke a method that it inherits.

EXAMPLE 1.8 Inclusion Polymorphism

```
1    public class TestRatio {
2      public static void main(String[] args) {
3        Ratio x = new Ratio(22, 7);
4        System.out.println("x.hashCode(): " + x.hashCode());
5      }
6    }
```
The output is:
```
        x.hashCode(): 1671711
```
At line 4, the Ratio object x invokes the hashCode() method that it inherits from the Object class.

Another kind of polymorphism occurs with generic methods, where an actual type is substituted in for a type parameter. This is illustrated in Example 1.9.

EXAMPLE 1.9 Parametric Polymorphism

```
1      public class TestSort {
2        public static void main(String[] args) {
3          String[] countries = {"CN", "IN", "US", "ID", "BR"};
4          print(countries);
5          Arrays.sort(countries);
6          print(countries);
7          Ratio[] ratios = new Ratio[3];
8          ratios[0] = new Ratio(22, 7);
9          ratios[1] = new Ratio(25, 8);
10         ratios[2] = new Ratio(28, 9);
11         print(ratios);
12         Arrays.sort(ratios);
13         print(ratios);
14       }
15
16       static <T> void print(T[] a) {  // generic method
17         for (T t : a) {
18           System.out.printf("%s ", t);
19         }
20         System.out.println();
21       }
22     }
```

Here is the output:

```
CN IN US ID BR
BR CN ID IN US
22/7 25/8 28/9
28/9 25/8 22/7
```

The print() method defined at line 16 is a *generic method*. It uses the *type parameter* T as a place-holder for an actual type, which will be determined at run time. When the generic method is invoked at lines 4 and 6, the type String is used in place of T. When it is invoked at lines 11 and 13, the type Ratio is used. This makes the method polymorphic, capable of printing arrays of String objects and arrays of Ratio objects.

The program also uses the generic sort() method that is defined in the java.util.Arrays class. It requires the type parameter T to be an extension of the Comparable interface, which both the String class and our Ratio class are.

Inclusion polymorphism and parametric polymorphism are both special cases of *universal polymorphism*. The other general kind of polymorphism is called *ad hoc polymorphism* which also has two special kinds, named *overloading polymorphism* and *coercion*. These are best illustrated with primitive types.

The plus operator (+) is polymorphically overloaded: It means integer addition when used in the form 22 + 33; it means floating point addition when used in the form 2.2 + 3.3; and it means string concatenation when used in the form name + ", Esq.".

Coercion occurs when a value of one type is implicitly converted to a value of another type when the context requires that other type. For example, when the compiler evaluates the expression 22 + 3.3, it interprets the plus operator as floating point addition, requiring both operands to be either type float or type double. So it "coerces" the 22 into being 22.0 and then performs the operation.

JAVADOC

A Java program is a main class together with the other classes that it uses. Most classes are part of the standard *Java Class Libraries* provided by Sun Microsystems, Inc. These libraries are orgainzed into several package hierarchies, known collectively as the *Application Programming Interface* (API).

The two most common package hierarchies are the java and javax hierarchies, parts of which are shown in Figure 1.8.

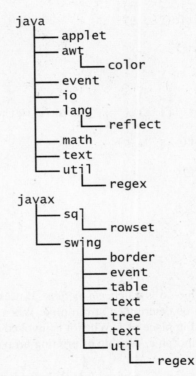

Figure 1.8 Parts of the java and javax package hierarchies

Complete documentation is provided for all the classes in the Java API. Also called *Java API Specification*, these javadocs are located at:

    http://java.sun.com/javase/6/docs/api/

The Javadoc for the String class, in the java.lang package, is shown in Figure 1.9 on page 17.

Review Questions

1.1   What is a requirements document?

1.2   What is the difference between the design stage and the implementation stage in the development of software?

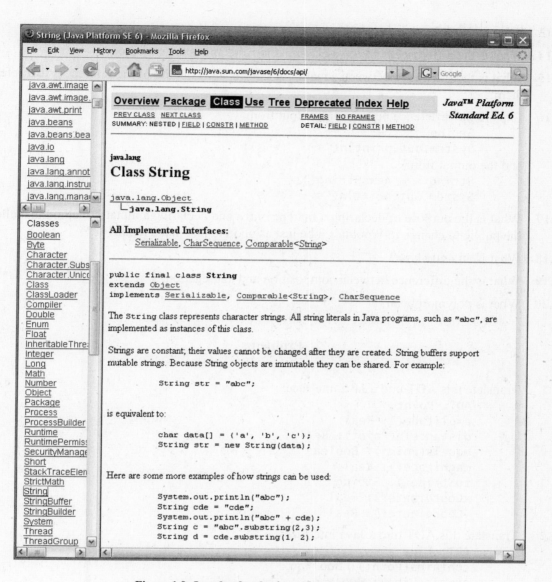

Figure 1.9 Javadoc for the `java.lang.String` class

1.3   What is the difference between the state and the behavior of a class?

1.4   What is an abstract data type?

1.5   What constitutes a Java program?

1.6   What kinds of members can a class have?

1.7   What is an implicit argument?

1.8   What is the purpose of the `toString()` method?

1.9   What is the purpose of the `equals()` method?

1.10   What's the difference among `public`, `protected`, and `private`?

1.11   What is a package?

1.12   What is the difference between an abstract class and an abstract data type?

1.13 What is the difference between a constructor and a method?

1.14 What is the difference between a class method and an instance method?

1.15 What is the difference between equality of objects and equality of the references that refer to them?

1.16 Explain the difference between the output from
```
String s;
System.out.println("s = " + s);
```
and the output from
```
String s = new String();
System.out.println("s = " + s);
```

1.17 What is the purpose of declaring a field private and declaring a mutator method that allows the public to change it. Wouldn't it be just as good to just make it public?

1.18 What is an enum type?

1.19 What is the difference between composition and aggregation?

1.20 What is polymorphism?

Problems

1.1 Translate this ADT into a Java interface:
```
ADT: Point
amplitude(): Real
distanceTo(Point): Real
equals(Point): Boolean
magnitude(): Real
toString(): String
xCoordinate(): Real
yCoordinate(): Real
```

1.2 Translate this ADT into a Java interface:
```
ADT: Line
contains(Point): Boolean
equals(Line): Boolean
isHorizontal(): Boolean
isVertical(): Boolean
slope(): Real
toString(): String
xIntercept(): Real
yIntercept(): Real
```

1.3 Translate this ADT into a Java interface:
```
ADT: Circle
area(): Real
center(): Point
circumference(): Real
contains(Point): Boolean
equals(Circle): Boolean
radius(): Real
toString(): String
```

1.4   Translate this ADT into a Java interface:

```
ADT: Polynomial
degree(): int
derivative(): Polynomial
equals(Point): Boolean
sum(Polynomial): Polynomial
toString(): String
valueAt(Real): Real
```

1.5   Implement the ADT in Problem 1.1 with a Java class, and draw its UML diagram.

1.6   Implement the ADT in Problem 1.2 with a Java class, and draw its UML diagram.

1.7   Implement the ADT in Problem 1.3 with a Java class, and draw its UML diagram.

1.8   Implement the ADT in Problem 1.4 with a Java class, and draw its UML diagram.

Answers to Review Questions

1.1   The requirements document of a software development project is a precise specification of what the software should do.

1.2   In the development of software, the design stage identifies the components (classes) to be used and the relationships among them. The implementation stage is where the computer progam code is actually written.

1.3   The state of a class consists of the values of its fields. The behavior of a class is defined by its methods.

1.4   An abstract data type is a specification of the type's operations: what an instance of that type can do.

1.5   A Java program is a Java class with a main() method? The main() method must have this header:
```
public static void main(String[] args)
```

1.6   A class member may be a field, a constructor, a method, a nested class, a nested interface, or an enum type.

1.7   The *implicit argument* of a method is the object to which the method invocation is bound.

1.8   The toString() method returns a String object that represents the state of its implicit argument.

1.9   The equals() method returns true if and only if states (contents) of its implicit and explicit arguments are the same.

1.10 A class member that is declared public is accessible from any other class. A class member that is declared protected is accessible only from its own class and subclasses (extensions). A class member that is declared private is accessible only from its own class.

1.11 A *package* is a namespace, that is, a name for a group of classes, interfaces, and enum types that can be used to distinguish those from other classes, interfaces, and enum types with the same name.

1.12 An abstract class is a Java class with at least one abstract method—a method that has no body. An abstract data type is a specification of a type's operations that could be implemented in any object-oriented programming language.

1.13 A *constructor* is a member function of a class that is used to create objects of that class. It has the same name as the class itself, has no return type, and is invoked using the new operator. A *method* is an ordinary member function of a class. It has its own name, a return type (which may be void), and is invoked using the dot operator.

1.14 A *class method* is declared static and is invoked using the class name. For example,
```
double y = Math.abs(x);
```
invokes the class method abs() that is defined in the Math class. An *instance method* is declared without the static modifier and is invoked using the name of the object to which it is bound. For example,

```
double x = random.nextDouble();
```
invokes the class method `nextDouble()` that is defined in the Random class and is bound to the object random which is an instance of that class.

1.15 Two objects should be equal if they have the same data values (i.e., the same *state*). Two references are equal if they refer to the same object. The condition (p == q) tests equality of the references p and q, not the equality of the objects to which they refer.

1.16 The output from the code
```
String s;
System.out.println("s = " + s);
```
is
```
s = null
```
The output from the code
```
String s = new String();
System.out.println("s = " + s);
```
is
```
s =
```
In the first case, the reference s is initialized by default to be `null`; there is no `String` object. In the second case, s is initialized to refer to the empty `String` object.

1.17 The advantage of forcing the public to use a mutator method to change a field is that you can control how the field is changed.

1.18 An enum type is a type, defined with the enum keyword that lists by name each possible value for the type.

1.19 When a type is composed of another type, the complete existence of that component type's objects is controlled by the composing type's object; the components are uniquely bound to it and cannout be changed by any outside object. With aggregation, the component elements exits outside of the collection, can be changed by other classes, and may even be components of other aggregates.

1.20 Polymorphism describes the way an object or variable may be treated in different contexts as though it has a different type. For example, inheritance allows an argument of type *B* to be passed to a parameter of type *A* if *B* extends *A*.

Solutions to Problems

1.1
```
public interface Point {
    public double amplitude();
    public double distanceTo(Point point);
    public boolean equals(Object object);
    public double magnitude();
    public String toString();
    public double xCoordinate();
    public double yCoordinate();
}
```

1.2
```
public interface Line {
    public boolean contains(Point point);
    public boolean equals(Object object);
    public boolean isHorizontal();
    public boolean isVertical();
    public double slope();
    public String toString();
    public double xIntercept();
    public double yIntercept();
}
```

1.3
```
public interface Circle {
  public double area();
  public Point center();
  public double circumference();
  public boolean contains(Point point);
  public boolean equals(Object object);
  public double radius();
  public String toString();
}
```

1.4
```
public interface Polynomial {
  public int degree();
  public Polynomial derivative();
  public boolean equals(Object object);
  public Polynomial sum(Polynomial polynomial);
  public String toString();
  public double valueAt(double x);
}
```

1.5
```
public class MyPoint implements Point {
  private double x, y;
  public static Point ORIGIN = new MyPoint();

  private MyPoint() {
  }

  public MyPoint(double x, double y) {
    this.x = x;
    this.y = y;
  }

  public double amplitude() {
    return Math.atan(y/x);
  }

  public double distanceTo(Point point) {
    if (point.equals(this)) {
      return 0.0;
    } else if (!(point instanceof MyPoint)) {
      throw new IllegalArgumentException("use a MyPoint object");
    } else {
      MyPoint that = (MyPoint)point;
      double dx = that.x - this.x;
      double dy = that.y - this.y;
      return Math.sqrt(dx*dx + dy*dy);
    }
  }

  public boolean equals(Object object) {
    if (object==this) {
      return true;
    } else if (!(object instanceof MyPoint)) {
      return false;
    }
    MyPoint that = (MyPoint)object;
    return (that.x == this.x && that.y == this.y);
  }
  public double magnitude() {
    return Math.sqrt(x*x + y*y);
  }
```

```java
    public String toString() {
      return String.format("(%.2f,%.2f)", x, y);
    }

    public double xCoordinate() {
      return x;
    }

    public double yCoordinate() {
      return y;
    }
}
```

1.6
```java
public class MyLine implements Line {
  private double m, b;  // slope, intercept
  public static Line X_AXIS = new MyLine();

  private MyLine() {
  }

  public MyLine (double m, double b) {
    this.m = m;
    this.b = b;
  }

  public boolean contains(Point point) {
    double x = point.xCoordinate();
    double y = point.yCoordinate();
    return y == m*x + b;
  }

  public boolean equals(Object object) {
    if (object==this) {
      return true;
    } else if (!(object instanceof MyLine)) {
      return false;
    }
    MyLine that = (MyLine)object;
    return (that.m == this.m && that.b == this.b);
  }

  public boolean isHorizontal() {
    return m == 0.0;
  }

  public boolean isVertical() {
    return m == Double.POSITIVE_INFINITY || m==Double.NEGATIVE_INFINITY;
  }

  public double slope() {
    return m;
  }

  public String toString() {
    return String.format("y = %.2fx + %.2f", m, b);
  }
```

```java
    public double xIntercept() {
      if (isHorizontal()) {
        throw new RuntimeException("this line is horizontal");
      }
      return -b/m;
    }

    public double yIntercept() {
      if (isVertical()) {
        throw new RuntimeException("this line is vertical");
      }
      return b;
    }
  }
```

1.7
```java
    public class MyCircle implements Circle {
      private Point c;   // center
      private double r;  // radius

      public MyCircle() {
      }

      public MyCircle(Point c, double r) {
        this.c = c;
        this.r = r;
      }

      public double area() {
        return Math.PI*r*r;
      }

      public Point center() {
        return c;
      }

      public double circumference() {
        return 2*Math.PI*r;
      }

      public boolean contains(Point point) {
        double x = point.xCoordinate();
        double y = point.yCoordinate();
        return x*x + y*y < r*r;
      }

      public boolean equals(Object object) {
        if (object==this) {
          return true;
        } else if (!(object instanceof MyCircle)) {
          return false;
        }
        MyCircle that = (MyCircle)object;
        return (that.c == this.c && that.r == this.r);
      }

      public double radius() {
        return r;
      }
```

```
                    public String toString() {
                      return String.format("[Center: %.2fx; Radius: %.2f]", c, r);
                    }
                  }
1.8               public class MyPolynomial implements Polynomial {
                    private double[] c;  // coefficients

                    public MyPolynomial(double[] a) {  // a[i] = coeffficient of x^i
                      int n = c.length;
                      c = new double[n];
                      System.arraycopy(a, 0, c, 0, n);
                    }
                    public int degree() {
                      return c.length - 1;
                    }

                    public Polynomial derivative() {
                      double da[] = new double[c.length-1];
                      for (int i=0; i<da.length; i++) {
                        da[i] = (i+1)*c[i+1];
                      }
                      return new MyPolynomial(da);
                    }

                    public boolean equals(Object object) {
                      if (object==this) {
                        return true;
                      } else if (!(object instanceof MyPolynomial)) {
                        return false;
                      }
                      MyPolynomial that = (MyPolynomial)object;
                      return java.util.Arrays.equals(that.c, this.c);
                    }

                    public Polynomial sum(Polynomial p) {
                      if (!(p instanceof MyPolynomial)) {
                        throw new IllegalArgumentException("use a MyPolynomial object");
                      }
                      MyPolynomial that = (MyPolynomial)p;
                      double[] pc = that.c;
                      int n = Math.max(c.length, pc.length);
                      MyPolynomial q = new MyPolynomial(new double[n]);
                      for (int i=0; i<n; i++) {
                        q.c[i] = c[i] + pc[i];
                      }
                      return q;
                    }

                    public String toString() {
                      StringBuilder buf = new StringBuilder();
                      int n = c.length;
                      if (n > 0 && c[0] != 0.0) {
                        buf.append(c[0]);
                      }
                      if (n > 1 && c[1] != 0.0) {
                        buf.append(String.format(" + %.2f", c[1]));
                      }
```

```
      for (int i=2; i<n; i++) {
        if (c[i] != 0.0) {
        buf.append(String.format(" + %.2f^%d", c[i], i));
        }
      }
      return buf.toString();
  }

  public double valueAt(double x) {
    double y = 0.0;
    for (int i=0; i<c.length; i++) {
      y += c[i]*Math.pow(x, i);
    }
    return y;
  }
}
```

CHAPTER 2

Arrays

An *array* is an object that consists of a sequence of elements that are numbered 0, 1, 2, . . . The element numbers are called *index numbers*. Array elements can be accessed by their index numbers using the *subscript operator* [], as a[0], a[1], a[2], and so on.

Arrays are widely used because they are so efficient.

PROPERTIES OF ARRAYS

Here are the main properties of arrays in Java:
1. Arrays are objects.
2. Arrays are created dynamically (at run time).
3. Arrays may be assigned to variables of type Object.
4. Any method of the Object class may be invoked on an array.
5. An array object contains a sequence of variables.
6. The variables are called the *components* or *elements* of the array.
7. If the component type is T, then the array itself has type T[].
8. An array type variable holds a reference to the array object.
9. The component type may itself be an array type.
10. An array *element* is a component whose type is not an array type.
11. An element's type may be either primitive or reference.
12. The *length* of an array is its number of components.
13. An array's length is set when the array is created, and it cannot be changed.
14. An array's length can be accessed as a public final instance variable.
15. Array index values must be integers in the range 0...length − 1.
16. An ArrayIndexOutOfBoundsException is thrown if Property 15 is violated.
17. Variables of type short, byte, or char can be used as indexes.
18. Arrays can be duplicated with the Object.clone() method.
19. Arrays can be tested for equality with the Arrays.equals() method.
20. Array objects implement Cloneable and java.io.Serializable.

Property 3 follows from Property 1. Although array types are not classes, they behave this way as extensions of the Object class. Property 7 shows that array types are not the same as class types. They are, in fact, derived types: For every class type T there is a corresponding array type T[]. Also, for each of the eight primitive types, the corresponding array type exists.

Property 9 allows the existence of arrays of arrays. Technically, Java allows multidimensional arrays only with primitive types. But for objects, an array of arrays is essentially the same thing. Since arrays themselves are objects, an array of arrays is an array of objects, and some of those component objects could also be nonarrays. (See Example 2.1.)

Note that a consequence of Property 13 is that changing a reference component value to null has no effect upon the length of the array; null is still a valid value of a reference component.

EXAMPLE 2.1 Some Array Definitions

Here are some valid array definitions:

```
1    public class ArrayDefs {
2      public static void main(String[] args) {
3        float x[];
4        x = new float[100];
5        args = new String[10];
6        boolean[] isPrime = new boolean[1000];
7        int fib[] = {0, 1, 1, 2, 3, 5, 8, 13};
8        short[][][] b = new short[4][10][5];
9        double a[][] = {{1.1,2.2}, {3.3,4.4}, null, {5.5,6.6}, null};
10       a[4] = new double[66];
11       a[4][65] = 3.14;
12       Object[] objects = {x, args, isPrime, fib, b, a};
13     }
14   }
```

Line 3 declares x[] to be an array of floats but does not allocate any storage for the array. Line 4 defines x[] to have 100 float components.

Line 5 declares args[] to be an array of 10 String objects. Note the two different (equivalent) ways to declare an array: The brackets may be a suffix on the type identifier or on the array identifier. Line 5 defines args[] to have 10 String components.

Line 6 defines isPrime[] to be an array of 1000 boolean variables.

Line 7 defines fib[] to be an array of 8 ints, initializing them to the 8 values listed. So for example, fib[4] has the value 3, and fib[7] has the value 13.

Line 8 defines b[][][] to be a three-dimensional array of 4 components, each of which is a two-dimensional array of 10 components, each of which is a one-dimensional array of 5 component elements of type short.

Line 9 defines a[][] to be an array of five components, each of which is an array of elements of type double. Only three of the five component arrays are allocated. Then line 10 allocates a 66-element array of doubles to a[4], and line 11 assigns 3.14 to its last element.

Line 12 defines the array objects to consist of six components, each of which is itself an array. The components of the first four component arrays are elements (nonarrays). But the components of the components b and a are not elements because they are also arrays. The actual elements of the objects array include 2, 5, and 13 (components of the component fib), null (components of the component a), and 2.2 and 3.14 (components of the components of the component a).

The array a[][] defined in Example 2.1 is called a *ragged array* because it is a two-dimensional array with rows of different lengths.

The element type of an array in Java can be a primitive type, a reference type, or an array type. The simplest, of course, are arrays of primitive type elements, such as x[], isPrime[], and fib[] in Example 2.1. These are arrays that can be sorted.

DUPLICATING AN ARRAY

Since it is an object, an array can be duplicated by invoking the `Object.clone()` method, as shown in Example 2.2.

EXAMPLE 2.2 Duplicating an Array

```
15    public class DuplicatingArrays {
16      public static void main(String[] args) {
17        int[] a = {22, 44, 66, 88};
18        print(a);
19        int[] b = (int[])a.clone();  // duplicate a[] in b[]
20        print(b);
21        String[] c = {"AB", "CD", "EF"};
22        print(c);
23        String[] d = (String[])c.clone();  // duplicate c[] in d[]
24        print(d);
25        c[1] = "XYZ";  // change c[], but not d[]
26        print(c);
27        print(d);
28      }
29
30      public static void print(int[] a) {
31        System.out.printf("{%d", a[0]);
32        for (int i = 1; i < a.length; i++) {
33          System.out.printf(", %d", a[i]);
34        }
35        System.out.println("}");
36      }
37
38      public static void print(Object[] a) {
39        System.out.printf("{%s", a[0]);
40        for (int i = 1; i < a.length; i++) {
41          System.out.printf(", %s", a[i]);
42        }
43        System.out.println("}");
44      }
45    }
```

The output is:

```
{22, 44, 66, 88}
{22, 44, 66, 88}
{AB, CD, EF}
{AB, CD, EF}
{AB, XYZ, EF}
{AB, CD, EF}
```

The array a[] contains four int elements. The array b[] is a duplicate of a[]. Similarly, the array d[] is a duplicate of the array c[], each containing three String elements. In both cases, the duplication is obtained by invoking the clone() method. Since it returns a reference to an Object, it must be cast to the array type being duplicated, int[] or String[].

The last part of the example shows that the cloned array d[] is indeed a separate copy of c[]: Changing c[1] to "XYZ" has no effect upon the value "CD" of d[1].

THE `java.util.Arrays` CLASS

Java includes a special "utility" class for processing arrays. The name of this class is `Arrays`, and it is defined in the `java.util` package.

EXAMPLE 2.3 Using the `java.util.Arrays` Class

This program imports the `Arrays` class from the `java.util` package to access the `sort()`, `binarySearch()`, `fill()`, and `equals()` methods. It also imports the `static` `print()` method from Example 2.2.

```
1     import java.util.Arrays;
2
3     public class TestArrays {
4       public static void main(String[] args) {
5         int[] a = {44, 77, 55, 22, 99, 88, 33, 66};
6         print(a);
7         Arrays.sort(a);
8         print(a);
9         int k = Arrays.binarySearch(a, 44);
10        System.out.printf("Arrays.binarySearch(a, 44): %d%n", k);
11        System.out.printf("a[%d]: %d%n", k, a[k]);
12        k = Arrays.binarySearch(a, 45);
13        System.out.printf("Arrays.binarySearch(a, 45): %d%n", k);
14        int[] b = new int[8];
15        print(b);
16        Arrays.fill(b, 55);
17        print(b);
18        System.out.println("Arrays.equals(a,b): " + Arrays.equals(a,b));
19      }
20    }
```

The output is

```
44 77 55 22 99 88 33 66
22 33 44 55 66 77 88 99
Arrays.binarySearch(a, 44): 2
a[2]: 44
Arrays.binarySearch(a, 45): -4
0 0 0 0 0 0 0 0
55 55 55 55 55 55 55 55
Arrays.equals(a,b): false
```

The array `a[]` is created and printed at lines 5–6. At line 7, the call `Arrays.sort(a)` sorts the elements of the array, putting them in ascending order, as we can see from the output from line 8.

At line 9, the `Arrays.binarySearch()` method is invoked. The second argument, 44, is the search target. The method returns the index 2, which is assigned to k at line 9. Line 11 verifies that 44 is indeed the value of `a[2]`.

The method is invoked again at line 13, this time searching for the target 45. The value is not found in the array, so the method returns a negative number, $k = -4$. When this happens, the index $i = -k - 1$ will be the position in the array where the target element should be inserted to maintain the ascending order of the array. Note that, in this case, $i = -k - 1 = 3$, and 45 should be inserted at `a[3]` since there are three elements in the array that are less than 45.

The output from line 17 shows how the `Arrays.fill()` method works: It filled the eight-element array `b[]` with the argument 55.

Finally, line 18 shows how the `Arrays.equals()` method works. It will return true only if the two arrays have the same element type (as a[] and b[] do: int[]), the same length (as a[] and b[] do: 8), and the same values at each element (a[] and b[] do not).

The `java.util.Arrays` class is outlined in more detail in page 95.

THE SEQUENTIAL SEARCH ALGORITHM

The *sequential search* (also called the *linear search*) is the simplest search algorithm. It is also the least efficient. It simply examines each element sequentially, starting with the first element, until it finds the key element or it reaches the end of the array.

If you were looking for someone on a moving passenger train, you would use a sequential search.

Here is the *sequential search algorithm*:

(Postcondition: either the index i is returned where $s_i = x$, or -1 is returned.)

1. Repeat steps 2–3, for $i = 0$ to $n - 1$.
2. (Invariant: none of the elements in the subsequence $\{s_0...s_{i-1}\}$ is equal to x.)
3. If $s_i = x$, return i.
4. Return -1.

It is implemented in Example 2.4.

EXAMPLE 2.4 The Sequential Search

```
1    public class TestBinarySearch {
2      public static void main(String[] args) {
3        int[] a = {22, 33, 44, 55, 66, 77, 88, 99};
4        ch02.ex02.DuplicatingArrays.print(a);
5        System.out.println("search(a, 44): " + search(a, 44));
6        System.out.println("search(a, 50): " + search(a, 50));
7        System.out.println("search(a, 77): " + search(a, 77));
8        System.out.println("search(a, 100): " + search(a, 100));
9      }
10
11     public static int search(int[] a, int x) {
12       // POSTCONDITIONS: returns an integer i;
13       //                 if i >= 0, then a[i] == x; otherwise x is not in a[];
14       for (int i=0; i<a.length; i++) {          // step 1
15         // INVARIANT: x is not among a[0]...a[i-1]   // step 2
16         if (a[i] == x) {                        // step 3
17           return i;
18         }
19       }
20       return -1;                                // step 4
21     }
22   }
```

The output is:

```
{22, 33, 44, 55, 66, 77, 88, 99}
search(a, 44): 2
search(a, 50): -1
search(a, 77): 5
search(a, 100): -1
```

The search() method returns the index of the target x: search(a, 44) returns 2, because a[2] = 44; search(a, 77) returns 5, because a[5] = 77. The method returns –1 when the target is not in the array: search(a, 50) returns –1, because 50 is not in the array.

The sequential search is correct. This means that it works. The following argument is a proof of that fact.

If $n = 0$, then the sequence is empty and the loop does not execute at all. Only step 4 executes, immediately returning –1. This satisfies the postconditions: x cannot equal any of the elements because there aren't any.

If $n = 1$, then the loop iterates only once, with $i = 0$. On that iteration, either $s_0 = x$ or $s_0 \neq x$. If $s_0 = x$, then 0 is returned and the postcondition is satisfied. If $s_0 \neq x$, then the loop terminates, step 4 executes, and –1 is returned, and that satisfies the postcondition because the single element of the sequence is not equal to x.

Suppose $n > 1$. We want to apply the First Principle of Mathematical Induction to deduce that the loop invariant must be true on every iteration of the loop. (See page 321.) That requires the verification of the invariant on the first iteration and the deduction of the invariant on iteration i from the corresponding invariant on iteration $i-1$.

On the first iteration of the loop, $i = 0$, and the loop invariant in step 2 is true "vacuously" because the subsequence $\{s_0...s_{i-1}\}$ is empty. Then in step 3, either $s_0 = x$ or $s_0 \neq x$. If $s_0 = x$, then 0 is returned and the postcondition is satisfied. If $s_0 \neq x$, then the loop continues on to a second iteration. Then $i = 1$, and the loop invariant in step 2 is again true because the subsequence $\{s_0...s_{i-1}\} = \{s_0\}$ and $s_0 \neq x$.

Suppose now that on iteration $i-1$, the loop invariant is true; that is, none of the elements in the subsequence $\{s_0..s_{i-1}\}$ is equal to x. If the loop continues on to the next iteration, then the condition $s_i = x$ at step 3 was not true. Thus, $s_i \neq x$. Therefore, none of the elements in the subsequence $\{s_0..s_i\}$ is equal to x, which is the loop invariant on the ith iteration

The sequential search runs in $O(n)$ time. This means that, on average, the running time is proportional to the number of elements in the array. So if everything else is the same, then applying the sequential search to an array twice as long will take about twice as long, on average. The following argument is a proof of that fact.

If x is in the sequence, say at $x = s_i$ with $i < n$, then the loop will iterate i times. In that case, the running time is proportional to i, which is $O(n)$ since $i < n$. If x is not in the sequence, then the loop will iterate n times, making the running time proportional to n, which is $O(n)$.

THE BINARY SEARCH ALGORITHM

The *binary search* is the standard algorithm for searching through a sorted sequence. It is much more efficient than the sequential search, but it does require that the elements be in order. It repeatedly divides the sequence in two, each time restricting the search to the half that would contain the element.

You might use the binary search to look up a word in a dictionary.

Here is the *binary algorithm*:

(Precondition: $s = \{s_0, s_1, \ldots, s_{n-1}\}$ is a sorted sequence of n values of the same type as x.)

(Postcondition: either the index i is returned where $s_i = x$, or –1 is returned.)

    1. Let ss be a subsequence of the sequence s, initially set equal to s.

    2. If the subsequence ss is empty, return –1.

3. (Invariant: If x is in the sequence s, then it must be in the subsequence ss.)
4. Let s_i be the middle element of ss.
5. If $s_i = x$, return its index i.
6. If $s_i < x$, repeat steps 2–7 on the subsequence that lies above s_i.
7. Repeat steps 2–7 on the subsequence of ss that lies below s_i.

It is implemented in Example 2.5.

EXAMPLE 2.5 The Binary Search

```
1    public class TestBinarySearch {
2      public static void main(String[] args) {
3        int[] a = {22, 33, 44, 55, 66, 77, 88, 99};
4        ch02.ex02.DuplicatingArrays.print(a);
5        System.out.println("search(a, 44): " + search(a, 44));
6        System.out.println("search(a, 50): " + search(a, 50));
7        System.out.println("search(a, 77): " + search(a, 77));
8        System.out.println("search(a, 100): " + search(a, 100));
9      }
10
11     public static int search(int[] a, int x) {
12       // POSTCONDITIONS: returns i;
13       //                    if i >= 0, then a[i] == x; otherwise i == -1;
14       int lo = 0;
15       int hi = a.length;
16       while (lo < hi) {                              // step 1
17         // INVARIANT: if a[j]==x then lo <= j < hi;  // step 3
18         int i = (lo + hi)/2;                         // step 4
19         if (a[i] == x) {
20           return i;                                  // step 5
21         } else if (a[i] < x) {
22           lo = i+1;                                  // step 6
23         } else {
24           hi = i;                                    // step 7
25         }
26       }
27       return -1;                                     // step 2
28     }
29   }
```

The output is the same as in Example 2.4.

The binary search is correct. The loop invariant is true on the first iteration because the current subsequence is the same as the original sequence. On every other iteration, the current subsequence was defined in the preceding iteration to be the half of the previous subsequence that remained after omitting the half that did not contain x. So if x was in the original sequence, then it must be in the current subsequence. Thus the loop invariant is true on every iteration.

On each iteration, either i is returned where $s_i = x$, or the subsequence is reduced by more than 50 percent. Since the original sequence has only a finite number of elements, the loop cannot continue indefinitely. Consequently, the algorithm terminates either by returning i from within the loop or at step 6 or step 7 where –1 is returned. If i is returned from within the loop, then $s_i = x$. Otherwise, the loop terminates when hi < lo; that is, when the subsequence is empty. In that case we know by the loop invariant that s_i is not in the original sequence.

The binary search runs in $O(\lg n)$ time. This means that, on average, the running time is proportional to the logarithm of the number of elements in the array. So if everything else is the same, if it takes an average of T milliseconds to run on an array of n elements, then will take an average of $2T$ milliseconds to run on an array of n^2 elements. For example, if it takes 3 ms to search 10,000 elements, then it should take about 6 ms to search 100,000,000 elements! The following argument is a proof of that fact.

Each iteration of the loop searches a subarray that is less than half as long as the subarray on the previous iteration. Thus the total number of iterations is no more than the number of times that the length n can be divided by 2. That number is $\lg n$. And the total running time is roughly proportional to the number of iterations that the loop makes.

Review Questions

2.1   What is the difference between a component and an element of an array?

2.2   What does it mean to say that Java does not allow multidimensional arrays?

2.3   What is an `ArrayIndexOutOfBoundsException` exception, and how does its use distinguish Java from other languages such as C and C++?

2.4   What types are valid for array indexes?

2.5   What's wrong with this definition:
```
Arrays arrays = new Arrays();
```

2.6   What is the simplest way to print an array of objects?

2.7   If the binary search is so much faster than the sequential search, why would the latter ever be used?

2.8   What happens if the sequential search is applied to an element that occurs more than once in the array?

2.9   What happens if the binary search is applied to an element that occurs more than once in the array?

Problems

2.1   Run a test program to see how the `Arrays.fill()` method handles an array of objects.

2.2   If the sequential search took 50 ms to run on an array of 10,000 elements, how long would you expect it to take to run on an array of 20,000 elements on the same computer?

2.3   If the binary search took 5 ms to run on an array of 1,000 elements, how long would you expect it to take to run on an array of 1,000,000 elements on the same computer?

2.4   The *interpolation search* is the same as the binary search except that in step 4 the element s_i is chosen so that the proportion of elements less than s_i in the subsequence ss equals the proportion that would be expected in a uniform distribution. For example, looking up the name "Byrd" in a phone book of 2,600 pages, one would open first near page 200 because one would expect about 2/26 of all the names to precede it. The interpolation search can be shown to run in $O(\lg \lg n)$ time. If it took 5 ms to run on an array of 1,000 elements, how long would you expect it to take to run on an array of 1,000,000 elements on the same computer?

2.5 Run a test driver for the binary search method in Example 2.5 on page 32 on an array of 10,000 elements and count the number of iterations.

2.6 Write and test this method:
```
boolean isSorted(int[] a)
// returns true iff a[0] <= a[1] <= ... <= a[a.length-1]
```

2.7 Write and test this method:
```
int minimum(int[] a)
// returns the minimum element of a[]
```

2.8 Write and test this method:
```
double mean(double[] a)
// returns the average value of all the elements in a[]
```

2.9 Write and test this method:
```
int[] withoutDuplicates(int[] a)
// returns the specified array after removing all duplicates
```

2.10 Write and test this method:
```
void reverse(int[] a)
// reverses the elements of a[]
```

2.11 Write and test this method:
```
Object[] concatenate(Object[] a, Object[] b)
// returns an array containing all of a[] followed by all of b[]
```

2.12 Write and test this method:
```
void shuffle(Object[] a)
// randomly permutes the elements of a[]
```

2.13 Write and test this method:
```
int[] tally(String string)
// returns an array a[] of 26 integers that count the frequencies
// of the (case insensitive) letters in the given string
```

2.14 Write and test this method:
```
double innerProduct(double[] x, double[] y)
// returns the algebraic inner product (the sum of the component-
// wise products) of the two given arrays as (algebraic) vectors
```

2.15 Write and test this method:
```
double[][] outerProduct(double[] x, double[] y)
// returns the algebraic outer product of the two given arrays
// as (algebraic) vectors: p[i][j] = a[i]*b[j]
```

2.16 Write and test this method:
```
double[][] product(double[][] a, double[][] b)
// returns the matrix product of the two given arrays a matrix:
// p[i][j] = Sum(a[i][k]*b[k][j]:k)
```

2.17 Write and test this method:
```
double[][] transpose(double[][] a)
// returns the transpose ta of the specified array as a matrix:
// ta[i][j] = a[j][i]
```

2.18 Write and test this method:
```
int[][] pascal(int size)
// returns Pascal's triangle of the given size
```

2.19 The *Sieve of Eratosthenes* is an array of `boolean` elements whose *i*th element is true if and only if *i* is a prime number. Use the following algorithm to compute and print a sieve of size 1000:

(Precondition: *p* is an array of *n* bits.)

(Postcondition: *p*[*i*] is true if and only if *i* is prime.)

1. Initialize *p*[0] and *p*[1] to be false, and all other *p*[*i*] to be true.
2. Repeat step 3 for each *i* from 3 to *n*, incrementing by 2.
3. If there is a prime ≤ the square root of *i* that divides *i*, set *p*[*i*] false.

2.20 Repeat Problem 2.19 using a `java.util.Vector` object.

2.21 Repeat Problem 2.19 using a `java.util.BitSet` object.

2.22 Define and test a `Primes` class with these methods:

```
public static void setLast(int last)      // sets last
public static void setLast()              // sets last=1
public static void sizeSize(int size)     // sets size of bitset
public static void sizeSize()             // sets bitset size=1000
public static boolean isPrime(int n)      // true if n is prime
public static int next()                  // next prime after last
public static void printPrimes()          // prints sieve
```

Use the `BitSet` implementation of the Sieve of Eratosthenes from Problem 2.21. Use these definitions:

```
public class Primes {
private static final int SIZE = 1000;
private static int size = SIZE;
private static BitSet sieve = new BitSet(size);
private static int last = 1;
```

including this *static initializer*, which implements the Sieve of Eratosthenes:

```
static {
  for (int i = 2; i < SIZE; i++) {
    sieve.set(i);
  }
  for (int n = 2; 2*n < SIZE; n++) {
    if (sieve.get(n)) {
      for (int m=n; m*n<SIZE; m++) {
        sieve.clear(m*n);
      }
    }
  }
}
```

2.23 Add the following method to the `Primes` class and then test it:

```
public static String factor(int n)
// precondition: n > 1
// returns the prime factorization of n;
// example:  factor(4840) returns "2*2*2*5*11*11"
```

2.24 Christian Goldbach (1690–1764) conjectured in 1742 that every even number greater than 2 is the sum of two primes. Write a program that tests the *Goldbach conjecture* for all even numbers less than 100. Use the `Primes` class from Problem 2.22. Your first 10 lines of output should look like this:

```
4 = 2+2
6 = 3+3
8 = 3+5
```

```
10 = 3+7  = 5+5
12 = 5+7
14 = 3+11 = 7+7
16 = 3+13 = 5+11
18 = 5+13 = 7+11
20 = 3+17 = 7+13
22 = 3+19 = 5+17 = 11+11
```

2.25 Pierre de Fermat (1601–1665) conjectured that there are infinitely many prime numbers of the form $n = 2^{2^p} + 1$ for some integer p. These numbers are called *Fermat primes*. For example, 5 is a Fermat prime because it is a prime number and it has the form $2^{2} + 1$. Write a program that finds all the Fermat primes that are in the range of the `int` type. Use the `Primes` class from Problem 2.22 and the `Math.pow()` method. Your first 5 lines of output should look like this:

```
2^2^0 + 1 = 3
2^2^1 + 1 = 5
2^2^2 + 1 = 17
2^2^3 + 1 = 257
2^2^4 + 1 = 65537
```

2.26 Charles Babbage (1792–1871) obtained the first government grant in history when in 1823 he persuaded the British government to provide £1000 to build his difference engine. In his grant proposal, Babbage gave the formula $x^2 + x + 41$ as an example of a function that his computer would tabulate. This particular function was of interest to mathematicians because it produces an unusual number of prime numbers. Primes that have this form $n = x^2 + x + 41$ for some integer x could be called *Babbage primes*. Write a program that finds all the Babbage primes that are less than 10,000. Use the `Primes` class from Problem 2.22. Your first five lines of output should look like this:

```
0        41 is prime
1        43 is prime
2        47 is prime
3        53 is prime
4        61 is prime
```

2.27 Two consecutive odd integers that are both prime are called *twin primes*. The *twin primes conjecture* is that there are infinitely many twin primes. Write a program that finds all the twin primes that are less than 1000. Use the `Primes` class from Problem 2.22. Your first five lines of output should look like this:

```
3        5
5        7
11       13
17       19
29       31
```

2.28 Test the conjecture that there is at least one prime between each pair of consecutive square numbers. (The *square numbers* are 1, 4, 9, 16, 25, . . .). Use the `Primes` class from Problem 2.22. Your first five lines of output should look like this:

```
1  < 2  < 4
4  < 5  < 9
9  < 11 < 16
16 < 17 < 25
25 < 29 < 36
```

2.29 The Minimite friar Marin Mersenne (1588–1648) undertook in 1644 the study of numbers of the form $n = 2^p - 1$, where p is a prime. He believed that most of these n are also primes, now called *Mersenne primes*. Write a program that finds all the Mersenne primes for $p < 30$. Use the `Primes` class from Problem 2.22. Your first five lines of output should look like this:

```
2        2^2-1 = 3 is prime
3        2^3-1 = 7 is prime
5        2^5-1 = 31 is prime
7        2^7-1 = 127 is prime
11       2^11-1 = 2047 is not prime
```

2.30   A number is said to be *palindromic* if it is invariant under reversion; that is, the number is the same if its digits are reversed. For example, 3456543 is palindromic. Write a program that checks each of the first 10,000 prime numbers and prints those that are palindromic. Use the `Primes` class from Problem 2.22.

Answers to Review Questions

2.1   An array *component* can be any type: primitive, reference, or array. An array *element* is a component that is not itself an array type. So in a two-dimensional array `a[][]`, the components of `a[]` are its row arrays, and the elements of `a[][]` are `double` variables.

2.2   A multidimensional array is one that has more than one index. A Java array has only one index variable. However, since a components indexed by that variable can itself be an array (with an index), the original array appears to have more than one index.

2.3   An `ArrayIndexOutOfBoundsException` object is an exception that gets thrown whenever a value less than 0 or greater than or equal to the array's length is attempted to be used as an index on the array. This give the programmer some control over the consequences of such a run-time error. In languages such as C++, such a run-time error normally causes the program to crash.

2.4   An array index can have type `byte`, `char`, `short`, or `int`.

2.5   The `Array` class cannot be instantiated because its constructor is declared `private`.

2.6   The simplest way to print an array of objects is to pass it to the `Arrays.toList()` method which produces a `List` object that can be printed directly with the `System.out.println()` method.

2.7   The binary search will probably not work unless the sequence is sorted first.

2.8   If the sequential search is applied to an element that occurs more than once in an array, it will return the index of the one that is closest to the beginning of the array.

2.9   If the binary search is applied to an element that occurs more than once in an array, it could return the index of any one of them. It depends upon how close their indexes are to multiples of midpoints of subintervals. For example, if the binary search is applied in an array of 10,000 elements, searching for a value that is repeated at locations 0–99, the search would return the index 77 on the 7th iteration.

Solutions to Problems

2.1
```
public class TestFill {
    public static void main(String[] args) {
        Object[] a = new Object[4];
        Arrays.fill(a, new Date());
        ch02.ex02.DuplicatingArrays.print(a);
        Arrays.fill(a, 22);
        ch02.ex02.DuplicatingArrays.print(a);
        Arrays.fill(a, "Yo!");
        ch02.ex02.DuplicatingArrays.print(a);
    }
```

2.2 The sequential search runs in linear time, which means that the time is proportional to the number of elements. So an array with twice as many elements would take twice as long to process: 20 ms.

2.3 The binary search runs in logarithmic time, so squaring the size of the problem should only double its running time. So an array with 1000^2 elements would take twice as long to process: 10 ms.

2.4 The interpolation search runs in hyperlogarithmic time, so squaring the size of the problem should have no appreciable effect on its running time. So an array with 1,000,000 elements would also take about 2 ms to process.

2.5
```java
public class TestBinarySearch {
    private static final int SIZE = 10000;
    private static final int START = 0;
    private static final int RANGE = 10000;
    private static Random random = new Random();
    private static int count = 0;

    public static void main(String[] args) {
      int[] a = new int[SIZE];
      load(a, START, RANGE);
      Arrays.sort(a);
      search(a, random.nextInt(10000));
      System.out.println(count + " iterations");
    }

    public static void load(int[] a, int start, int range) {
      for (int i = 0; i < a.length; i++) {
        a[i] = start + random.nextInt(range);  // random 5-digit numbers
      }
    }

    public static int search(int[] a, int x) {
      int lo = 0;
      int hi = a.length;
      while (lo < hi) {
        ++count;
        int i = (lo + hi)/2;
        if (a[i] == x) {
          return i;
        } else if (a[i] < x) {
          lo = i+1;
        } else {
          hi = i;
        }
      }
      return -1;
    }
}
```

2.6
```java
boolean isSorted(int[] a) {
  if (a.length < 2) {
    return true;
  }
  for (int i = 1; i < a.length; i++) {
    if (a[i] < a[i-1]) {
      return false;
    }
  }
  return true;
}
```

2.7
```
int minimum(int[] a) {
  int min = a[0];
  for (int i = 1; i < a.length; i++) {
    if (a[i] < min) {
      min = a[i];
    }
  }
  return min;
}
```

2.8
```
int mean(int[] a) {
  double sum=0.0;
  for (int i = 0; i < a.length; i++) {
    sum += a[i];
  return sum/a.length;
}
```

2.9
```
int[] withoutDuplicates(int[] a) {
  int n = a.length;
  if (n < 2) {
    return a;
  }
  for (int i = 0; i < n-1; i++) {
    for (int j = i+1; j < n; j++) {
      if (a[j] == a[i]) {
        --n;
        System.arraycopy(a, j+1, a, j, n-j);
        --j;
      }
    }
  }
  int[] aa = new int[n];
  System.arraycopy(a, 0, aa, 0, n);
  return aa;
}
```

2.10
```
void reverse(int[] a) {
  int n = a.length;
  if (n < 2) {
    return;
  }
  for (int i = 0; i < n/2; i++) {
    swap(a, i, n-i-1);
  }
}
void swap(int[] a, int i, int j) {
  // swaps a[i] with a[j]:
  int ai = a[i];
  int aj = a[j];
  a[i] = aj;
  a[j] = ai;
}
```

2.11
```
Object[] concatenate(Object[] a, Object[] b) {
  Object[] c = new Object[a.length+b.length];
  for (int i = 0; i < a.length; i++) {
    c[i] = a[i];
  }
  for (int i = 0; i < b.length; i++) {
    c[i+a.length] = b[i];
  }
```

```
          return c;
        }

2.12    void shuffle(Object[] a) {
          Random random = new Random();
          int n = a.length;
          for (int i = 0; i < n; i++) {
            ch02.pr10.TestReverse.swap(a,i,random.nextInt(a.length));
          }
        }

2.13    int[] tally(String s) {
          int[] frequency = new int[26];
          for (int i = 0; i < s.length(); i++) {
            char ch = Character.toUpperCase(s.charAt(i));
            if (Character.isLetter(ch)) {
              ++frequency[(int)ch - (int)'A'];  // count ch
            }
          return frequency;
        }

2.14    double innerProduct(double[] x, double[] y) {
          double sum = 0.0;
          for (int i = 0; i < x.length && i < y.length; i++)
            sum += x[i]*y[i];
          return sum;
        }

2.15    double[][] outerProduct(double[] x, double[] y) {
          double[][] z = new double[x.length][y.length];
          for (double xi : x) {
            for (double yj : y) {
              z[i][j] = xi*yj;
            }
          }
          return z;
        }

2.16    double[][] product(double[][] x, double[][] y) {
          double[][] z = new double[x.length][y[0].length];
          for (int i = 0; i < x.length; i++) {
            for (int j = 0; j < y[0].length; j++) {
              double sum = 0.0;
              for (int k = 0; k < x[0].length; k++) {
                sum += x[i][k]*y[k][j];
              }
              z[i][j] = sum;
            }
          }
          return z;
        }

2.17    double[][] transpose(double[][] x) {
          double[][] y = new double[x[0].length][x.length];
          for (int i = 0; i < x[0].length; i++) {
            for (int j = 0; j < x.length; j++) {
              y[i][j] = x[j][i];
            }
          }
          return y;
        }
```

2.18
```java
int[][] pascal(int n) {
  int[][] p = new int[n][n];
  for (int j = 0; j < n; j++) {
    p[j][0] = p[j][j] = 1;
  }
  for (int i = 2; i < n; i++) {
    for (int j = 1; j < i; j++) {
      p[i][j] = p[i-1][j-1] + p[i-1][j];
    }
  }
  return p;
}
```

2.19
```java
public class TestSieve {
  private static final int SIZE=1000;
  private static boolean[] isPrime = new boolean[SIZE];

  public static void main(String[] args) {
    initializeSieve();
    printSieve();
  }

  private static void initializeSieve() {
    for (int i = 2; i < SIZE; i++) {
      isPrime[i] = true;
    }
    for (int n = 2; 2*n < SIZE; n++) {
      if (isPrime[n]) {
        for (int m = n; m*n <SIZE; m++) {
          isPrime[m*n] = false;
        }
      }
    }
  }

  private static void printSieve() {
    int n=0;
    for (int i = 0; i < SIZE; i++) {
      if (isPrime[i]) {
        System.out.printf("%5d%s", i, ++n%16==0?"\n":"");
      }
    }
    System.out.printf("%n%d primes less than %d%n", n, SIZE);
  }
}
```

2.20
```java
public class TestSieve {
  private static final int SIZE=1000;
  private static Vector<Boolean> isPrime = new Vector<Boolean>(SIZE);

  public static void main(String[] args) {
    initializeSieve();
    printSieve();
  }

  private static void initializeSieve() {
    isPrime.add(false);  // 0 is not prime
    isPrime.add(false);  // 1 is not prime
    for (int i = 2; i < SIZE; i++) {
      isPrime.add(true);
    }
```

```
            for (int n = 2; 2*n < SIZE; n++) {
              if ((isPrime.get(n))) {
                for (int m = n; m*n < SIZE; m++) {
                  isPrime.set(m*n, false);
                }
              }
            }
          }

          private static void printSieve() {
            int n=0;
            for (int i = 0; i < SIZE; i++) {
              if (isPrime.get(i)) {
                System.out.printf("%5d%s", i, ++n%16==0?"\n":"");
              }
            }
            System.out.printf("%n%d primes less than %d%n", n, SIZE);
          }
        }
```

2.21
```
        public class TestSieve {
          private static final int SIZE=1000;
          private static BitSet isPrime = new BitSet(SIZE);

          public static void main(String[] args) {
            initializeSieve();
            ch02.pr20.TestSieve.printSieve();
          }

          private static void initializeSieve() {
            for (int i = 2; i < SIZE; i++) {
              isPrime.set(i);
            }
            for (int n = 2; 2*n < SIZE; n++) {
              if (isPrime.get(n)) {
                for (int m = n; m*n <SIZE; m++) {
                  isPrime.clear(m*n);
                }
              }
            }
          }

          private static void printSieve() {
            int n=0;
            for (int i = 0; i < SIZE; i++) {
              if (isPrime.get(i)) {
                System.out.printf("%5d%s", i, ++n%16==0?"\n":"");
              }
            }
            System.out.printf("%n%d primes less than %d%n", n, SIZE);
          }
        }
```

2.22
```
        public class Primes {
          private static final int SIZE = 1000;
          private static int size = SIZE;
          private static BitSet sieve = new BitSet(size);
          private static int last = 1;
```

```
        static {
          for (int i=2; i<SIZE; i++) {
            sieve.set(i);
          }
          for (int n=2; 2*n<SIZE; n++) {
            if (sieve.get(n)) {
              for (int m=n; m*n<SIZE; m++) {
                sieve.clear(m*n);
              }
            }
          }
        }
        public static void setLast(int n) {
          last = n;
        }
        public static void setLast() {
          last = 1;
        }
        public static void setSize(int n) {
          size = n;
        }
        public static void setSize() {
          size = 1000;
        }
        public static boolean isPrime(int n) {
          return sieve.get(n);
        }
        public static int next() {
          while (++last<size) {
            if (sieve.get(last)) {
              return last;
            }
          }
          return -1;
        }
        public static void printPrimes() {
          int n=0;
          for (int i=0; i<SIZE; i++) {
            if (sieve.get(i)) {
              System.out.print((n++%10==0?"\n":"\t")+i);
            }
          }
          System.out.println("\n" + n + " primes less than " + SIZE);
        }
      }
```

2.23
```
      public static String factor(int n) {
        public static String factor(int n) {
          String primes="";
          int p = next();
          while (n > 1) {
            if (n%p==0) {
              primes += (primes.length()==0?"":"*") + p;
              n /= p;
            }
            else p = next();
            if (p == -1) {
              primes += " OVERFLOW";
              break;
            }
```

```
        }
        setLast();
        return primes;
    }
```

2.24
```
    public class TestGoldbach {
        public static void main(String[] args) {
            Primes.setSize(1000);
            System.out.println("4 = 2+2");
            for (int n = 6; n < 100; n += 2) {
                System.out.print(n);
                for (int p = 3; p <= n/2; p += 2) {
                    if (Primes.isPrime(p) && Primes.isPrime(n-p)) {
                        System.out.print(" = "+p+"+"+(n-p));
                    }
                }
                System.out.println();
            }
        }
    }
```

2.25
```
    public class TestFermat {
        public static void main(String[] args) {
            Primes.setSize(1000);
            for (int p = 0; p < 5; p++) {
                int n = (int)Math.pow(2,Math.pow(2,p)) + 1;
                if (Primes.isPrime(n)) {
                    System.out.println("p = "+p+", n = 2^2^p = "+n);
                }
            }
        }
    }
```

2.26
```
    public class TestBabbage {
        public static void main(String[] args) {
            Primes.setSize(1000);
            for (int x = 0; x < 50; x++) {
                System.out.print(x);
                int n = x*x + x + 41;
                if (Primes.isPrime(n)) {
                    System.out.println("\t"+n+" is prime");
                } else {
                    System.out.println();
                }
            }
        }
    }
```

2.27
```
    public class TestTwinPrimes {
        public static void main(String[] args) {
            Primes.setSize(1000);
            int n = Primes.next();
            while (n < 0.9*N) {
                if (Primes.isPrime(n+2)) {
                    System.out.println(n + "\t" + (n+2));
                }
                n = primes.next();
            }
        }
    }
```

2.28
```
public class TestSquares {
   public static void main(String[] args) {
      Primes.setSize(1000);
      for (int n = 1; n < 100; n++) {
         for (int i = n*n+1; i < (n+1)*(n+1); i++) {
            if (Primes.isPrime(i)) {
               System.out.printf("%d < %d < %d%n", n*n, i, (n+1)*(n+1));
               break;
            }
         }
      }
   }
}
```

2.29
```
public class TestMersenne {
   public static void main(String[] args) {
      Primes.setSize(1000);
      for (int p = Primes.next(); p < 30; p = Primes.next()) {
         int n = (int)Math.round(Math.pow(2,p)) - 1;
         System.out.printf("%d\t2^%d-1%d", p, p, n);
         if (Primes.isPrime(n)) {
            System.out.println(" is prime ");
         } else {
            System.out.println(" is not prime ");
         }
      }
   }
}
```

2.30
```
boolean isPalindromic(int n) {
   if (n < 0) {
      return false;
   }
   int p10=1;
   // make p10 is the greatest power of 10 that is < n
   while (p10 < n) {
      p10 *= 10;
   }
   p10 /= 10;
   while (n > 9) {
      if (n/p10 != n%10) {
         return false;
      }
      n /= 10;    // remove rightmost digit from n
      p10 /= 10;
      n %= p10;   // remove leftmost digit from n
   }
   return true;  // single digit integers are palindromic
}
```

CHAPTER 3

Linked Data Structures

Arrays work well for unordered sequences, and even for ordered sequences if they don't change much. But if you want to maintain an ordered list that allows quick insertions and deletions, you should use a linked data structure. This chapter shows how to do that.

MAINTAINING AN ORDERED ARRAY

Chapter 2 outlines how the binary search can find elements very quickly in an array that is sorted. This suggests that we should keep our arrays in sorted order. But inserting new elements in an ordered array is difficult. The main problem is that we have to shift all the larger elements forward to make room for the new element to be placed in its correct ordered position. This can be done by the insert() method shown in Example 3.1.

EXAMPLE 3.1 Inserting into an Ordered Array

```
1    void insert(int[] a, int n, int x) {
2      // preconditions: a[0] <= ... <= a[n-1], and n < a.length;
3      // postconditions: a[0] <= ... <= a[n], and x is among them;
4      int i = 0;
5      while (i < n && a[i] <= x) {
6        ++i;
7      }
8      System.arraycopy(a, i, a, i+1, n-i);  // copies a[i..n) into a[i+1..n+1)
9      a[i] = x;
10   }
```

The insert() method takes three arguments: the array a[], the number n of elements that are already sorted in the array, and the new element x to be inserted among them. The preconditions at line 2 specify that the first n elements of the array are in ascending order and that the array has room for at least one more element. The postconditions at line 3 specify that the array is still in ascending order and that x has been successfully inserted among them.

The code at lines 4–7 searches the array for the correct position for x to be inserted. It should be the smallest index i for which a[i] > x. For example, if x = 50 for the array shown in Figure 3.1, then the correct position for x is at index i = 1, because a[0] <= x < a[1].

After the correct position i has been located for x, the insert() method shifts the elements that are greater than x one position to the right. This is accomplished by the call

```
System.arraycopy(a, i, a, i+1, n-i);
```

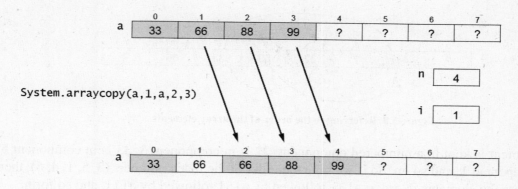

System.arraycopy(a,1,a,2,3)

n 4

i 1

Figure 3.1 Making room for the new element

at line 8. The `arraycopy()` method is a `static` method in the `System` class. It is usually the most efficient way to copy elements between arrays or within a single array. Its five arguments are: the source array, the index of the first element to be copied from the source array, the destination array, the index in the destination array where the first element is to be copied, and the number of elements to be copied. If n = 4 and i = 1, as shown in Figure 3.1, then the call is

                System.arraycopy(a, 1, a, 2, 3);
This shifts elements {a[1], a[2], a[3]} = {66, 88, 99} into elements {a[2], a[3], a[4]}.

Finally, x is inserted into a[i] at line 9, as shown in Figure 3.2.

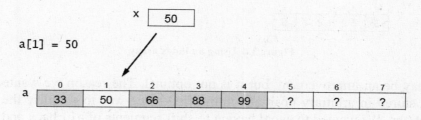

x 50

a[1] = 50

Figure 3.2 Copying x into its correct position

The `insert()` method may have to move a lot of data. For example, if n = 1000 and x is less than all of those elements, then the method will move all 1000 elements. On average, inserting into a sorted array of n elements will move $n/2$ elements. So this is a $\Theta(n)$ operation.

Deleting an element is simply the reverse of the insertion process. It too will have to move $n/2$ elements, on average. So deletion is also a $\Theta(n)$ operation.

INDIRECT REFERENCE

One solution to the data movement problem that is intrinsic to dynamic ordered arrays is to use an auxiliary index array to keep track of where the elements actually are. This solution requires more space (a second array) and makes the code a bit more complicated. But it eliminates the need to move the elements. It allows the elements to be stored at an arbitrary position in the array, using the auxiliary index array to locate them for ordered access.

The main idea is shown in Figure 3.3. The elements {22, 33, 44, 55, 66} are kept in arbitrary positions in the array a[], and their order is determined by some auxiliary mechanism.

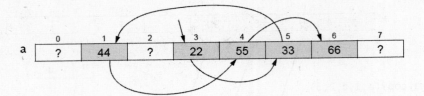

Figure 3.3 Referring to the order of the array elements

Each element is kept in a numbered component: 22 is in component 3, 33 is in component 5, 44 is in component 1, and so on. So if we save the order of the index numbers (3, 5, 1, 4, 6), then we can access the elements in order: a[3] followed by a[5] followed by a[1], and so forth.

An *index array* is an array whose elements are index values for another array. By storing the index numbers 3, 5, 1, 4, 6 in an index array k[] (shown in Figure 3.4), we can use them to access the data elements 22, 33, 44, 55, 66 in order.

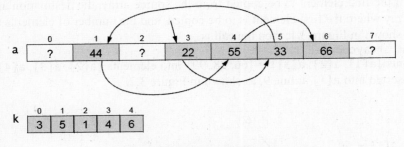

Figure 3.4 Using an index array

Now this may be an improvement, but it is not optimal. The reason we wanted to allow the element to be stored in arbitrary positions in the first place was to simplify the insertion and deletion operations. We wanted to avoid having to shift segments of a[] back and forth. But the solution shown in Figure 3.4 merely transfers that obligation from a[] to k[]. If we had to insert the element 50, we could put it at position a[0] or a[2] or any place after a[6], but we would then have to insert its index into the index array k[] between k[2] and k[3] to keep track of the order of the elements.

A better solution is to use the same array positions in the index array k[] as we are using in the data array a[]. Since the index array is keeping track of the correct order of the index numbers of the data elements, it can be used to do the same for the index numbers themselves.

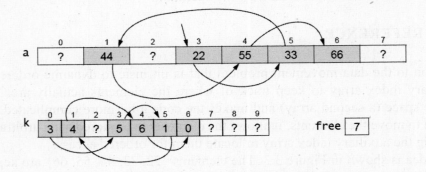

Figure 3.5 Using an index array

In Figure 3.5, the index array k[] keeps track of the order of the elements in a[]. The starting index 3 is stored in k[0]. That begins the chain of indexes: k[0] = 3, k[3] = 5, k[5] = 1, k[1] = 4, k[4] = 6, k[6] = 0. The index 0 signals the end of the ordered sequence. The index sequence 0, 3, 5, 1, 4, 6 gives us the data elements in order: a[3] = 22, a[5] = 33, a[1] = 44, a[4] = 55, a[6] = 66.

The extra variable free, shown Figure 3.5, saves the index of a free location in both the index array k[] and the data array a[]. The value 7 means that k[7] and a[7] should be used next.

The implementation of an index array solves the problem of having to shift segments of array elements back and forth during deletions and insertions. For example, to insert x = 50 in Figure 3.5, we first traverse the sequence to find the index i of the largest element that is less than x: i = 1. Then just follow these three steps:

```
a[free] = x;       // put x into the next free position
k[free] = k[i];    // store the next index in that position in k[]
k[i] = free++;     // store the index of x in k[] and increment free
```

The results are shown in Figure 3.6.

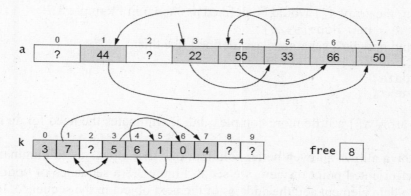

Figure 3.6 Inserting an element

The Java code for this algorithm is shown in Example 3.2. This improves the insert() method shown in Example 3.2, because its only data movement is the actual insertion of x into the array a[] at line 5.

EXAMPLE 3.2 Inserting into an Array that Is Indirectly Ordered

```
1    void insert(int x) {
2        int i=0;
3        while (k[i] != 0 && a[k[i]] < x) {
4            i = k[i];
5        }
6        a[free] = x;
7        k[free] = k[i];
8        k[i] = free++;
9    }
```

The while loop at lines 3–5 is similar to the while loop at lines 5–7 in Example 3.1 on page 46: it finds the first index i for which a[k[i]] > x. At line 6, x is inserted in the next free location in the array a[]. At line 7, the index of the next location after x is stored in k[free]. At line 8, the index of x is copied into k[i], and then free is incremented to the index of the next free location.

Note that this code assumes that the array is large enough to accommodate all elements that might be inserted. In practice, we would probably include a resize() method.

LINKED NODES

The values of the index array k[] in Figure 3.6 are used as locators, addressing the actual data array a[]. We don't really need a separate array for them. Their relative positions in the index array match the positions of the corresponding data elements. So we can combine them into a single array of data-address pairs, as shown in Figure 3.7:

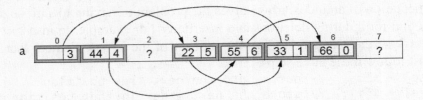

Figure 3.7 Storing the indexes with their elements in the same array

In this version, the array a[] would be defined as shown in Example 3.7.

```
Node[] a = new Node[size];
```

where Node would now be a separate class, defined like this:

```
class Node {
   int data;
   int next;
}
```

This makes the array a[] a little more complex, but it eliminates the need for an auxiliary array altogether.

Fortunately, Java allows an even better solution, one that allows us to eliminate both arrays! Taking an object-oriented point of view, we see in Figure 3.8 a sequence of Node objects. Each object contains a data element and the address of the next object in the sequence. In Java, objects are directly accessed by their addresses. That's what an object reference is: the address of where the object is stored in memory. So by reinterpreting the meaning of "address," as a memory address (i.e., object reference) instead of an array index, we can simplify the structure to the one shown in Figure 3.8. Here, the arrows represent object references (i.e., memory addresses).

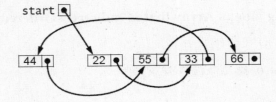

Figure 3.8 Using objects for the elements and their references

Now, instead of an array a[], we need only keep track of the single start reference. The Java runtime system does all the rest of the bookkeeping. The code is given in Example 3.3.

EXAMPLE 3.3 A Node Class

```
1   class Node {
2      int data;
3      Node next;
```

data [22] next [●]→

Node

Figure 3.9 A Node object

```
4
5        Node(int data) {
6            this.data = data;
7        }
8    }
```

Notice that the Node class is now *self-referential*: Its next field is declared to have type Node. Each Node object contains a field that is a reference to a Node object.

The other field in the Node class is its data field, declared at line 2 here to be an int. Of course in general this field could be any type we want—whatever type values we have to store in the list.

The Node class in Example 3.3 also includes a one-argument constructor, at line 5. Note that, since we have explicitly defined a constructor that takes at least one argument, the compiler will *not* implicitly define a no-argument constructor. Therefore, since we have *not* explicitly defined a no-argument constructor, none will exist. That means that the only way a Node object can be created is with the one-argument constructor (at line 5); that is, we must provide a data value for each new Node object that we create.

Figure 3.9 shows a typical Node object. Its data field contains the integer 22, and its next field contains a reference to another Node object (not shown). Although it is common to use an arrow like this to represent an object reference, it is good to keep in mind that the actual value of the reference is the memory address of the object to which it refers. In other programming languages, such variables are called *pointers*; hence their common depiction as arrows.

Recall that in Java each reference variable either locates an object or is null. The value null means that the variable does not refer to any object. The memory address that is stored in a null reference variable is 0x0 (the hexadecimal value 0); no object is ever stored at that address. Figure 3.10 shows a Node object whose next field is null.

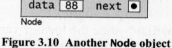

Node

Figure 3.10 Another Node object

Example 3.4 shows how the five-element list could be built.

EXAMPLE 3.4 Constructing a Linked List

```
1    Node start = new Node(22);
2    start.next = new Node(33);
3    start.next.next = new Node(44);
4    start.next.next.next = new Node(55);
5    start.next.next.next.next = new Node(66);
```

Figure 3.11 Initializing start

At line 1, we create a node containing the data value 22 and initialize our start variable to it. The result is shown in Figure 3.11. Note that the start variable is merely a reference to the Node object. Also note that the next reference in the Node object is null, indicated by the black dot with no arrow emanating from it. The node's next field is null because the constructor (defined at line 5 in Example 3.3 on page 50) does not initialize it. In Java, every class field that is an object reference (i.e., its type is either a class or an interface) is automatically initialized to null, unless it is initialized by its constructor to some existing object.

In the figures that follow, each Node object is shown as a box with two parts: the left side contains the integer data, and the right side contains the next reference. This simply abbreviates the versions shown in Figure 3.9.

Continuing the code in Example 3.4, at line 2, the start node's next field is assigned to a new Node object containing the data 33. Now the list has two nodes, as shown in Figure 3.12.

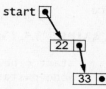

Figure 3.12 Adding a node

The next node is added to the end of the list at line 3. To do that, we have to assign it to the `next` field of the node that contains 33. But the only node to which we have external access (i.e., the only node that has a variable name) is the first node. Its name is `start`. So we have to use the expression `start.next.next` to refer to the `next` field of the node that contains 33.

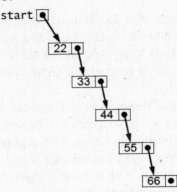

Similarly, the fourth node is added at line 4 using the expression `start.next.next.next`, and the fifth node is added at line 5 using the expression `start.next.next.next.next`. That finally gives us the five-node list shown in Figure 3.13.

Figure 3.13 The five-node list

The code in Example 3.4 is clumsy and unsuited for generalization. Obviously, if we wanted to build a linked list of 50 nodes, this approach would be unworkable. The solution is to use a local reference variable that can "walk through" the list, locating one node after the other and thereby giving local access to the nodes. Traditionally, the variable p (for "pointer") is used for this purpose. Since it will refer to individual nodes, it should be declared to be a `Node` reference, like this:

```
Node p;
```
And since our only access to the nodes is from the `start` node, we should initialize p like this:
```
Node p=start;
```
This is shown in Figure 3.14. Then the assignment
```
p = p.next;
```
will advance the locator variable p to the next node, as shown in Figure 3.15. This same assignment can thus be executed as many times as is needed to advance through the linked list.

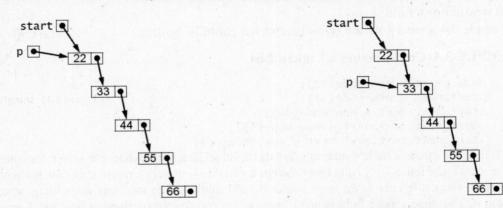

Figure 3.14 Initializing p at the start node   **Figure 3.15 Advancing p to the second node**

Example 3.5 shows how we could have used this technique to build the linked list in the first place.

EXAMPLE 3.5 Constructing a Linked List

```
1    start = new Node(22);
2    Node p=start;
3    p.next = new Node(33);
4    p = p.next;
```

```
5       p.next = new Node(44);
6       p = p.next;
7       p.next = new Node(55);
8       p = p.next;
9       p.next = new Node(66);
```

This code may not seem much better than the other version in Example 3.4. But one big advange is that it is easily managed within a loop. For example, the same list can be built with the three lines of code in Example 3.6.

EXAMPLE 3.6 Using a for Loop

```
1       Node start = new Node(22), p = start;
2       for (int i=0; i<4; i++) {
3           p = p.next = new Node(33+11*i);
4       }
```

Obviously, this form could just as easily build a linked list of 50 nodes. Each step in the execution of this code is shown in Figure 3.16.The reference variable p is analogous to an array index i: It advances through the nodes of a linked list just as i advances through the elements of an array. Consequently, it is natural to use p in a for loop, just as we would use the array index i. For example, compare Example 3.7 with Example 3.8.

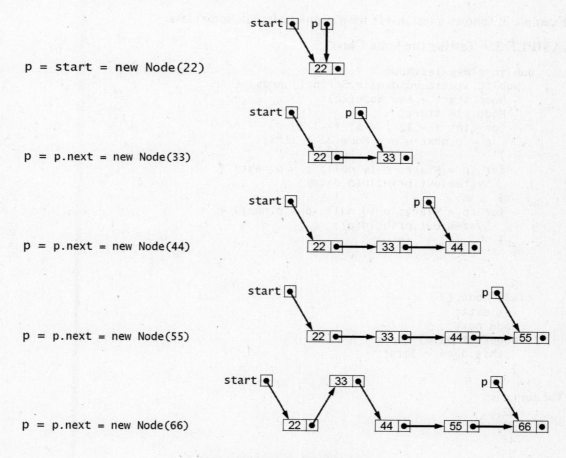

p = start = new Node(22)

p = p.next = new Node(33)

p = p.next = new Node(44)

p = p.next = new Node(55)

p = p.next = new Node(66)

Figure 3.16 Trace of Example 3.6

EXAMPLE 3.7 Using a for Loop to Print a Linked List

```
1    for (Node p = start; p != null; p = p.next) {
2       System.out.println(p.data);
3    }
```

EXAMPLE 3.8 Using a for Loop to Print an Array

```
1    for (int i=0; i < n; i++) {
2       System.out.println(a[i]);
3    }
```

In both listings, the for loop prints one element on each iteration. The for statement has a three-part control mechanism. The first part declares the control variable (p for the list, i for the array) and initializes it to the first element:

```
        Node p=start
        int i=0
```

The second part gives the continuation condition, asserting that there are more elements:

```
        p != null
        i < n
```

The third part gives the update expression, advancing the control variable to the next element:

```
        p = p.next
        i++
```

In each of these parts, the two versions are analogous.

Example 3.9 shows a test driver for a simple external Node class.

EXAMPLE 3.9 Testing the Node Class

```
1    public class TestNode {
2      public static void main(String[] args) {
3        Node start = new Node(22);
4        Node p = start;
5        for (int i = 1; i < 5; i++) {
6          p = p.next = new Node(22 + 11*i);
7        }
8        for (p = start; p != null; p = p.next) {
9          System.out.println(p.data);
10       }
11       for (p = start; p != null; p = p.next) {
12         System.out.println(p);
13       }
14     }
15   }
16
17   class Node {
18     int data;
19     Node next;
20     Node(int data) {
21       this.data = data;
22     }
23   }
```

The output is:

```
        22
        33
        44
        55
        66
```

```
Node@7182c1
Node@3f5d07
Node@f4a24a
Node@cac268
Node@a16869
```

The first node is constructed at line 3. Then the `for` loop at lines 5–7 constructs the other four nodes. The second `for` loop at lines 8–10 prints the node data in the first five lines of output. The third `for` loop at lines 11–13 gives the actual memory addresses of the five `Node` objects.

When you use an object reference like p in a string expression such as

```
System.out.println(p);
```

the system automatically invokes that object's `toString()` method. Unless it has been overridden, the version of the `toString()` method that is defined in the `Object` class will execute, as it did in the program in Example 3.9. The string returned by that version merely contains the object's type (`Node`) followed by the @ sign and the memory address of the object (7182c1). So the last five lines of output report that the five `Node` objects are stored at the (hexadecimal) memory addresses 0x7182c1, 0x3f5d07, 0xf4a24a, 0xcac268, and 0xa16869. These then are the actual values stored in the reference variables `start`, `start.next`, `start.next.next`, `start.next.next.next`, and `start.next.next.next.next`.

You can see from Figure 3.17 why we usually draw linked lists using arrows to represent the `Node` references. Showing the actual memory address values instead requires more effort to see which node references which. Moreover, those memory address values are runtime dependent: They will be different on different computers, and maybe even on the same computer at different times.

One final note: At line 6 we use the chained assignment

```
p = p.next = new Node(22+11*i);
```

It is important to remember the order of operations in such a statement. Here, the first thing that happens is the evaluation of the expression 22 + 11*i. When i is 1, that evaluates to 33; when i is 4, it evaluates to 66. After the value is obtained, it is passed to the `Node` class constructor at line 5 of Example 3.3 on page 50. That constructs a node with that value in its `data` field and `null` in its `next` field. The constructor returns a reference to the `Node` object. It is that reference that is assigned first to `p.next`, and then to `p`. The key is that the assignments are made from right to left. So we know that p is not updated until after its `next` field is. So, first the `next` field is set to point to the new node, and then the loop control variable p is advanced to that next node.

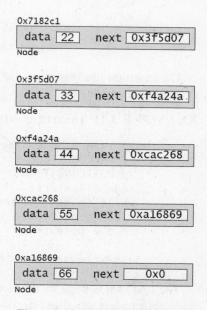

Figure 3.17 The five Node objects

INSERTING AN ELEMENT INTO A LINKED LIST

Recall how new elements were inserted into the linked list that was built in Figure 3.16 on page 53. To simplify the process, we add a two-argument constructor to our `Node` class, as shown in Example 3.10 on page 56. This allows us to create the node and insert it all at once.

Figure 3.18 illustrates the invocation of the two-argument `Node` constructor. It shows `next` as a reference to a `Node` object and x as an `int` with value 50. Passing these two arguments to the constructor creates a new `Node` object that contains 50 and whose `next` field points to the same object that the given `next` pointer points to. The constructor then returns a reference to the new `Node` object, which is assigned to q.

The code for inserting an element into a nonempty linked list is given in Example 3.11. To appreciate its simplicity, compare it with the equivalent method in Example 3.2 on page 49.

EXAMPLE 3.10 A Node Class with Two Constructors

```
1   class Node {
2      int data;
3      Node next;
4
5      Node(int data) {
6         this.data = data;
7      }
8
9      Node(int data, Node next) {
10         this.data = data;
11         this.next = next;
12      }
13   }
```

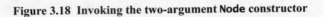

Figure 3.18 Invoking the two-argument Node constructor

The insertion has two steps: (1) find the list node p that should precede the new node; (2) create and attach the new node.

EXAMPLE 3.11 Inserting into a Nonempty Sorted Linked List of Integers

```
1    void insert(Node start, int x) {
2       // PRECONDITIONS: the list is in ascending order, and x > start.data;
3       // POSTCONDITIONS: the list is in ascending order, and it contains x;
4       Node p = start;
5       while (p.next != null) {
6          if (p.next.data > x)  break;
7          p = p.next;
8       }
9       p.next = new Node(x,p.next);
10    }
```

The first step is done by the loop at lines 5–8. The variable p is declared at line 4 to be a reference to Node objects. It is initialized to point to the start node, which contains 22 in Figure 3.19. The loop control condition (p.next != null) at line 5 will allow the loop to iterate until p points to the last element in the list. At that point, p.next will be null, stopping the loop. But inside the loop, at line 6, the condition (p.next.data > x) will stop the loop prematurely, before p reaches any nodes that should come after the new node. This is how the list remains in ascending order: New elements are always inserted between the elements that are less than it and those that are greater than it.

The assignment p = p.next at line 7 is the standard mechanism for traversing a linked list. On each iteration of the while loop, this assignment moves p to point to the next node in the list.

The actual insertion is done by the statement at line 9. The expression new Node(x,p.next) creates the new node and initializes its two fields, as we saw previously in Figure 3.18. In that version, it assigned the new node's reference to q. The statement at line 7 assigns it to p.next instead. This changes the next pointer of the p node (the node containing 44): it was pointing to the node containing 55; now it points to the new node that contains 50.

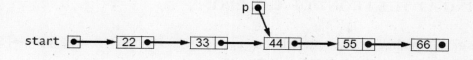

$$\text{p.next = new Node(50,p.next)}$$

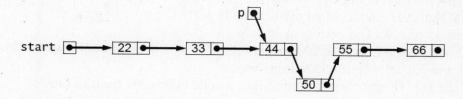

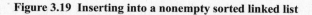

Figure 3.19 Inserting into a nonempty sorted linked list

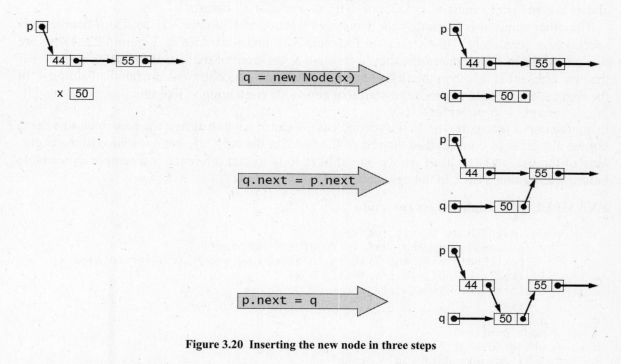

Figure 3.20 Inserting the new node in three steps

This second stage of the insertion could be done by several separate statements, like this:

```
Node q = new Node(x);
q.next = p.next;
p.next = q;
```

These separate steps are illustrated Figure 3.20. Once we understand this process, we might as well use the power of Java and write it in the single statement

```
p.next = new Node(x, p.next);
```

without the clutter of the extra variable q.

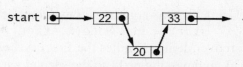

Figure 3.21 Inserting 20 incorrectly

INSERTING AT THE FRONT OF THE LIST

The insert() method in Example 3.11 on page 56 includes the extra precondition that x be greater than the first element in the list (start.data). To see why that precondition is needed, look at what the method would do if x were 20 instead of 50. In that case, the break condition at line 6 would be true on the first iteration of the while loop, leaving p pointing at the start node when the new node gets inserted at line 9. The result, as shown in Figure 3.21 on page 57, is that 20 gets inserted between 22 and 33, instead of where it belongs at the front of the list. The problem is that we lack a node to precede the new one.

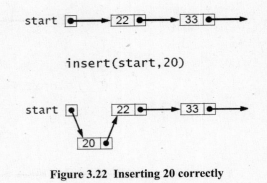

Figure 3.22 Inserting 20 correctly

One way to solve this problem is to restructure the linked list itself so that it maintains a "dummy" head node that precedes the first real data node. This uses a little extra space, but it allows the insert() method in Example 3.11 to work for all cases.

The other solution is to modify the insert() method in Example 3.11 so that it handles this special case separately. This is done in Example 3.12 and illustrated in Figure 3.22. There are two situations in which the insert should be done at the front of the list: if the list is empty or if the new element is less than the first element of the list. Both conditions are handled at line 4. In the first case, we could simply reset start to a new node containing x, like this:

        start = new Node(x);

using the one-arg constructor. In the second case, we also have to assign the new node to start, but we also have to connect it to the rest of the list. But the only reference we have to the beginning of the list is start itself, so we would have to hold that reference in a temporary variable before reassigning start to the new node.

EXAMPLE 3.12 Linked List Insertion

```
1    Node insert(Node start, int x) {
2      // precondition: the list is in ascending order;
3      // postconditions: the list is in ascending order, and it contains x;
4      if (start == null || start.data > x) {
5        start = new Node(x,start);
6        return start;
7      }
8      Node p=start;
9      while (p.next != null) {
10       if (p.next.data > x)  break;
11       p = p.next;
12     }
13     p.next = new Node(x,p.next);
14     return start;
15   }
```

Using the two-argument constructor obviates the need for that extra temporary assignment:

        start = new Node(x,start);

Moreover, it also handles the first case, where the list was empty, because in that case, start is null, and passing null to the second parameter is equivalent to using the one-arg constructor:

```
         start = new Node(x, null);  // equivalent
         start = new Node(x);        // equivalent
```
So once again, the two-argument constructor provides the best solution.

Note that unlike the simpler version in Example 3.11, the complete `insert()` method in Example 3.12 has to return the `start` node reference, because that reference may be changed at line 5.

DELETING FROM A SORTED LINKED LIST

Implementing an ordered list with a linked structure makes insertion far more efficient because it eliminates the need to shift elements. The same is true for deletion.

Like the `insert()` method, the `delete()` method has two main parts: (1) find the element; (2) delete it. It also handles the special case at the front of the list separately. Example 3.13 shows the `delete()` method.

EXAMPLE 3.13 Linked List Deletion

```
1   Node delete(Node start, int x) {
2     // precondition: the list is in ascending order;
3     // postconditions: the list is in ascending order, and if it did
4     // contains x, then the first occurrence of x has been deleted;
5     if (start == null || start.data > x) {  // x is not in the list
6       return start;
7     } else if (start.data == x) {       // x is the first element in the list
8       return start.next;
9     }
10    for (Node p = start; p.next != null; p = p.next) {
11      if (p.next.data > x) {
12        break;                          // x is not in the list
13      } else if (p.next.data == x) {    // x is in the p.next node
14        p.next = p.next.next;           // delete it
15        break;
16      }
17    }
18    return start;
19  }
```

If the list is empty, then `start == null` and nothing has to be done. Also, if the first element is greater than x, then since the list is sorted, all the elements must be greater than x, so x is not in the list. Both of these cases are handled first at line 5.

If the first element in the list equals x, then it is deleted at line 8. This is done by returning `start.next` to `start`, as shown in Figure 3.23. If no other reference is pointing to the original `start` node, then it will be deleted by the Java "garbage collector."

If the first element of the list is less than x, then the `for` loop at line 10 searches for the first element that is greater than or equal to x. If it finds one greater, then the method breaks at line 12 and returns without changing the list. If it finds an element equal to x, then it deletes it at line 14. This is illustrated in Figure 3.24.

NESTED CLASSES

In Java, a class member may be a field, a constructor, a method, an interface, or another class. A class that is a member of another class is called a *nested class*.

Figure 3.23 Deleting the first element from a sorted linked list

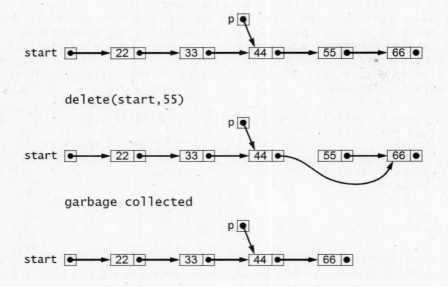

Figure 3.24 Deleting any other element from a sorted linked list

If the only place where a class Y will be used is within another class X, then class Y should be nested within class X. This is an important example of the *information hiding* principle that we have applied in other contexts.

If X is any type (class or interface) and Y is any other type nested within X, then every member of X is accessible from Y and every member of Y is accessible from X. This is illustrated in Example 3.14.

The Main class in Example 3.14 has a private nested class named Nested. Both classes have a private int field. Main declares and initializes m at line 2; Nested declares and initializes n at line 15. The Nested class also defines a private method f() at line 17.

EXAMPLE 3.14 Accessibility from Nested Classes

```
1    public class Main {
2      private int m = 22;
3
4      public Main() {
5        Nested nested = new Nested();
6        System.out.println("Outside of Nested; nested.n = " + nested.n);
7        nested.f();
8      }
9
10     public static void main(String[] args) {
11       new Main();
12     }
13
14     private class Nested {
15       private int n = 44;
16
17       private void f() {
18         System.out.println("Inside of Nested; m = " + m);
19       }
20     }
21   }
```

The output is:
```
        Outside of Nested; nested.n = 44
        Inside of Nested; m = 22
```
The main() method invokes the Main() constructor at line 11. That instantiates the Nested class at line 5. The private field n of the Nested class is accessed at line 6, and the private method f() of the Nested class is accessed at line 7. This shows that private members of a nested class are accessible from its enclosing class. Symmetrically, the private members of the enclosing class are accessible from within its nested class, as demonstrated by line 18.

The UML symbol for the nesting of one class inside another uses a circle with a plus sign inside in place of the arrowhead, as shown in Figure 3.25.

Since all members of a private nested class are still accessible from anywhere else in the enclosing class,

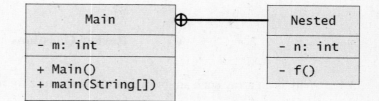

Figure 3.25 UML diagram for a nested class

those members are usually declared without any access modifier (private, protected, or public), for simplicity.

Normally, a nested class should be declared static unless its instances need to access nonstatic members of its enclosing class. (A nested class that is nonstatic is called an *inner class*.)

The Node class defined in Example 3.10 on page 56 is used only within the context of the linked lists that are being implemented. So it should be nested inside its List class. Moreover, since nodes have no need to access List methods or fields, the Node class should be declared as a static nested class. This is done at line 12 in Example 3.15 and is illustrated in Figure 3.26.

EXAMPLE 3.15 Nesting the Node Class within a LinkedList Class

```
1   public class LinkedList {
2     private Node start;
3
4     public void insert(int x) {
5       // Insert lines 2-14 of Example 3.12 on page 58
6     }
7
8     public void delete(int x) {
9       // Insert lines 2-18 of Example 3.13 on page 59
10    }
11
12    private static class Node {
13      // Insert lines 2-12 of Example 3.10 on page 56
14    }
15  }
```

Hiding the Node class within the LinkedList class encapsulates the LinkedList class, making it self-contained and concealing its implementation details. A developer could change the implementation without having to modify any code outside of that class.

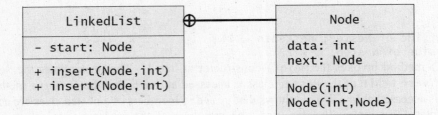

Figure 3.26 A Node class nested within a LinkedList class

Review Questions

3.1 Why is an array such an inefficient data structure for a dynamic sorted list?

3.2 What is an index array?

3.3 If linked lists are so much better than arrays, why are arrays used at all?

3.4 Why does insertion at the front of a linked list have to be done differently from insertion elsewhere?

3.5 Why are the lists backwards in the BigInt class?

Problems

3.1 Write and test this method, similar to the insert() method in Example 3.1 on page 46:
```
void delete(int[] a, int n, int x)
// precondition: 0 <= n < a.length;
// postconditions: the first occurrence of x among
//                 {a[0], ..., a[n-1]} has been deleted;
```

For example, if a[] is the array {33, 55, 77, 99, 77, 55, 33, 0}, then delete(a, 6, 55) will change a[] to {33, 77, 99, 77, 55, 33, 0, 0}.

3.2   Write and test this method:
```
int size(Node list)
// returns: the number of nodes in the specified list;
```
For example, if list is {33, 55, 77, 99}, then size(list) will return 4.

3.3   Write and test this method:
```
int sum(Node list)
// returns: the sum of the integers in the specified list;
```
For example, if list is {25, 45, 65, 85}, then sum(list) will return 220.

3.4   Write and test this method:
```
void removeLast(Node list)
// precondition: the specified list has at least two nodes;
// postcondition: the last node in the list has been deleted;
```
For example, if list is {22, 44, 66, 88}, then removeLast(list) will change it to {22, 44, 66}.

3.5   Write and test this method:
```
Node copy(Node list)
// returns: a new list that is a duplicate of the specified list;
```
Note that the new list must be completely independent of the specified list. Changing one list should have no effect upon the other.

3.6   Write and test this method:
```
Node sublist(Node list, int p, int q)
// returns: a new list that contains copies of the q-p nodes of the
//    specified list, starting with node number p (starting with 0);
```
For example, if list is {22, 33, 44, 55, 66, 77, 88, 99}, then sublist(list, 2, 7) will return the new list {44, 55, 66, 77, 88}. Note that the two lists must be completely independent of each other. Changing one list should have no effect upon the other.

3.7   Write and test this method:
```
void append(Node list1, Node list2)
// precondition: list1 has at least one node;
// postcondition: list1 has list2 appended to it;
```
For example, if list1 is {22, 33, 44, 55} and list2 is {66, 77, 88, 99}, then append(list1, list2) will change list1 to {22, 33, 44, 55, 44, 55, 66, 77, 88}. Note that no new nodes are created by this method.

3.8   Write and test this method:
```
Node concat(Node list1, Node list2)
// returns: a new list that contains a copy of list1, followed by
//    a copy of list2;
```
For example, if list1 is {22, 33, 44, 55} and list2 is {66, 77, 88, 99}, then concat(list1, list2) will return the new list {22, 33, 44, 55, 44, 55, 66, 77, 88}. Note that the three lists should be completely independent of each other. Changing one list should have no effect upon the others.

3.9   Write and test this method:
```
void set(Node list, int i, int x)
// replaces the value of element number i with x;
```
For example, if list is {22, 33, 44, 55, 66, 77, 88, 99}, then set(list, 2, 50) will change list to {22, 33, 50, 55, 66, 44, 88, 99}.

3.10   Write and test this method:

```
int get(Node list, int i)
// returns the value of element number i;
```

For example, if list is {22, 33, 44, 55, 66, 77, 88, 99}, then get(list, 2) will return 44.

3.11   Write and test this method:

```
void put(Node list, int i, int x)
// inserts x as element number i;
```

For example, if list is {22, 33, 44, 55, 66, 77, 88, 99}, then put(list, 3, 50) will change list to {22, 33, 44, 50, 55, 66, 44, 88, 99}. Hint: if i = 0, replace the value of the first node with x, and insert a new node immediately after it that contains the previous fist value.

3.12   Write and test this method:

```
void swap(Node list, int i, int j)
// swaps the ith element with the jth element;
```

For example, if list is {22, 33, 44, 55, 66, 77, 88, 99}, then swap(list, 2, 5) will change list to {22, 33, 77, 55, 66, 44, 88, 99}.

3.13   Write and test this method:

```
Node merged(Node list1, Node list2)
// precondition: list1 and list2 are both in ascending order;
// returns: a new list that contains all the elements of list1 and
//    list2 in ascending order;
```

For example, if list1 is {22, 33, 55, 88} and list2 is {44, 66, 77, 99}, then merged(list1, list2) will return the new list {22, 33, 44, 55, 66, 77, 88, 99}. Note that the three lists should be completely independent of each other. Changing one list should have no effect upon the others.

3.14   Write and test this method:

```
void rotateLeft(Node list)
// moves the first element of the specified list to its end;
```

For example, if list is {22, 33, 44, 55, 66, 77, 88, 99}, then rotateLeft(list) will change list to {33, 44, 55, 66, 77, 88, 99, 22}. Note that no new nodes are created by this method.

Answers to Review Questions

3.1   Arrays are inefficient for implementing dynamic sorted lists because the insert and delete operations require moving half the elements, on average.

3.2   An index array is an array whose elements are index values into another array.

3.3   Linked lists provide no direct access. To find the 100th element, you have to move sequentially through the first 99 elements.

3.4   Insertion at the front of a linked list has to be done differently because the link to the new node is the start link; it is not p.next for any node p (unless you use a dummy head node).

3.5   We had to define the linked lists backwards in the BigInt class because the digits of an integer are processed from right to left in the common arithmetic operations.

Solutions to Problems

3.1
```
void delete(int[] a, int n, int x) {
  int i = 0;  // find the first index i for which a[i] > x:
  while (i < n && a[i] <= x) {
    ++i;
  }
  if (i < n-1) {
    System.arraycopy(a, i, a, i-1, n-i);
  }
  a[n-1] = 0;
}
```

3.2
```
int size(Node list) {
  int count = 0;
  while (list != null) {
    ++count;
    list = list.next;
  }
  return count;
}
```

3.3
```
int sum(Node list) {
  int sum = 0;
  while (list != null) {
    sum += list.data;
    list = list.next;
  }
  return sum;
}
```

3.4
```
void removeLast(Node list) {
  if (list == null || list.next == null) {
    throw new IllegalStateException();
  }
  while (list.next.next != null) {
    list = list.next;
  }
  list.next = null;
}
```

3.5
```
Node copy(Node list) {
  if (list == null) {
    return null;
  }
  Node clone = new Node(list.data);
  for (Node p=list, q=clone; p.next != null; p=p.next, q=q.next) {
    q.next = new Node(p.next.data);
  }
  return clone;
}
```

3.6
```
Node sublist(Node list, int p, int q) {
  if (m < 0 || n < m) {
    throw new IllegalArgumentException();
  } else if (n == m) {
    return null;
  }
  for (int i=0; i<m; i++) {
    list = list.next;
  }
```

```
            Node clone = new Node(list.data);
            Node p=list, q=clone;
            for (int i=m+1; i<n; i++) {
              if (p.next == null) {
                throw new IllegalArgumentException();
              }
              q.next = new Node(p.next.data);
              p = p.next;
              q = q.next;
            }
            return clone;
          }
```

3.7
```
          void append(Node list1, Node list2) {
            if (list1 == null) {
              throw new IllegalStateException();
            }
            while (list1.next != null) {
              list1 = list1.next;
            }
            list1.next = list2;
          }
```

3.8
```
          Node concat(Node list1, Node list2) {
            Node list3 = new Node(0), p=list1, q=list3;
            while (p != null) {
              q.next = new Node(p.data);
              p = p.next;
              q = q.next;
            }
            p = list2;
            while (p != null) {
              q.next = new Node(p.data);
              p = p.next;
              q = q.next;
            }
            return list3.next;  // discard dummy head node
          }
```

3.9
```
          void set(Node list, int i, int x) {
            if (i < 0) {
              throw new IllegalArgumentException();
            }
            for (int j=0; j<i; j++) {
              if (list == null) {
                throw new IllegalStateException();
              }
              list = list.next;
            }
            list.data = x;
            return;
          }
```

3.10
```
          int void get(Node list, int i) {
            // returns the value of element number i;
            Node p = list;
            int j = 0;
            while (j < i && p != null) {
              ++j;
              p = p.next;
            }
```

```
              if (p == null) {
                throw new java.util.NoSuchElementException();
              }
              return p.data;
            }
```

3.11
```
            void put(Node list, int i, int x) {
              // inserts x as element number i;
              if (list == null) {
                throw new java.util.NoSuchElementException("list is empty");
              } else if (i == 0) {
                list.next = new Node(list.data, list.next);
                list.data = x;
              } else {
                Node p = list;
                int j = 1;
                while (j < i && p != null) {
                  ++j;
                  p = p.next;
                }
                if (p == null) {
                  String error=String.format("the list has onlt %d elements",j-1);
                  throw new java.util.NoSuchElementException(error);
                }
                p.next = new Node(x, p.next);
              }
            }
```

3.12
```
            void swap(Node list, int i, int j) {
              if (i < 0 || j < 0) {
                throw new IllegalArgumentException();
              } else if (i == j) {
                return;
              }
              Node p=list, q=list;
              for (int ii=0; ii<i; ii++) {
                if (p == null) {
                  throw new IllegalStateException();
                }
                p = p.next;
              }
              for (int jj=0; jj<j; jj++) {
                if (q == null) {
                  throw new IllegalStateException();
                }
                q = q.next;
              }
              int pdata = p.data, qdata = q.data;
              p.data = qdata;
              q.data = pdata;
              return;
            }
```

3.13
```
            Node merged(Node list1, Node list2) {
              Node list = new Node(0), p = list, p1 = list1, p2 = list2;
              while (p1 != null && p2 != null) {
                if (p1.data < p2.data) {
                  p = p.next = new Node(p1.data);
                  p1 = p1.next;
                } else {
                  p = p.next = new Node(p2.data);
                  p2 = p2.next;
```

```
              }
            }
            while (p1 != null) {
              p = p.next = new Node(p1.data);
              p1 = p1.next;
            }
            while (p2 != null) {
              p = p.next = new Node(p2.data);
              p2 = p2.next;
            }
            return list.next;
          }
3.14      void rotateLeft(Node list) {
            Node p = list, q = list;
            while (p != null) {
              p = p.next;
              if (p != null) {
                p = p.next;
              }
              q = q.next;
            }
            // now q = middle node:
            Node m = q;
            p = list;
            Node t=p.next, tt=m.next;
            while (m.next != null) {
              tt = m.next;
              p.next = m;
              p = m.next = t;
              t = p.next;
              m = tt;
            }
            p.next = m;
          }
```

CHAPTER 4

The Java Collections Framework

The Java Collections Framework (JCF) is a group of classes and interfaces in the `java.util` package. Its main purpose is to provide a unified framework for implementing common data structures so that the resulting classes can be used in a consistent, efficient, and intuitive manner. This chapter outlines how these types can be used.

THE INHERITANCE HIERARCHY

A *collection* is an object that contains other objects, which are called the *elements* of the collection. The JCF specifies four general types of collections: `List`, `Queue`, `Set`, and `Map`. These are defined as interfaces and are extended and implemented with other interfaces and classes in the `java.util` package.

The relationships among the main classes and interfaces in the JCF are summarized in Figure 4.1. The interfaces are shown on the right in italics, and the classes that implement them are on their left. The dashed lines indicate direct implementation. Inheritance, both between classes and between interfaces is shown by solid lines. For example, the `AbstractList` class extends the `AbstractCollection` class, and the `List` interface extends the `Collection` interface. Note that some of the class names have the prefix `Abstract`, which indicates that they include abstract methods that are implemented by their subclasses.

The four main types in the JCF are `List`, `Queue`, `Set`, and `Map`. A *list* is a sequence of elements. A *queue* is a first-in-first-out collection, like a waiting line. A *set* is an unstructured collection of distinct elements. A *map* is a collection of component pairs that works like an index or dictionary, where the first component is used to "look up" the information stored in the second component.

The hierarchy shows that the `Deque`, `SortedSet`, and `SortedMap` interfaces extend the `Queue`, `Set`, and `Map` interfaces, respectively. These are more specialized types. A `Deque` is a double-ended queue, allowing insertions and deletions at both ends. The `SortedSet` and `SortedMap` interfaces work only with objects that can be compared, like strings.

The JCF implements the interfaces with several different data structures. The simplest structure is an indexed structure, that is, an array, which is used by the `ArrayList`, the `ArrayDeque`, the `HashSet`, and the `HashMap` classes. Other implementations use a linked structure. The `LinkedList` class uses a doubly linked linear structure, the `PriorityQueue` class uses a heap tree, the `TreeSet` and `TreeMap` classes use a linked binary search tree, and the `LinkedHashSet`,

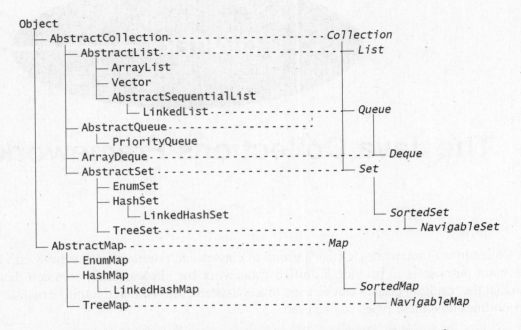

Figure 4.1 The inheritance hierarchy for the Java Collections Framework

and `LinkedHashMap` classes use a hybrid linked array structure. The specialized `EnumSet` and `EnumMap` classes use a bit string. These twelve implementations are summarized in Table 4.1.

Data Structure	List	Queue	Set	Map
Indexed	ArrayList	ArrayDeque	HashSet	HashMap
Linked	LinkedList	PriorityQueue	TreeSet	TreeMap
Indexed with links			LinkedHashSet	LinkedHashMap
Bit string			EnumSet	EnumMap

Table 4.1 Data structures used by the concrete classes in the JCF

The `java.util` package includes four other container classes that were created prior to the introduction of the JCF in Java version 1.2. They are the `Vector`, `Stack`, `Dictionary`, and `Hashtable` classes. Since they are not quite consistent with the JCF, they are now regarded as "legacy classes." The `Vector` and `Stack` classes have been superseded by the `ArrayList` class, and the `Dictionary` and `Hashtable` classes by the `HashMap` class.

THE `Collection` INTERFACE

The `Collection` interface provides a basis for most of the other interfaces and classes in the JCF. It specifies 15 methods, as shown in the Javadoc page in Figure 4.2 on page 71. Some of these methods are obvious: for example, the `clear()`, `contains()`, `isEmpty()`, and `size()` methods. The `equals()` and `hashCode()` methods are inherited from the `Object` class and are meant to be overridden.

The `add()` method may work differently for different implementations. For collections that prohibit duplicate elements, this method should add the specified object only if it is not already an element. For collections that allow duplicate elements, the method should add the specified

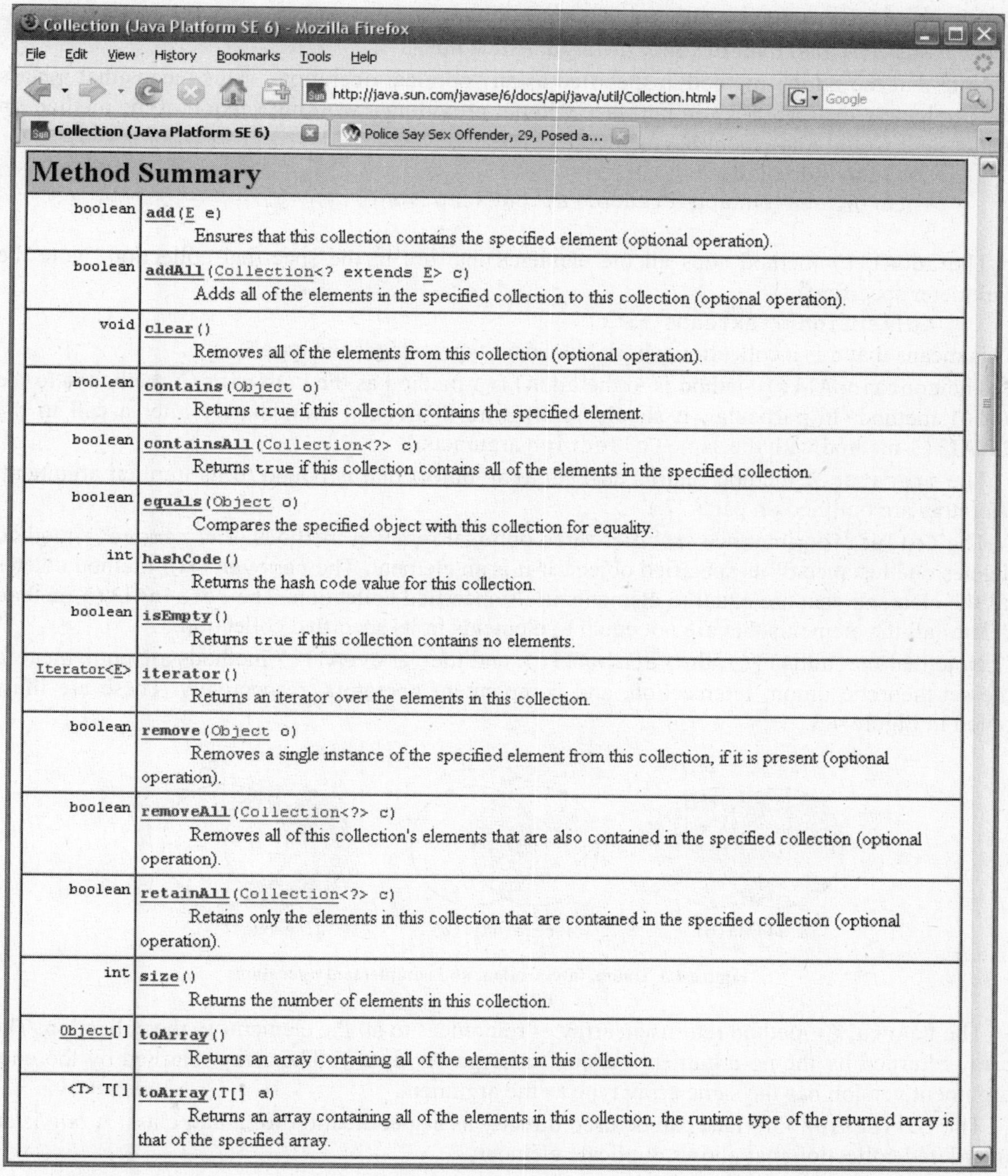

Method Summary

boolean	**add**(E e) Ensures that this collection contains the specified element (optional operation).
boolean	**addAll**(Collection<? extends E> c) Adds all of the elements in the specified collection to this collection (optional operation).
void	**clear**() Removes all of the elements from this collection (optional operation).
boolean	**contains**(Object o) Returns true if this collection contains the specified element.
boolean	**containsAll**(Collection<?> c) Returns true if this collection contains all of the elements in the specified collection.
boolean	**equals**(Object o) Compares the specified object with this collection for equality.
int	**hashCode**() Returns the hash code value for this collection.
boolean	**isEmpty**() Returns true if this collection contains no elements.
Iterator<E>	**iterator**() Returns an iterator over the elements in this collection.
boolean	**remove**(Object o) Removes a single instance of the specified element from this collection, if it is present (optional operation).
boolean	**removeAll**(Collection<?> c) Removes all of this collection's elements that are also contained in the specified collection (optional operation).
boolean	**retainAll**(Collection<?> c) Retains only the elements in this collection that are contained in the specified collection (optional operation).
int	**size**() Returns the number of elements in this collection.
Object[]	**toArray**() Returns an array containing all of the elements in this collection.
<T> T[]	**toArray**(T[] a) Returns an array containing all of the elements in this collection; the runtime type of the returned array is that of the specified array.

Figure 4.2 Methods specified by the `java.util.Collection` interface

object, possibly as a duplicate. In either case, the method should return true if and only if it changed the collection.

The "contract" imposed by the interface requires any class that implements the add() method to throw an exception if the collection does not contain the specified object after the method has been called. For example, if an implement prohibits `null` elements, then the method should throw a `NullPointerException` if the argument is `null`.

Note that the `add()` method is specified as an "optional operation." This means that a class can implement the `Collection` interface without providing a working version of the method. In that case, it would implement the method like this:

```
boolean add(E o) {
    throw new UnsupportedOperationException();
}
```

The `addAll()` method adds all the elements that are in the specified collection. Note the parameter specifier:

```
Collection<? extends E> c
```

This means that c is a collection whose elements' type extends the type E.

The `containsAll()` method is to the `addAll()` method as the `contains()` method is to the `add()` method. In particular, it should return true if invoked immediately after a call to the `addAll()` method with the same `Collection` argument.

The `iterator()` method returns an `Iterator` object that is bound to its implicit argument. (Iterators are outlined on page 77.)

The `Collection` interface specifies three optional removal methods. The `remove()` method deletes one instance of its specified object, if it is an element. The `removeAll()` method deletes all the elements that are equal to elements in its specified collection. The `retainAll()` method deletes all the elements that are not equal to elements in its specified collection.

Note that the `addAll()`, the `retainAll()`, and the `removeAll()` methods are equivalent to the set-theoretic union, intersection, and complement operators, respectively. These are illustrated in Figure 4.3.

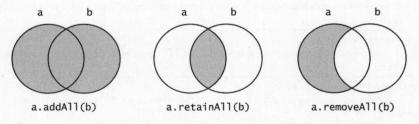

Figure 4.3 Union, intersection, and complement operations

The `toArray()` method returns an array of references to all the elements in the collection. The array returned by the no-argument version has type `Object[]`. The array returned by the one-argument version has the same array type as the argument.

The `Collection` interface can be used directly as a specification for a Bag class. A *bag* is an unordered collection that allows duplicate elements.

THE `HashSet` CLASS

The `HashSet` class is probably the simplest of all the concrete classes in the JCF. Its instances represent ordinary sets of unique elements (no duplicates). In fact, a set can be defined simply as a collection of unique elements. It extends the `AbstractSet` class. That class implements the `Set` interface, which extends the `Collection` interface. (See Figure 4.1 on page 70.)

The Set interface specifies the same 15 methods that the Collection interface specifies. (See Figure 4.2 on page 71.) The only difference is that the "contract" further stipulates that implementing classes are obliged to ensure that duplicate elements cannot be added to the collection.

The AbstractSet class implements the equals() method, the hashCode() method, and the removeAll() method, designating the other 12 methods as abstract. This means that the concrete EnumSet, HashSet, and TreeSet classes have their own specialized implementations of those 12 methods.

The HashSet class gets its name from the fact that collections of this type maintain no order among their elements; they are all mixed up, like hash.

EXAMPLE 4.1 Testing the HashSet Class

This example tests 10 of the 15 methods of the HashSet class.

```
1    public class TestHashSet {
2      public static void main(String[] args) {
3        Set<String> set = new HashSet<String>();
4        System.out.printf("set.isEmpty(): %b%n", set.isEmpty());
5        Collections.addAll(set, "CN", "FR", "GB", "RU", "US");
6        System.out.println(set);
7        System.out.printf("set.size(): %d%n", set.size());
8        System.out.printf("set.contains(\"GB\"): %b%n", set.contains("GB"));
9        System.out.printf("set.contains(\"JP\"): %b%n", set.contains("JP"));
10       System.out.printf("set.isEmpty(): %b%n", set.isEmpty());
11       set.add("BR");
12       System.out.println(set);
13       set.remove("FR");
14       System.out.println(set);
15       String[] array = set.toArray(new String[0]);
16       for (String string : array) {
17         System.out.printf("%s ", string);
18       }
19       System.out.println("");
20       Set<String> g8 = new HashSet<String>();
21       Collections.addAll(g8, "CA", "DE", "FR", "GB", "IT", "JP", "RU", "US");
22       System.out.println(g8);
23       g8.retainAll(set);
24       System.out.println(g8);
25       set.removeAll(g8);
26       System.out.println(set);
27       set.addAll(g8);
28       System.out.println(set);
29       set.clear();
30       System.out.println(set);
31     }
32   }
```

The output is:

```
set.isEmpty(): true
[FR, US, RU, GB, CN]
set.size(): 5
set.contains("GB"): true
set.contains("JP"): false
set.isEmpty(): false
[FR, US, RU, BR, GB, CN]
[US, RU, BR, GB, CN]
US RU BR GB CN
```

```
[JP, FR, US, RU, GB, DE, IT, CA]
[US, RU, GB]
[BR, CN]
[US, RU, BR, GB, CN]
[]
```

The `set` object is instantiated at line 3 as a `HashSet` of `String` elements. The `isEmpty()` method is tested at line 4 and again at line 10.

At line 5, the collection is loaded with five elements. This is done by the static `addAll()` method defined in the `java.util.Collections` class. Note that the order with which the five elements are printed at line 6 is different from the order with which they were added to the set. This illustrates the "hash" nature of the set.

The `size()` and `contains()` methods are tested at lines 7–9. The `add()` method is tested at line 11, and the `remove()` method is tested at line 13.

At line 15, the one-argument `toArray()` method is used to generate a `String` array of the same elements that are in the collection. The `for` loop at lines 16–18 confirms that the array contains the same elements.

Lines 20–21 create and load a second set, named g8. This is then used together with the set collection to test the `retainAll()`, `removeAll()`, and `addAll()` methods at lines 23–28.

Finally, the `clear()` method is tested at line 29.

GENERIC COLLECTIONS

The `<String>` symbol used twice in line 3 of Example 4.1 means that the elements of the collection must be `String` type:

```
3        Set<String> set = new HashSet<String>();
```

The types `Set<String>` and `HashSet<String>` are called *parameterized types* or *generic types*. Specifying the element type this way causes the compiler to prevent any non-`String` objects from being inserted into the collection, making it *type-safe*.

Note that the parametrized type `HashSet<String>` extends the parametrized type `Set<String>` because the type `HashSet` extends the type `Set`. But `HashSet<String>` is not an extension of `HashSet<Object>` or of `Set<Object>`.

The JCF uses type parameters in most of its classes and interfaces. For example, the complete `Queue<E>` interface is shown in Example 4.2.

EXAMPLE 4.2 The Queue Interface

```
1    public interface Queue<E> extends Collection<E> {
2        boolean offer(E o);
3        E poll();
4        E remove();
5        E peek();
6        E element();
7    }
```

The expression `Queue<E> extends Collection<E>` at line 1 means that `Queue<E>` is a specialized collection of elements of some type E, to be specified later. Whatever type that is, it must also be the type for the parameter o in the `offer()` method at line 2 and the return type for the other four methods specified at lines 3–6.

The variable E used in lines 1–6 of Example 4.2 is called a *type parameter*. Like a method parameter, it stands for a type that can be substituted for it. The actual type that is substituted for the type parameter is called a *type argument*. For example:

```
Queue<String> stringQueue = new Queue<String>();
```

Here, the collection `stringQueue` is instantiated by substituting the type argument `String` for the type parameter E.

EXAMPLE 4.3 Using Type Arguments

This program uses two special user-defined types at line 3: an `enum` Month type defined at line 11 and a generic `Pair` type defined at lines 13–32:

```
1    public class TestPairClass {
2      public static void main(String[] args) {
3        Pair<Month, Integer> christmas = new Pair<Month,Integer>(Month.DEC, 25);
4        System.out.println(christmas);
5        Month month = christmas.getFirst();
6        int day = christmas.getSecond();
7        System.out.printf("%d %s%n", day, month);
8      }
9    }
10
11   enum Month { JAN, FEB, MAR, APR, MAY, JUN, JUL, AUG, SEP, OCT, NOV, DEC }
12
13   class Pair<S, T> {
14     private S first;
15     private T second;
16
17     public Pair(S first, T second) {
18       this.first = first;
19       this.second = second;
20     }
21
22     public S getFirst() {
23       return first;
24     }
25
26     public T getSecond() {
27       return second;
28     }
29
30     public String toString() {
31       return "(" + first + ", " + second + ")";
32     }
33   }
```

The output is:

```
(DEC, 25)
25 DEC
```

The generic class is defined at line 13. It has two type parameters: S and T. In the code at lines 14, 15, 17, 22, and 26, these two type parameters are used as place holders for actual types.

Note that the <S,T> expression is not used in the constructor definition at line 18. But the <> construct is required when the constructor is invoked, as at line 3.

If you compile a program using nongeneric JCF classes (i.e., without specifying a type arguments for the element type) you're likely to get a compiler message like this:

```
uses unchecked or unsafe operations.
Note: Recompile with -Xlint:unchecked for details.
```

You can avoid that simply by specifying an element type; even Object itself, like this:

```
List<Object> list = new ArrayList<Object>();
```

GENERIC METHODS

In addition to generic types, type parameters can also be used to define *generic methods*, identified by the generic parameter specifier <T> placed in front of the return type.

EXAMPLE 4.4 A Generic Method

```
1    public class TestPrint {
2      public static void main(String[] args) {
3        args = new String[]{"CA", "US", "MX", "HN", "GT"};
4        print(args);
5      }
6
7      static <E> void print(E[] a) {
8        for (E ae : a) {
9          System.out.printf("%s ", ae);
10       }
11       System.out.println();
12     }
13   }
```

The output is:

```
CA US MX HN GT
```

The method is identified as generic by the <E> specifier at line 7. This allows the type parameter E to be used in place of an actual type in the method block at line 8.

GENERIC WILDCARDS

The symbol ? can be used as a wildcard, in place of a generic variable. It stands for "unknown type," and is called the *wildcard type*.

EXAMPLE 4.5 A Universal print() Method

```
1    static void print(Collection<?> c) {
2      for (Object o : c) {
3        System.out.printf("%s ", o);
4      }
5      System.out.println();
6    }
```

This method can be used to print any type of collection, for example, a HashSet<String> or a Queue<Date>.

Note that if we used Collection<Object> instead of Collection<?> at line 1, then the method would only apply to collections whose element type is specified as Object. For example, it could not be used to print a HashSet<String> because that is not an extension of Collection<Object>.

The wildcard type can be used more selectively to limit the range of types that can be used in its place. For example, if you wanted to restrict the `print()` method in Example 4.5 to extensions of a `Person` class, then you would replace line 1 with:

```
1    static void print(Collection<? extends Person> c) {
```

The expression `? extends Person` is called a *bounded wildcard type*.

ITERATORS

An *iterator* is an object that provides access to the elements of a `Collection` object. It acts like a finger, pointing to one element at a time, much like the cursor of a text editor points to one character at a time. And like a cursor, an iterator has the capability of moving from one element to the next and of deleting its current element.

The analogy between iterators and cursors is not complete. Most iterators cannot jump around the way cursors can. On the other hand, it is possible to have several independent iterators traversing the same collection.

The algorithm that determines each "next" element in the iterator's path is an intrinsic property of the iterator itself. Moreover, it is possible to have several different iterator classes defined for the same collection class, each with its own traversal algorithms.

The requirements for an iterator are specified in the `java.util.Iterator` interface, shown in Figure 4.4.

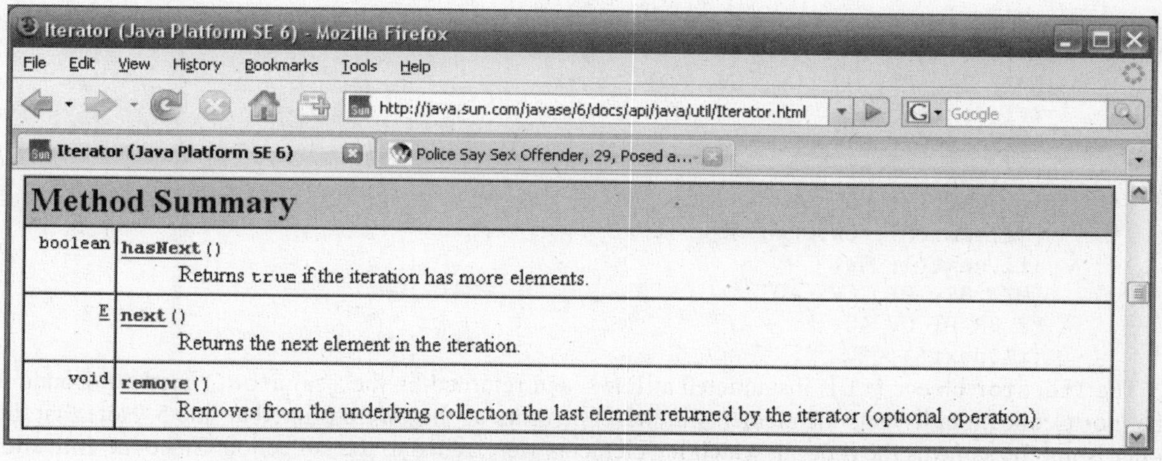

Figure 4.4 Methods specified by the `java.util.Iterator` interface

The `next()` method returns the current element of the collection to which the iterator is bound. Each time the `next()` method is invoked, it advances the iterator to the next element in the collection.

The `hasNext()` method returns `true` unless the iterator has reached the end of its traversal. This predicate is used to determine whether the `next()` method can be called again.

The `remove()` method deletes the last element returned by the `next()` method. This means that `next()` must be called before each call to `remove()`, designating the element to be deleted.

Normally, iterators are obtained by means of a call to the collection's `iterator()` method that is required by the `Collection` interface. (See Figure 4.2 on page 71.) It returns a new iterator, bound to the collection and initialized to its first element.

EXAMPLE 4.6 Using an Iterator

```
 1    public class TestIterators {
 2      public static void main(String[] args) {
 3        Set<String> port = new HashSet<String>();
 4        Collections.addAll(port, "AO", "BR", "CV", "GW", "MO", "MZ", "PT");
 5        System.out.println(port);
 6        Iterator it1 = port.iterator();
 7        System.out.printf("it1.next(): %s%n", it1.next());
 8        System.out.printf("it1.next(): %s%n", it1.next());
 9        System.out.printf("it1.next(): %s%n", it1.next());
10        System.out.printf("it1.next(): %s%n", it1.next());
11        it1.remove();
12        System.out.println(port);
13        System.out.printf("it1.next(): %s%n", it1.next());
14        it1.remove();
15        System.out.println(port);
16        Iterator it2 = port.iterator();
17        while(it2.hasNext()) {
18          System.out.printf("%s ", it2.next());
19        }
20        System.out.println("");
21        System.out.printf("it1.next(): %s%n", it1.next());
22      }
23    }
```

The output is:

```
[MZ, BR, PT, MO, GW, CV, AO]
it1.next(): MZ
it1.next(): BR
it1.next(): PT
it1.next(): MO
[MZ, BR, PT, GW, CV, AO]
it1.next(): GW
[MZ, BR, PT, CV, AO]
MZ BR PT CV AO
it1.next(): CV
```

The Iterator object it1 is instantiated at line 6 and returned by the iterator() method. Bound to the port collection, it visits the elements in the same order as they were printed at line 5. Note that this order is not the same as the order in which the elements were added to the collection. Since the collection is a set, its elements have no intrinsic order. It is the iterator itself that computes the traversal sequence. You can see from the output from line 5 that the toString() method (invoked implicitly by the println() method) uses the same traversal sequence, obviously using its own iterator to build the string.

The it1 iterator's remove() method is invoked at lines 11 and 14. This causes it to delete the "current" element, which in each case is the last element returned by a call to next(). At line 11, the last next() call was at line 10, which returned the MO element; so MO is deleted by remove() at line 11. Similarly, at line 14, the last next() call was at line 13, which returned the GW element; so GW is deleted by remove() at line 14. These deletions are evident from the output produced by the while loop at lines 17–19. Notice that that loop uses the independent iterator it2 to traverse the collection.

Note that the code at lines 16–19 make a complete traversal of the collection. This is guaranteed by the instantiation of the new iterator at line 16 and the use of the hasNext() method to control the loop.

The last output, generated at line 21, confirms that the two iterators it1 and it2 are independent. The action of it2 had no effect on it1, which returns the CV element at line 21.

The iterator it2 in Example 4.6 used a while loop to traverse the collection. Iterators can be used in a for loop the same way:

```
for (Iterator it = countries.iterator(); it.hasNext(); ) {
    System.out.printf("%s ", it.next());
}
```

This is analogous to using a for loop to traverse an array:

```
for (int i = 0; i < countries.length; i++) {
    System.out.printf("%s ", countries[i]);
}
```

Java 5.0 introduced the *for-each construct* for simplifying for loops:

```
for (String country : countries) {
    System.out.printf("%s ", country);
}
```

Here, the String variable country takes the place of the indexed expression countries[i]. This same code also replaces the iterator loop! Thus, the program in Example 4.6 works the same way if we replace lines 16–19 with this simpler for-each loop:

```
for (String country : port) {
    System.out.printf("%s ", country);
}
```

This code implicitly invokes the port collection's iterator() method, generating an implicit iterator, which then implicitly invokes the hasNext() and next() methods within the loop to traverse the collection. The declared variable country takes the place of the expression it.next() inside the loop.

Figure 4.5 illustrates the iterator it2 that traverses the port collection in Example 4.6. The essential feature is that the iterator locates one element at a time in the collection. It is up to the collection's iterator() method to determine the algorithm by which its iterator traverses the collection.

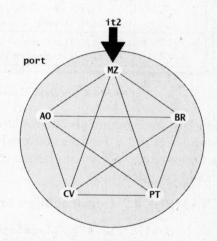

Figure 4.5 The iterator it2 on the set port

THE TreeSet CLASS

In addition to the Set interface, the TreeSet class also implements 6 methods specified by the SortedSet interface (Figure 4.6) and 13 methods specified by its NavigableSet extension (Figure 4.7). These additional 19 methods require implementing classes to maintain an ordering mechanism among their elements, allowing them to be compared for size.

In Java, there are two ways for objects to be compared: either by means of their natural ordering or by the application of an external Comparator object. Classes whose objects enjoy a natural order implement the comparable interface. These include the wrapper classes (Integer, Double, etc.), the BigInteger and BigDecimal classes in the java.math package, and the String class.

User-defined orderings can be defined for a class by implementing the Comparator interface, which is part of the JCF. It specifies a compare() method, which returns an int that indicates

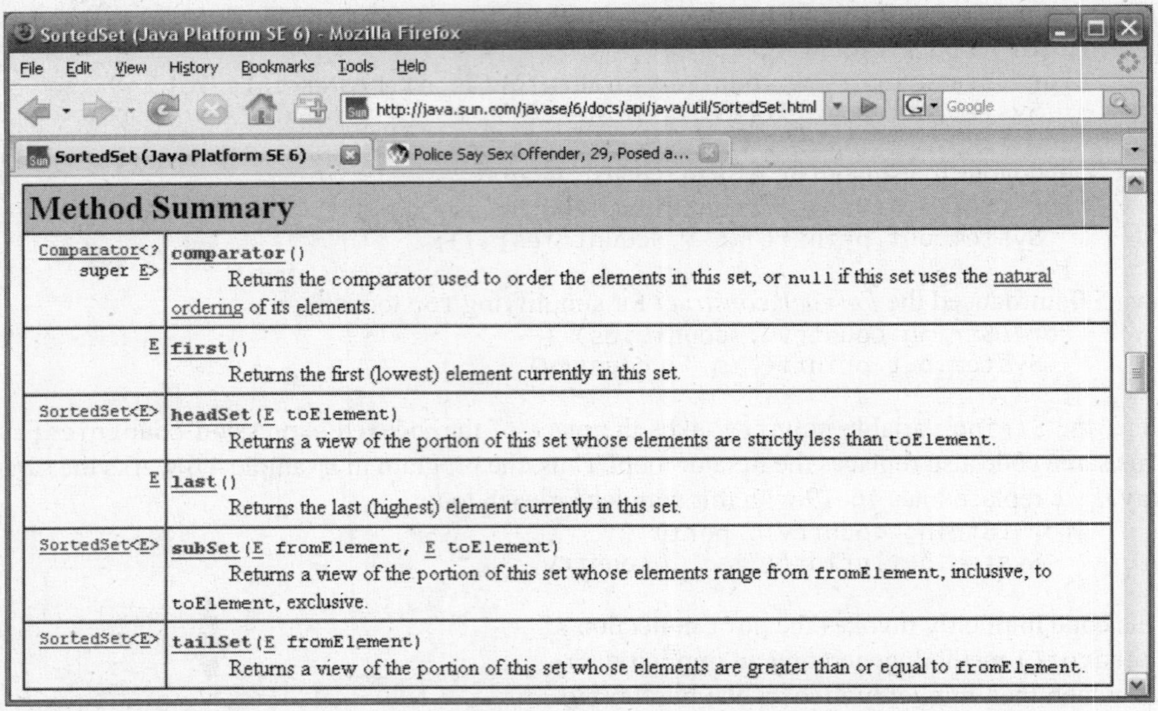

Figure 4.6 Specialized methods specified by the `java.util.SortedSet` interface

how its two arguments are ordered: `compare(x,y) > 0` means that x is greater than y, `compare(x,y) < 0` means that x is less than y, and `compare(x,y) == 0` means that x equals y. A `Comparator` object can be passed to a `SortedSet` constructor to specify how the elements should be ordered.

EXAMPLE 4.7 Constructing a TreeSet Collection with a Comparator Object

```
1   public class TestTreeSetWithComparator {
2     public static void main(String[] args) {
3       SortedSet<String> ital = new TreeSet<String>(new RevStringComparator());
4       Collections.addAll(ital, "IT", "VA", "SM", "CH");
5       System.out.println(ital);
6     }
7   }
8
9   class RevStringComparator implements Comparator<String> {
10    public int compare(String s1, String s2) {
11      StringBuilder sb1 = new StringBuilder(s1);
12      StringBuilder sb2 = new StringBuilder(s2);
13      String s1rev = sb1.reverse().toString();
14      String s2rev = sb2.reverse().toString();
15      return s1rev.compareTo(s2rev);
16    }
17  }
```

The output is:

        [VA, CH, SM, IT]

The separate `RevStringComparator` class implements the `Comparator` interface for `String` objects. It defines its `compare()` method by applying the `String` class's `CompareTo()` method to the reversed

NavigableSet (Java Platform SE 6) - Mozilla Firefox

File Edit View History Bookmarks Tools Help

http://java.sun.com/javase/6/docs/api/java/util/NavigableSet.h |G▾| Google

NavigableSet (Java Platform SE 6)   Police Say Sex Offender, 29, Posed a…

Method Summary

E	**ceiling**(E e) Returns the least element in this set greater than or equal to the given element, or null if there is no such element.
Iterator<E>	**descendingIterator**() Returns an iterator over the elements in this set, in descending order.
NavigableSet<E>	**descendingSet**() Returns a reverse order view of the elements contained in this set.
E	**floor**(E e) Returns the greatest element in this set less than or equal to the given element, or null if there is no such element.
SortedSet<E>	**headSet**(E toElement) Returns a view of the portion of this set whose elements are strictly less than toElement.
NavigableSet<E>	**headSet**(E toElement, boolean inclusive) Returns a view of the portion of this set whose elements are less than (or equal to, if inclusive is true) toElement.
E	**higher**(E e) Returns the least element in this set strictly greater than the given element, or null if there is no such element.
Iterator<E>	**iterator**() Returns an iterator over the elements in this set, in ascending order.
E	**lower**(E e) Returns the greatest element in this set strictly less than the given element, or null if there is no such element.
E	**pollFirst**() Retrieves and removes the first (lowest) element, or returns null if this set is empty.
E	**pollLast**() Retrieves and removes the last (highest) element, or returns null if this set is empty.
NavigableSet<E>	**subSet**(E fromElement, boolean fromInclusive, E toElement, boolean toInclusive) Returns a view of the portion of this set whose elements range from fromElement to toElement.
SortedSet<E>	**subSet**(E fromElement, E toElement) Returns a view of the portion of this set whose elements range from fromElement, inclusive, to toElement, exclusive.
SortedSet<E>	**tailSet**(E fromElement) Returns a view of the portion of this set whose elements are greater than or equal to fromElement.
NavigableSet<E>	**tailSet**(E fromElement, boolean inclusive) Returns a view of the portion of this set whose elements are greater than (or equal to, if inclusive is true) fromElement.

Figure 4.7 Specialized methods specified by the java.util.NavigableSet interface

strings. As a result, the SortedSet collection orders its elements by applying alphabetical ordering to their reversed strings. Since AV < HC < MS < TI (alphabetically), the order of the four inserted elements is as shown in the output from line 5.

If the TreeSet collection is instantiated without an explicit Comparator object, then it uses its elements' natural ordering.

EXAMPLE 4.8 Testing the TreeSet Class

```
1    public class TestTreeSet {
2      public static void main(String[] args) {
3        NavigableSet<String> engl = new TreeSet<String>();
4        Collections.addAll(engl, "IN", "US", "PK", "NG", "PH", "GB", "ZA");
5        System.out.println(engl);
6        engl.add("KE");
7        System.out.println(engl);
8        SortedSet<String> head = engl.headSet("KE");
9        SortedSet<String> mid = engl.subSet("KE", "US");
10       SortedSet<String> tail = engl.tailSet("US");
11       System.out.printf("%s %s %s%n", head, mid, tail);
12       System.out.printf("engl.first(): %s%n", engl.first());
13       System.out.printf("engl.last(): %s%n", engl.last());
14     }
15   }
```

The output is:
```
[GB, IN, NG, PH, PK, US, ZA]
[GB, IN, KE, NG, PH, PK, US, ZA]
[GB, IN] [KE, NG, PH, PK] [US, ZA]
engl.first(): GB
engl.last(): ZA
engl.lower("KE"): IN
engl.higher("KE"): NG
```

The set engl is instantiated as a TreeSet of String elements at line 3 and loaded with seven elements at line 4. An eighth element is added at line 6. The outputs from lines 5 and 7 confirm that the TreeSet is maintaining its elements in their natural (alphabetical) order.

Lines 8–13 illustrate some of the specialized methods implemented by the TreeSet class. (See Figure 4.6 on page 80.) The headSet() method returns the sorted subset of all elements that precede its argument. The subSet() method returns the sorted subset of elements that begin with its first argument and precede its second argument. The tailSet() method returns the sorted subset of all elements that do not precede its argument. Note that these three methods adhere to the Java's "left-continuous" policy that whenever a linear segment is to be specified by two bounding points a and b, the segment will include the lower element a and exclude the upper element b. For example, the subset [KE, NG, PH, PK] returned by the call engl.subSet("KE", "US") at line 9 includes the lower element KE and excludes the upper element US.

The intrinsic difference between the HashSet and TreeSet classes is their backing data structure. The HashSet class uses a hash table (outlined in Chapter 8), which uses each element's hashCode() to compute its location in the set. The TreeSet class uses a balanced binary search tree (outlined in Chapter 12) to store its elements. The advantages and disadvantages of these two data structures are summarized in Table 4.2.

These relative advantages and disadvantages make the choice easy: If you want to preserve the natural order of the elements in your set, use the TreeSet class; otherwise, use the HashSet

Data structure	Advantage	Disadvantage
Hash table	Access time is independent of the size *n* of the collection	Elements are stored in random order.
Search tree	Elements are accessible in their natural order	Access time is proportional to log*n*

Table 4.2 Hash tables versus search trees

class. In practice, the slower access time of the `TreeSet` class is usually not noticeable, unless the set is really large. For example, if $n < 1000$, there's really no disadvantage in using the `TreeSet` class.

THE `LinkedHashSet` CLASS

The `LinkedHashSet` class is the same as the `HashSet` class, except that it maintains a doubly linked list of the elements in the order in which they are inserted. This overcomes the random ordering of the `HashSet` class. The only disadvantage is slightly slower insertion and deletion times, which in most cases would be unnoticeable.

EXAMPLE 4.9 Testing the `LinkedHashSet` Class

```
1    public class TestLinkedHashSet {
2      public static void main(String[] args) {
3        Set<String> ital = new LinkedHashSet<String>();
4        Collections.addAll(ital, "IT", "VA", "SM", "CH");
5        System.out.println(ital);
6        ital.remove("VA");
7        System.out.println(ital);
8        ital.add("VA");
9        System.out.println(ital);
10     }
11   }
```

The output is:
```
[IT, VA, SM, CH]
[IT, SM, CH]
[IT, SM, CH, VA]
```

This program creates the same `ital` set as in Example 4.8 on page 82. The output from line 5 confirms that its access order matches the order in which the elements were inserted. The output from line 9 shows that the `add()` method inserts at the end of the linked list.

THE `EnumSet` CLASS

The `EnumSet` class is designed for elements of an `enum` type (*enumerated type*). For example,
```
enum Day { SUN, MON, TUE, WED, THU, FRI, SAT }
```
If an application uses sets of days, then those sets can be implemented most efficiently as `EnumSet` objects using an enum type like this.

In addition to the 15 methods required by the `Set` interface, the `EnumSet` class also implements the 13 additional methods specified in its Javadoc page, shown in Figure 4.8. Notice that each of these methods returns an `EnumSet` object, and every one except `clone()` is a `static` method. These are used to instantiate the sets, like this:
```
EnumSet<Day> weekdays = EnumSet.range(Day.MON, Day.FRI);
EnumSet<Day> weekend = EnumSet.of(Day.SUN, Day.SAT);
```

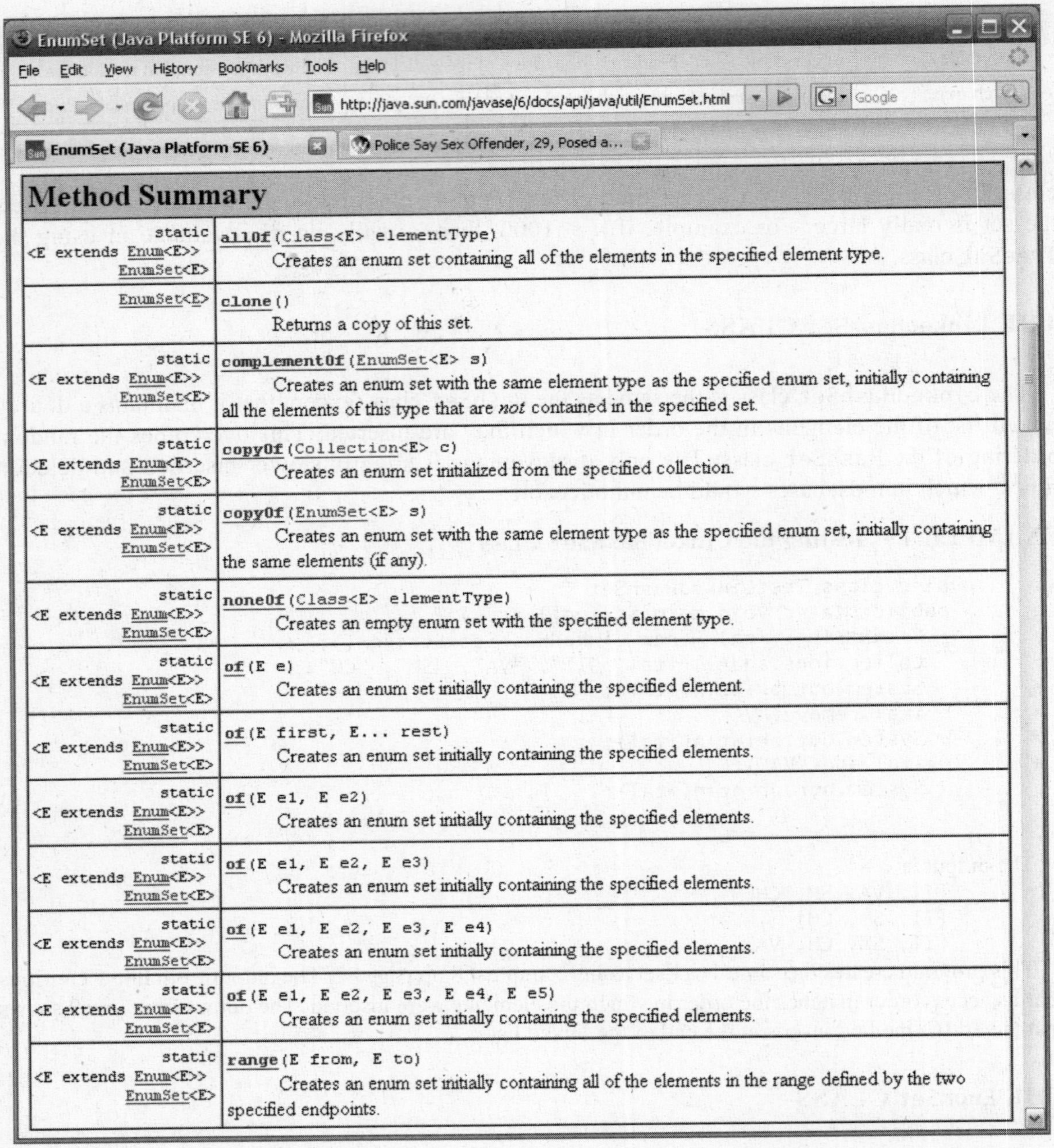

Method Summary

static <E extends Enum<E>> EnumSet<E>	**allOf**(Class<E> elementType) Creates an enum set containing all of the elements in the specified element type.
EnumSet<E>	**clone**() Returns a copy of this set.
static <E extends Enum<E>> EnumSet<E>	**complementOf**(EnumSet<E> s) Creates an enum set with the same element type as the specified enum set, initially containing all the elements of this type that are *not* contained in the specified set.
static <E extends Enum<E>> EnumSet<E>	**copyOf**(Collection<E> c) Creates an enum set initialized from the specified collection.
static <E extends Enum<E>> EnumSet<E>	**copyOf**(EnumSet<E> s) Creates an enum set with the same element type as the specified enum set, initially containing the same elements (if any).
static <E extends Enum<E>> EnumSet<E>	**noneOf**(Class<E> elementType) Creates an empty enum set with the specified element type.
static <E extends Enum<E>> EnumSet<E>	**of**(E e) Creates an enum set initially containing the specified element.
static <E extends Enum<E>> EnumSet<E>	**of**(E first, E... rest) Creates an enum set initially containing the specified elements.
static <E extends Enum<E>> EnumSet<E>	**of**(E e1, E e2) Creates an enum set initially containing the specified elements.
static <E extends Enum<E>> EnumSet<E>	**of**(E e1, E e2, E e3) Creates an enum set initially containing the specified elements.
static <E extends Enum<E>> EnumSet<E>	**of**(E e1, E e2, E e3, E e4) Creates an enum set initially containing the specified elements.
static <E extends Enum<E>> EnumSet<E>	**of**(E e1, E e2, E e3, E e4, E e5) Creates an enum set initially containing the specified elements.
static <E extends Enum<E>> EnumSet<E>	**range**(E from, E to) Creates an enum set initially containing all of the elements in the range defined by the two specified endpoints.

Figure 4.8 Specialized methods implemented by the `java.util.EnumSet` class

EXAMPLE 4.10 Testing the EnumSet Class

```
1    public class TestEnumSet {
2
3      public static enum Month { JAN, FEB, MAR, APR, MAY, JUN,
4        JUL, AUG, SEP, OCT, NOV, DEC }
5
```

```
 6      public static void main(String[] args) {
 7        EnumSet<Month> spring = EnumSet.range(Month.MAR, Month.JUN);
 8        System.out.println(spring);
 9        System.out.println(EnumSet.complementOf(spring));
10        EnumSet<Month> shortMonths =
11            EnumSet.of(Month.SEP, Month.APR, Month.JUN, Month.NOV, Month.FEB);
12        System.out.println(shortMonths);
13        shortMonths.addAll(spring);
14        System.out.println(shortMonths);
15      }
16    }
```

The output is:

```
[MAR, APR, MAY, JUN]
[JAN, FEB, JUL, AUG, SEP, OCT, NOV, DEC]
[FEB, APR, JUN, SEP, NOV]
[FEB, MAR, APR, MAY, JUN, SEP, NOV]
```

The `enum` type `Month` is defined at line 3. Variables of that type can have only those 12 specified values (or `null`). At line 7, the `EnumSet` `spring` is instantiated by invoking the `static range()` method of the `EnumSet` class. Notice that this method does not adhere to Java's "left-continuous" policy (see page 82): the resulting set includes both of the specified elements `MAR` and `JUN`.

The `EnumSet` class's `complementOf()` and `of()` methods are invoked at lines 9 and 11, respectively. These work as described in the Javadoc, shown in Figure 4.8 on page 84. The `addAll()` method is tested at line 13, producing the union of the `shortMonths` and `spring` sets.

THE `List` INTERFACE

A *list* is a linearly ordered data structure in which every element (except possibly the first) has a predecessor element and every element (except possibly the last) has a successor element. List elements are usually numbered in sequence: x_0, x_1, x_2, . . . The numbers are called *indexes* or *subscripts*. Unlike sets, list data structures usually allow duplicate elements.

The `List` interface extends the `Collection` interface. (See Figure 4.1 on page 70.) In addition to the 15 methods specified by the `Collection` interface (Figure 4.2 on page 71), the `List` interface also specifies these 10 additional methods:

```
voidadd(int index, E element)
boolean addAll(int index, Collection<? extends E> c)
E get(int index)
int indexOf(Object o)
int lastIndexOf(Object o)
ListIterator<E> listIterator()
ListIterator<E> listIterator(int index)
E remove(int index)
E set(int index, E element)
List<E> subList(int fromIndex, int toIndex)
```

These methods use indexed access into the list.

The indexed `addAll()` method has a second parameter with this generic type:

```
Collection<? extends E>
```

The `?` symbol, called a *generic wildcard*, means that the type is unknown. The expression `? extends E` means the unknown type must be an extension of the collection's element type `E`.

The `ListIterator<E>` type is outlined on page 87.

THE `ArrayList` AND `Vector` CLASSES

The `ArrayList` class uses an array to implement the `List` interface. When the array becomes full, the `add()` method resizes it by replacing it with one that is twice as big. That is time-consuming, but it happens infrequently.

The array index allows the `get()` and `set()` methods to run in constant time, independent of the size of the collection. Also, the no-argument `add()` method runs in *amortized constant time*, which means that the time it takes to insert *n* elements is (on average) proportional to *n*. It does so by appending the new elements to the end of the list.

The indexed `add()` and `remove()` methods have to shift subsequences of elements back and forth in the array to accommodate the inserted elements and to fill the gaps left by the deleted elements. Consequently, these operations run in *linear time*, which means that the time is (on average) proportional to the size of the collection.

The `Vector` class is similar to the `ArrayList` class, using a resizable array to store its elements. It has 45 methods, including the 3 that it inherits from the `AbstractList` class. In addition to those 3, the 15 methods specified by the `Collection` interface (Figure 4.2 on page 71), and the 10 methods specified by the `List` interface, it implements these 17 `Vector` methods:

```
void addElement(E obj)
int capacity()
void copyInto(Object[] anArray)
E elementAt(int index)
Enumeration<E> elements()
void ensureCapacity(int minCapacity)
E firstElement()
int indexOf(Object o, int index)
void insertElementAt(E obj, int index)
E lastElement()
int lastIndexOf(Object o, int index)
void removeAllElements()
boolean removeElement(Object obj)
void removeElementAt(int index)
void setElementAt(E obj, int index)
void setSize(int newSize)
void trimToSize()
```

These date back to Java 1.0, which preceded the JCF. Most of them are redundant. For example, the `removeElement(Object)` method is the same as the `remove(Object)` method specified by the `Collection` interface, and the `removeElementAt(int)` method is the same as the `remove(int)` method specified by the `List` interface.

THE `LinkedList` CLASS

The `LinkedList` class uses a doubly linked list to implement the `List` interface. In addition to the 25 methods specified by the `Collection` and `List` interfaces, this class also implements these 11 other methods:

```
void addFirst(E o)
void addLast(E o)
E element()
```

```
E getFirst()
E getLast()
boolean offer(E o)
E peek()
E poll()
E remove()
E removeFirst()
E removeLast()
```

The add, get, and remove methods that refer to first and last access the first element and last element of the list, respectively. For example, the call

```
list.addFirst(x);
```

would add the object x to the front of the list, making it the first element.

Note that the three remove methods listed here are all obviated by the remove(int) method specified by the List interface. The LinkedList methods remove() and removeFirst() are the same as the List method remove(0).

The other five new methods (element(), offer(), peek(), poll(), and remove()) are outlined below.

THE ListIterator INTERFACE

The ListIterator interface extends the Iterator interface by specifying the six additional methods shown in Figure 4.9. These extra methods require ListIterator objects to be *bidirectional*. Thus, previous(), hasPrevious(), and previousIndex() act the same way as next(), hasNext(), and nextIndex(), respectively, except in the reverse direction.

The ListIterator interface also adds two more "optional requirements": the add() and set() methods, to accompany the optional remove() method. Recall (page 72) that the purpose of specifying an "optional" method in an interface is to recommend the method signature for that method if it is implemented. To avoid implementing the method, the class can simply throw a new UnsupportedOperationException object, as shown on page 72.

THE Queue INTERFACE

A *queue* is a waiting line. In computing, a queue is a linear data structure that allows insertions only at one end and deletions only at the other end. As a dynamic data structure, this embodies the first-in-first-out (FIFO) protocol. The most familiar use of the queue data structure is a *print queue*, which temporarily holds print jobs for a printer.

The Queue interface was added to the JCF with Java 5.0. Reflecting the print queue prototype, the Javadoc states that a queue is a "collection designed for holding elements prior to processing." It specifies five specialized methods in addition to the 15 methods specified by the Collection interface, overriding the add() method. (See Figure 4.10 on page 89.)

The add() and offer() methods insert the specified element at the back of the queue. The only difference between them is their behavior when the queue is full: add() throws an unchecked exception, while offer() returns false.

The element() and peek() methods return the element at the front of the queue. The only difference between them is their behavior when the queue is empty: element() throws a NoSuchElementException, while peek() returns null.

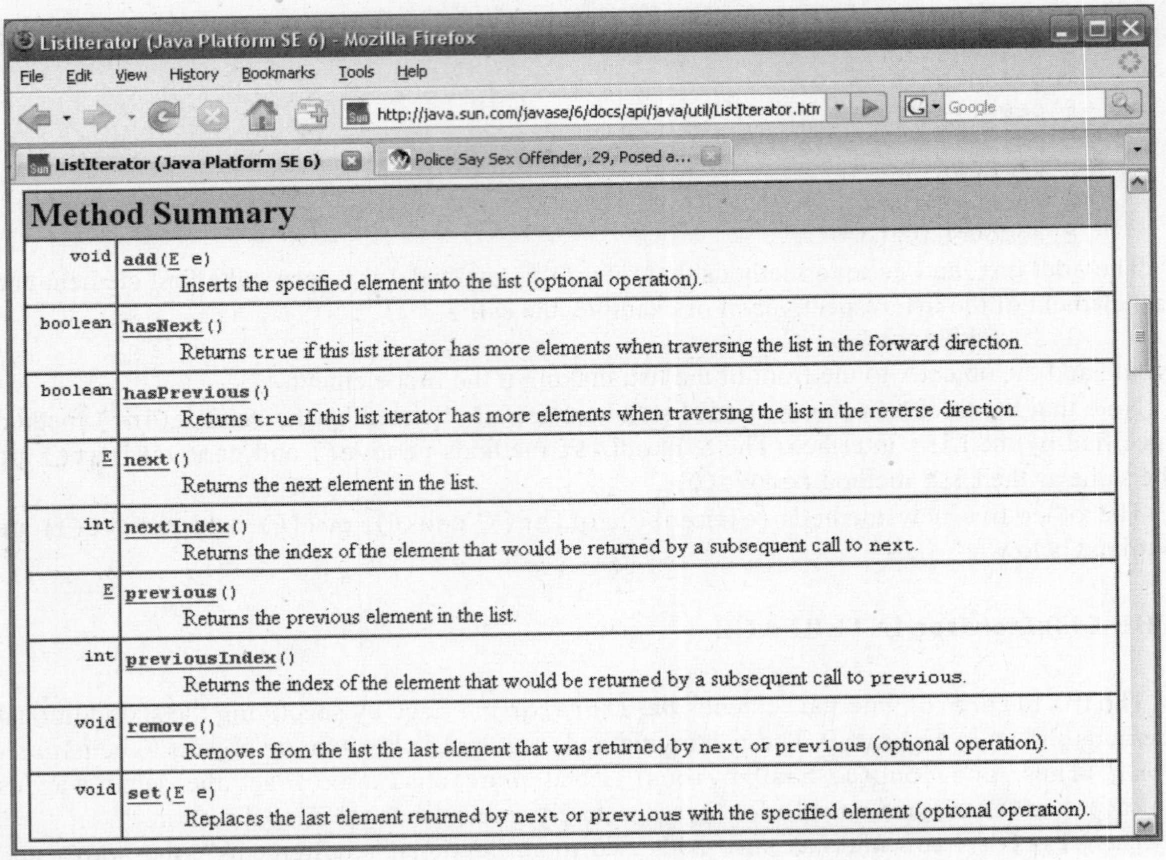

Figure 4.9 The `java.util.ListIterator` interface

The `remove()` and `poll()` methods delete and return the element at the front of the queue. The only difference between them is their behavior when the queue is empty: `remove()` throws a `NoSuchElementException`, while `poll()` returns `null`.

The `AbstractQueue` class implements 5 of the 20 required methods of the `Queue` interface: `add()`, `addAll()`, `clear()`, `element()`, and `remove()`. The purpose of this class (as with all abstract classes) is to serve as a partial implementation, to be completed in a concrete extension by implementing the other required methods. The Javadoc for the `AbstractQueue` class states: "A `Queue` implementation that extends this class must minimally define a method `Queue.offer(E)` which does not permit insertion of null elements, along with methods `Queue.peek()`, `Queue.poll()`, `Collection.size()`, and a `Collection.iterator()` supporting `Iterator.remove()`."

EXAMPLE 4.11 Implementing a LinkedQueue Class

```
1    public class TestQueue {
2      public static void main(String[] args) {
3        Queue<String> queue = new LinkedQueue<String>();
4        Collections.addAll(queue, "AR", "BO", "CO", "EC");
5        System.out.println(queue);
6        String firstOut = queue.remove();
```

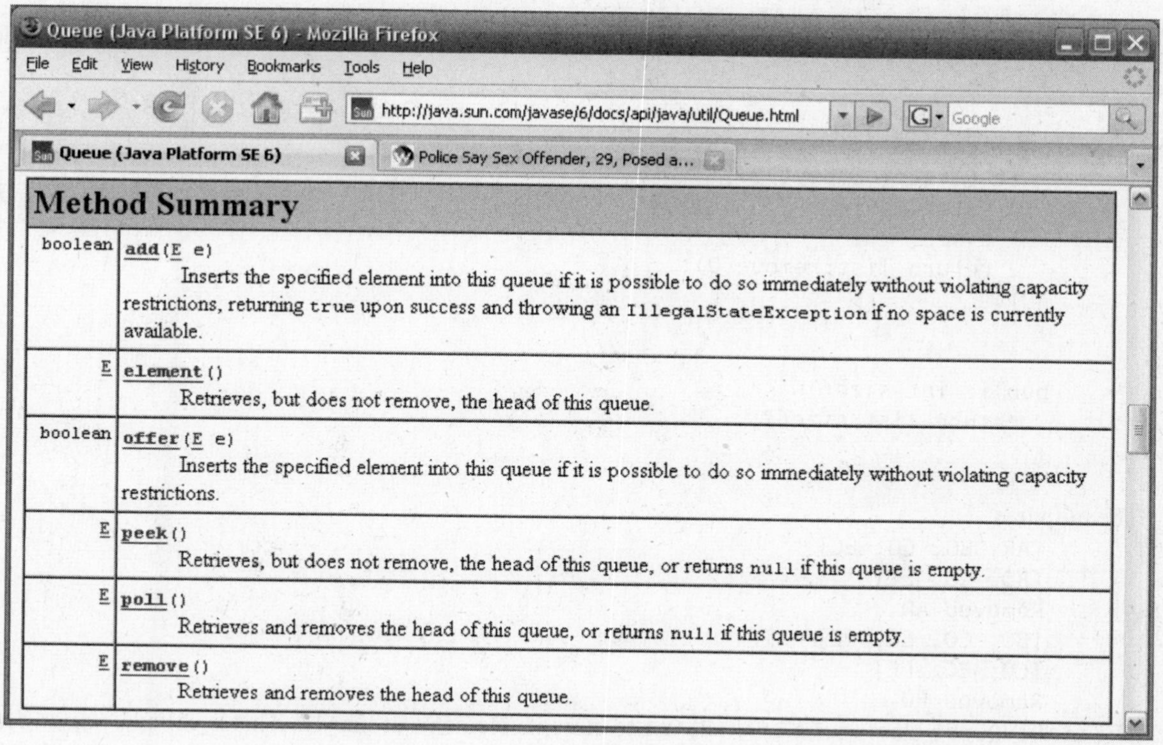

Method Summary

boolean	**add**(E e) Inserts the specified element into this queue if it is possible to do so immediately without violating capacity restrictions, returning `true` upon success and throwing an `IllegalStateException` if no space is currently available.
E	**element**() Retrieves, but does not remove, the head of this queue.
boolean	**offer**(E e) Inserts the specified element into this queue if it is possible to do so immediately without violating capacity restrictions.
E	**peek**() Retrieves, but does not remove, the head of this queue, or returns `null` if this queue is empty.
E	**poll**() Retrieves and removes the head of this queue, or returns `null` if this queue is empty.
E	**remove**() Retrieves and removes the head of this queue.

Figure 4.10 Specialized methods specified by the `java.util.Queue` interface

```
7          System.out.println(queue);
8          System.out.printf("Removed %s%n", firstOut);
9          queue.add("PE");
10         System.out.println(queue);
11         String secondOut = queue.remove();
12         System.out.println(queue);
13         System.out.printf("Removed %s%n", secondOut);
14       }
15     }
16
17     class LinkedQueue<E> extends AbstractQueue<E> implements Queue<E> {
18       private List<E> list = new LinkedList<E>();
19
20       public Iterator<E> iterator() {
21         return list.iterator();
22       }
23
24       public boolean offer(E e) {
25         if (e == null) {
26           return false;
27         } else {
28           list.add(e);
29           return true;
30         }
31       }
32
```

```
33        public E peek() {
34          return list.get(0);
35        }
36
37        public E poll() {
38          if (list.isEmpty()) {
39            return null;
40          } else {
41            return list.remove(0);
42          }
43        }
44
45        public int size() {
46          return list.size();
47        }
48    }
```

The output is:

```
[AR, BO, CO, EC]
[BO, CO, EC]
Removed AR
[BO, CO, EC, PE]
[CO, EC, PE]
Removed BO
```

The LinkedQueue class uses a LinkedList to store its elements at line 18. This is called *composition* of classes; a LinkedQueue object is composed of a LinkedList object. It allows the composing class's methods to be implemented using the component class's methods. Thus, offer() uses list.add() at line 28, peek() uses list.get() at line 34, poll() uses list.remove() at line 41, and size() uses list.size() at line 46.

The action of the main() method illustrates the FIFO nature of a queue: Insert elements at the back and remove them from the front. Thus, the first in (AR) was the first out (at line 6), and the second in (BO) was the second out (at line 11).

THE PriorityQueue CLASS

A *priority queue* is the same as an ordinary queue except for its removal algorithm: Instead of removing the element that has been in the queue the longest, it removes the element that has the highest priority. This of course, requires its elements to be prioritized. In other words, the elements have to have some ordering mechanism; either a natural order, such as alphabetic order for strings, or an order imposed by a Comparator object. (See page 79.)

The PriorityQueue class extends the AbstractQueue class, implementing the Queue interface. To accommodate the priority protocol, it includes a constructor for specifying a Comparator, a constructor for specifying a SortedSet source of elements, and an accessor method for obtaining the elements' comparator:

```
PriorityQueue(int initialCapacity, Comparator<? super E> comparator)
PriorityQueue(SortedSet<? extends E> c)
Comparator<? super E> comparator()
```

Note that the first of these two constructors requires the collection's initialCapacity to be specified. That is because the PriorityQueue class is implemented with a heap data structure, which uses an array to store its elements. (See Chapter 13.)

EXAMPLE 4.12 Testing the PriorityQueue Class

```
1    public class TestPriorityQueue {
2      public static void main(String[] args) {
3        Queue<String> queue = new PriorityQueue<String>();
4        Collections.addAll(queue, "CO", "UY", "EC", "AR");
5        System.out.printf("Removed %s%n", queue.remove());
6        System.out.printf("Removed %s%n", queue.remove());
7        queue.add("PE");
8        queue.add("BO");
9        System.out.printf("Removed %s%n", queue.remove());
10       System.out.printf("Removed %s%n", queue.remove());
11     }
12   }
```

The output is:

```
Removed AR
Removed CO
Removed BO
Removed EC
```

The queue collection is instantiated at line 3 as a PriorityQueue of Strings. Consequently, the remove() method always removes the element that comes first alphabetically.

THE Deque INTERFACE AND ArrayDeque CLASS

A deque (pronounced "deck") is a double-ended queue, that is, a linear data structure that allows insertions and deletions at both ends but nowhere else.

The Deque interface extends the Queue interface. (See Figure 4.1 on page 70.) In addition to the 15 methods specified by the Collection interface and the 5 more methods specified by the Queue interface, the Deque interface specifies these 17 methods:

```
void           addFirst(E e)
void           addLast(E e)
Iterator<E>    descendingIterator()
E              getFirst()
E              getLast()
boolean        offerFirst(E e)
boolean        offerLast(E e)
E              peekFirst()
E              peekLast()
E              pollFirst()
E              pollLast()
E              pop()
void           push(E e)
E              removeFirst()
E              removeLast()
boolean        removeFirstOccurrence(Object o)
boolean        removeLastOccurrence(Object o)
```

Notice how these methods come in pairs, one each for each end of the deque: first for the front of the deque, and last for the back.

The descendingIterator() method is the same as the iterator() method, except that it moves in the opposite direction.

The `pop()` and `push()` methods are the same as the `removeFirst()` and `addFirst()` methods, respectively. They are the traditional names for the insert and delete methods for a *stack* data structure, which is a deque that allows access at only one end. (See Chapter 5.)

The `ArrayDeque` class implements the `Deque` interface by using a resizable array to store its elements. The `Deque` interface and its `ArrayDeque` implementation were added to the JCF with Java 6.

EXAMPLE 4.13   Using the ArrayDeque Class

```
1   public class TestArrayDeque {
2     public static void main(String[] args) {
3       Deque<String> deque = new ArrayDeque<String>();
4       Collections.addAll(deque, "GB", "DE", "FR", "ES");
5       System.out.println(deque);
6       System.out.println("deque.getFirst(): " + deque.getFirst());
7       System.out.println(deque);
8       System.out.println("deque.removeFirst(): " + deque.removeFirst());
9       System.out.println(deque);
10      System.out.println("deque.addFirst(\"IT\"):");
11      deque.addFirst("IT");
12      System.out.println(deque);
13      System.out.println("deque.getLast(): " + deque.getLast());
14      System.out.println(deque);
15      System.out.println("deque.removeLast(): " + deque.removeLast());
16      System.out.println(deque);
17      System.out.println("deque.addLast(\"IE\"):");
18      deque.addLast("IE");
19      System.out.println(deque);
20    }
21  }
```

The output is:
```
[GB, DE, FR, ES]
deque.getFirst(): GB
[GB, DE, FR, ES]
deque.removeFirst(): GB
[DE, FR, ES]
deque.addFirst("IT"):
[IT, DE, FR, ES]
deque.getLast(): ES
[IT, DE, FR, ES]
deque.removeLast(): ES
[IT, DE, FR]
deque.addLast("IE"):
[IT, DE, FR, IE]
```
The program tests the `get()`, `add()`, and `remove()` methods from both ends of the deque.

THE Map INTERFACE AND ITS IMPLEMENTING CLASSES

A *map* (also called a *dictionary* or *look-up table*) is a collection whose elements are key-value pairs. A *key* is a unique element that acts as an identifier for its *value*, which is an element that typically holds several components of data.

The information shown in Table 4.3 provides a good example. If these data were stored in a map data structure, then each row would be stored in a separate key-value pair. The keys would be the strings in the ISO column. The value for each key would be the rest of the data for the country that is uniquely identified by that key. These data could be the fields of a

Name	ISO	Language	Area	Population	Age
Austria	AT	German	83,870	8,192,880	40.9
Poland	PL	Polish	312,685	38,536,869	37.0
France	FR	French	547,030	60,876,136	39.1
Germany	DE	German	357,021	82,422,299	42.6
Italy	IT	Italian	301,230	58,133,509	42.2
Portugal	PT	Portuguese	92,391	10,605,870	38.5
Sweden	SE	Swedish	449,964	9,016,596	40.9

Table 4.3 A table of seven records

Country object, using the Country class defined in Example 4.14.

The Map interface is defined like this:

```
public interface Map<K,V>
```

Its type parameters are the key type K and the value type V. The type Map<String,Country> could be used for the records in Table 4.3, using the String class for K and a Country class for V. (See page 74.)

The Map interface is shown in Figure 4.11 on page 94. It specifies 14 methods. Note that this interface does not extend the Collection interface. (See Figure 4.1 on page 70.) Sets, lists, and queues are collections of individual elements, which are not key-value pairs.

The two subinterfaces and five implementing classes of the Map interface are analogous to the corresponding subinterfaces and implementing classes of the Set interface. Like the AbstractSet class, the AbstractMap class implements only those methods that are either independent of the underlying data structure or can be implemented using the other methods. Like the EnumSet, HashSet, LinkedHashSet, and TreeSet classes, the EnumMap, HashMap, LinkedHashMap, and TreeMap implement the abstract methods.

The EnumMap class is defined like this:

```
public class EnumMap<K extends Enum<K>,V> extends AbstractMap<K,V>
```

The expression K extends Enum<K> means that only enum types can be used for the key type K.

EXAMPLE 4.14 Using the EnumMap Class

```
1    public class TestEnumMap {
2      public static void main(String[] args) {
3        Map<EuCodes,Country> eu = new EnumMap<EuCodes,Country>(EuCodes.class);
4        eu.put(EuCodes.AT, new Country("Austria","German",83870,8192880,40.9));
5        eu.put(EuCodes.PL, new Country("Poland","Polish",312685,38536869,37.0));
6        eu.put(EuCodes.FR, new Country("France","French",547030,60876136,39.1));
7        System.out.println(eu.size());
8        System.out.println(eu.keySet());
9        System.out.println(eu.get(EuCodes.PL));
10       }
11     }
12
13     enum EuCodes { AM, AT, BY, BE, BG, HR, CY, CZ, DK, EE, FI, FR, GE,
14         DE, GR, HU, IS, IE, IT, LV, LI, LT, LU, MK, MT, MD, MC, NL,
15         NO, PL, PT, RO, RU, SK, SI, ES, SE, CH, TR, UA, GB, VA }
16
17     class Country {
18       private String name;
19       private String language;
```

```
20      private int area;
21      private int population;
22      private double avAge;
23
24      Country(String name, String lang, int area, int pop, double avAge) {
25        this.name = name;
26        this.language = lang;
27        this.area = area;
28        this.population = pop;
29        this.avAge = avAge;
30      }
```

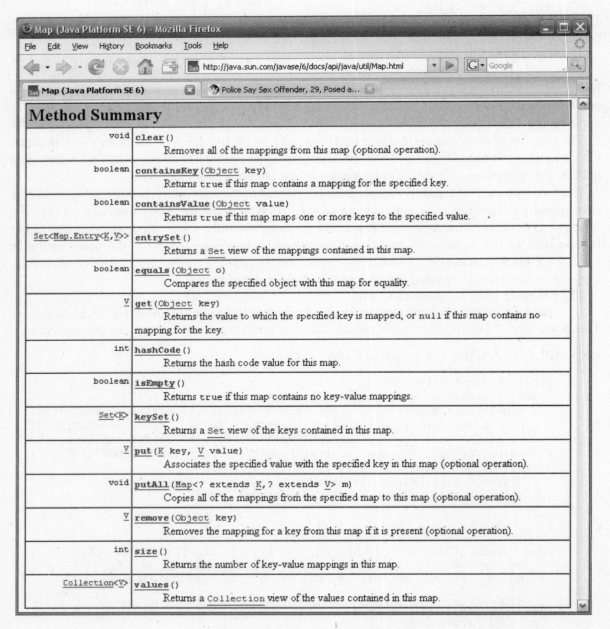

Figure 4.11 The java.util.Map interface

```
31
32          public String toString() {
33             return "[" + name + ": " + language + ", " + area + ", " + population
34                + ", " + avAge + "]";
35          }
36       }
```

The output is:

```
3
[AT, FR, PL]
[Poland: Polish, 312685, 38536869, 37.0]
```

The program uses two other classes: EuCodes at lines 13–15, and Country at lines 17–36. These are the type arguments for the type parameters K and V at line 3.

Three key-value pairs are inserted at lines 3–6. The size(), keySet(), and get() methods are tested at lines 7–9. The get() method illustrates the look-up table nature of a map: the call

```
          eu.get(EuCodes.PL)
```

looks up the record (the "value") for the key EuCodes.PL and returns it as:

```
          [Poland: Polish, 312685, 38536869, 37.0]
```

The JCF implements four extensions of the AbstractMap class: the EnumMap class, the HashMap class, the LinkedHashMap class, and the TreeMap class. Their distinctions are the same as the distinctions among the corresponding four extensions of the AbstractSet class. The HashMap class allows any class to be the key type. Its LinkedHashMap extension maintains a doubly linked list of all its elements, allowing ordered key access according the order of insertion. The TreeMap class allows ordered key access according to either the key type's natural order or a Comparator object passed to its constructor.

THE Arrays CLASS

The java.util.Arrays class contains static methods for processing arrays, including methods for converting arrays to collections and vice versa. The class is briefly outlined on page 29.

Most of the methods in the Arrays class are overloaded with separate versions for the generic array type T[] and for each of the nine specific array types: boolean[], byte[], char[], double[], float[], int[], long[], Object[], and short[]. In addition, most of these have a separate version for a subarray. For example, here are the 18 overloaded versions of the sort() method:

```
    void        sort(boolean[] a)
    void        sort(boolean[] a, int fromIndex, int toIndex)
    void        sort(byte[] a)
    void        sort(byte[] a, int fromIndex, int toIndex)
    void        sort(c[] a)
    void        sort(byte[] a, int fromIndex, int toIndex)
    void        sort(double[] a)
    void        sort(double[] a, int fromIndex, int toIndex)
    void        sort(int[] a)
    void        sort(int[] a, int fromIndex, int toIndex)
    void        sort(float[] a)
    void        sort(float[] a, int fromIndex, int toIndex)
    void        sort(long[] a)
    void        sort(long[] a, int fromIndex, int toIndex)
```

```
void        sort(Object[] a)
void        sort(Object[] a, int fromIndex, int toIndex)
void        sort(short[] a)
void        sort(short[] a, int fromIndex, int toIndex)
<T> void    sort(T[] a, Comparator<? super T> c)
<T> void    sort(T[] a, int fromIndex, int toIndex,
                 Comparator<? super T> c)
```

(There is no sort() method for boolean arrays.)

The eight different method() categories are:

```
binarySearch()
copyOf()
copyOfRange()
equals()
fill()
hashCode()
sort()
toString()
```

In addition, there is a single asList() method that returns an ArrayList collection containing the elements passed to it, like this:

```
List<String> list = Arrays.asList("CA", "US", "MX");
```

THE Collections CLASS

The java.util.Collections class provides over 50 static utility methods that implement algorithms for sorting, searching, shuffling, and maintaining collections, among other tasks.

EXAMPLE 4.15 Using Utility Methods from the Collections Class

This program illustrates the addAll(), swap(), sort(), binarySearch(), and reverse() methods that are defined in the Collections, class:

```
1    public class TestCollections {
2      public static void main(String[] args) {
3        List g8 = new ArrayList();
4        Collections.addAll(g8, "US", "DE", "JP", "FR", "GB", "RU", "CA", "IT");
5        System.out.println(g8);
6        Collections.swap(g8, 2, 4);
7        System.out.println(g8);
8        Collections.sort(g8);
9        System.out.println(g8);
10       int k = Collections.binarySearch(g8, "CN");
11       System.out.println(k);
12       if (k < 0) {
13         g8.add(-k - 1, "CN");
14       };
15       System.out.println(g8);
16       Collections.reverse(g8);
17       System.out.println(g8);
18     }
19   }
```

The output is:

```
[US, DE, JP, FR, GB, RU, CA, IT]
[US, DE, GB, FR, JP, RU, CA, IT]
[CA, DE, FR, GB, IT, JP, RU, US]
```

```
        -2
        [CA, CN, DE, FR, GB, IT, JP, RU, US]
        [US, RU, JP, IT, GB, FR, DE, CN, CA]
```
At line 4, the addAll() method is used to load eight strings into the empty list g8. At line 6, the "JP" and "GB" elements are swapped, and then the list is sorted at line 8.

At line 10, the binarySearch() method searches for the string "CN". The negative output signals that it is not there. The value of k tells where to insert it to keep the list sorted: at index –k – 1.

Finally, at line 16, the reverse() method reverses the entire list.

AUTOBOXING

Java 5.0 introduced *autoboxing*, which means that a primitive value can be added to a collection without explicitly "wrapping" it in an object; it will be wrapped, or "boxed" automatically. It will also be unwrapped when extracted. This is illustrated in Example 4.16.

EXAMPLE 4.16 Using Autoboxing

This program creates a list of five integers as an ArrayList<Integer> object:

```
1     import java.util.*;
2
3     public class TestAutoboxing {
4       public static void main(String[] args) {
5         List<Integer> list = new ArrayList<Integer>();
6         Collections.addAll(list, 22, 33, 44, 55, 66);
7         System.out.printf("list:         %s%n", list);
8         System.out.printf("list.size(): %s%n", list.size());
9         System.out.printf("list.get(2): %s%n", list.get(2));
10        int n = list.get(2);
11        System.out.printf("n:            %d%n", n);
12        list.remove(2);
13        System.out.printf("list:         %s%n", list);
14        System.out.printf("list.size(): %s%n", list.size());
15        list.remove(new Integer(66));
16        System.out.printf("list:         %s%n", list);
17        System.out.printf("list.size(): %s%n", list.size());
18      }
19    }
```

The output is:
```
        list:         [22, 33, 44, 55, 66]
        list.size(): 5
        list.get(2): 44
        n:            44
        list:         [22, 33, 55, 66]
        list.size(): 4
        list:         [22, 33, 55]
        list.size(): 3
```
At line 6, the addAll() method from the Collections class inserts five Integer objects into list. The primitive int values, 22, 33, 44, 55, and 66 are "boxed" automatically, instantiating the five wrapper objects to hold them.

At line 10, the element at index 2, which is the Integer object that holds the primitive int value 44, is accessed by the get() method. It is automatically "unboxed" during its assignment to the int variable n.

The remove() method is overloaded in the JCF: One version takes an int argument that specifies the position of the element to be removed, and one version takes a reference to an object that equals() the element to be removed. These two versions are invoked at lines 12 and 15. At line 12, the element at index 2, which is the object that holds 44, is removed. At line 15, the element that `equals()` the object that holds 66 is removed.

Note that this would not work:

```
list.remove(22);  // ERROR: the argument refers to index 22
```

Autoboxing occurs only when the types would otherwise be mismatched.

Autoboxing, which might better be called "autowrapping," also works in other contexts where an explicit instantiation of a wrapper class would otherwise be required. For example:

```
Double pi = 3.14159;  // OK
```

Note that automatic implicit instantiation (also called *promotion*) also occurs when a primitive expression is combined with a `String` object by means of the concatenation operator +. For example:

```
System.out.println("circumference = " + 2*pi*r);  // OK
```

In this case, the value of the `double` expression 2*pi*r is automatically wrapped in a new `Double` object, whose `toString()` method is then invoked to produce the `String` object that is concatenated with the `String` literal "circumference = ". This suggests that the alternative,

```
System.out.printf("circumference = %f%n", 2*pi*r);  // BETTER
```

should be preferred.

Review Questions

4.1   What is the Java Collections Framework?

4.2   What are the four main types defined in the Java Collections Framework?

4.3   What is a queue?

4.4   What is a deque?

4.5   What is a legacy class?

4.6   Which collection classes are implemented with an indexed structure (i.e., a simple array)?

4.7   Which collection classes are implemented with a linked structure?

4.8   Which collection classes are implemented with a linked indexed structure?

4.9   What is an `ArrayList` object?

4.10   What is a `LinkedList` object?

4.11   What is the `Collection` interface?

4.12   What set-theoretic methods are supported by the Java Collections Framework?

4.13   What is an iterator?

4.14   How are iterators similar to array indexes?

4.15   How are iterators different from array indexes?

4.16   How can the `Arrays` class be used to initialize a collection?

4.17   How can the `Collections` class be used to initialize a collection?

4.18   What is a generic class?

4.19   What is a generic method?

4.20   What is a generic type parameter?

4.21   What is a constrained generic type parameter?

4.22   What is a generic type argument?

4.23   What is autoboxing?

Problems

4.1   Write and test this method:
```
int chars(List<String> strings)
// returns the total number of characters in all the strings
```

4.2   Write and test this method, using an iterator:
```
void print(Collection c)
// prints all the elements of the collection c
```
Note that this has the same effect as in Example 4.4 on page 76.

4.3   Write and test this generic method:
```
<E> int frequency(Collection<E> c, E e) {
// returns the number of occurrences of e in c
```
   a.   using an iterator.
   b.   using an enhanced for loop.

4.4   Write and test this generic method:
```
<E> E getLast(List<E> list) {
// returns the last element of the list
```
   a.   using an iterator.
   b.   using an enhanced for loop.

4.5   Write and test this generic method:
```
<E> E getElementAt(List<E> list, int index) {
// returns the list element at the specified index
```
   a.   using an iterator.
   b.   using an enhanced for loop.

4.6   Write and test this client method:
```
<E> Collection<E> toCollection(E[] a)
// returns a generic Collection that contains the elements
// of the specified array
```

Answers to Review Questions

4.1   The *Java Collections Framework* is a group of interrelated interfaces and classes that support the creation and use of lists, sets, and iterators.

4.2   The four main types are List, Queue, Set, and Map.

4.3   A *queue* is a first-in-first-out collection that allows elements to be added at only one end (the back) and removed only from the other end (the front).

4.4   A *deque* is a double-ended queue that allows elements to be added and removed only from its two ends (the front and back).

4.5   A *legacy class* is a class that has been superseded by another class.

4.6 The `ArrayList`, `ArrayDeque`, `ArrayDeque`, and `HashMap` classes are implemented with an array.

4.7 The `LinkedList`, `PriorityQueue`, `TreeSet`, and `TreeMap` classes are implemented with a linked structure (either a linked list or a tree).

4.8 The `LinkedHashSet` class and the `LinkedHashMap` class are implemented with a linked indexed structure.

4.9 An `ArrayList` object is an instance of the `java.util.ArrayList` class. As a member of the Java Collections Framework, it supports all the methods of the `Collection` interface. As an indexed structure, it provides direct access to its elements by their index numbers.

4.10 A `LinkedList` object is an instance of the `java.util.LinkedList` class. As a member of the Java Collections Framework, it supports all the methods of the `Collection` interface. As a linked structure, it allows elements to be added and removed in constant time, independent of the size of the list.

4.11 The `Collection` interface is a Java interface that specifies the 15 methods listed in Figure 4.2 on page 71.

4.12 The four set-theoretic methods specified by the `Collection` interface are listed in Figure 4.2 on page 71: `addAll()` for unions, `removeAll()` for complements, `retainAll()` for intersections, and `containsAll()` for testing the subset relation.

4.13 An *iterator* is an object that moves about on a collection, providing access to its elements.

4.14 An iterator can be used to traverse a collection with a `for` loop, in the same way that an index can be used to traverse an array.

4.15 An array index provides *direct access* (i.e., random access) into an array. An iterator provides only *sequential access*.

4.16 The `java.util.Arrays` class includes an `asList()` method that returns a `List` object whose elements are the same as those in the array passed to it. (See Example 4.15 on page 96.)

4.17 The `java.util.Collections` class includes an `addAll()` method that adds all elements that are passed to it. (See Example 4.15 on page 96.) The method takes a variable number of arguments (i.e., it is a *varargs method*).

4.18 A *generic class* is a class that uses generic type parameters, that is, parametrized types. (See page 96.)

4.19 A *generic method* is a method that uses generic type parameters, that is, parametrized types.

4.20 A *generic type parameter* is a symbol used in a class or method definition that represents a type. When applied, an actual class or interface name must be substituted for the parameter.

4.21 A *constrained generic type parameter* is a generic type parameter that is constrained by an `extends` clause.

4.22 A *generic type argument* is a class or interface name that is being substituted for a generic type parameter in a generic class or generic method.

4.23 The term "autoboxing" refers to the automatic implicit instantiation of a wrapper class thereby allowing the value of a fundamental type expression to be used where an object is expected, for example, in the `Collections.addAll()` method. (See Example 4.16 on page 97.)

Solutions to Problems

4.1
```
int chars(List<String> strings) {
    int chars = 0;
    for (String s : strings) {
      chars += s.length();
    }
    return chars;
```

4.2

```java
        }
void print(Collection c) {
  for (Iterator it = c.iterator(); it.hasNext(); ) {
    System.out.printf("%s ", it.next());
  }
  System.out.println();
}
```

4.3 **a.**

```java
<E> int frequency(Collection<E> c, E e) {
  int f = 0;
  for (Iterator<E> it = c.iterator(); it.hasNext(); ) {
    if (it.next().equals(e)) {
      ++f;
    }
  }
  return f;
}
```

b.

```java
<E> int frequency(Collection<E> c, E e) {
  int f = 0;
  for (E ce : c) {
    if (ce.equals(x)) {
      ++f;
    }
  }
  return f;
}
```

4.4 **a.**

```java
<E> E getLast(List<E> list) {
  E last = null;
  for (Iterator<E> it = list.iterator(); it.hasNext(); ) {
    last = it.next();
  }
  return last;
}
```

b.

```java
<E> E getLast(List<E> list) {
  E last = null;
  for (E e : list) {
    last = e;
  }
  return last;
}
```

4.5 **a.**

```java
<E> E getElementAt(List<E> list, int index) {
  E element = null;
  int i=0;
  for (Iterator<E> it = list.iterator(); it.hasNext() && i++<=index;){
    element = it.next();
  }
  return element;
}
```

b.

```java
<E> E getElementAt(List<E> list, int index) {
  E element = null;
  int i=0;
  for (E e : list) {
    if (i++ == index) {
      return e;
    }
  }
  return null;
}
```

4.6

```
<E> Collection<E> toCollection(E[] a) {
  Collection<E> c = new ArrayList<E>();
  for (E ae : a) {
    c.add(ae);
  }
  return c;
}
```

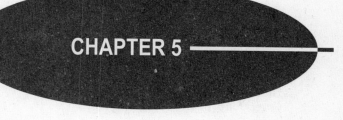

CHAPTER 5 ————

Stacks

A *stack* is a collection that implements the last-in-first-out (LIFO) protocol. This means that the only accessible object in the collection is the last one that was inserted. A stack of books is a good analogy: You can't take a book from the stack without first removing the books that are stacked on top of it.

STACK OPERATIONS

The fundamental operations of a stack are:
1. Add an element onto the top of the stack.
2. Access the current element on the top of the stack.
3. Remove the current element on the top of the stack.

These three operations are usually named *push*, *peek*, and *pop*, respectively.

THE JCF Stack CLASS

As shown in Figure 4.1 on page 70, the Java Collections Framework includes a `Vector` class, which is a specialized `List` type. Prior to the development of the JCF, Java extended the `Vector` class to a `Stack` class. But that class is now considered obsolete because it isn't consistent with the JCF. Instead, the Java API recommends using the `ArrayDeque` class for stacks, like this:

```
Deque<String> stack = new ArrayDeque<String>();
```

This provides all the normal functionality of a stack, while being consistent with the JCF. (See page 91.)

EXAMPLE 5.1 Testing a String Stack

```
1    public class TestStringStack {
2      public static void main(String[] args) {
3        Deque<String> stack = new ArrayDeque<String>();
4        stack.push("GB");
5        stack.push("DE");
6        stack.push("FR");
7        stack.push("ES");
8        System.out.println(stack);
9        System.out.println("stack.peek(): " + stack.peek());
```

```
10        System.out.println("stack.pop(): " + stack.pop());
11        System.out.println(stack);
12        System.out.println("stack.pop(): " + stack.pop());
13        System.out.println(stack);
14        System.out.println("stack.push(\"IE\"): ");
15        stack.push("IE");
16        System.out.println(stack);
17      }
18    }
```

The output is:

```
[ES, FR, DE, GB]
stack.peek(): ES
stack.pop(): ES
[FR, DE, GB]
stack.pop(): FR
[DE, GB]
stack.push("IE"):
[IE, DE, GB]
```

The push, peek, and pop operations are illustrated at lines 4, 9, and 10, respectively.

A Stack INTERFACE

The operational requirements of a stack (peek, pop, and push) can be formalized as a Java interface:

EXAMPLE 5.2 A Stack Interface

```
1    public interface Stack<E> {
2        public boolean isEmpty();
3        public E peek();
4        public E pop();
5        public void push(E element);
6        public int size();
7    }
```

The symbol E is a *type parameter*. (See page 76.) It stands for the deferred element type for the stack.

In addition to the three required stack operations, this interface also specifies an isEmpty() method and a size() method.

The Stack interface shown in Example 5.2 is a *generic type*. (See page 76.) The expression <E> at line 1 means that the element type E is unspecified.

AN INDEXED IMPLEMENTATION

There are several ways to implement the Stack interface. The simplest is an indexed implementation, using an ordinary array.

EXAMPLE 5.3 An ArrayStack Implementation

```
1    public class ArrayStack<E> implements Stack<E> {
2        private E[] elements;
3        private int size;
4        private static final int INITIAL_CAPACITY = 100;
5
```

```
6      public ArrayStack() {
7        elements = (E[]) new Object[INITIAL_CAPACITY];
8      }
9
10     public ArrayStack(int capacity) {
11       elements = (E[]) new Object[capacity];
12     }
13
14     public boolean isEmpty() {
15       return (size == 0);
16     }
17
18     public E peek() {
19       if (size == 0) {
20         throw new java.util.EmptyStackException();
21       }
22       return elements[size-1];  // top of stack
23     }
24
25     public E pop() {
26       if (size == 0) {
27         throw new java.util.EmptyStackException();
28       }
29       E element = elements[--size];
30       elements[size] = null;
31       return element;
32     }
33
34     public void push(E element) {
35       if (size == elements.length) {
36         resize();
37       }
38       elements[size++] = element;
39     }
40
41     public int size() {
42       return size;
43     }
44
45     private void resize() {
46       assert size == elements.length;
47       Object[] a = new Object[2*size];
48       System.arraycopy(elements, 0, a, 0, size);
49       elements = (E[])a;
50     }
51   }
```

Since this class is implementing the generic type Stack<E>, it too is a generic type. Thus, the type parameter E is used wherever the element type has to be specified. For example, at line 29, the local variable element is declared to have type E.

This ArrayStack implementation uses a "backing array" elements[] to store the stack's elements. It is declared at line 2 to have type E[], that is, an array of elements of type E. The other class field is the integer size, which keeps a count of the number of elements in the stack.

The class defines the static constant INITIAL_CAPACITY at line 4 to be the number 100. This is used only to specify the initial size of the backing array at line 7. The choice of 100 is arbitrary; any reasonably small positive integer would suffice.

Two constructors are defined: the default (no-argument) constructor at line 6 and the one-argument constructor at line 10. Both merely allocate the backing array, using either the default INITIAL_CAPACITY (line 7) or a user-specified capacity (line 11).

Notice how arrays are allocated in a generic collection:

```
7          elements = (E[]) new Object[INITIAL_CAPACITY];
```

Since generic arrays are not supported in Java, this simpler approach

```
          elements = new E[INITIAL_CAPACITY];   // ERROR!
```

will not compile. Instead, we have to allocate the backing array as an array of Object elements, and then cast that array with (E[]) in order to assign it to the elements field, which has type E[]. This subterfuge may generate a compiler warning, which can be ignored.

The implementations of the five methods required by the Stack interface are pretty straightforward. The size() method at line 41 is an *accessor method* that simply returns the value of the size field. The isEmpty() method at line 14 returns true or false according to whether or not the value of size is 0.

The peek() method at line 18 throws an exception if the stack is empty. Otherwise, it returns the top element on the stack: elements[size-1].

The pop() method at line 25 is almost the same as the peek() method. But before returning the top element, it must remove it by decrementing the size field at line 29 and replacing the top element with null at line 30. This last step is done so that no references will be left to an inaccessible object.

The push() method at line 34 is essentially the reverse of the pop() method. At line 38, the element is added to the array at the next available position, at elements[size], and then the size counter is post-decremented.

If the array is full, then the size counter will equal elements.length. If that condition holds when push() is called, the array is doubled by a call to the private resize() method at line 36. This creates the temporary array a[] at line 47, copies all the elements into it at line 48, and then assigns the elements field to it at line 49.

Note the use of the assert statement at line 46. If the condition size == elements.length does not hold at that point, the program will abort with an error message, just like an uncaught exception. Of course, that should never happen, because the resize() method is private, and the only place where it is called within this class is at line 36, inside the if block for that same condition. The purpose of including the assert statement here is merely "insurance," to guard against possible future modifications of the class that might inadvertently involve the resize() method when that condition is not true.

The ArrayStack class implemented in Example 5.3 can be tested the same way the Stack class is tested in Example 5.1 on page 103. The push(), peek(), and pop() calls should work the same way. The println() calls cannot be executed for the ArrayStack class because it has no toString() method. But that's proper, because a stack really should not allow access to any of its elements other than the one on top.

A LINKED IMPLEMENTATION

The main alternative to an indexed implementation is a linked implementation, using a linked list. (See Chapter 3.)

EXAMPLE 5.4 A LinkedStack Implementation

```
1     public class LinkedStack<E> implements Stack<E> {
2       private Node<E> head = new Node<E>();  // dummy node
3       private int size;
4
```

```
5       public boolean isEmpty() {
6         return (size == 0);
7       }
8
9       public E peek() {
10        if (size == 0) {
11          throw new java.util.EmptyStackException();
12        }
13        return head.prev.element;  // top of stack
14      }
15
16      public E pop() {
17        if (size == 0) {
18          throw new java.util.EmptyStackException();
19        }
20        E element = head.prev.element;
21        head.prev = head.prev.prev;
22        head.prev.next = head;
23        --size;
24        return element;
25      }
26
27      public void push(E element) {
28        head.prev = head.prev.next = new Node<E>(element, head.prev, head);
29        ++size;
30      }
31
32      public int size() {
33        return size;
34      }
35
36      private static class Node<E> {
37        E element;
38        Node<E> prev;
39        Node<E> next;
40
41        Node() {
42          this.prev = this.next = this;
43        }
44
45        Node(E element, Node<E> prev, Node<E> next) {
46          this.element = element;
47          this.prev = prev;
48          this.next = next;
49        }
50      }
51    }
```

This class implements a doubly linked list, using the private inner Node class defined at lines 36–50. Each node contains an element field and two link fields: one pointed to the previous node in the list and one pointing to the next node. The constructor defined at line 41 constructs a *dummy node* with null element and with both links pointing to the node itself. The three-argument constructor defined at line 45 allows all three fields to be initialized.

The LinkedStack class defines two fields at lines 2–3: its head node link and its size counter. Note that this implements the empty stack as a single dummy node with its prev and next links pointing to the node itself. The advantage of self-pointers is that we avoid null pointers, obviating special cases in the push() and pop() methods.

When the stack is not empty, the top element will always be in the node referenced by the head.prev link. Thus, both peek() and pop() return head.prev.element.

To remove the top element, pop() deletes the node that contains it. This requires resetting two pointers, which is done at lines 21–22:

```
21          head.prev = head.prev.prev;
22          head.prev.prev.next = head;
```

The push() method constructs a new node containing the specified element at line 28, and then it resets both the head.prev.next and the head.prev links to point to it. Note that the chained assignment works from right to left, first assigning the new node reference to head.prev.next and then to head.prev. That order of operations is critical because the existing head.prev.next node is not accessible after head.prev is changed.

ABSTRACTING THE COMMON CODE

The ArrayStack and LinkedStack implementations of the Stack interface are quite different. Nevertheless, they do have some identical code. The size() method and the isEmpty() method are the same. Their implementation does not depend upon whether the backing structure is indexed or linked.

When parts of an implementation are independent of the underlying data structure, it is advantageous to implement those parts separately in an abstract class.

EXAMPLE 5.5 An AbstractStack Class

```
1     public abstract class AbstractStack<E> implements Stack<E> {
2       protected int size;
3
4       public boolean isEmpty() {
5         return (size == 0);
6       }
7
8       abstract public E peek();
9
10      abstract public E pop();
11
12      abstract public void push(E element);
13
14      public int size() {
15        return size;
16      }
17    }
```

The three methods that depend upon the implementation's backing structure are declared abstract (lines 8, 10, and 12). This of course requires the class itself to be declared abstract.

Notice at line 2 that the size field is declared protected instead of private so that it can be accessed by the extending concrete classes.

With the AbstractStack class implemented as shown in Example 5.5, we can now simplify the two concrete implementations from Example 5.3 on page 104 and Example 5.4 on page 106. We need only add the expression extends AbstractStack<E> to each class header, and then we can remove their isEmpty() and size() methods and their declaration of the size field. This of course is the strategy used by the JCF. (See Figure 4.1 on page 70.)

APPLICATION: AN RPN CALCULATOR

Although the stack data structure is one of the simplest, it is essential in certain important applications. Some of these are illustrated in the following examples.

An arithmetic expression is said to be in *postfix* notation (also called *reverse Polish notation*, or *RPN*) if each operator is placed after its operands. For example, the postfix expression for 3*(4 + 5) is 3 4 5 + *. [The expression 3*(4 + 5) is called an *infix expression*.] Postfix expressions are easier to process by machine than are infix expressions. Calculators that process postfix expressions are called *RPN calculators*.

EXAMPLE 5.6 An RPN Calculator

This program parses postfix expressions, performing the indicated arithmetic. It uses a stack to accumulate the operands.

```
1    public class Calculator {
2      public static void main(String[] args) {
3        Deque<String> stack = new ArrayDeque<String>();
4        Scanner in = new Scanner(System.in);
5        while (true) {
6          String input = in.nextLine();
7          char ch = input.charAt(0);
8          if (ch == '+' || ch == '-' || ch == '*' || ch == '/') {
9            double y = Double.parseDouble(stack.pop());
10           double x = Double.parseDouble(stack.pop());
11           double z = 0;
12           switch (ch) {
13             case '+':  z = x + y;  break;
14             case '-':  z = x - y;  break;
15             case '*':  z = x * y;  break;
16             case '/':  z = x / y;
17           }
18           System.out.printf("\t%.2f %c %.2f = %.2f%n", x, ch, y, z);
19           stack.push(new Double(z).toString());
20         } else if (ch == 'q' || ch == 'Q') {
21           return;
22         } else {
23           stack.push(input);
24         }
25       }
26     }
27   }
```

Here is one run:

```
3
4
5
+
        4.00 + 5.00 = 9.00
*
        3.00 * 9.00 = 27.00
10
/
        27.00 / 10.00 = 2.70
1
-
        2.70 - 1.00 = 1.70
Q
```

At line 3, the program instantiates a stack of strings, like the one in Example 5.1 on page 103. Then it goes into an infinite `while` loop at line 5, interactively reading a string on each iteration at line 6.

If the user inputs anything other than +, -, *, /, q, or Q, the program assumes it is a number and pushes it onto the stack at line 23. If it is one of the four arithmetic operations, then the top two numbers are popped off the stack at lines 9–10 and the operation is applied to them. The result is printed at line 18 and then pushed onto the stack at line 19.

The program ends when the user enters q or Q (for "quit").

Human readers tend to prefer infix to postfix notation for arithmetic expressions. The following example converts a given infix expression to postfix.

EXAMPLE 5.7 Converting Infix to Postfix

```
1    public class TestScanner {
2      public static void main(String[] args) {
3        Deque<String> stack = new ArrayDeque<String>();
4        String line = new Scanner(System.in).nextLine();
5        System.out.println(line);
6        Scanner scanner = new Scanner(line);
7        while (scanner.hasNext()) {
8          if (scanner.hasNextInt()) {
9            System.out.print(scanner.nextInt() + " ");
10         } else {
11           String str = scanner. next();
12           if ("+-*/".indexOf(str) >= 0) {
13             stack.push(str);
14           } else if (str.equals(")")) {
15             System.out.print(stack.pop() + " ");
16           }
17         }
18       }
19       while (!stack.isEmpty()) {
20         System.out.print(stack.pop() + " ");
21       }
22       System.out.println();
23     }
24   }
```

The output is:

```
( 80 - 30 ) * ( 40 + 50 / 10 )
80 30 - 40 50 10 / + *
```

The output shows that the program parsed the infix expression (80 – 30) * (40 + 50 / 10) to generate its postfix equivalent 80 30 – 40 50 10 / + *.

The program uses a stack, declared at line 3, and a scanner, declared at line 6. The scanner extracts integer and string tokens from the input line. If the token is an integer, it is printed immediately, at line 9. If it is one of the four strings "+", "-", "*", or "/", it is pushed onto the stack at line 13. If it is the strings ")", then the top element of the stack is popped off and printed at line 15. After the input line has been completely parsed, the remaining elements are popped from the stack and printed at lines 19–21.

Review Questions

5.1   Why are stacks called LIFO structures?

5.2   Would it make sense to call a stack

a. a LILO structure?

b. a FILO structure?

5.3 What is

    a. prefix notation?

    b. infix notation?

    c. postfix notation?

5.4 Determine whether each of the following is true about postfix expressions:

    a. $x\,y+z+=x\,y\,z++$

    b. $x\,y+z-=x\,y\,z-+$

    c. $x\,y-z+=x\,y\,z+-$

    d. $x\,y-z-=x\,y\,z--$

Problems

5.1 Trace the following code, showing the contents of the `stack` after each invocation:

```
Stack stack = new Stack();
stack.push(new Character('A'));
stack.push(new Character('B'));
stack.push(new Character('C'));
stack.pop();
stack.pop();
stack.push(new Character('D'));
stack.push(new Character('E'));
stack.push(new Character('F'));
stack.pop();
stack.push(new Character('G'));
stack.pop();
stack.pop();
stack.pop();
```

5.2 Translate each of the following prefix expressions into infix:

    a. $-/+*a\,b\,c\,d\,e$

    b. $/-a\,b*c+d\,e$

    c. $/a+b*c-d\,e$

5.3 Translate the prefix expressions in Problem 5.2 into postfix.

5.4 Translate each of the following infix expressions into prefix:

    a. $(a+b)-(c/(d+e))$

    b. $a/((b/c)*(d-e))$

    c. $(a/(b/c))*(d-e)$

5.5 Translate the infix expressions in Problem 5.4 into postfix.

5.6 Translate each of the following postfix expressions into prefix:

    a. $a\,b+c\,d-/e+$

    b. $a\,b\,c+d\,e-*-$

    c. $a\,b\,c\,d\,e////$

5.7 Translate the postfix expressions in Problem 5.6 into infix.

5.8   Write this client method using only the push(), peek(), pop(), and isEmpty() methods:
```
public static <E> Deque<E> reversed(Deque<E> stack)
// returns a new stack that contains the same elements as the given
// stack, but in reversed order
```

5.9   Write this client method using only the push(), peek(), pop(), and isEmpty() methods:
```
public static <E> Deque<E> reversed(Deque<E> stack)
// returns a new stack that contains the same elements as the given
// stack, but in reversed order, and leaves the given stack in its
// original state
```

5.10 Write this client method using only the push(), peek(), pop(), and isEmpty() methods:
```
public static <E> void reverse(Deque<E> stack)
// reverses the contents of the specified stack
```

5.11 Write this client method using only the push(), peek(), pop(), and isEmpty() methods:
```
public static <E> E penultimate(Deque<E> stack)
// returns the second from the top element of the specified stack
```

5.12 Write this client method using only the push(), peek(), pop(), and isEmpty() methods:
```
public static <E> E popPenultimate(Deque<E> stack)
// removes and returns the second element of the specified stack
```

5.13 Write this client method using only the push(), peek(), pop(), and isEmpty() methods:
```
public static <E> E bottom(Deque<E> stack)
// returns the bottom element of the specified stack
```

5.14 Write this client method using only the push(), peek(), pop(), and isEmpty() methods:
```
public static <E> E popBottom(Deque<E> stack)
// removes and returns the bottom element of the specified stack
```

5.15 Add this member method to the ArrayStack class shown in Example 5.3 on page 104:
```
public void reverse()
// reverses the contents of this stack
```

5.16 Add this member method to the LinkedStack class shown in Example 5.4 on page 106:
```
public void reverse()
// reverses the contents of this stack
```

5.17 Add this member method to the ArrayStack class shown in Example 5.3 on page 104:
```
public E penultimate()
// returns the second from the top element of this stack
```

5.18 Add this member method to the LinkedStack class shown in Example 5.4 on page 106:
```
public E penultimate()
// returns the second from the top element of this stack
```

5.19 Add this member method to the ArrayStack class shown in Example 5.3 on page 104:
```
public E popPenultimate()
// removes and returns the second element of this stack
```

5.20 Add this member method to the LinkedStack class shown in Example 5.4 on page 106:
```
public E popPenultimate()
// removes and returns the second element of this stack
```

5.21 Add this member method to the ArrayStack class shown in Example 5.3 on page 104:
```
public E bottom()
// returns the bottom element of this stack
```

5.22 Add this member method to the LinkedStack class shown in Example 5.4 on page 106:
```
public E bottom()
// returns the bottom element of this stack
```

5.23 Add this member method to the `ArrayStack` class shown in Example 5.3 on page 104:
```
public E popBottom()
// removes and returns the bottom element of this stack
```

5.24 Add this member method to the `LinkedStack` class shown in Example 5.4 on page 106:
```
public E popBottom()
// removes and returns the bottom element of this stack
```

Answers to Review Questions

5.1 Stacks are called LIFO structures because the last element that is inserted into a stack is always the first element to be removed. LIFO is an acronym for last-in-first-out.

5.2　**a.** No, because a LILO structure would mean last-in-last-out, which is just the opposite of the "last-in-first-out" protocol.

　　b. Yes, because a FILO structure would mean first-in-last-out, which is the same as a last-in-first-out protocol.

5.3　**a.** The prefix notation for arithmetic expressions places binary operators ahead of both of their operands. For example, the expression "$x + 2$" is written "$+ x\ 2$" in prefix notation. The standard functional notation used in mathematics uses prefix notation: $f(x)$, $\sin x$, and so on.

　　b. The infix notation for arithmetic expressions places binary operators between their operands. Infix notation is the usual format for arithmetic expressions, for example, $x + 2$.

　　c. The postfix notation for arithmetic expressions places binary operators after both of their operands. For example, the expression "$x + 2$" is written "$x\ 2\ +$" in postfix notation. The factorial function in mathematics uses postfix notation: $n!$.

5.4　**a.** True, because $(x + y) + z = x + (y + z)$.

　　b. True, because $(x + y) - z = x + (y - z)$.

　　c. False, because $(x - y) + z \neq x - (y + z)$.

　　d. False, because $(x - y) - z \neq x - (y - z)$.

Solutions to Problems

5.1　$A \rightarrow AB \rightarrow ABC \rightarrow AB \rightarrow A \rightarrow AD \rightarrow ADE \rightarrow ADEF \rightarrow ADE \rightarrow ADEG \rightarrow ADEF \rightarrow ADE$

5.2　**a.** $(a * b + c) / d - e$
　　b. $(a - b) / (c * (d + e))$
　　c. $a / (b + (c * (d - e)))$

5.3　**a.** $a\ b * c + d / e -$
　　b. $a\ b - c\ d\ e + * /$
　　c. $a\ b\ c\ d\ e - * + /$

5.4　**a.** $(a + b) - (c / (d + e)) = - + a\ b / c + d\ e$
　　b. $a / ((b / c) * (d - e)) = / a * / b\ c - d\ e$
　　c. $(a / (b / c)) * (d - e) = * / a / b\ c - d\ e$

5.5　**a.** $(a + b) - (c / (d + e)) = a\ b + c\ d\ e + / -$
　　b. $a / ((b / c) * (d - e)) = a\ b\ c / d\ e - * /$
　　c. $(a / (b / c)) * (d - e) = a\ b\ c / / * d\ e - *$

5.6　**a.** $(a + b) / (c - d) + e$
　　b. $a - (b + c) * (d - e)$
　　c. $a / (b / (c / (d / e)))$

5.7   **a.** $+/+ab-cde$

         b. $-a*+bc-de$

         c. $/a/b/c/de$

5.8
```java
public static <E> Deque<E> reversed(Deque<E> stack) {
    // returns a new stack that contains the same elements as the given
    // stack, but in reversed order
    Deque<E> stack1 = new ArrayDeque<E>();
    while(!stack.isEmpty()) {
       stack1.push(stack.pop());
    }
    return stack1;
}
```

5.9
```java
public static <E> Deque<E> reversed(Deque<E> stack) {
    // returns a new stack that contains the same elements as the given
    // stack, but in reversed order, and leaves the given stack in its
    // original state
    Deque<E> stack1 = new ArrayDeque<E>();
    Deque<E> stack2 = new ArrayDeque<E>();
    while(!stack.isEmpty()) {
       stack1.push(stack.peek());
       stack2.push(stack.pop());
    }
    while(!stack2.isEmpty()) {
       stack.push(stack2.pop());
    }
    return stack1;
}
```

5.10
```java
public static <E> void reverse(Deque<E> stack) {
    // reverses the contents of the specified stack
    Deque<E> stack1 = new ArrayDeque<E>();
    Deque<E> stack2 = new ArrayDeque<E>();
    while(!stack.isEmpty()) {
       stack1.push(stack.pop());
    }
    while(!stack1.isEmpty()) {
       stack2.push(stack1.pop());
    }
    while(!stack2.isEmpty()) {
       stack.push(stack2.pop());
    }
}
```

5.11
```java
public static <E> E penultimate(Deque<E> stack) {
    // returns the second from the top element of the specified stack
    E x1 = stack.pop();
    E x2 = stack.peek();
    stack.push(x1);
    return x2;
}
```

5.12
```java
public static <E> E popPenultimate(Deque<E> stack) {
    // removes and returns the second element of the specified stack
    E x1 = stack.pop();
    E x2 = stack.pop();
    stack.push(x1);
    return x2;
}
```

5.13
```java
public static <E> E bottom(Deque<E> stack) {
    // returns the bottom element of the specified stack
    Deque<E> stack1 = new ArrayDeque<E>();
```

```
        while(!stack.isEmpty()) {
          stack1.push(stack.pop());
        }
        E x = stack1.peek();
        while(!stack1.isEmpty()) {
          stack.push(stack1.pop());
        }
        return x;
      }
```

5.14
```
      public static <E> E popBottom(Deque<E> stack) {
        // removes and returns the bottom element of the specified stack
        Deque<E> stack1 = new ArrayDeque<E>();
        while(!stack.isEmpty()) {
          stack1.push(stack.pop());
        }
        E x = stack1.pop();
        while(!stack1.isEmpty()) {
          stack.push(stack1.pop());
        }
        return x;
      }
```

5.15
```
      public void reverse() {
        // reverses the contents of the this stack
        for (int i=0; i<size/2; i++) {
          E e = elements[i];
          elements[i] = elements[size-1-i];
          elements[size-1-i] = e;
        }
      }
```

5.16
```
      public void reverse() {
        // reverses the contents of the this stack
        Node<E> p = head;
        for (int i=0; i<=size; i++) {
          Node<E> q = p.next;
          p.next = p.prev;
          p = p.prev = q;
        }
      }
```

5.17
```
      public E penultimate() {
        // returns the second from the top element of this stack
        if (size < 2) {
          throw new java.util.NoSuchElementException();
        }
        return elements[size-2];
      }
```

5.18
```
      public E penultimate() {
        // returns the second from the top element of this stack
        if (size < 2) {
          throw new java.util.NoSuchElementException();
        }
        return head.prev.prev.element;   // second from top of stack
      }
```

5.19
```
      public E popPenultimate() {
        // removes and returns the second element of this stack
        if (size < 2) {
          throw new java.util.NoSuchElementException();
        }
        E element = elements[size-2];
```

```
                    elements[size-2] = elements[size-1];
                    elements[size-1] = null;
                    --size;
                    return element;
                  }
5.20              public E popPenultimate() {
                    // removes and returns the second element of this stack
                    if (size < 2) {
                      throw new java.util.NoSuchElementException();
                    }
                    E element = head.prev.prev.element;
                    head.prev.prev = head.prev.prev.prev;
                    head.prev.prev.next = head.prev;
                    --size;
                    return element;
                  }
5.21              public E bottom() {
                    // returns the bottom element of this stack
                    if (size == 0) {
                      throw new java.util.EmptyStackException();
                    }
                    return elements[0];   // bottom of stack
                  }
5.22              public E bottom() {
                    // returns the bottom element of this stack
                    if (size == 0) {
                      throw new java.util.EmptyStackException();
                    }
                    return head.next.element;   // bottom of stack
                  }
5.23              public E popBottom() {
                    // removes and returns the bottom element of this stack
                    if (size == 0) {
                      throw new java.util.EmptyStackException();
                    }
                    E element = elements[0];
                    for (int i=0; i<size-2; i++) {
                      elements[i] = elements[i+1];
                    }
                    elements[size-1] = null;
                    --size;
                    return element;
                  }
5.24              public E popBottom() {
                    // removes and returns the bottom element of this stack
                    if (size == 0) {
                      throw new java.util.EmptyStackException();
                    }
                      E element = head.next.element;
                    head.next = head.next.next;
                    head.next.prev = head;
                    --size;
                    return element;
                  }
```

Queues

A *queue* is a collection that implements the first-in-first-out (FIFO) protocol. This means that the only accessible object in the collection is the first one that was inserted. The most common example of a queue is a waiting line.

QUEUE OPERATIONS

The fundamental operations of a queue are:
1. Add an element to the back of the queue.
2. Access the current element at the front of the queue.
3. Remove the current element at the front of the queue.
Some authors use the terms *enqueue* and *dequeue* for the add and remove operations.

THE JCF Queue INTERFACE

As shown in Figure 4.1 on page 70, the Java Collections Framework includes a Queue interface, which is implemented by four classes: the LinkedList class, the AbstractQueue class, the PriorityQueue class, and the ArrayDeque class. For simple FIFO queues, the ArrayDeque class is the best choice:

```
Queue<String> queue = new ArrayDeque<String>();
```
This provides all the normal functionality of a queue. (See page 91.)

EXAMPLE 6.1 Testing a String Queue

```
1    public class TestStringStack {
2      public static void main(String[] args) {
3        Queue<String> queue = new ArrayDeque<String>();
4        queue.add("GB");
5        queue.add("DE");
6        queue.add("FR");
7        queue.add("ES");
8        System.out.println(queue);
9        System.out.println("queue.element(): " + queue.element());
10       System.out.println("queue.remove(): " + queue.remove());
11       System.out.println(queue);
12       System.out.println("queue.remove(): " + queue.remove());
13       System.out.println(queue);
14       System.out.println("queue.add(\"IE\"): ");
15       queue.add("IE");
```

```
16          System.out.println(queue);
17          System.out.println("queue.remove(): " + queue.remove());
18          System.out.println(queue);
19       }
20    }
```

The output is:

```
[GB, DE, FR, ES]
queue.element(): GB
queue.remove(): GB
[DE, FR, ES]
queue.remove(): DE
[FR, ES]
queue.add("IE"):
[FR, ES, IE]
queue.remove(): FR
[ES, IE]
```

The add, element, and remove operations are illustrated at lines 4, 9, and 10, respectively.

By comparing the output in Example 6.1 with that of Example 5.1 on page 103, it is easy to see that the only operational difference between a queue and a stack is the access point. With a queue, it is at the front, where the "oldest" element—the one that has been there the longest—is found. With a stack, it is at the top, where the "youngest" element—the one that arrived most recently—is found.

Notice that for the ArrayDeque class, the toString() method (invoked automatically by the println() method at line 8) displays the queue from front to back, and the stack from top to bottom. So in both cases, the access point is at the left end of the display.

A SIMPLE Queue INTERFACE

The operational requirements of a queue can be formalized by this simple Java interface:

EXAMPLE 6.2 A Queue Interface

```
1    public interface Queue<E> {
2       public void add(E element);
3       public E element();
4       public boolean isEmpty();
5       public E remove();
6       public int size();
7    }
```

In addition to the three required queue operations, this interface also specifies an isEmpty() method and a size() method.

Compare the Queue interface shown in Example 6.2 with the JCF's Queue interface, shown in Figure 4.10 on page 89. It includes offer(), peek(), and poll() methods. In most situations, these are the same operations as the add(), element(), and remove() methods, respectively. If a limited-capacity queue is full, the add() method throws an IllegalStateException, while the offer() method merely returns false. If the queue is empty, the element() the remove() methods throw a NoSuchElementException, while the peek() and poll() methods merely returns null.

AN INDEXED IMPLEMENTATION

Like stacks and other linear data structures, queues can be implemented using an ordinary array. The ArrayQueue class shown in Example 6.3 is similar to the ArrayStack class shown in Example 5.3 on page 104.

EXAMPLE 6.3 An ArrayQueue Implementation

```
1   public class ArrayQueue<E> implements Queue<E> {
2     private E[] elements;
3     private int front;
4     private int back;
5     private static final int INITIAL_CAPACITY = 4;
6
7     public ArrayQueue() {
8       elements = (E[]) new Object[INITIAL_CAPACITY];
9     }
10
11    public ArrayQueue(int capacity) {
12      elements = (E[]) new Object[capacity];
13    }
14
15    public void add(E element) {
16      if (size() == elements.length - 1) {
17        resize();
18      }
19      elements[back] = element;
20      if (back < elements.length - 1) {
21        ++back;
22      } else {
23        back = 0;   //wrap
24      }
25    }
26
27    public E element() {
28      if (size() == 0) {
29        throw new java.util.NoSuchElementException();
30      }
31      return elements[front];
32    }
33
34    public boolean isEmpty() {
35      return (size() == 0);
36    }
37
38    public E remove() {
39      if (size() == 0) {
40        throw new java.util.NoSuchElementException();
41      }
42      E element = elements[front];
43      elements[front] = null;
44      ++front;
45      if (front == back) {  // queue is empty
46        front = back = 0;
47      }
```

```
48          if (front == elements.length) {  // wrap
49            front = 0;
50          }
51          return element;
52        }
53
54        public int size() {
55          if (front <= back) {
56            return back - front;
57          } else {
58            return back - front + elements.length;
59          }
60        }
61
62        private void resize() {
63          int size = size();
64          int len = elements.length;
65          assert size == len;
66          Object[] a = new Object[2*len];
67          System.arraycopy(elements, front, a, 0, len - front);
68          System.arraycopy(elements, 0, a, len - front, back);
69          elements = (E[])a;
70          front = 0;
71          back = size;
72        }
73    }
```

Instead of storing the size counter, this implementation stores front and back indexes into the array. The front element of the queue is always at elements[front], and the back element of the queue is always at elements[back-1] (except when back = 0). The front index is advanced each time an element is removed from the queue (at line 44), and the back index is advanced each time an element is added (at line 21). In both cases, when the index reaches the end of the array, it is "advanced" to 0. This "wraps" the queue around the end of the array, like a ring, allowing array elements to be reused.

AN INDEXED IMPLEMENTATION

We can use a doubly linked list to implement the Queue interface the same way we implemented the Stack interface in Example 5.4 on page 106.

EXAMPLE 6.4 A LinkedQueue Class

```
1    public class LinkedQueue<E> implements Queue<E> {
2      private Node<E> head = new Node<E>();  // dummy node
3      private int size;
4
5      public void add(E element) {
6        head.prev = head.prev.next = new Node<E>(element, head.prev, head);
7        ++size;
8      }
9
10     public E element() {
11       if (size == 0) {
12         throw new java.util.EmptyStackException();
13       }
14       return head.next.element;  // front of queue  // next <--> prev
15     }
```

```
16
17      public boolean isEmpty() {
18        return (size == 0);
19      }
20
21      public E remove() {
22        if (size == 0) {
23          throw new java.util.EmptyStackException();
24        }
25        E element = head.next.element;    // next  <-->  prev
26        head.next = head.next.next;       // next  <-->  prev
27        head.next.prev = head;            // next  <-->  prev
28        --size;
29        return element;
30      }
31
32      public int size() {
33        return size;
34      }
35
36      private static class Node<E> {
37        E element;
38        Node<E> prev;
39        Node<E> next;
40
41        Node() {
42          this.prev = this.next = this;
43        }
44
45        Node(E element, Node<E> prev, Node<E> next) {
46          this.element = element;
47          this.prev = prev;
48          this.next = next;
49        }
50      }
51    }
```

The only changes that need to be made to the LinkedStack class (other than the method names) are at lines 14 and 25–27, where the next and prev fields are swapped.

APPLICATION: A CLIENT-SERVER SYSTEM

Queues are used to implement the FIFO protocol. That is common in client-server application. For example, when cars on a toll road arrive at a toll plaza, the cars are the clients, and the toll booths are the servers. If the rate at which the cars pass through the toll booths is slower than their arrival rate, then a waiting-line builds up. That is a queue.

EXAMPLE 6.5 A Client-Server Simulation

This simulation illustrates *object-oriented programming* (OOP). Java objects are instantiated to represent all the interacting clients and servers. To that end, we first define Client and Server classes.

This is an event-driven simulation, where clients arrive for service at random times and services have random durations. Each client will have an arrival time, a time when service starts, and a time when it ends. All time values will be integers.

```
1    public class Client {
2      private int id;
3      private int startTime;
4
5      public Client(int id, int time) {
6        this.id = id;
7        System.out.printf("%s arrived at time %d.%n", this, time);
8      }
9
10     public void setStartTime(int time) {
11       startTime = time;
12     }
13
14     public String toString() {
15       return "#" + id;
16     }
17   }
```

To trace the simulation, we have the Client constructor print its arrival time (at line 7).

Each server serves at most one client at a time, so the Server class has a client field that references that server's client, or is null when the server is idle.

Each Server object also stores the time when it will stop serving its current client. That time is computed by adding its service time (a positive random integer) to the time when it begins serving that client. The random number generator used to generate those service times is stored as a random field in the Server object. A server's actual service time varies with each client. But the server's average service time is a fixed property of the server, initialized when the Server object is constructed (at line 10):

```
1    public class Server {
2      private Client client;
3      private int id;
4      private int stopTime = -1;
5      private double meanServiceTime;
6      private ExpRandom random;
7
8      public Server(int id, double meanServiceTime) {
9        this.id = id;
10       this.meanServiceTime = meanServiceTime;
11       this.random = new ExpRandom(meanServiceTime);
12     }
13
14     public double getMeanServiceTime() {
15       return meanServiceTime;
16     }
17
18     public int getStopTime() {
19       return stopTime;
20     }
21
22     public boolean isIdle() {
23       return client == null;
24     }
25
26     public void startServing(Client client, int time) {
27       this.client = client;
28       this.client.setStartTime(time);
29       this.stopTime = time + random.nextInt();
30       System.out.printf("%s started serving client %s at time %d.%n",
31           this, client, time);
32     }
```

```
33
34      public void stopServing(int time) {
35        System.out.printf("%s stopped serving client %s at time %d.%n",
36            this, client, time);
37        client = null;
38      }
39
40      public String toString() {
41        return "Server " + "ABCDEFGHIJKLMNOPQRSTUVWXYZ".charAt(id);
42      }
43    }
```

The startServing() method (lines 26–32) assigns a new client to the server, stores the start time in the Client object, computes and stores the stop time in its own stopTime field, and prints a report of those actions. The stopServing() method (lines 34–38) stores the stop time in the Client object and prints another report.

For a simulation to be realistic, it must use randomly generated numbers to simulate the natural uncertainty of the real word. Those random numbers should have the same distribution as the natural uncertainties that they represent. Service times and time between client arrivals both tend to be distributed exponentially. That means that the probability that the time t is less than a number x is $p = 1 - e^{-\lambda x}$. But the Math.random() method returns numbers that are uniformly distributed in the range $0 \le p < 1$. So to convert the random number p to the exponentially distributed random variable x, we solve the equation, obtaining $x = -(1/\lambda)\ln(1 - p)$. The constant $1/\lambda$ is the mean of the distribution. Thus we code the nextDouble() method as shown at line 9:

```
1     public class ExpRandom extends java.util.Random {
2       private double mean;
3
4       public ExpRandom(double mean) {
5         this.mean = mean;
6       }
7
8       public double nextDouble() {
9         return -mean*Math.log(1 - Math.random());
10      }
11
12      public int nextInt() {
13        return (int)Math.ceil(nextDouble());
14      }
15    }
```

The actual simulation is performed by the main class shown below. It sets four constants for the simulation at lines 2–5: the number of servers, the number of clients arriving for service, the mean service time among the servers, and the mean time between arrivals for the clients.

The queue is to hold the clients that have arrived for service and are waiting for an unoccupied server. The simulation instantiates two random exponentially distributed number generators (lines 7–8) and separate arrays for the Server and Client objects (lines 9–10):

```
1     public class Simulation {
2       private static final int SERVERS = 3;
3       private static final int CLIENTS = 20;
4       private static final double MEAN_SERVICE_TIME = 25;
5       private static final double MEAN_ARRIVAL_TIME = 4;
6       private static Queue<Client> queue = new ArrayDeque<Client>();
7       private static ExpRandom randomService = new ExpRandom(MEAN_SERVICE_TIME);
8       private static ExpRandom randomArrival = new ExpRandom(MEAN_ARRIVAL_TIME);
9       private static Server[] servers = new Server[SERVERS];
10      private static Client[] clients = new Client[CLIENTS];
```

```
11
12      public Simulation() {
13        String fmt = "%-27s %6d%n";
14        System.out.printf(fmt, "Number of servers:", SERVERS);
15        System.out.printf(fmt, "Number of clients:", CLIENTS);
16        System.out.printf(fmt, "Mean service time:", MEAN_SERVICE_TIME);
17        System.out.printf(fmt, "Mean interarrival time:", MEAN_ARRIVAL_TIME);
18        for (int i=0; i<SERVERS; i++) {
19          double meanServiceTime = randomService.nextDouble();
20          servers[i] = new Server(i, meanServiceTime);
21          System.out.printf("Mean service time for %s: %4.1f%n",
22              servers[i], servers[i].getMeanServiceTime());
23        }
24        int nextArrivalTime = 0;
25        for (int t=0, clientId=0; clientId < CLIENTS; t++) {
26          if (t == nextArrivalTime) {
27            nextArrivalTime = t + randomArrival.nextInt();
28            Client client = clients[clientId] = new Client(++clientId, t);
29            queue.add(client);
30            System.out.println("\tClient queue: " + queue);
31          }
32          for (Server server : servers) {
33            if (t == server.getStopTime()) {
34              server.stopServing(t);
35            }
36            if (server.isIdle() && !queue.isEmpty()) {
37              Client client = (Client)queue.remove();
38              System.out.println("\tClient queue: " + queue);
39              server.startServing(client,t);
40            }
41          }
42        }
43      }
44
45      public static void main(String[] args) {
46        new Simulation();
47      }
48    }
```

The output for one run was:

```
        Number of servers:            3
        Number of clients:           12
        Mean service time:           25
        Mean interarrival time:       4
        Mean service time for Server A: 17.2
        Mean service time for Server B: 51.7
        Mean service time for Server C: 24.5
        #1 arrived at time 0.
                Client queue: [#1]
                Client queue: []
        Server A started serving client #1 at time 0.
        #2 arrived at time 2.
                Client queue: [#2]
                Client queue: []
        Server B started serving client #2 at time 2.
        #3 arrived at time 4.
                Client queue: [#3]
                Client queue: []
```

```
Server C started serving client #3 at time 4.
#4 arrived at time 6.
        Client queue: [#4]
#5 arrived at time 7.
        Client queue: [#4, #5]
#6 arrived at time 11.
        Client queue: [#4, #5, #6]
Server A stopped serving client #1 at time 11.
        Client queue: [#5, #6]
Server A started serving client #4 at time 11.
#7 arrived at time 12.
        Client queue: [#5, #6, #7]
#8 arrived at time 16.
        Client queue: [#5, #6, #7, #8]
#9 arrived at time 23.
        Client queue: [#5, #6, #7, #8, #9]
#10 arrived at time 30.
        Client queue: [#5, #6, #7, #8, #9, #10]
Server C stopped serving client #3 at time 30.
        Client queue: [#6, #7, #8, #9, #10]
Server C started serving client #5 at time 30.
Server B stopped serving client #2 at time 33.
        Client queue: [#7, #8, #9, #10]
Server B started serving client #6 at time 33.
#11 arrived at time 34.
        Client queue: [#7, #8, #9, #10, #11]
#12 arrived at time 36.
        Client queue: [#7, #8, #9, #10, #11, #12]
```

The simulation main loop is at lines 25–42. It iterates once for each clock tick t, and continues until all the clients have arrived. If it is time for a new client to arrive, then lines 27–30 execute, setting the next arrival time, creating a new Client object, and adding the new client to the queue. Then at lines 32–41, each Server object is updated. If it is time for an active server to finish serving its client, then its stopserving() method is invoked. If a server is idle and there are clients waiting in the queue, then the next client in the queue is removed from the queue and that server begins serving it.

The output shows the progress of one run. Client #4 is the first client to have to wait in the queue, followed by #5 and #6. At time t = 11, Server A finishes serving Client #1 and begins serving Client #4, who therefore leaves the queue at that time.

By the time the next server (Server C) becomes free, at time t = 30, four more clients have arrived and are waiting in the queue. Then C begins to serve #5. At time t = 33, Server B finishes with #2 and begins serving #6. Then the queue grows back to six clients waiting when the simulation finishes at time t = 36.

The simulation in Example 6.5 is called a *time-driven simulation* because its main loop iterates once for each tick of the clock. In contrast, an *event-driven* simulation is one in which the main loop iterates once for each event: a job arrival, a service begin, or a service end. Event-driven simulations are usually simpler, but they require all servers to perform at the same rate.

Review Questions

6.1 Why are queues called FIFO structures?

6.2 Would it make sense to call a queue
   a. a LILO structure?
   b. a FILO structure?

6.3 What are the advantages and disadvantages of the linked implementation of a queue relative to the contiguous implementation?

Problems

6.1 Trace the following code, showing the contents of the queue q after each call:

```
ArrayQueue q;
q.enqueue("A");
q.enqueue("B");
q.enqueue("C");
q.dequeue();
q.dequeue();
q.enqueue("D");
q.enqueue("E");
q.enqueue("F");
q.dequeue();
q.enqueue("G");
q.dequeue();
q.dequeue();
q.dequeue();
```

6.2 Write this client method using only the methods specified in the Queue interface:

```
public static <E> Queue<E> reversed(Queue<E> queue) {
// returns a new queue that contains the same elements as the given
// queue, but in reversed order
```

6.3 Write this client method using only the methods specified in the Queue interface:

```
public static <E> Queue<E> reversed(Queue<E> queue) {
// returns a new queue that contains the same elements as the given
// queue, but in reversed order, and leaves the given queue in its
// original state
```

6.4 Write this client method using only the methods specified in the Queue interface:

```
public static <E> void reverse(Queue<E> queue) {
// reverses the elements in the specified queue
```

6.5 Write this client method using only the methods specified in the Queue interface:

```
public static <E> E secondElement(Queue<E> queue) {
// returns the second element in the specified queue, leaving the
// queue in its original state
```

6.6 Write this client method using only the methods specified in the Queue interface:

```
public static <E> E lastElement(Queue<E> queue) {
// returns the last element in the specified queue, leaving the
// queue in its original state
```

6.7 Write this client method using only the methods specified in the Queue interface:

```
public static <E> void removeLastElement(Queue<E> queue) {
// removes the last element in the specified queue
```

6.8 Write this client method using only the methods specified in the Queue interface:

```
public static <E> Queue<E> merge(Queue<E> q1, Queue<E> q2) {
// returns a new queue that contains the same elements as the two
// specified queues, alternately merged together, leaving the two
// specified queues in their original state
```

6.9   Add this member method to the `ArrayQueue` class shown in Example 6.3 on page 119:
```
public void reverse()
// reverses the contents of this queue
```

6.10   Add this member method to the `LinkedQueue` class shown in Example 6.4 on page 120:
```
public void reverse()
// reverses the contents of this queue
```

6.11   Add this member method to the `ArrayQueue` class shown in Example 6.3 on page 119:
```
public E second() {
// returns the second element of this queue
```

6.12   Add this member method to the `LinkedQueue` class shown in Example 6.4 on page 120:
```
public E second() {
// returns the second element of this queue
```

6.13   Add this member method to the `ArrayQueue` class shown in Example 6.3 on page 119:
```
public E removeSecond() {
// removes and returns the second element of this queue
```

6.14   Add this member method to the `LinkedQueue` class shown in Example 6.4 on page 120:
```
public E removeSecond() {
// removes and returns the second element of this queue
```

Answers to Review Questions

6.1   Queues are called FIFO structures because the first element that is inserted into a queue is always the first element to be removed. FIFO is an acronym for first-in-first-out.

6.2   **a.**   Yes, because a LILO structure would mean last-in-last-out which is just the same as a first-in-first-out protocol.

   b.   No, because a FILO structure would mean first-in-last-out which is the opposite of the first-in-first-out protocol.

6.3   The advantage of the linked implementation is that it essentially eliminated the possibility of queue *overflow*, that is, the number of calls to the `add()` method is limited only by the amount of computer memory available to the new operator. The only real disadvantage is that the linked implementation uses pointers, so it is more complicated than the contiguous implementation.

Solutions to Problems

6.1   A → AB → ABC → BC → C → CD → CDE → CDEF → DEF → DEFG → EFG → FG → G

6.2
```
public static <E> Queue<E> reversed(Queue<E> queue) {
  // returns a new queue that contains the same elements as the given
  // queue, but in reversed order
  Queue<E> queue1 = new ArrayDeque<E>();
  Deque<E> stack = new ArrayDeque<E>();
  while(!queue.isEmpty()) {
    stack.push(queue.remove());
  }
  while(!stack.isEmpty()) {
    queue1.add(stack.pop());
  }
  return queue1;
}
```

6.3
```
public static <E> Queue<E> reversed(Queue<E> queue) {
    // returns a new queue that contains the same elements as the given
    // queue, but in reversed order, and leaves the given queue in its
    // original state
    Queue<E> queue1 = new ArrayDeque<E>();
    Deque<E> stack = new ArrayDeque<E>();
    for (int i=0; i<queue.size(); i++) {
        stack.push(queue.element());
        queue.add(queue.remove());
    }
    while(!stack.isEmpty()) {
        queue1.add(stack.pop());
    }
    return queue1;
}
```

6.4
```
public static <E> void reverse(Queue<E> queue) {
    // returns a new queue that contains the same elements as the given
    // queue, but in reversed order, and leaves the given queue in its
    // original state
    Deque<E> stack = new ArrayDeque<E>();
    while(!queue.isEmpty()) {
        stack.push(queue.remove());
    }
    while(!stack.isEmpty()) {
        queue.add(stack.pop());
    }
}
```

6.5
```
public static <E> E secondElement(Queue<E> queue) {
    // returns the second element in the specified queue, leaving the
    // queue in its original state
    queue.add(queue.remove());
    E element = queue.element();
    for (int i=1; i<queue.size(); i++) {
        queue.add(queue.remove());
    }
    return element;
}
```

6.6
```
public static <E>  E lastElement(Queue<E> queue) {
    // returns the last element in the specified queue, leaving the
    // queue in its original state
    for (int i=1; i<queue.size(); i++) {
        queue.add(queue.remove());
    }
    E element = queue.element();
    queue.add(queue.remove());
    return element;
}
```

6.7
```
public static <E> void removeLastElement(Queue<E> queue) {
    // removes the last element in the specified queue
    for (int i=1; i<queue.size(); i++) {
        queue.add(queue.remove());
    }
    queue.remove();
}
```

6.8
```
public static <E> Queue<E> merge(Queue<E> queue1, Queue<E> queue2) {
    // returns a new queue that contains the same elements as the two
    // specified queues, alternately merged together, leaving the two
    // specified queues in their original state
```

```
              Queue<E> queue3 = new ArrayDeque<E>();
              int n1 = queue1.size();
              int n2 = queue2.size();
              int n = Math.min(n1, n2);
              for (int i = 0; i < n; i++) {
                queue3.add(queue1.element());
                queue1.add(queue1.remove());
                queue3.add(queue2.element());
                queue2.add(queue2.remove());
              }
              for (int i = 0; i < n1 - n; i++) {
                queue3.add(queue1.element());
                queue1.add(queue1.remove());
              }
              for (int i = 0; i < n2 - n; i++) {
                queue3.add(queue2.element());
                queue2.add(queue2.remove());
              }
              return queue3;
            }
```

6.9
```
            public void reverse() {
              // reverses the contents of this queue
              resize();
              int n = size();
              for (int i=0; i<n/2; i++) {
                E e = elements[i];
                elements[i] = elements[n-1-i];
                elements[n-1-i] = e;
              }
            }
```

6.10
```
            public void reverse() {
              // reverses the contents of this queue
              Node<E> p = head;
              for (int i=0; i<=size; i++) {
                Node<E> q = p.next;
                p.next = p.prev;
                p = p.prev = q;
              }
            }
```

6.11
```
            public E second() {
              // returns the second element of this queue
              if (size() < 2) {
                throw new java.util.NoSuchElementException();
              }
              int len = elements.length;
              if (front + 1 == len) {
                return elements[0];
              } else {
                return elements[front+1];
              }
            }
```

6.12
```
            public E second() {
              // returns the second element of this queue
              if (size < 2) {
                throw new java.util.NoSuchElementException();
              }
              return head.next.next.element;
            }
```

6.13
```
public E removeSecond() {
   // removes and returns the second element of this queue
   if (size() < 2) {
     throw new java.util.NoSuchElementException();
   }
   int len = elements.length;
   E e;
   if (front + 1 == len) {
     e = elements[0];
     elements[0] = elements[len-1];
     elements[len-1] = null;
     front = 0;
   } else {
     e = elements[front+1];
     elements[front+1] = elements[front];
     elements[front] = null;
     ++front;
   }
   return e;
}
```

6.14
```
public E removeSecond() {
   // removes and returns the second element of this queue
   if (size() < 2) {
     throw new java.util.NoSuchElementException();
   }
   E element = head.next.next.element;
   head.next.next = head.next.next.next;
   head.next.next.prev = head.next;
   --size;
   return e;
}
```

CHAPTER 7

Lists

A *list* is a collection of elements that are accessible sequentially: the first element, followed by the second element, followed by the third element, and so on. This is called *sequential access* or *linked access* (as opposed to direct or indexed access). A good example is a line of train cars on a track: To get to the fourth car from the first car, you have to go through the second and third cars in that order. This example also illustrates how insertions and deletions are managed in a list. The only changes needed are to the two cars that are adjacent to location where the insertion or deletion is made. None of the other cars is affected.

THE JCF List INTERFACE

The List interface specified by the Java Collections Framework is outlined on page 85. It adds 10 methods to the 15 methods specified by the Collection interface that it extends.

From the JCF inheritance hierarchy shown in Figure 4.1 on page 70, you can see that the Queue, Deque, and Set interfaces all extend the List interface. Consequently, all of the List, Queue, Deque, and Set classes implement the List interface. This includes the concrete classes outlined in Chapter 4: ArrayList, Vector, LinkedList, PriorityQueue, ArrayDeque, EnumSet, HashSet, LinkedHashSet, and TreeSet.

As Table 4.1 on page 70 shows, the JCF provides both linked and indexed implementations of the List interface: the LinkedList class uses sequential access, while the ArrayList class provides direct access.

EXAMPLE 7.1 Testing a List Class

This program illustrates some of the methods specified by the List interface:

```
1   public class TestStringList {
2     public static void main(String[] args) {
3       List<String> list = new ArrayList<String>();
4       Collections.addAll(list, "GB", "DE", "FR", "ES");
5       System.out.println(list);
6       list.add(3, "DE");
7       System.out.println(list);
8       System.out.println("list.get(3): " + list.get(3));
9       System.out.println("list.indexOf(\"DE\"): " + list.indexOf("DE"));
10      System.out.println("list.indexOf(\"IE\"): " + list.indexOf("IE"));
11      System.out.println("list.subList(1, 5): " + list.subList(1, 5));
12      list.remove("DE");
13      System.out.println(list);
14    }
15  }
```

The output is:

```
[GB, DE, FR, ES]
[GB, DE, FR, DE, ES]
list.get(3): DE
list.indexOf("DE"): 1
list.indexOf("IE"): -1
list.subList(1, 5): [DE, FR, DE, ES]
[GB, FR, DE, ES]
```

The `list` object is created at line 3 as an `ArrayList` of `String` objects. It uses the `static addAll()` method of the `Collections` class at line 4 to load four strings into it. The two-argument `add()` method is tested at line 6, inserting the string "DE" as element number 2. Note that, unlike sets, lists allow duplicate elements.

At line 8, the `get()` method is used to obtain element number 3. Lines 9–10 illustrate the `indexOf()` method, returning the index number of the specified element. Note that it returns the index of the first occurrence of the element; DE occurs at both index 1 and index 3.

The call `list.subList(1, 5)` at line 11 returns the sublist of elements indexed from 1 up to (but not including) 5. As long as the two indexes are in range, the size of the sublist will always be their difference; in this case, $5 - 1 = 4$ elements.

At line 12, the call `list.remove("DE")` removes the first occurrence of DE.

THE RANGE-VIEW OPERATION `sublist()`

The `sublist()` method illustrated in Example 7.1 is far more powerful than what that example suggests. It provides a "view" into its list, against which other `List` methods may be applied. When used in the chained-invocation mode, like this

```
list.sublist(1, 5).get(2)
```

it allows the attached method to apply to the list itself while restricting its context to the sublist. Thus, that call, for example, would return element number 2 of the sublist, which is actually element number 3 of the list itself.

EXAMPLE 7.2 Using the `sublist()` Method as a Range-View Operation

```
1    public class TestSubList {
2      public static void main(String[] args) {
3        List<String> list = new ArrayList<String>();
4        Collections.addAll(list, "A","B","C","D","E","F","G","H","I","J");
5        System.out.println(list);
6        System.out.println("list.subList(3,8): " + list.subList(3,8));
7        System.out.println("list.subList(3,8).get(2): "
8            + list.subList(3,8).get(2));
9        System.out.println("list.subList(3,8).set(2,\"B\"):");
10       list.subList(3,8).set(2, "B");
11       System.out.println(list);
12       System.out.println("list.indexOf(\"B\"): " + list.indexOf("B"));
13       System.out.println("list.subList(3,8).indexOf(\"B\"): "
14           + list.subList(3,8).indexOf("B"));
15       System.out.println(list);
16       System.out.println("Collections.reverse(list.subList(3,8)):");
17       Collections.reverse(list.subList(3,8));
18       System.out.println(list);
19       System.out.println("Collections.rotate(list.subList(3,8), 2):");
20       Collections.rotate(list.subList(3,8), 2);
21       System.out.println(list);
```

```
22        System.out.println("Collections.fill(list.subList(3,8), \"X\"):");
23        Collections.fill(list.subList(3,8), "X");
24        System.out.println(list);
25        list.subList(3,8).clear();
26        System.out.println(list);
27      }
28    }
```

The output is:

```
[A, B, C, D, E, F, G, H, I, J]
list.subList(3,8): [D, E, F, G, H]
list.subList(3,8).get(2): F
list.subList(3,8).set(2,"B"):
[A, B, C, D, E, B, G, H, I, J]
list.indexOf("B"): 1
list.subList(3,8).indexOf("B"): 2
[A, B, C, D, E, B, G, H, I, J]
Collections.reverse(list.subList(3,8)):
[A, B, C, H, G, B, E, D, I, J]
Collections.rotate(list.subList(3,8), 2):
[A, B, C, E, D, H, G, B, I, J]
Collections.fill(list.subList(3,8), "X"):
[A, B, C, X, X, X, X, X, I, J]
[A, B, C, I, J]
```

The call list.subList(3,8) at line 6 returns the sublist [D, E, F, G, H].

The call list.subList(3,8).get(2) at line 8 returns F, which is element number 2 in that sublist.

The call list.subList(3,8).set(2,"B") at line 10 replaces that element with B in the list.

The call list.indexOf("B") at line 12 returns 1 because the first B in the list is element number 1.

The call list.subList(3,8).indexOf("B") at line 14 returns 2 because the first B in that sublist is element number 2 of the sublist.

The call Collections.reverse(list.subList(3,8)) at line 17 reverses the five-element sublist [D,E,B,G,H] within the original list, changing [A,B,C,D,E,B,G,H,I,J] to [A,B,C,H,G,B,E,D,I,J].

The call Collections.rotate(list.subList(3,8),2) at line 20 rotates the five-element sublist [H,G,B,E,D] to [E,D,H,G,B], changing the whole list to [A,B,C,E,D,H,G,B,I,J].

The call Collections.fill(list.subList(3,8),"X") at line 23 replaces the five-element sublist [E,D,H,G,B] to [X,X,X,X,X], changing the whole list to [A,B,C,X,X,X,X,X,I,J].

The call list.subList(3,8).clear() at line 25 deletes the five-element sublist [X,X,X,X,X] from the list, changing it to [A,B,C,I,J].

LIST ITERATORS

Collection iterators are outlined on page 77. The JCF defines the ListIterator interface as an extension of the Iterator interface. It specifies an additional six methods that reflect the bidirectional nature of a list iterator. All nine methods are shown in Figure 7.1 on page 135.

The standard way to obtain a list iterator on a list is to invoke its listIterator() method, just as invoking its iterator() method returns an ordinary (unidirectional) iterator.

EXAMPLE 7.3 Using the sublist() Method as a Range-View Operation

```
1    public class TestSubList {
2      public static void main(String[] args) {
3        List<String> list = new ArrayList<String>();
4        Collections.addAll(list, "A","B","C","D","E","F","G","H");
5        System.out.println(list);
```

```
6      ListIterator<String> it = list.listIterator();
7      System.out.println("it.nextIndex(): " + it.nextIndex());
8      System.out.println("it.next(): " + it.next());
9      System.out.println("it.previousIndex(): " + it.previousIndex());
10     System.out.println("it.nextIndex(): " + it.nextIndex());
11     System.out.println("it.next(): " + it.next());
12     System.out.println("it.next(): " + it.next());
13     System.out.println("it.previous(): " + it.previous());
14     System.out.println("it.previousIndex(): " + it.previousIndex());
15     System.out.println("it.nextIndex(): " + it.nextIndex());
16     System.out.println("it.previous(): " + it.previous());
17     System.out.println("it.next(): " + it.next());
18     System.out.println("it.next(): " + it.next());
19     System.out.println("it.next(): " + it.next());
20     System.out.println("it.add(\"X\"):");
21     it.add("X");
22     System.out.println(list);
23     System.out.println("it.next(): " + it.next());
24     System.out.println("it.set(\"Y\"):");
25     it.set("Y");
26     System.out.println(list);
27     System.out.println("it.next(): " + it.next());
28     System.out.println("it.remove():");
29     it.remove();
30     System.out.println("it.next(): " + it.next());
31     System.out.println(list);
32   }
33 }
```

The output is:

```
[A, B, C, D, E, F, G, H]
it.nextIndex(): 0
it.next(): A
it.previousIndex(): 0
it.nextIndex(): 1
it.next(): B
it.next(): C
it.previous(): C
it.previousIndex(): 1
it.nextIndex(): 2
it.previous(): B
it.next(): B
it.next(): C
it.next(): D
it.add("X"):
[A, B, C, D, X, E, F, G, H]
it.next(): E
it.set("Y"):
[A, B, C, D, X, Y, F, G, H]
it.next(): F
it.remove():
it.next(): G
[A, B, C, D, X, Y, G, H]
```

The output shows the effects of the nine `ListIterator` methods. At lines 7 and 10, the `nextIndex()` method returns the index number of the iterator's current element: first 0, and then 1. Similarly, the `previousIndex()` method returns the index number of the iterator's previous element. The `next()` and `previous()` methods move the iterator up and down the list. At line 21, the `add()` method inserts a new

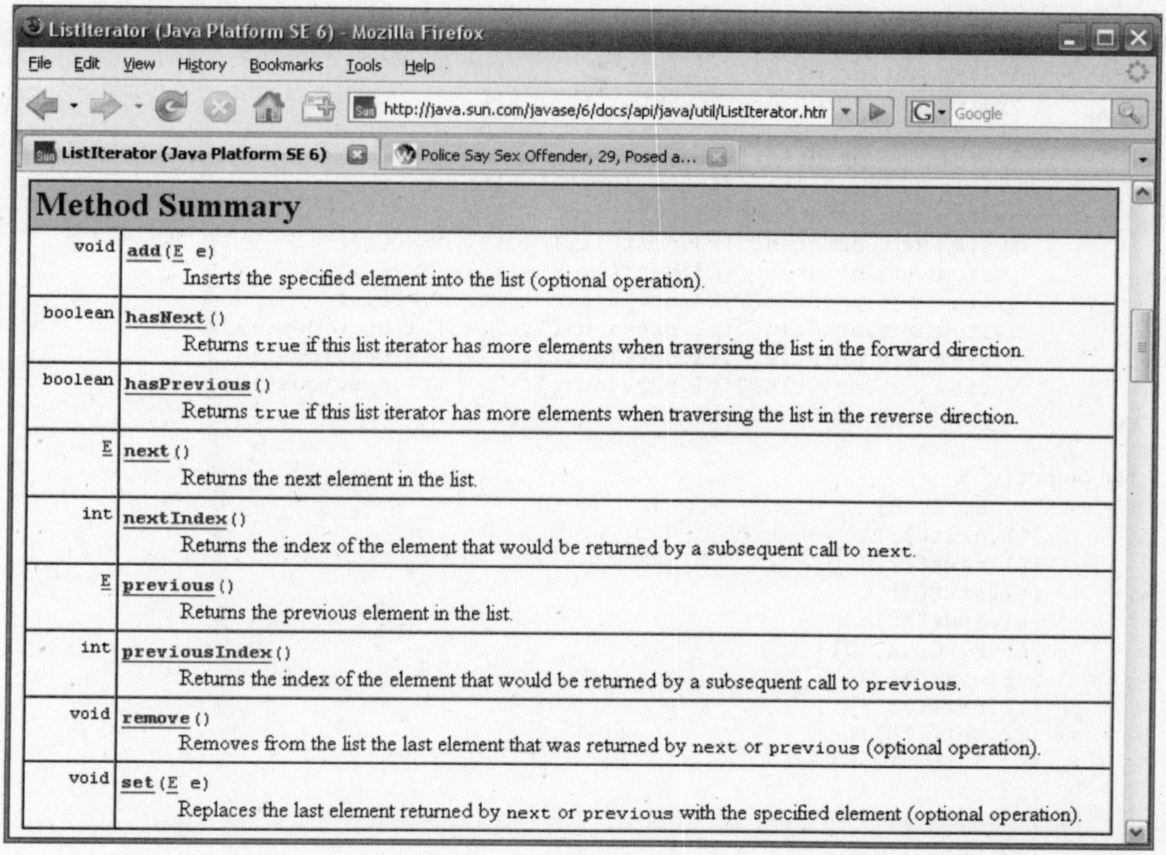

Figure 7.1 Methods specified by the `java.util.ListIterator` interface

element X immediately after that last element referenced by the next() method, which was D. At line 25, the set() method changes the last element referenced by the next() method, from E to Y. At line 29, the remove() method deletes the last element referenced by the next() method, which was F.

Like a finger tracing through some text, an iterator is an object bound to a collection that moves independently of other iterators on the same collection.

EXAMPLE 7.4 Using Several `ListIterator` Objects Iterating on the Same List Object

This program illustrates some of the methods that are specific to the `ArrayList` class:

```java
1   public class TestingSeveralIterators {
2     public static void main(String[] args) {
3       List<String> list = new ArrayList<String>();
4       Collections.addAll(list, "A", "B", "C", "D");
5       System.out.println(list);
6       ListIterator<String> it1 = list.listIterator();
7       System.out.println("it1.next(): " + it1.next());
8       System.out.println("it1.next(): " + it1.next());
9       System.out.println("it1.next(): " + it1.next());
10      System.out.println("it1.add(\"X\"):");
11      it1.add("X");
12      System.out.println(list);
```

```
13      ListIterator<String> it2 = list.listIterator();
14      System.out.println("it2.next(): " + it2.next());
15      System.out.println("it2.next(): " + it2.next());
16      System.out.println("it2.set(\"Y\"):");
17      it2.set("Y");
18      System.out.println(list);
19      ListIterator<String> it3 = list.listIterator();
20      System.out.println("it3.next(): " + it3.next());
21      System.out.println("it3.next(): " + it3.next());
22      System.out.println("it3.next(): " + it3.next());
23      System.out.println("it3.next(): " + it3.next());
24      System.out.println("it1.previous(): " + it1.previous());
25      System.out.println("it1.previous(): " + it1.previous());
26      System.out.println("it1.previous(): " + it1.previous());
27    }
28  }
```

The output is:

```
[A, B, C, D]
it1.next(): A
it1.next(): B
it1.next(): C
it1.add("X"):
[A, B, C, X, D]
it2.next(): A
it2.next(): B
it2.set("Y"):
[A, Y, C, X, D]
it3.next(): A
it3.next(): Y
it3.next(): C
it3.next(): X
it1.previous(): X
it1.previous(): C
it1.previous(): Y
```

The first iterator it1 advances past the first three elements and then inserts X between C and D at line 11. The second iterator it2 advances past the first two elements and then changes B and Y at line 17. The third iterator it3 advances past the first four elements, including the changed element Y and the inserted element X. Finally, the first iterator it1 backs up over the previous three elements, including the inserted element X and the changed element Y.

OTHER LIST TYPES

The JCF defines a concrete LinkedList class. (See page 86.) But that may not be exactly what you need for certain applications. In those cases, the AbstractList class can be extended to obtain a custom-made list class that is consistent with the JCF.

EXAMPLE 7.5 A Ring Class

This defines a list class that uses a circular, singly linked list. It is similar to the LinkedList class, except that the next() method is able to wrap around from the end of the list to the beginning, thus forming a circle or "ring."

```
1   public class Ring<E> extends AbstractList<E> implements List<E> {
2       private Node<E> end;
3       private int size;
```

```
 4
 5      public boolean add(E element) {
 6        if (size == 0) {
 7          end = new Node<E>(element, null);
 8          end.next = end;
 9        } else {
10          end = end.next = new Node<E>(element, end.next);
11        }
12        ++size;
13        return true;
14      }
15
16      public E get(int index) {
17        if (index < 0 || index >= size) {
18          throw new IndexOutOfBoundsException();
19        }
20        Node<E> p = end.next;
21        for (int i=0; i<index; i++) {
22          p = p.next;
23        }
24        return p.element;
25      }
26
27      public Iterator<E> iterator() {
28        return new RingIterator();
29      }
30
31      public String toString() {
32        Node<E> p = end.next;
33        StringBuilder buf = new StringBuilder("[" + p.element);
34        while (p != end) {
35          p = p.next;
36          buf.append(", " + p.element);
37        }
38        buf.append("]");
39        return buf.toString();
40      }
41
42      public int size() {
43        return size;
44      }
45
46      private class RingIterator implements Iterator<E> {
47        private Node<E> last;
48        private Node<E> preLast = end;
49
50        public boolean hasNext() {
51          return size > 0;
52        }
53
54        public E next() {
55          if (last == null) {
56            last = preLast.next;
57          } else {
58            preLast = last;
59            last = last.next;
60          }
```

```
61              return last.element;
62          }
63
64          public void remove() {
65              if (last == null) {
66                  throw new IllegalStateException();
67              }
68              if (size == 1) {
69                  end = preLast = null;
70              } else {
71                  preLast.next = last.next;
72              }
73              if (last == end) {
74                  end = preLast;
75              }
76              last = null;
77              --size;
78          }
79      }
80
81      private static class Node<E> {
82          E element;
83          Node<E> next;
84
85          Node(E element, Node<E> next) {
86              this.element = element;
87              this.next = next;
88          }
89      }
90  }
```

The class defines nine members: the two fields: end and size; the five methods: add(), get(), iterator(), size(), and toString(); and the two classes: RingIterator and Node. The RingIterator class extends the Iterator class to support the iterator() method. Instances of the Node class are used to hold the list's data and to maintain their links.

The AbstractList class, which this Ring class extends, requires only its get() and size() methods to be overridden. For our specific purposes, we also override the add(), iterator(), and toString() methods. We plan to use this class to solve the Josephus problem (in Example 7.6), and for that we'll need to add elements to the ring, iterate around the ring, and print the ring.

The end field references the node that references the "beginning" node in the list, that is, it points to the beginning of the list. Since we are using only one link per node (a "singly linked list"), we have to have direct access to the predecessor of any node that might have to be deleted. The end reference is null when the list is empty.

The size field keeps count of how many elements are in the list. Initially 0, it is incremented in the add() method (line 12), decremented in the iterator's remove() method (line 77), and returned in the size() method (line 43).

The add() method invokes the Node class's constructor (lines 7 and 10) to create a new node for the specified element. If the list is empty, it sets its end field to a single node that points to itself. Otherwise, the new node is inserted immediately after the end node, and then the new reference is set to that new node. This way, new elements are always added to the "end" of the ring. (See Figure 7.2.)

The get() method is required by the AbstractList class. It uses a reference pointer p at line 20 to count the specified number of nodes to return access to the element with the specified index number.

The iterator() method uses the RingIterator constructor at line 28 to return an iterator on the ring. The RingIterator class has two fields, both Node references. The last field points to the last node

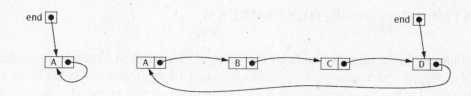

Figure 7.2 The end reference in the Ring class

accessed by the iterator's `next()` method. It will be `null` initially and immediately after each call to the iterator's `remove()` method. The `preLast` field points to the node that points to the `last` node. It is used by the `remove()` method.

The iterator's `hasNext()` method returns true at line 51, unless the list is empty. In a circular list, every element has a next element.

The `next()` method serves two purposes. If called immediately after a call to `remove()`, then it resets the `last` field (line 56), which the `remove()` method leaves `null`. Otherwise, it simply advances the `preLast` and `last` pointers (lines 58–59).

The purpose of the `remove()` method at line 64 is to delete the last element accessed by the `next()` method. Normally, it does that simply by resetting one link—the preceding node's `next` field (line 71). But it also has several special cases to handle. If its invocation does not immediately follow a call to `next()`, then it's in an illegal state, and thus throws an `IllegalStateException` at line 66. If the list has only one element, then removing it should leave the list in its original empty state by nullifying its `preLast` field (line 69). In that case, the `Ring` class's end field is also nullified. If the element being deleted is the one referenced by the `Ring` class's `end` field, then that field is reset to the element's predecessor at line 74. Finally, `last` is nullified at line 76 to mark the fact that the `next()` method was not the last one called in the iterator.

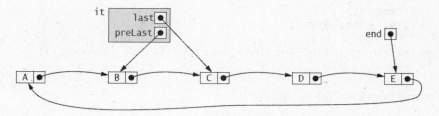

Figure 7.3 The last and preLast references in the RingIterator class

Figure 7.3 illustrates how the `last` and `preLast` pointers work in an iterator on a `Ring` list. This shows the state of the list immediately after a call to `next()` has returned the element C. An immediate call to `remove()` would delete the C node by resetting the B node's `next` reference to point to the D node, as shown in Figure 7.4.

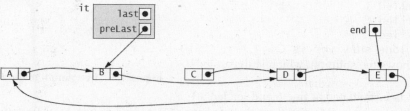

Figure 7.4 After a call to it.remove()

Note the efficiency of this operation: To delete C, only one link has to be reset, and one link is nullified.

APPLICATION: THE JOSEPHUS PROBLEM

This problem is based upon a report by the historian Joseph ben Matthias (Josephus) on the outcome of a suicide pact that he had made between himself and 40 soldiers as they were besieged by superior Roman forces in 67 A.D. Josephus proposed that each man slay his neighbor. This scheme necessarily leaves one to kill himself. Josephus cleverly contrived to be that one, thus surviving to tell the tale.

The solution to the problem is generated by the Josephus program in Example 7.6. It uses the Ring class from Example 7.5 on page 136.

EXAMPLE 7.6 The Josephus Problem

```
1   public class Josephus {
2       public static final int SOLDIERS = 8;
3       public static final String ALPHA = "ABCDEFGHIJKLMNOPQRSTUVWXYZ";
4
5       public static void main(String[] args) {
6         Ring<String> ring = new Ring<String>();
7         for (int i=0; i<SOLDIERS; i++) {
8           ring.add(ALPHA.substring(i, i+1));
9         }
10        System.out.println(ring);
11        Iterator<String> it = ring.iterator();
12        String killer = it.next();
13        while (ring.size() > 1) {
14          String victim = it.next();
15          System.out.println(killer + " killed " + victim);
16          it.remove();
17          killer = it.next();
18        }
19        System.out.println("The lone survivor is " + it.next());
20      }
21  }
```

Here is the output from a run for 11 soldiers:

```
[A, B, C, D, E, F, G, H, I, J, K]
A killed B
C killed D
E killed F
G killed H
I killed J
K killed A
C killed E
G killed I
K killed C
G killed K
The lone survivor is G
```

This output shows the solution, which is illustrated in Figure 7.5.

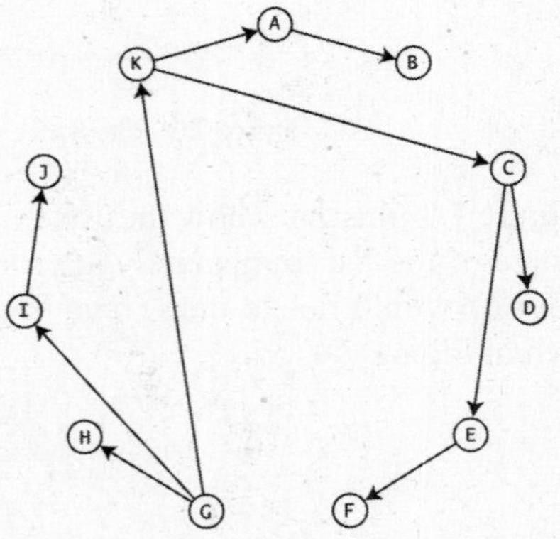

Figure 7.5 The solution to the Josephus problem

The Ring list is instantiated at line 6 and loaded at lines 7–9. The iterator it is obtained from the iterator() method at line 11. After advancing past A at line 12, it advances past B at line 14, removes B at line 16, and then advances past C at line 17. The while loop continues until only one soldier remains. Each iteration advances it past two elements, naming them killer and victim, and removes the victim node.

APPLICATION: A Polynomial CLASS

A *polynomial* is a mathematical function of the form:

$$p(x) = a_0 x^n + a_1 x^{n-1} + a_2 x^{n-2} + \cdots + a_{n-1} x + a_n$$

The greatest exponent, *n*, is called the *degree* of the polynomial. For example, $p(x) = 7x^4 - 2$ is a polynomial of degree 4. The simplest polynomials are *constant polynomials* such as $p(x) = 6$ (degree 0) and *linear polynomials* such as $p(x) = 9x + 6$ (degree 1). The unique *zero polynomial* $p(x) = 0$ is defined to have degree −1. In this section we present a Polynomial class whose instances represent mathematical polynomials and which supports the usual algebraic operations on polynomials.

A polynomial can be regarded as a sum of distinct terms. A *term* is a mathematical function of the form $t(x) = cx^e$, where *c* is any real number and *e* is any nonnegative integer. The number *c* is called the *coefficient*, and the number *e* is called the *exponent*.

To define a class whose objects represent polynomials, we use a linked list of Term objects. For example, the polynomial $p(x) = 3x^2 - 2x + 5$ could be represented as a list of three elements, where the first element represents the term $3x^2$, the second element represents the term $-2x$, and the third element represents the (constant) term 5.

EXAMPLE 7.7 A Polynomial Class

```
1    public class Polynomial {
2       private List<Term> list = new LinkedList<Term>();
3       public static final Polynomial ZERO = new Polynomial();
4
5       private Polynomial() {  // default constructor
6       }
7
8       public Polynomial(double coef, int exp) {
9          if (coef != 0.0) {
10            list.add(new Term(coef, exp));
11         }
12      }
13
14      public Polynomial(Polynomial p) {  // copy constructor
15         for (Term term : p.list) {
16            this.list.add(new Term(term));
17         }
18      }
19
20      public Polynomial(double... a) {
21         for (int i=0; i<a.length; i++) {
22            if (a[i] != 0.0) {
23               list.add(new Term(a[i], i));
24            }
25         }
26      }
27
28      public int degree() {
29         if (list.isEmpty()) {
30            return -1;
31         } else {
32            return list.get(list.size()-1).exp;
33         }
34      }
```

```java
35
36     public boolean isZero() {
37       return list.isEmpty();
38     }
39
40     public Polynomial plus(Polynomial p) {
41       if (this.isZero()) {
42         return new Polynomial(p);
43       }
44       if (p.isZero()) {
45         return new Polynomial(this);
46       }
47       Polynomial q = new Polynomial();
48       ListIterator<Term> it = list.listIterator();
49       ListIterator<Term> itp = p.list.listIterator();
50       while (it.hasNext() && itp.hasNext()) {
51         Term term = it.next();
52         Term pTerm = itp.next();
53         if (term.exp < pTerm.exp) {
54           q.list.add(new Term(term));
55           itp.previous();
56         } else if (term.exp == pTerm.exp) {
57           q.list.add(new Term(term.coef + pTerm.coef, term.exp));
58         } else {  // (term.exp > pTerm.exp)
59           q.list.add(new Term(pTerm));
60           it.previous();
61         }
62       }
63       while (it.hasNext()) {
64         q.list.add(new Term(it.next()));
65       }
66       while (itp.hasNext()) {
67         q.list.add(new Term(itp.next()));
68       }
69       return q;
70     }
71
72     public String toString() {
73       if (this.isZero()) {
74         return "0";
75       }
76       Iterator<Term> it = list.iterator();
77       StringBuilder buf = new StringBuilder();
78       boolean isFirstTerm = true;
79       while (it.hasNext()) {
80         Term term = it.next();
81         double c = term.coef;
82         int e = term.exp;
83         if (isFirstTerm) {
84           buf.append(String.format("%.2f", c));
85           isFirstTerm = false;
86         } else {
87           if (term.coef < 0) {
88             buf.append(String.format(" - %.2f", -c));
89           } else {
90             buf.append(String.format(" + %.2f", c));
91           }
```

```
92              }
93              if (e == 1) {
94                  buf.append("x");
95              } else if (e > 1) {
96                  buf.append("x^" + e);
97              }
98          }
99          return buf.toString();
100     }
101
102     private static class Term {
103         private double coef;
104         private int exp;
105
106         public Term(double coef, int exp) {
107             if (coef == 0.0 || exp < 0) {
108                 throw new IllegalArgumentException();
109             }
110             this.coef = coef;
111             this.exp = exp;
112         }
113
114         public Term(Term that) {  // copy constructor
115             this(that.coef, that.exp);
116         }
117     }
118 }
```

Instead of using *inheritance* by extending a List class, this Polynomial class uses *composition*, declaring a list field at line 2. This design gives the user more control over the class by limiting it to only those methods actually defined in the class. Of course, those methods are mostly implemented by means of List methods. The list backing structure is declared to be a LinkedList<Term> collection. So each element of the list is a Term object. The list stores the polynomial's nonzero terms in increasing order of their exponents.

The Term class is defined as an *inner class* at lines 102–117, that is, a static member class. It has two fields, coef and exp (for the coefficient and the exponent of the term), and two constructors. The second constructor (line 114) is a *copy constructor*, creating a duplicate of the term passed to it. It uses the this keyword to invoke the two-argument constructor defined at line 106.

The Polynomial class has four constructors and four methods. The *default constructor* (also called the "no-arg constructor") defined at line 8 is declared to be private. This prevents it from being used outside of its class. Its purpose is to construct the Polynomial object that represents the zero polynomial, and it is invoked at line 3 to do that. To ensure that that object is unique, we prevent it from being constructed anywhere else.

The constructor at line 8 creates a Polynomial object that represents a single term, such as $88.8x^{44}$. The constructor at line 14 is a copy constructor, which duplicates the object passed to it. The constructor at line 20 uses the Java "var-args" syntax to allow a variable number of arguments, in this case of type double. This is the same as a single argument of type double[]. That constructor creates a polynomial whose coefficients are the nonzero values in the array, each one generating a term of the form $c_n x^n$, where $c_n = a[n]$. For example, the array $\{4, 0, 7, 0, 0, 0, 3\}$ would produce the Polynomial object that represents $4 + 7x^2 + 3x^6$.

The degree() method at line 28 returns the polynomial's highest exponent. Since the terms are maintained in the list in increasing order of their exponents, the degree of the polynomial is the simply the exp field of the last element in the list. That element has index list.size()-1, so the expression at line 32 does the job.

The `plus()` method at line 40 returns a new object that represents the sum of the implicit argument (`this`) and the explicit argument (`p`). That result, instantiated as q at line 44, is built by means of the three `while` loops ate lines 50–68. The first loop repeatedly compares the exponents of a term from each polynomial (`this` and `p`), duplicates the one with the smaller exponent, and adds it to q. If the two terms are equal, then their coefficients are added (at line 57) to form the new term. The loops use iterators to traverse the two lists. Since the term whose coefficient was not yet used has to be accessed again on the next iteration, its iterator has to be backed up (at lines 55 and 60). Consequently, we need the bidirectional iterators provided by the `listIterator()` method.

The `toString()` method uses a unidirectional iterator to traverse the list at line 80 to generate a string representation of the `Polynomial` object.

EXAMPLE 7.8 Testing the Polynomial Class

```
1    public class TestPolynomial {
2      public static void main(String[] args) {
3        Polynomial p = new Polynomial(3, -8, 0, 0, 2, 1);
4        Polynomial q = new Polynomial(0, 5, 6, 9);
5        System.out.println("p: " + p);
6        System.out.println("p.degree(): " + p.degree());
7        System.out.println("q: " + q);
8        System.out.println("q.degree(): " + q.degree());
9        System.out.println("p.plus(q): " + p.plus(q));
10       System.out.println("q.plus(p): " + q.plus(p));
11       System.out.println("p.plus(q).degree(): " + p.plus(q).degree());
12       Polynomial z = new Polynomial(0);
13       System.out.println("z: " + z);
14       System.out.println("z.degree(): " + z.degree());
15       System.out.println("p.plus(z): " + p.plus(z));
16       System.out.println("z.plus(p): " + z.plus(p));
17       System.out.println("p:         " + p);
18       Polynomial t = new Polynomial(8.88, 44);
19       System.out.println("t: " + t);
20       System.out.println("t.degree(): " + t.degree());
21     }
22   }
```

The output is:

```
p: 3.00 - 8.00x + 2.00x^4 + 1.00x^5
p.degree(): 5
q: 5.00x + 6.00x^2 + 9.00x^3
q.degree(): 3
p.plus(q): 3.00 - 3.00x + 6.00x^2 + 9.00x^3 + 2.00x^4 + 1.00x^5
q.plus(p): 3.00 - 3.00x + 6.00x^2 + 9.00x^3 + 2.00x^4 + 1.00x^5
p.plus(q).degree(): 5
z: 0
z.degree(): -1
p.plus(z): 3.00 - 8.00x + 2.00x^4 + 1.00x^5
z.plus(p): 3.00 - 8.00x + 2.00x^4 + 1.00x^5
p:         3.00 - 8.00x + 2.00x^4 + 1.00x^5
t: 8.88x^44
t.degree(): 44
```

The var-args constructor is tested at lines 3–4, and the two-argument constructor is tested at line 18. The other testing includes checking (at lines 9–10) that the `plus()` method is commutative: $p + q = q + p$, and (at lines 14–16) that the zero polynomial z satisfies the defining condition $p + z = z + p = p$.

Review Questions

7.1   What is the difference between the `Collection` interface and the `List` interface?

7.2   What is the difference between the `AbstractCollection` class and the `AbstractList` class?

7.3   What is the difference between the `AbstractList` class and the `AbstractSequentialList` class?

7.4   What is the difference between the `Iterator` interface and the `ListIterator` interface?

7.5   What is the difference between the `ArrayList` class and the `LinkedList` class?

7.6   What is the difference between an `ArrayList` object and a `Vector` object?

7.7   In deciding whether to use an `ArrayList` or a `LinkedList` in an application, what factors make one choice better than the other?

Problems

7.1   Implement the following method:
```
        public static void loadRandomLetters(LinkedList list, int n)
        // fills list with n randomly generated capital letters
```

7.2   Write a method that uses an iterator to print the contents of a linked list, one object per line.

7.3   Write a method that uses an iterator to print the contents of a linked list in reverse order, one object per line.

7.4   Write the following method:
```
        public static void exchange(LinkedList list, int i, int j)
        // swaps the elements indexed at i and j
```

7.5   Modify the solution to the Josephus Problem (Example 7.6 on page 140) so that it also uses a `SKIP` parameter to generate the output. The value of `SKIP` is a constant nonnegative integer that specifies whom each soldier should kill. For example, if `skip = 2`, then A would kill D (skipping over B and C), E would kill H, and so forth. The original solution is then the special case where `skip = 0`. Assume that no one commits suicide. So if a killer's target turns out to be himself, he would kill the next man in the list.

7.6   Write and test this method for the `Polynomial` class:
```
        public double valueAt(double x)
        // returns the y-value of p at the specified x-value
```

7.7   Write and test this method for the `Polynomial` class:
```
        public Polynomial times(double factor)
        // returns a new polynomial that is equal to this polynomial
```

Answers to Review Questions

7.1   The `List` interface includes these 10 methods that work with indexes:
```
        public void       add(int index, Object object);
        public boolean    addAll(int index, Collection collection);
        public Object     get(int index);
        public int        indexOf(Object object);
        public int        lastIndexOf(Object object);
```

```
public ListIterator  listIterator();
public ListIterator  listIterator(int index);
public Object        remove(int index);
public Object        set(int index, Object object);
public List          subList(int start, int stop);
```

7.2 The AbstractList class implements the methods of the List interface, including the 10 index methods listed above in the answer to Question 7.1 which are not in the AbstractCollection class.

7.3 The AbstractSequentialList class is designed to serve as a base class for linked list classes. It specifies the two abstract methods listIterator() and size() which must be implemented by any concrete subclass.

7.4 The ListIterator class extends the Iterator class in a way that is analogous to the way the AbstractSequentialList class extends the AbstractList class. (See the answer to Question 7.2 above.) Ordinary Iterator objects are unidirectional iterators that iterate on array lists; ListIterator objects are bidirectional iterators that iterate on linked lists.

7.5 Instances of the ArrayList class use contiguous, indexed, direct access (array) storage. Instances of the LinkedList class use linked (sequential) access storage. So array lists provide faster access, while linked lists provide faster modifications (insertions and removals).

7.6 There isn't much difference between an ArrayList object and a Vector object: They both provide direct indexed access. As part of the Java Collections Framework, the ArrayList class was introduced more recently, in Java 1.2, and so it is probably more preferred. The Vector class has about twice as many methods, but many are redundant and consequently a bit confusing.

7.7 An ArrayList object should be preferred when frequent lookups are expected. A LinkedList object should be preferred when frequent additions and/or removals are expected. (See the answer to Question 7.6 above.)

Solutions to Problems

7.1
```
void loadRandomLetters( LinkedList list, int n) {
  list.clear();
   while (0 < n--)
     list.add("" + (char)('A' + (int)(Math.random()*26)));
}
```

7.2
```
void printForward(LinkedList list) {
   for (ListIterator itr=list.listIterator(); itr.hasNext(); )
     System.out.println(itr.next());
}
```

7.3
```
void printBackward(LinkedList list) {
   ListIterator itr=list.listIterator(list.size());
   while (itr.hasPrevious())
     System.out.println(itr.previous());
}
```

7.4
```
void exchange(LinkedList list, int i, int j) {
   Object ithObj = list.get(i);
   Object jthObj = list.get(j) ;
   list.set(i,jthObj);
   list.set(j,ithObj);
}
```

7.5 The solution to the generalized Josephus Problem:
```
public class Josephus {
   public static final int SOLDIERS = 11;
   public static final int SKIP = 2;
   public static final String ALPHA = "ABCDEFGHIJKLMNOPQRSTUVWXYZ";
```

```
            public static void main(String[] args) {
            Ring<String> ring = new Ring<String>();
            for (int i=0; i<SOLDIERS; i++) {
              ring.add(ALPHA.substring(i, i+1));
            }
            System.out.println(ring);
            Iterator<String> it = ring.iterator();
            String killer = it.next();
            String victim = null;
            while (ring.size() > 1) {
              for (int i = 0; i <= SKIP; i++) {
                victim = it.next();
              }
              if (victim == killer) {
                victim = it.next();
              }
              System.out.println(killer + " killed " + victim);
              it.remove();
              killer = it.next();
            }
            System.out.println("The lone survivor is " + it.next());
          }
        }
```

7.6
```
        public double valueAt(double x) {
          // returns the y-value p(x) of p at the specified x-value
          // This implements Horner's method.
          if (this.isZero()) {
            return 0.0;
          }
          ListIterator<Term> it = list.listIterator();
          Term term = null;
          while (it.hasNext()) {  // move to last element
            term = it.next();
          }
          term = it.previous();
          double y = term.coef;
          int n = term.exp;
          while (it.hasPrevious()) {
            term = it.previous();
            y *= Math.pow(x, n - term.exp);
            y += term.coef;
            n = term.exp;
          }
          y *= Math.pow(x, n);
          return y;
        }
```

7.7
```
        public Polynomial times(double factor) {
          // returns a new polynomial that is equal to this polynomial
          if (this.isZero() || factor == 0.0) {
            return ZERO;
          }
          Polynomial p = new Polynomial(this);
          for (Term t : p.list) {
            t.coef *= factor;
          }
          return p;
        }
```

CHAPTER 8

Hash Tables

A *hash table* (also called a *map*, a *lookup table*, an *associative array*, or a *dictionary*) is a container that allows direct access by any index type. It works like an array or vector except that the index variable need not be an integer. A good analogy is a dictionary; the index variable is the word being looked up, and the element that it indexes is its dictionary definition.

A table is a sequence of pairs. The first component of the pair is called the *key*. It serves as the index into the table, generalizing the subscript integer used in arrays. The second component is called the *value* of its key component. It contains the information being looked up. In the dictionary example, the key is the word being looked up, and the value is that word's definition (and everything else listed for that word).

A table is also called a map because we think of the keys being mapped into their values, like a mathematical function: $f(key) = value$. Tables are also called an associative arrays because they can be implemented using two parallel arrays; the keys in one array and the values in the other.

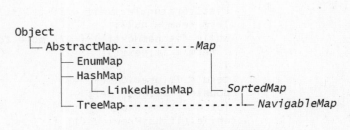

Figure 8.1 The Map classes of the JCF

THE JAVA Map INTERFACE

The Java Collections Framework includes a Map interface, as shown in Figure 8.1. It is defined in the java.util package like this:

```java
public interface Map {
    int size();
    boolean isEmpty();
    boolean containsKey(Object key);
    boolean containsValue(Object value);
    Object get(Object key);
    Object put(Object key, Object value);
    Object remove(Object key);
    void putAll(Map map);
    void clear();
```

148

```
        public Set keySet();
        public Collection values();
        public Set entrySet();
        public interface Entry {
           Object getKey();
           Object getValue();
           Object setValue(Object value);
           boolean equals(Object o);
           int hashCode();
        }
        boolean equals(Object o);
        int hashCode();
     }
```

THE HashMap CLASS

As the class hierarchy in Figure 8.1 shows, Java defines four implementations of its Map interface: the AbstractMap class, the HashMap class, the TreeMap class, and the WeakHashMap class.

EXAMPLE 8.1 A German-English Dictionary

This program uses the HashMap class to build a German-English dictionary:

```
1    public class TestDictionary {
2      public static void main(String[] args) {
3        Map map = new HashMap();
4        map.put("Tag","day");
5        map.put("Hut","hat");
6        map.put("Uhr","clock");
7        map.put("Rad","wheel");
8        map.put("Ohr","ear");
9        map.put("Tor","gate");
10       System.out.println("map=" + map);
11       System.out.println("map.size()=" + map.size());
12       System.out.println("map.keySet()=" + map.keySet());
13       System.out.println("map.values()=" + map.values());
14       System.out.println("map.get(\"Uhr\")=" + map.get("Uhr"));
15       System.out.println("map.remove(\"Rad\")=" + map.remove("Rad"));
16       System.out.println("map.get(\"Rad\")=" + map.get("Rad"));
17       System.out.println("map=" + map);
18       System.out.println("map.size()=" + map.size());
19     }
20   }
```

The output is:

```
        map={Rad=wheel, Uhr=clock, Ohr=ear, Tor=gate, Hut=hat, Tag=day}
        map.size()=6
        map.keySet()=[Rad, Uhr, Ohr, Tor, Hut, Tag]
        map.values()=[wheel, clock, ear, gate, hat, day]
        map.get("Uhr")=clock
        map.remove("Rad")=wheel
        map.get("Rad")=null
        map={Uhr=clock, Ohr=ear, Tor=gate, Hut=hat, Tag=day}
        map.size()=5
```

The put() method inserts key/value pairs into the table. For example,

```
            map.put("Tag","day");
```

inserts the key/value pair ("Tag","day"), where "Tag" is the key and "day" is the value.

The first call to println() invokes the HashMap.toString() method, printing the entire Map object. The second call to println() invokes the HashMap.size() method, showing that the Map object has six key/value elements. The next call to println() invokes the HashMap.keySet() method, which returns a Set object containing all the keys (the six German words). The next call to println() invokes the HashMap.values() method, which returns a Collection object containing all the values (the six English words). The next call to println() invokes the HashMap.get() method, which returns the value for a given key. This call returns the value object "clock" for the key object "Uhr". The next call to println() invokes the HashMap.remove() method, which deletes the ("Rad","wheel") pair, which is confirmed by the next call: map.get("Rad") returns null, indicating that there is no key/value pair in map whose key is "Rad". The last two lines prints the entire map again and its size, revealing that the ("Rad","wheel") pair has indeed been deleted.

The order in which the key/value pairs were stored in the HashMap object in Example 8.1 seems to be random and unrelated to the order in which the pairs were inserted. The next example verifies this.

EXAMPLE 8.2 Java HashMap Objects Are Hash Tables

This program creates two independent HashMap objects and loads them with the same key/value pairs but in different orders:

```
1    public class TestHashTable {
2      public static void main(String[] args) {
3        Map map1 = new HashMap();
4        map1.put("Tor","gate");
5        map1.put("Rad","wheel");
6        map1.put("Tag","day");
7        map1.put("Uhr","clock");
8        map1.put("Hut","hat");
9        map1.put("Ohr","ear");
10       System.out.println("map1=" + map1);
11       Map map2 = new HashMap();
12       map2.put("Rad","wheel");
13       map2.put("Uhr","clock");
14       map2.put("Ohr","ear");
15       map2.put("Tag","day");
16       map2.put("Tor","gate");
17       map2.put("Hut","hat");
18       System.out.println("map2=" + map2);
19     }
```

The output is:

```
        map1={Rad=wheel, Uhr=clock, Ohr=ear, Tor=gate, Hut=hat, Tag=day}
        map2={Rad=wheel, Uhr=clock, Ohr=ear, Tor=gate, Hut=hat, Tag=day}
```

The order in which the key/value pairs are stored in the HashMap table is reflected by the output from the toString() method. That stored order is same in both tables, independent of the order in which they were inserted. Note that it is also the same stored order in the HashMap table in Example 8.1.

JAVA HASH CODES

The order in which the key/value pairs are stored in a HashMap table depends only upon the capacity of the table and the values of objects' the hash codes. Recall (Chapter 4) that every object in Java is given an intrinsic *hash code*, which is computed from the actual hard data stored in the object. The Object.hashCode() method returns that code for each object.

EXAMPLE 8.3 Hash Codes of Some String Objects

This program prints the intrinsic hash codes of the `String` objects stored in the previous programs:

```
1    public class TestHashCodes {
2      public static void main(String[] args) {
3        printHashCode("Rad");
4        printHashCode("Uhr");
5        printHashCode("Ohr");
6        printHashCode("Tor");
7        printHashCode("Hut");
8        printHashCode("Tag");
9      }
10
11     private static void printHashCode(String word) {
12       System.out.printf("%s: %s%n", word, word.hashCode());
13     }
14   }
```

The output is:

```
Rad: 81909
Uhr: 85023
Ohr: 79257
Tor: 84279
Hut: 72935
Tag: 83834
```

The fact that all six codes are relatively close 5-digits integers reflects the fact that these `String` objects all have length 3.

HASH TABLES

A *hash table* is a table that uses a special function to compute the location of data values from their key values instead of storing the keys in the table. The special function is called the *hash function* for the table. Since the lookup time is independent of the size of the table, hash tables have very fast access time.

Java defined a `Hashtable` class in its `java.util` package. But it has essentially been upgraded to the `HashMap` class. That is, a `HashMap` table can do everything that a `Hashtable` object can do. Moreover, the `HashMap` class is more consistent with rest of the Java Collections Framework.

A general hash table looks like the one pictured in Figure 8.2: an array of `Objects` indexed by their hash values. This requires that the range of the hash function match the range of index values in the array. This is almost always managed by simply using the remainder operator modulo the size of the array:

Figure 8.2 Hash table

EXAMPLE 8.4 Mapping Keys into a Hash Table of Size 11

This program prints hash code values for `String` objects to be stored in a hash table of size 11:

```
1    public class TestHashing {
2      private static final int MASK = 0x7FFFFFFF; //  = 2^32-1
3      private static final int CAPACITY = 11;
4
```

```
5      public static void main(String[] args) {
6        printHash("Rad");
7        printHash("Uhr");
8        printHash("Ohr");
9        printHash("Tor");
10       printHash("Hut");
11       printHash("Tag");
12     }
13
14     private static void printHash(String word) {
15       System.out.println("hash(" + word + ") = " + hash(word));
16     }
17
18     private static int hash(Object object) {
19       return (object.hashCode() & MASK) % CAPACITY;
20     }
21   }
```

The output is:
```
hash(Rad) = 3
hash(Uhr) = 4
hash(Ohr) = 2
hash(Tor) = 8
hash(Hut) = 5
hash(Tag) = 3
```

The hash function values are computed at line 19, where CAPACITY is 11 and MASK is 2147483647, expressed in hexadecimal as 0x7FFFFFFF. The operation n & MASK simply removes the sign from whatever integer n has. This is the right thing to do in Java before using the remainder operator to compute an array index because (unlike C++) Java may give a negative result to m % CAPACITY if m is negative. So the resulting value returned by the hash() function in this example is guaranteed to be in the range of 0 to 10.

The first five strings hash into index values 3, 4, 2, 8, and 5, so they would be stored in those locations in the hash table. But the sixth string ("Tag") also hashes to 3, causing a collision with "Rad", which would already be stored in component 3. The most common algorithm to apply when such collisions occur is to simply put the new item in the next available component. That would be component 6 in this example, since "Uhr" would already be in component 4 and "Hut" would already be in component 5. This "collision resolution" algorithm is called *linear probing*.

The HashMap class uses a hash function just like the one in Example 8.4 to implement its accessor methods: containsKey(), get(), put(), remove(), and entrySet(). Its sets the hash table size at 101 initially. With that knowledge, we can see why the six strings in the previous examples were stored in the order indicated.

EXAMPLE 8.5 Mapping Keys into a Hash Table of Size 101

This program is identical to the one in Example 8.4 except that the hash table CAPACITY is 101 instead of 11:

```
1    public class TestHashing {
2      private static final int MASK = 0x7FFFFFFF; //  = 2^32-1
3      private static final int CAPACITY = 101;
4
5      public static void main(String[] args) {
6        printHash("Rad");
7        printHash("Uhr");
8        printHash("Ohr");
```

```
9          printHash("Tor");
10         printHash("Hut");
11         printHash("Tag");
12       }
13
14     private static void printHash(String word) {
15         System.out.println("hash(" + word + ") = " + hash(word));
16       }
17
18     private static int hash(Object object) {
19         return (object.hashCode() & MASK) % CAPACITY;
20       }
21     }
```

The output is:
```
hash(Rad) = 99
hash(Uhr) = 82
hash(Ohr) = 73
hash(Tor) = 45
hash(Hut) = 13
hash(Tag) = 4
```
The result is that the items are stored in reverse order from which they are accessed.

HASH TABLE PERFORMANCE

A hash table of size 101 that contain six elements will perform very well. It is very unlikely to have any collisions, so the access functions are immediate, running in constant time $O(1)$. This is *direct access*, just like an array.

But a hash table of size 101 that contains 100 elements is likely to perform very poorly because there will have been many collisions in the process of storing its elements. For example, if the string "Lob" had 60 collisions before a free component was found for it, then each time it is accessed, it will take 60 "probes" to find it. That kind of performance is close to $O(n)$ —not much better than a linked list.

The solution to the problem described here is to prevent the hash table from becoming too full. This is done by resizing it whenever it reaches a threshold size.

The measure of fullness depends upon two parameters: The *size* of the hash table is the actual number of elements in the table; the *capacity* of the table is the number of components that it has. The ratio of these two parameters is called the *load factor*. In the first example cited in this section, the size was 6 and the capacity was 101, resulting in a load factor of 6/101 = 5.94 percent. In the second example, the size was 100, resulting in a load factor of 100/101 = 99.01 percent.

The HashMap class automatically resizes its hash table when the load factor reaches a specific *threshold* value. This threshold value can be set when the hash table is created, using the constructor
```
     public HashMap(int initialCapacity, float loadFactor)
```
which also allows the initial capacity to be set. If you use a constructor that does not take one or the other of these two arguments, then the default values of capacity 101 and load threshold 75 percent will be used.

COLLISION RESOLUTION ALGORITHMS

The collision resolution algorithm used in the previous examples is called *linear probing*. When a new item hashes to a table component that is already in use, the algorithm specifies to increment the index until an empty component is found. This may require a "wraparound" back to the beginning of the hash table.

EXAMPLE 8.6 Linear Probing

This program extends the program in Example 8.4. It keeps track of which table components are used and the load factor after each hashing.

```
1     public class Ex1406
2     public class TestLinearProbing {
3       private static final int MASK = 0x7FFFFFFF; // 2^32-1
4       private static final int CAPACITY = 11;
5       private static int size = 0;
6       private static boolean[] used = new boolean[CAPACITY];
7
8       public static void main(String[] args) {
9         printHash("Rad");
10        printHash("Uhr");
11        printHash("Ohr");
12        printHash("Tor");
13        printHash("Hut");
14        printHash("Tag");
15        printHash("Eis");
16        printHash("Ast");
17        printHash("Zug");
18        printHash("Hof");
19        printHash("Mal");
20      }
21
22      private static void printHash(String word) {
23        System.out.printf("hash(%s) = %d, load = %d%%%n",
24                word, hash(word), 100*size/CAPACITY);
25      }
26
27      private static int hash(Object object) {
28        ++size;
29        int h = (object.hashCode() & MASK) % CAPACITY;
30        while (used[h]) {
31          System.out.printf("%d, ", h);
32          h = (h+1)%CAPACITY;
33        }
34        used[h] = true;
35        return h;
36      }
37    }
```

The output is:

```
hash(Rad) = 3, load = 9%
hash(Uhr) = 4, load = 18%
hash(Ohr) = 2, load = 27%
hash(Tor) = 8, load = 36%
hash(Hut) = 5, load = 45%
3, 4, 5, hash(Tag) = 6, load = 54%
```

```
5, 6, hash(Eis) = 7, load = 63%
3, 4, 5, 6, 7, 8, hash(Ast) = 9, load = 72%
9, hash(Zug) = 10, load = 81%
3, 4, 5, 6, 7, 8, 9, 10, hash(Hof) = 0, load = 90%
2, 3, 4, 5, 6, 7, 8, 9, 10, 0, hash(Mal) = 1, load = 100%
```

The size field contains the number of items hashed into the table. The used[] array flags which components are occupied in the table. The printHash() method prints the hash table index and the resulting load factor as a percent. When linear probing kicks in, each successive index number probe is printed.

As seen in Example 8.4, the collision occurs with the insertion of "Tag" at line 14. This program shows that it had three collisions (at index numbers 3, 4, and 5) before finding a free hash location at index 6. After that insertion, the table is 54 percent full.

Every item after that also collides. And of course, as the table fills up, the number of collisions becomes more frequent. The last item, "Mal", has 10 collisions. That means that thereafter, every time this item is accessed it will have to search every one of the 11 items before it is found; clearly an $O(n)$ process.

Notice the index "wraparound" on the insertion of "Mal": 2, 3, 4, 5, 6, 7, 8, 9, 10, 0, 1.

Another collision resolution algorithm that usually performs better than linear probing is called *quadratic probing*. This algorithm jumps over items in its probing, with the result that the used components are more uniformly distributed with fewer large clusters. That improves performance because the resulting probe chains are shorter.

EXAMPLE 8.7 Quadratic Probing

This program is the same as the program in Example 8.6 except for the modified hash() function shown here.

```
38    public class TestQuadraticProbing {
39      private static final int MASK = 0x7FFFFFFF; // 2^32-1
40      private static final int CAPACITY = 11;
41      private static int size = 0;
42      private static boolean[] used = new boolean[CAPACITY];
43
44      public static void main(String[] args) {
45        printHash("Rad");
46        printHash("Uhr");
47        printHash("Ohr");
48        printHash("Tor");
49        printHash("Hut");
50        printHash("Tag");
51        printHash("Eis");
52        printHash("Ast");
53        printHash("Zug");
54        printHash("Hof");
55        printHash("Mal");
56      }
57
58      private static void printHash(String word) {
59        System.out.printf("hash(%s) = %d, load = %d%%%n",
60                word, hash(word), 100*size/CAPACITY);
61      }
62
63      private static int hash(Object object) {
64        ++size;
```

```
65      int h = (object.hashCode() & MASK) % CAPACITY;
66      if (used[h]) {
67        int h0 = h;
68        int jump = 1;
69        while (used[h]) {
70          System.out.printf("%d, ", h);
71          h = (h0 + jump*jump)%CAPACITY;  // squared increment
72          ++jump;
73        }
74      }
75      used[h] = true;
76      return h;
77    }
78  }
```

The output is:

```
hash(Rad) = 3, load = 9%
hash(Uhr) = 4, load = 18%
hash(Ohr) = 2, load = 27%
hash(Tor) = 8, load = 36%
hash(Hut) = 5, load = 45%
3, 4, hash(Tag) = 7, load = 54%
5, hash(Eis) = 6, load = 63%
3, 4, 7, hash(Ast) = 1, load = 72%
hash(Zug) = 9, load = 81%
```

The essential difference here is in the sequence of index numbers probed within the while loop when a collision occurs. Instead of searching linearly, it uses a squared increment. For example, when the insertion of "Ast" collides at index 3, linear probing continued probing at indexes 4, 5, 6, 7, 8, and 9 (in Example 8.6). But with quadratic probing, only indexes 3, 4, 7, and 1 (= 12 mod 11) are probed, using successive jumps of 1, 4, and 9 (1^2, 2^2, and 3^2). Linear probing required 50 percent more probes.

The price that the quadratic probing algorithm pays for its improved performance is that it is more likely to result in an infinite loop. That happens in Example 8.7 with the next insertion. The string "Hof" hashes initially to index 3. After eight collisions, the linear probing algorithm found a free cell at index 0 (= 11 mod 11). But the probe sequence used on this item by the quadratic probing algorithm is the same as for "Ast": 3, 4, 7, 1, 8, 6, 6, 8 1, 7, 4, 3, 4, ... This is computed from the unmodulated quadratic sequence 3, 4, 7, 12, 19, 28, 39, 52, 67, 84, 103, 124, 147, ... This continues indefinitely, probing only the six indexes 3, 4, 7, 1, 8, and 6, all of which have already been used. So even though the table is only 81% full, the insertion fails. That can't happen with linear probing.

SEPARATE CHAINING

Instead of devising a more effective collision resolution algorithm, we can avoid collisions altogether by allowing more than one item per table component. This method is called *separate chaining*, because is uses linked lists ("chains") to hold the multiple items. In this context, the table components are usually called "buckets."

EXAMPLE 8.8 Separate Chaining

Here is how part of a definition for a HashTable class might look, using separate chaining:

```
1   public class HashTable {
2     private static final int MASK = 0x7FFFFFFF; // 2^32-1
```

```
3        private static int capacity = 101;
4        private static int size = 0;
5        private static float load = 0.75F;
6        private static LinkedList[] buckets;
7
8        HashTable() {
9          buckets = new LinkedList[capacity];
10         for (int i = 0; i < capacity; i++) {
11           buckets[i] = new LinkedList();
12         }
13       }
14
15       HashTable(int capacity, float load) {
16         this();
17         this.capacity = capacity;
18         this.load = load;
19       }
20
21       Object put(Object key, Object value) {
22         int h = hash(key);
23         LinkedList bucket=buckets[h];
24         Object oldValue = null;
25         for (ListIterator it = bucket.iterator(); it.hasNext(); ) {
26           Map.Entry entry = it.next();
27           if (entry.getKey().equals(key)) {
28             break;
29           }
30         }
31         if (entry.getKey().equals(key)) {
32           oldValue = entry.setValue(value);
33         } else {
34           bucket.add(new Entry(key,value));
35         }
36         return oldValue;
37       }
38
39     // more methods...
40   }
```

Note that put() serves two different purposes. If the table already has an entry with the given key, it only changes the value of that entry. Otherwise, it adds a new entry with that key/value pair.

The java.util.HashMap class uses separate chaining in a way that is similar to that shown in Example 8.8.

APPLICATIONS

Tables are widely used in systems programming. Moreover, they are the primary building blocks of relational databases.

Here is an example in applications programming.

EXAMPLE 8.9 A Concordance

A *concordance* is a list of words that appear in a text document along with the numbers of the lines on which the words appear. It is just like an index of a book except that it lists line numbers instead of page numbers. Concordances are useful for analyzing documents to find word frequencies and associations that are not evident from reading the document directly.

This program builds a concordance for a text file. The run here uses this particular text taken from Shakespeare's play *Julius Caesar*. The first part of the resulting concordance is shown on the right.

This output results from obtaining a Set "view" of the concordance and then iterating through the set, printing one element per line. Each element is a Map.Entry object whose Key is the word from the text (in all uppercase letters) and whose Value is the listing of line numbers where the word was found. For example, the word "man" was found on lines 10, 15, 22, and 27. Line 10 is

```
        For Brutus is an honourable man;
```

Here is the Concordance class:

```
1   public class Concordance {
2     private Map<String,String> map = new HashMap<String,String>();
3
4     public Concordance(String file) {
5       int lineNumber = 0;
6       try {
7         Scanner input = new Scanner(new File(file));
8         while (input.hasNextLine()) {
9           String line = input.nextLine();
10          ++lineNumber;
11          StringTokenizer parser = new StringTokenizer(line, ",.;:()-!?' ");
12          while (parser.hasMoreTokens()) {
13            String word = parser.nextToken().toUpperCase();
14            String listing = map.get(word);
15            if (listing == null) {
16              listing = "" + lineNumber;
17            } else {
18              listing += ", " + lineNumber;
19            }
20            map.put(word,listing);
21          }
22        }
23        input.close();
24      } catch(IOException e) {
25        System.out.println(e);
26      }
27    }
28
29    public void write(String file) {
30      try {
31        PrintWriter output = new PrintWriter(file);
32        for (Map.Entry<String,String> entry : map.entrySet()) {
33          output.println(entry);
34        }
35        output.close();
36      } catch(IOException e) {
37        System.out.println(e);
38      }
39    }
40  }
```

The hash table is defined at line 2. It has type java.util.HashMap<String,String>, which means that both its key and value fields have type String. Its constructor at line 4 takes the name of the input file as its argument. It uses a java.util.Scanner object to read the file line by line. Each line is parsed by a java.util.StringTokenizer object named parser, defined at line 11. Note that the parser uses as

Shakespeare.txt

```
Friends, Romans, countrymen, lend me your ears!
I come to bury Caesar, not to praise him.
The evil that men do lives after them,
The good is oft interred with their bones;
So let it be with Caesar. The noble Brutus
Hath told you Caesar was ambitious;
If it were so, it was a grievous fault;
And grievously hath Caesar answer'd it.
Here, under leave of Brutus and the rest, --
For Brutus is an honourable man;
So are they all, all honourable men.
Come I to speak in Caesar's funeral.
He was my friend, faithful and just to me.
But Brutus says he was ambitious;
And Brutus is an honourable man.
He hath brought many captives home to Rome.
Whose ransoms did the general coffers fill:
Did this in Caesar seem ambitious?
When that the poor have cried, Caesar hath wept;
Ambition should be made of sterner stuff.
Yet Brutus says he was ambitious;
And Brutus is an honourable man.
You all did see that on the Lupercal
I thrice presented him with a kingly crown,
Which he did thrice refuse: was this ambition?
Yet Brutus says he was ambitious;
And, sure, is an honourable man.
I speak not to disprove what Brutus spoke,
But here I am to speak what I do know.
You all did love him once, not without cause.
What cause withholds you, then, to mourn for him?
O judgement! thou art fled to brutish beasts,
And men have lost their reason!
```

Shakespeare.out

```
STUFF=20
THE=3, 4, 5, 9, 17, 19, 23
GRIEVOUS=7
GRIEVOUSLY=8
WHOSE=17
REASON=33
AND=8, 9, 13, 15, 22, 27, 33
FAULT=7
KINGLY=24
COUNTRYMEN=1
MOURN=31
FRIENDS=1
GOOD=4
LEAVE=9
ROME=16
CROWN=24
SHOULD=20
INTERRED=4
WEPT=19
FOR=10, 31
FRIEND=13
BUT=14, 29
BRUTUS=5, 9, 10, 14, 15, 21, 22, 26, 28
MAN=10, 15, 22, 27
CAUSE=30, 31
SURE=27
PRESENTED=24
YOU=6, 23, 30, 31
SEE=23
BONES=4
LIVES=3
REFUSE=25
HERE=9, 29
```

Figure 8.3 The concordance in Example 8.9

delimiters all of the 11 characters in the string ",.;:()-!?'". Each parsed word is used as a key in the hash table. The corresponding value is the string of line numbers that is accumulated at lines 16 and 18.

The `write()` method at line 29 uses a for-each loop to print the concordance to the specified file. At line 32, the map's `entrySet()` method returns a set of elements of type `Map.Entry<String,String>`. These are the key/value pairs that are stored in the hash table. Each key is a word from the input file and its entry is the list of the line numbers of the lines where that word appears in the text.

Here is the test program:

```
1    public class TestConcordance {
2       public static final String PATH = "B:\\DSWJ2\\src\\ch08\\ex09\\";
3       public static final String IN_FILE = "Shakespeare.txt";
4       public static final String OUT_FILE = "Shakespeare.out";
5
6       public static void main(String[] args) {
7          Concordance c = new Concordance(PATH+IN_FILE);
8          c.write(PATH+OUT_FILE);
9       }
10   }
```

The output from the program in Example 8.9 demonstrates a critical feature of hash tables: Their contents are not ordered. To obtain an alphabetized printout of the concordance, we would have to sort it.

THE `TreeMap` CLASS

The `TreeMap` class extends the `AbstractMap` class and implements the `SortedMap` interface. It is called a *tree map* because its backing structure is a binary search tree instead of a hash table.

Shakespeare.out

```
A=7, 24
AFTER=3
ALL=11, 11, 23, 30
AM=29
AMBITION=20, 25
AMBITIOUS=6, 14, 18, 21, 26
AN=10, 15, 22, 27
AND=8, 9, 13, 15, 22, 27, 33
ANSWER=8
ARE=11
ART=32
BE=5, 20
BEASTS=32
BONES=4
BROUGHT=16
BRUTISH=32
BRUTUS=5, 9, 10, 14, 15, 21, 22, 26, 28
BURY=2
BUT=14, 29
CAESAR=2, 5, 6, 8, 12, 18, 19
CAPTIVES=16
CAUSE=30, 31
COFFERS=17
COME=2, 12
COUNTRYMEN=1
CRIED=19
CROWN=24
D=8
DID=17, 18, 23, 25, 30
DISPROVE=28
DO=3, 29
EARS=1
EVIL=3
```

Figure 8.4 The ordered concordance in Example 8.10

But it is still a map with key/value entries. As a binary search tree structure, it sacrifices its $O(1)$ access time, but its keys are ordered.

EXAMPLE 8.10 An Ordered Concordance

By replacing HashMap with TreeMap at line 2 in the Concordance class of Example 8.9, we obtain an ordered concordance:

```
2        private Map<String,String> map = new HashMap<String,String>();
```

Part of the output from the same test program is shown in Figure 8.4.

Review Questions

8.1   What is the difference between a table and a vector?

8.2   Why is a table also called a map?

8.3   Why is a table also called an associative array?

8.4   Why is a table also called a dictionary?

8.5   What is a concordance?

8.6   What is a hash table?

8.7   What is the difference between the Java Hashtable class and the Java HashMap class?

8.8   The first two examples showed that the order of insertion into a hash table is irrelevant if there are no collisions. What if there are?

8.9   What are the advantages and disadvantages of quadratic probing compared to linear probing?

8.10   What are the advantages and disadvantages of using a `HashMap` compared to a `TreeMap`?

Problems

8.1   Run a program similar to the one in Example 8.1 on page 149 to insert the following 16 entries into the German-English dictionary:

```
map.put("Ast","gate");
map.put("Eis","ice");
map.put("Hof","court, yard, farm");
map.put("Hut","hat");
map.put("Lob","praise");
map.put("Mal","mark, signal");
map.put("Mut","courage");
map.put("Ohr","ear");
map.put("Ost","east");
map.put("Rad","wheel");
map.put("Rat","advice, counsel");
map.put("Tag","day");
map.put("Tor","gate");
map.put("Uhr","clock");
map.put("Wal","whale");
map.put("Zug","procession, train");
```

Words.txt

```
A
AFTER
ALL
AM
AN
AND
ARE
BE
BROUGHT
BUT
COME
DID
DO
FOR
HATH
HAVE
HE
HERE
HIM
I
IF
IN
IS
IT
LET
MADE
MANY
OF
ON
TO
```

8.2   Modify the `Concordance` class so that it filters out common words (pronouns, adverbs, etc.) whose listing would not contribute to new insights into the document. Store the common words in a separate file like the one shown in Figure 8.5.

8.3   Modify the program in Example 8.1 on page 149 so that it stores the words in alphabetical order. Have it load the same data as in Problem 8.1 above and then print the table's contents in alphabetical order.

8.4   Implement a `FrequencyTable` class for producing a list of words together with their frequency of occurrence in a specified text file.

Figure 8.5 Words

Answers to Review Questions

8.1   A vector provides direct access to its elements by means of its integer index. A table provides direct access to its elements by means of a key field, which can be of any ordinal type: `int`, `double`, `string`, and so forth.

8.2   A table is also called a map because, like a mathematical function, it maps each key value into a unique element.

8.3   A table is also called an associative array because it acts like an array (see Answer 8.1) in which each key value is associated with its unique element. Like a mathematical function, it maps each key value into a unique element.

8.4   A table is also called a dictionary because it is used the same way as an ordinary natural language dictionary: to look up elements, as one would look up words in a dictionary.

8.5   A *concordance* is a list of words that appear in a text document along with the numbers of the lines on which the words appear. (See page 157.)

8.6 A *hash table* is a table that uses a special function to compute the location of data values from their key values instead of storing the keys in the table. (See page 151.)

8.7 Not much. The Java Hashtable class has generally been superseded by the Java HashMap class, which conforms a little better to the Java Collections Framework.

8.8 If there are collisions, then the order of insertion is relevant.

8.9 Quadratic probing generally results in fewer collisions because the probes jump over gaps in the index range. But unlike linear probing, quadratic probing can cause infinite loops even when the table is not full.

8.10 A HashMap object is a hash table implemented with separate chaining and a default load threshold of 75 percent, so it provides nearly $O(1)$ access time for insertions, deletions, and searches. A TreeMap object is a balanced binary search tree implemented as a red-black tree, so it provides nearly $O(\lg n)$ access time for insertions, deletions, and searches. So a HashMap is faster, but a TreeMap is ordered.

Solutions to Problems

8.1 Inserting 16 entries into the German-English dictionary:

```java
public class Testing {
    public static void main(String[] args) {
        Map map = new HashMap(11);
        map.put("Ast","branch");
        map.put("Eis","ice");
        map.put("Hof","court, yard, farm");
        map.put("Hut","hat");
        map.put("Lob","praise");
        map.put("Mal","mark, signal");
        map.put("Mut","courage");
        map.put("Ohr","ear");
        map.put("Ost","east");
        map.put("Rad","wheel");
        map.put("Rat","advice, counsel");
        map.put("Tag","day");
        map.put("Tor","gate");
        map.put("Uhr","clock");
        map.put("Wal","whale");
        map.put("Zug","procession, train");
        System.out.println("map=" + map);
        System.out.println("map.keySet()=" + map.keySet());
        System.out.println("map.size()=" + map.size());
    }
}
```

8.2 A Concordance that filters out common words:

```java
public class Concordance {
    private Map<String,String> map = new TreeMap<String,String>();
    private Set<String> words = new TreeSet<String>();

    public Concordance(String source, String filter) {
        int lineNumber = 0;
        try {
            Scanner input = new Scanner(new File(filter));
            while (input.hasNextLine()) {
                String line = input.nextLine();
                StringTokenizer parser = new StringTokenizer(line);
                words.add(parser.nextToken().toUpperCase());
            }
```

```
                    input = new Scanner(new File(source));
                while (input.hasNextLine()) {
                  String line = input.nextLine();
                  ++lineNumber;
                  StringTokenizer parser = new StringTokenizer(line,",.;:()-!?' ");
                  while (parser.hasMoreTokens()) {
                    String word = parser.nextToken().toUpperCase();
                    if (words.contains(word)) {
                      continue;
                    }
                    // insert lines 14-40 from Example 8.9
```

8.3 A sorted German-English dictionary:

```
            public class TestDictionary {
              private static Map map;
              public static void main(String[] args) {
                map = new TreeMap();
                load();
                dump();
              }

              private static void load() {
                map.put("Ast","branch");
                map.put("Eis","ice");
                map.put("Hof","court, yard, farm");
                map.put("Hut","hat");
                map.put("Lob","praise");
                map.put("Mal","mark, signal");
                map.put("Mut","courage");
                map.put("Ohr","ear");
                map.put("Ost","east");
                map.put("Rad","wheel");
                map.put("Rat","advice, counsel");
                map.put("Tag","day");
                map.put("Tor","gate");
                map.put("Uhr","clock");
                map.put("Wal","whale");
                map.put("Zug","procession, train");
              }

              private static void dump() {
                Set set = map.entrySet();
                for (Map.Entry<String,String> entry : map.entrySet()) {
                  System.out.println(entry);
                }
              }
            }
```

8.4 A frequency table:

```
            public class FrequencyTable {
              private Map<String,String> map = new TreeMap<String,String>();

              public FrequencyTable(String file) {
                int lineNumber = 0;
                try {
                  Scanner input = new Scanner(new File(file));
                  while (input.hasNextLine()) {
                    String line = input.nextLine();
                    ++lineNumber;
                    StringTokenizer parser = new StringTokenizer(line,",.;:()-!?' ");
```

```
        while (parser.hasMoreTokens()) {
          String word = parser.nextToken().toUpperCase();
          String frequency = (String)map.get(word);
          if (frequency==null) {
            frequency = "1";
          } else {
            int n=Integer.parseInt(frequency);
            ++n;
            frequency = "" + n;
          }
          map.put(word, frequency);
          // insert lines 21-40 from Example 8.9
```

CHAPTER 9

Recursion

A *recursive* function is one that calls itself. This powerful technique produces repetition without using loops (e.g., `while` loops or `for` loops). Thus it can produce substantial results from very little code. Recursion allows elegantly simple solutions to difficult problems. But it can also be misused, producing inefficient code. Recursive code is usually produced from recursive algorithms.

SIMPLE RECURSIVE FUNCTIONS

EXAMPLE 9.1 The Factorial Function

The *factorial* function is defined mathematically by

$$n! = \begin{cases} 1, \text{ if } n = 0 \\ n(n-1)!, \text{ if } n > 0 \end{cases}$$

This is a recursive definition because the factorial "recurs" on the right side of the equation. The function is defined in terms of itself.

The first 10 values of the factorial function are shown in Table 9.1. The first value, 0!, is defined by the upper half of the definition: 0! = 1 (for $n = 0$). All the rest of the values are defined by the lower half of the definition:

For $n = 1$, $1! = n! = n(n-1)! = 1(1-1)! = 1(0)! = 1(1) = 1$.
For $n = 2$, $2! = n! = n(n-1)! = 2(2-1)! = 2(1)! = 2(1) = 2$.
For $n = 3$, $3! = n! = n(n-1)! = 3(3-1)! = 3(2)! = 3(2) = 6$.
For $n = 4$, $4! = n! = n(n-1)! = 4(4-1)! = 4(3)! = 4(6) = 24$.
For $n = 5$, $5! = n! = n(n-1)! = 5(5-1)! = 5(4)! = 5(24) = 120$.

Notice how rapidly this function grows.

n	$n!$
0	1
1	1
2	2
3	6
4	24
5	120
6	720
7	5,040
8	40,310
9	362,880

Table 9.1 Factorials

EXAMPLE 9.2 Recursive Implementation of the Factorial Function

When a function is defined recursively, its implementation is usually a direct translation of its recursive definition. The two parts of the recursive definition of the factorial function translate directly into two Java statements:

```
1    public static int f(int n) {
2      if (n==0) {
3        return 1;          // basis
4      }
```

```
5        return n*f(n-1);  // recursive part
6    }
```

Here is a simple test driver for the factorial method:

```
1    public static void main(String[] args) {
2      for (int n=0; n<10; n++) {
3        System.out.println("f("+n+") = "+f(n));
4      }
5    }
```

It prints the same values as shown in Table 9.1.

EXAMPLE 9.3 Iterative Implementation of the Factorial Function

The factorial function is also easy to implement iteratively:

```
1    public static int f(int n) {
2      int f = 1;
3      for (int i = 2; i <= n; i++) {
4        f *= i;
5      }
6      return f;
7    }
```

Note that the function header is identical to that used in Example 9.2; only the body is different. This allows us to use the same test driver for both implementations. The output should be the same.

BASIS AND RECURSIVE PARTS

To work correctly, every recursive function must have a *basis* and a *recursive part*. The basis is what stops the recursion. The recursive part is where the function calls itself.

EXAMPLE 9.4 The Basis and Recursive Parts of the Factorial Function

In the Java method that implements the factorial function in Example 9.2, the basis and the recursive parts are labeled with comments. The recursive part invokes the method, passing a smaller value of n. So starting with a positive value like 5, the values on the successive invocations will be 4, 3, 2, 1, and 0. When 0 is passed, the basis executes, thereby stopping the recursion and beginning the chain of returns, returning 1, 1, 2, 6, 24, and finally 120.

EXAMPLE 9.5 The Fibonacci Numbers

The *Fibonacci numbers* are 1, 1, 2, 3, 5, 8, 13, 21, 34, 55, ... Each number after the second is the sum of the two preceding numbers. This is a naturally recursive definition:

$$F_n = \begin{cases} 0, \text{if } n = 0 \\ 1, \text{if } n = 1 \\ F_{n-1} + F_{n-2}, \text{if } n > 1 \end{cases}$$

The first 15 values of the Fibonacci sequence are shown in Table 9.2. The first two values, F_0 and F_1, are defined by the first two parts of the definition: $F_0 = 0$ (for $n = 0$) and $F_1 = 1$ (for $n = 1$). These two parts form the basis of the recursion. All the other values are defined by the recursive part of the definition:

n	F_n
0	0
1	1
2	1
3	2
4	3
5	5
6	8
7	13
8	21
9	34
10	55
11	89
12	144
13	233
14	377

Table 9.2 Fibonacci numbers

For $n = 2$, $F_2 = F_n = F_{n-1} + F_{n-2} = F_{(2)-1} + F_{(2)-2} = F_1 + F_0 = 1 + 0 = 1$.
For $n = 3$, $F_3 = F_n = F_{n-1} + F_{n-2} = F_{(3)-1} + F_{(3)-2} = F_2 + F_1 = 1 + 1 = 2$.
For $n = 4$, $F_4 = F_n = F_{n-1} + F_{n-2} = F_{(4)-1} + F_{(4)-2} = F_3 + F_2 = 2 + 1 = 3$.
For $n = 5$, $F_5 = F_n = F_{n-1} + F_{n-2} = F_{(5)-1} + F_{(5)-2} = F_4 + F_3 = 3 + 2 = 5$.
For $n = 6$, $F_6 = F_n = F_{n-1} + F_{n-2} = F_{(6)-1} + F_{(6)-2} = F_5 + F_4 = 5 + 3 = 8$.
For $n = 7$, $F_7 = F_n = F_{n-1} + F_{n-2} = F_{(7)-1} + F_{(7)-2} = F_6 + F_5 = 8 + 5 = 13$.

EXAMPLE 9.6 Recursive Implementation of the Fibonacci Function

```
1    public static int fib(int n) {
2      if (n < 2) {
3        return n;                    // basis
4      }
5      return fib(n-1) + fib(n-2);  // recursive part
6    }
```

Here is a simple test driver for the Fibonacci method:

```
1    public static void main(String[] args) {
2      for (int n = 0; n < 16; n++) {
3        System.out.println("fib(" + n + ") = " + fib(n));
4      }
5    }
```

It prints the same values as shown in Table 9.2.

TRACING A RECURSIVE CALL

Hand tracing the execution of a method usually helps clarify it.

EXAMPLE 9.7 Tracing the Recursive Factorial Function

Here is a trace of the call f(5) to the recursive factorial function defined in Example 9.2:

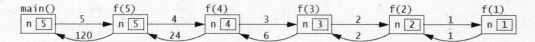

Figure 9.1 Tracing the recursive factorial function

The call originates in the main() function, passing 5 to the f() function. There, the value of the parameter n is 5, so it calls f(4), passing 4 to the f() function. There the value of the parameter n is 4, so it calls f(3), passing 3 to the f() function. This process continues (recursively) until the call f(1) is made from within the call f(2). There, the value of the parameter n is 1, so it returns 1 immediately, without making any more calls. Then the call f(2) returns 2*1 = 2 to the call f(3). Then the call f(3) returns 3*2 = 6 to the call f(4). Then the call f(4) returns 4*6 = 24 to the call f(5). Finally, the call f(5) returns the value 120 to main().

The trace in Example 9.7 shows that the call f(n) to the recursive implementation of the factorial function will generate $n - 1$ recursive calls. This is clearly very inefficient compared to the iterative implementation shown in Example 9.3.

EXAMPLE 9.8 Tracing the Recursive Fibonacci Function

The Fibonacci function (Example 9.6) is more heavily recursive than the factorial function (Example 9.2) because it includes two recursive calls. The consequences can be seen from the trace of the call fib(5), shown in Figure 9.2 on page 168. The call originates in the main() function, passing 5 to the fib() function. There, the value of the parameter n is 5, so it calls fib(4) and fib(3), passing 4 and 3, respectively. Each of these calls then makes two more recursive calls, continuing down to the basis calls f(1) and f(0). Each of these basis calls returns 1. The recursive calls then return the sum of the two values returned to them, ultimately resulting in the value 8 being returned to main().

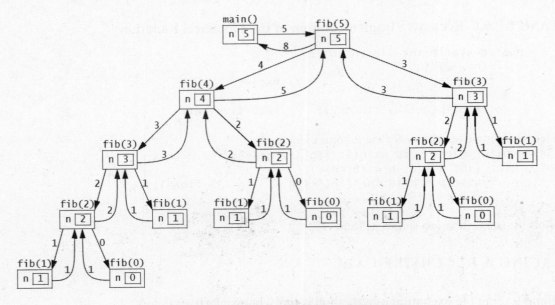

Figure 9.2 Tracing the recursive Fibonacci function

THE RECURSIVE BINARY SEARCH

The nonrecursive binary search algorithm is given on page 31. It uses the *divide-and-conquer strategy*, each time splitting the sequence in half and continuing the search on one half. This is naturally recursive.

EXAMPLE 9.9 The Recursive Binary Search

Here is the *recursive binary search algorithm*:
(Precondition: $s = \{s_0, s_1, \ldots, s_{n-1}\}$ is a sorted sequence of n ordinal values of the same type as x.)
(Postcondition: either the index i is returned where $s_i = x$, or -1 is returned.)
    1.   If the sequence is empty, return -1.
    2.   Let s_i be the middle element of the sequence.
    3.   If $s_i = x$, return its index i.
    4.   If $s_i < x$, apply the algorithm on the subsequence that lies above s_i.
    5.   Apply the algorithm on the subsequence of s that lies below s_i.
It is implemented in Example 9.10.

The recursive binary search runs in $O(\lg n)$ time. The running time is proportional to the number of recursive calls made. Each call processes a subsequence that is half as long as the previous one. So the number of recursive calls is the same as the number of times that n can be divided in two, namely $\lg n$.

EXAMPLE 9.10 Testing the Recursive Binary Search

```
1    public class TestBinarySearch {
2      public static void main(String[] args) {
3        int[] a = {22, 33, 44, 55, 66, 77, 88, 99};
4        print(a);
5        System.out.println("search(a, 44): " + search(a, 44));
6        System.out.println("search(a, 50): " + search(a, 50));
7        System.out.println("search(a, 77): " + search(a, 77));
8        System.out.println("search(a, 100): " + search(a, 100));
9      }
10
11     public static void print(int[] a) {
12       System.out.printf("{%d", a[0]);
13       for (int i = 1; i < a.length; i++) {
14         System.out.printf(", %d", a[i]);
15       }
16       System.out.println("}");
17     }
18
19     public static int search(int[] a, int x) {
20       return search(a, 0, a.length-1, x);
21     }
22
23     public static int search(int[] a, int lo, int hi, int x) {
24       // PRECONDITION:    a[0] <= a[1] <= ... <= a[a.length-1];
25       // POSTCONDITIONS: returns i;
26       //                 if i >= 0, then a[i] == x; otherwise i == -1;
27       if (lo > hi) {
28         return -1;  // basis
29       }
30       int i = (lo + hi)/2;
31       if (a[i] == x) {
32         return i;
33       } else if (a[i] < x) {
34         return search(a, i+1, hi, x);
35       } else {
36         return search(a, lo, i-1, x);
37       }
38     }
39   }
```

The output is:

```
{22, 33, 44, 55, 66, 77, 88, 99}
search(a, 44): 2
search(a, 50): -1
search(a, 77): 5
search(a, 100): -1
```

The search() method returns the index of the target x: search(a, 44) returns 2 because a[2] = 44 and search(a, 77) returns 5 because a[5] = 77. The method returns –1 when the target is not in the array: search(a, 50) returns –1 because 50 is not in the array.

BINOMIAL COEFFICIENTS

The *binomial coefficients* are the coefficients that result from the expansion of a binomial expression of the form $(x + 1)^n$. For example,

$$(x + 1)^6 = x^6 + 6x^5 + 15x^4 + 20x^3 + 15x^2 + 6x + 1$$

The seven coefficients generated here are 1, 6, 15, 20, 15, 6, and 1.

The French mathematician Blaise Pascal (1623–1662) discovered a recursive relationship among the binomial coefficients. By arranging them in a triangle, he found that each interior number is the sum of the two directly above it. (See Figure 9.3.) For example, $15 = 5 + 10$.

Let $c(n,k)$ denote the coefficient in row number n and column number k (counting from 0). For example, $c(6,2) = 15$. Then Pascal's recurrence relation can be expressed as

$$c(n, k) = c(n-1, k-1) + c(n-1, k), \text{ for } 0 < k < n$$

For example, when $n = 6$ and $k = 2$, $c(6,2) = c(5,1) + c(5,2)$.

EXAMPLE 9.11 Recursive Implementation of the Binomial Coefficient Function

```
1    public static int c(int n, int k) {
2      if (k==0 || k==n) {
3        return 1;    // basis
4      }
5      return c(n-1,k-1) + c(n-1,k);  // recursion
6    }
```

The basis for the recursion covers the left and right sides of the triangle, where $k = 0$ and where $k = n$.

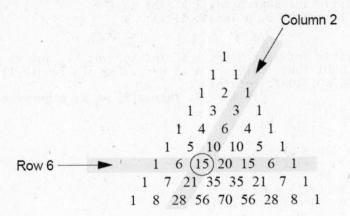

Figure 9.3 Pascal's triangle

The binomial coefficients are the same as the *combination* numbers used in combinatorial mathematics and computed explicitly by the formula

$$c(n, k) = \frac{n!}{k!(n-k)!} = \left(\frac{n}{1}\right)\left(\frac{n-1}{2}\right)\left(\frac{n-2}{3}\right)\dots\left(\frac{n-k+1}{k}\right)$$

In this context, the combination is often written $c(n, k) = \binom{n}{k}$ and is pronounced "n choose k." For example, "8 choose 3" is $\binom{8}{3} = (8/1)(7/2)(6/3) = 56$.

EXAMPLE 9.12 Iterative Implementation of the Binomial Coefficient Function

This version implements the explicit formula given above. The expression on the right consists of k factors, so it is computed by a loop iterating k times:

```
1    public static int c(int n, int k) {
2      if (n < 2 || k == 0 || k == n) {
3        return 1;
4      }
5      int c = 1;
```

```
6      for (int j = 1; j <= k; j++) {
7        c = c*(n-j+1)/j;
8      }
9      return c;
10   }
```

THE EUCLIDEAN ALGORITHM

The *Euclidean Algorithm* computes the greatest common divisor of two positive integers. Appearing as Proposition 2 in Book VII of Euclid's *Elements* (c. 300 B.C.), it is probably the oldest recursive algorithm. As originally formulated by Euclid, it says to subtract repeatedly the smaller number n from the larger number m until the resulting difference d is smaller than n. Then repeat the same steps with d in place of n and with n in place of m. Continue until the two numbers are equal. Then that number will be the greatest common divisor of the original two numbers.

Figure 9.4 applies this algorithm to find the greatest common divisor of 494 and 130 to be 26. This is correct because $494 = 26 \cdot 19$ and $130 = 26 \cdot 5$.

```
    494
   −130
    364
   −130
    234
   −130     130
    104    −104     104
            26     −26
                    78
                   −26
                    52
                   −26
                    26
```

Figure 9.4 The Euclidean algorithm

EXAMPLE 9.13 Recursive Implementation of the Euclidean Algorithm

Each step in the algorithm simply subtracts the smaller number from the larger. This is done recursively by calling either gcd(m,n-m) or gcd(m-n,n):

```
1    public static int gcd(int m, int n) {
2      if (m==n) {
3        return n;                // basis
4      } else if (m<n) {
5        return gcd(m,n-m);       // recursion
6      } else {
7        return gcd(m-n,n);       // recursion
8      }
9    }
```

For example, the call gcd(494,130) makes the recursive call gcd(364,130), which makes the recursive call gcd(234,130), which makes the recursive call gcd(104,130), which makes the recursive call gcd(104,26), which makes the recursive call gcd(78,26), which makes the recursive call gcd(52,26), which makes the recursive call gcd(26,26), which returns 26. The value 26 is then successively returned all the way back up the chain to the original call gcd(494,130), which returns it to its caller.

INDUCTIVE PROOF OF CORRECTNESS

Recursive functions are usually proved correct by the principle of *mathematical induction*. This principle states that an infinite sequence of propositions can be proved to be true by verifying that (*i*) the first statement is true, and (*ii*) the truth of every other statement in the sequence can be derived from the assumption that its preceding statements are true. Part (*i*) is called the *basis step* and part (*ii*) is called the *inductive step*. The assumption that the preceding statements are true is called the *inductive hypothesis*.

   The recursive factorial function is correct. To prove this fact, we first verify the basis. The call f(0) returns the correct value 1 because of the first part:

```
if (n < 2) {
    return 1;
}
```

Next, we assume that the function returns the correct value for all integers less than some $n > 0$. Then the second part

```
return n*f(n-1);
```

will return the correct value $n!$ because (by the inductive hypothesis) the call f(n-1) will return $(n-1)!$ and $n! = n\cdot(n-1)$.

   Note that we are using the "strong" principle of mathematical induction here (also called the *second principle of mathematical induction*). In this version, the inductive hypothesis allows us to assume that *all* the preceding statements are true. In the "weak" (or "first") principle, we are allowed to assume that only the single preceding statement is true. But since these two principles are equivalent (i.e., they are both valid methods of proof), it is usually better to apply strong induction.

   The Euclidean algorithm is correct. We can use (strong) induction to prove this fact. (See page 322.) If m and n are equal, then that number is their greatest common divisor. So the function returns the correct value in that case because of the part

```
if (m == n) {
    return n;
}
```

If m and n are not equal, then the function returns either gcd(m,n-m) or gcd(m-n,n). To see that this too is the correct value, we need only realize that all three pairs (m,n), (m,n-m), and (m-n,n) will always have the same greatest common divisor. This fact is a theorem from number theory.

COMPLEXITY ANALYSIS

   The complexity analysis of a recursive algorithm depends upon the solubility of its recurrence relation. The general technique is to let $T(n)$ be the number of steps required to carry out the algorithm on a problem of size n. The recursive part of the algorithm translates into a recurrence relation on $T(n)$. Its solution is then the complexity function for the algorithm.

   The recursive factorial function runs in $O(n)$ time. Let $T(n)$ be the number of recursive calls made from the initial call f(n) to the function in Example 9.2 on page 165. Then $T(0) = T(1) = 0$, because if $n < 2$, no recursive calls are made. If $n > 1$, then the line

```
return n*f(n-1);
```

executes, making the recursive call f(n-1). Then the total number of recursive calls is 1 plus the number of calls that are made from f(n-1). That translates into the recurrence relation

$$T(n) = 1 + T(n-1)$$

   The solution to this recurrence is

$$T(n) = n-1, \text{ for } n > 0$$

This conclusion is obtained in two stages: First we *find* the solution; then we use induction to *prove* that it is correct. The simplest technique for finding the solution to a recurrence relation is to make a table of values and look for a pattern. This recurrence relation says that each value of $T(n)$ is 1 more than the previous value. So the solution $f(n) = n-1$ is pretty obvious.

Now to prove that $T(n) = n - 1$ for all $n > 0$, let $f(n) = n - 1$ and apply the (weak) principle of mathematical induction. The basis case is where $n = 1$. In that case, $T(n) = T(1) = 0$ and $f(n) = f(1) = (1) - 1 = 0$. For the inductive step, we assume that $T(n) = f(n)$ for some $n > 0$ and then deduce from that assumption that $T(n + 1) = f(n + 1)$:

$$T(n + 1) = 1 + T(n) = 1 + f(n) = 1 + (n - 1) = n$$
$$f(n + 1) = (n + 1) - 1 = n$$

That completes the proof.

Now that we have determined that the complexity function for this recursive implementation of the factorial function $T(n) = n - 1$, we can conclude that this implementation "will run in $O(n)$ time." This means that its execution time will be proportional to the size of its argument n. If it takes 3 milliseconds to compute 8!, then it should take about 6 milliseconds to compute 16!.

DYNAMIC PROGRAMMING

In most cases, recursion is very inefficient because of its frequent function calls. So an iterative implementation may be better if it is not too complex. Another alternative is to implement the recurrence relation by storing previously computed values in an array instead of recomputing them with recursive function calls. This method is called *dynamic programming*.

EXAMPLE 9.14 Dynamic Programming Implementation of the Fibonacci Function

```
1   public static int fib(int n) {
2     if (n < 2) {
3       return n;
4     }
5     int[] f = new int[n];
6     f[0] = 0;
7     f[1] = 1;
8     for (int i=2; i<n; i++) {      // store the Fibonacci numbers
9       f[i] = f[i-1] + f[i-2];
10    }
11    return f[n-1] + f[n-2];
12  }
```

This implementation uses a dynamic array `f[]` of n integers to store the first n Fibonacci numbers.

THE TOWERS OF HANOI

We have seen important examples of functions that are more naturally defined and more easily understood by using recursion. For some problems, recursion is the only reasonable method of solution.

The Towers of Hanoi puzzle is a classic example of a problem whose solution demands recursion. The game consists of a board with three vertical pegs labeled A, B, and C, and a sequence of *n* disks with holes in their centers. (See Figure 9.5.) The radii of the disks are in an

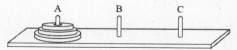

Figure 9.5 The Towers of Hanoi puzzle

arithmetic progression (e.g., 5cm, 6cm, 7cm, 8cm, . . .) and are mounted on peg A. The rule is that no disk may be above a smaller disk on the same peg. The objective of the game is to move all the disks from peg A to peg C, one disk at a time, without violating the rule.

The general solution to the Towers of Hanoi game is naturally recursive:

- Part I: Move the smaller $n-1$ disks from peg A to peg B.
- Part II: Move the remaining disk from peg A to peg C.
- Part III: Move the smaller $n-1$ disks from peg B to peg C.

The first and third steps are recursive: Apply the complete solution to n–1 disks. The basis to this recursive solution is the case where $n = 0$. In that case, do nothing.

The solution for the case of $n = 1$ disk is:

1. Move the disk from peg A to peg C.

The solution for the case of $n = 2$ disks is:

1. Move the top disk from peg A to peg B.
2. Move the second disk from peg A to peg C.
3. Move the top disk from peg B to peg C.

The solution for the case of $n = 3$ disks is:

1. Move the top disk from peg A to peg C.
2. Move the second disk from peg A to peg B.
3. Move the top disk from peg C to peg B.
4. Move the remaining disk from peg A to peg C.
5. Move the top disk from peg B to peg A.
6. Move the second disk from peg B to peg C.
7. Move the top disk from peg A to peg C.

Here, steps 1–3 constitute Part I of the general solution, step 4 constitutes Part II, and steps 5–7 constitute Part III.

Since the general recursive solution requires the substitution of different peg labels, it is better to use variables. Then, naming this three-step algorithm $hanoi(n, x, y, z)$, it becomes:

- Part I: Move the smaller $n-1$ disks from peg x to peg z.
- Part II: Move the remaining disk from peg x to peg y.
- Part III: Move the smaller $n-1$ disks from peg z to peg y.

The general solution is implemented in Example 9.15.

EXAMPLE 9.15 The Towers of Hanoi

This program prints the solution to the Towers of Hanoi problem of moving three disks from peg A to peg C via peg B:

```
1   public class TestHanoiTowers {
2     public static void main(String[] args) {
3       HanoiTowers(3, 'A', 'B', 'C');
4     }
5
6     public static void HanoiTowers(int n, char x, char y, char z) {
7       if (n==1) {                 // basis
8         System.out.printf("Move top disk from peg %c to peg %c.%n", x, z);
9       } else {
10        HanoiTowers(n-1, x, z, y);   // recursion
11        HanoiTowers(1, x, y, z);     // recursion
12        HanoiTowers(n-1, y, x, z);   // recursion
13      }
14    }
15  }
```

The output is:

```
Move top disk from peg A to peg C.
Move top disk from peg A to peg B.
Move top disk from peg C to peg B.
Move top disk from peg A to peg C.
Move top disk from peg B to peg A.
Move top disk from peg B to peg C.
Move top disk from peg A to peg C.
```

To solve the problem for three disks, the call at line 3 passes 3 to n, 'A' to x, 'B' to y, and 'C' to z. Since n > 1, line 10 executes next, passing 2 to n, 'A' to x, 'B' to z, and 'C' to y. Again, since n > 1, line 10 executes next, passing 1 to n, 'A' to x, 'B' to y, and 'C' to z. In that call, n = 1, so line 8 executes, printing the first line of output:

```
Move top disk from peg A to peg C.
```

That call returns to where the previous call left off at line 10, proceeding to line 11, where n = 2, x = 'A', y = 'C', and z = 'B'. That prints the second line of output:

```
Move top disk from peg A to peg B.
```

Then line 12 executes, this time passing 1 to n, 'C' to x, 'A' to y, and 'B' to z. In that call, n = 1 again, so line 8 executes, printing the third line of output:

```
Move top disk from peg C to peg B.
```

That call returns to where the second recursive call had left off at line 12. Since that is the last executable statement in the method, it also returns, back to where the first recursive call had left off at line 10. So it proceeds to line 11 with n = 3, x = 'A', y = 'B', and z = 'C'. That prints the fourth line of output:

```
Move top disk from peg A to peg C.
```

Then line 12 executes, passing 2 to n, 'B' to x, 'A' to y, and 'C' to z.

That call, HanoiTowers(2, 'B', 'A', 'C'), recursively moves the stack of two disks from peg B to to peg C via peg A and generates the last three lines of output:

```
Move top disk from peg B to peg A.
Move top disk from peg B to peg C.
Move top disk from peg A to peg C.
```

Since the previous four moves had already transferred the largest disk from peg A to peg C, this completes the task.

MUTUAL RECURSION

When a function calls itself, it is called *direct recursion*. Another form of recursion is when a function calls other functions that call other functions that eventually call the original function. This is called *indirect recursion*. Its most common form is when two functions call each other. This is called *mutual recursion*. (See Figure 9.6.)

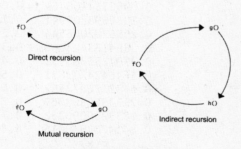

Figure 9.6 Types of recursion

EXAMPLE 9.16 The Sine and Cosine Functions Computed by Mutual Recursion

The sine and cosine functions from trigonometry can be defined in several different ways, and there are several different algorithms for computing their values. The simplest (although not the most efficient) is via mutual recursion. It is based upon the identities:

$$\sin 2\theta = 2\sin\theta\cos\theta$$
$$\cos 2\theta = 1 - 2(\sin\theta)^2$$

and the two Taylor polynomials:

$$\sin x \approx x - x^3/6$$

$$\cos x \approx 1 - x^2/2$$

which are close approximations for small values of x.

```
1    public class TestMutualRecursion {
2      public static void main(String[] args) {
3        String fmt1 = "%18s%18s%18s%n";
4        String fmt2 = "%18.13f%18.13f%18.13f%n";
5        System.out.printf(fmt1, "s(x)      ", "Math.sin(x)  ", "error        ");
6        for (double x = 0.0; x < 1.0; x += 0.1) {
7          System.out.printf(fmt2, s(x), Math.sin(x), Math.sin(x) - s(x));
8        }
9        System.out.printf(fmt1, "c(x)      ", "Math.cos(x)  ", "error        ");
10       for (double x = 0.0; x < 1.0; x += 0.1) {
11         System.out.printf(fmt2, c(x), Math.cos(x), c(x) - Math.cos(x));
12       }
13     }
14
15     public static double s(double x) {
16       if (-0.005 < x && x < 0.005) {
17         return x - x*x*x/6;      // basis
18       }
19       return 2*s(x/2)*c(x/2);   // recursion
20     }
21
22     public static double c(double x) {
23       if (-0.005 < x && x < 0.005) {
24         return 1.0 - x*x/2;       // basis
25       }
26       return 1 - 2*s(x/2)*s(x/2);  // recursion
27     }
28   }
```

The output is:

s(x)	Math.sin(x)	error
0.0000000000000	0.0000000000000	0.0000000000000
0.0998334166464	0.0998334166468	0.0000000000005
0.1986693307941	0.1986693307951	0.0000000000009
0.2955202066544	0.2955202066613	0.0000000000069
0.3894183423069	0.3894183423087	0.0000000000018
0.4794255385991	0.4794255386042	0.0000000000051
0.5646424733831	0.5646424733950	0.0000000000120
0.6442176872362	0.6442176872377	0.0000000000015
0.7173560908969	0.7173560908995	0.0000000000027
0.7833269096232	0.7833269096275	0.0000000000043
0.8414709848016	0.8414709848079	0.0000000000063

c(x)	Math.cos(x)	error
1.0000000000000	1.0000000000000	0.0000000000000
0.9950041652781	0.9950041652780	0.0000000000000
0.9800665778414	0.9800665778412	0.0000000000002
0.9553364891277	0.9553364891256	0.0000000000021
0.9210609940036	0.9210609940029	0.0000000000007
0.8775825618932	0.8775825618904	0.0000000000028
0.8253356149179	0.8253356149097	0.0000000000082
0.7648421872857	0.7648421872845	0.0000000000013
0.6967067093499	0.6967067093472	0.0000000000027
0.6216099682760	0.6216099682707	0.0000000000054
0.5403023058779	0.5403023058681	0.0000000000098

This works because on each recursive call x is divided by 2, and eventually it reaches the basis criterion (-0.005 < x && x < 0.005), which stops the recursion.

Review Questions

9.1   A recursive function must have two parts: its *basis* and its *recursive part*. Explain what each of these is and why it is essential to recursion.

9.2   How many recursive calls will the call `f(10)` to the recursive factorial function (Example 9.2 on page 165) generate?

9.3   How many recursive calls will the call `fib(6)` to the recursive Fibonacci function (Example 9.6 on page 167) generate?

9.4   What are the advantages and disadvantages of implementing a recursive solution instead of an iterative solution?

9.5   What is the difference between direct recursion and indirect recursion?

Problems

9.1   Write and test a recursive function that returns the sum of the squares of the first n positive integers.

9.2   Write and test a recursive function that returns the sum of the first n powers of a base b.

9.3   Write and test a recursive function that returns the sum of the first n elements of an array.

9.4   Write and test a recursive function that returns the maximum among the first n elements of an array.

9.5   Write and test a recursive function that returns the maximum among the first n elements of an array, using at most $\lg n$ recursive calls.

9.6   Write and test a recursive function that returns the power x^n.

9.7   Write and test a recursive function that returns the power x^n, using at most $2 \lg n$ recursive calls.

9.8   Write and test a recursive function that returns the integer binary logarithm of an integer n (i.e., the number of times n can be divided by 2).

9.9   Write and test a recursive boolean function that determines whether a string is a palindrome. (A *palindrome* is a string of characters that is the same as the string obtained from it by reversing its letters.)

9.10 Write and test a recursive function that returns a string that contains the binary representation of a positive integer.

9.11 Write and test a recursive function that returns a string that contains the hexadecimal representation of a positive integer.

9.12 Write and test a recursive function that prints all the permutations of the first n characters of a string. For example, the call `print("ABC",3)` would print

```
ABC
ACB
BAC
BCA
CBA
CAB
```

9.13 Implement the Fibonacci function iteratively (without using an array).

9.14 Implement the recursive Ackermann function:
$A(0, n) = n + 1$
$A(m, 0) = A(m - 1, 1)$, if $m > 0$
$A(m, n) = A(m - 1, A(m, n - 1))$, if $m > 0$ and $n > 0$

9.15 Prove Pascal's recurrence relation (page 170).

9.16 Trace the recursive implementation of the Euclidean Algorithm (Example 9.13 on page 171) on the call `gcd(385, 231)`.

9.17 Implement the Euclidean Algorithm (page 171) iteratively.

9.18 Implement the recursive Euclidean Algorithm using the integer remainder operator % instead of repeated subtraction.

9.19 Implement the Euclidean Algorithm iteratively using the integer remainder operator % instead of repeated subtraction.

9.20 Use mathematical induction to prove that the recursive implementation of the Fibonacci function (Example 9.6 on page 167) is correct.

9.21 Use mathematical induction to prove that the recursive function in Problem 9.4 is correct.

9.22 Use mathematical induction to prove that the recursive function in Problem 9.5 is correct.

9.23 Use mathematical induction to prove that the recursive function in Problem 9.8 is correct.

9.24 Use mathematical induction to prove that the recursive function in Problem 9.12 is correct.

9.25 The *computable domain* of a function is the set of inputs for which the function can produce correct results. Determine empirically the computable domain of the factorial function implemented in Example 9.2 on page 165.

9.26 Determine empirically the computable domain of the `sum(b,n)` function implemented in Problem 9.2 on page 177, using $b = 2$.

9.27 Determine empirically the computable domain of the Fibonacci function implemented in Example 9.3 on page 166.

9.28 Determine empirically the computable domain of the recursive binomial coefficient function (Example 9.11 on page 170).

9.29 The Towers of Hanoi program performs 7 disk moves for 3 disks. How many disk moves are performed for:
  a. 5 disks?
  b. 6 disks?
  c. *n* disks?

9.30 Prove the formula that you derived in previous problem.

9.31 Determine empirically the computable domain of the Ackermann function (Problem 9.14).

9.32 Show the recursive call tree for the call `hanoi(4,'A','B','C')` in Example 9.15 on page 174.

9.33 Modify the program in Example 9.16 on page 175 so that the results are more accurate by narrowing the bases so that recursion continues until $|x| < 0.00005$.

9.34 Modify the program in Example 9.16 on page 175 so that the results are obtained in fewer iterations by using the more accurate Taylor approximations
$$\sin x \approx x - x^3/6 + x^5/120$$
$$\cos x \approx 1 - x^2/2 + x^4/24$$

9.35 Use these formulas to implement the hyperbolic sine and hyperbolic cosine functions recursively:

$$\sinh 2x = 2\sinh x \cosh x$$
$$\cosh 2x = 1 + 2(\sinh x)^2$$
$$\sin x \approx x + x^3/6$$
$$\cos x \approx 1 + x^2/2$$

Compare your results with the corresponding values of the `Math.sinh()` and `Math.cosh()` methods.

9.36 Use these trigonometric formulas to implement the tangent function recursively:

$$\tan 2\theta = 2\tan\theta / (1 - \tan^2\theta)$$
$$\tan x \approx x + x^3/3$$

Compare your results with the corresponding values of the `Math.tan()` method.

9.37 Implement a recursive function that evaluates a polynomial $a_0 + a_1 x + a_2 x^2 + \cdots + a_3 x^3$, where the $n+1$ coefficients a_i are passed to the function in an array along with the degree n.

Answers to Review Questions

9.1 The basis of a recursive function is its starting point in its definition and its final step when it is being called recursively; it is what stops the recursion. The recursive part of a recursive function is the assignment that includes the function on the right side of the assignment operator, causing the function to call itself; it is what produces the repetition. For example, in the factorial function, the basis is $n! = 1$ if $n = 0$, and the recursive part is $n! = n(n-1)$ if $n > 0$.

9.2 The call `factorial(10)` will generate 10 recursive calls.

9.3 The call `f(6)` to the Fibonacci function will generate $14 + 8 = 22$ recursive calls because it calls `f(5)` and `f(4)`, which generate 14 and 8 recursive calls, respectively.

9.4 A recursive solution is often easier to understand than its equivalent iterative solution. But recursion usually runs more slowly than iteration.

9.5 Direct recursion is where a function calls itself. Indirect recursion is where a group of functions call each other.

Solutions to Problems

9.1 A recursive function that returns the sum of the first n squares:
```
int sum(int n) {
  if (n == 0) {
    return 0;                 // basis
  }
  return sum(n-1) + n*n;  // recursion
}
```

9.2 A recursive function that returns the sum of the first n powers of a base b:
```
double sum(double b, int n) {
  if (n == 0) {
    return 1;                 // basis
  }
  return 1 + b*sum(b,n-1);  // recursion
}
```
Note that this solution implements Horner's method: $1 + b*(1 + b*(1 + b*(1 + \cdots + b)))$.

9.3   A recursive function that returns the sum of the first *n* elements of an array:

```
double sum(double[] a, int n) {
  if (n == 0) {
    return 0.0;              // basis
  }
  return sum(a,n-1) + a[n-1];  // recursion
}
```

9.4   A recursive function that returns the maximum among the first *n* elements of an array:

```
double max(double[] a, int n) {
  if (n == 1) {
    return a[0];            // basis
  }
  double m = max(a,n-1);    // recursion
  if (a[n-1] > m) {
    return a[n-1];
  } else {
    return m;
  }
}
```

9.5   A recursive function that returns the maximum among the first *n* elements of an array and makes no more than lg*n* recursive calls:

```
double max(double[] a, int lo, int hi) {
  if (lo >= hi) {
    return a[lo];
  }
  int mid = (lo + hi)/2;              // middle index
  double m1 = max(a, lo, mid);        // recursion on a[lo..mid]
  double m2 = max(a, mid + 1, hi);    // recursion on a[mid+1..hi]
  return (m1>m2? m1: m2);             // maximum of {m1,m2}
}
```

9.6   A recursive function that returns the power x^n:

```
double pow(double x, int n) {
  if (n == 0) {
    return 1.0;              // basis
  }
  return x*pow(x,n-1);       // recursion
}
```

9.7   A recursive function that returns the power x^n and makes no more than lg*n* recursive calls:

```
double pow(double x, int n) {
  if (n == 0) {
    return 1.0;            // basis
  }
  double p = pow(x,n/2);
  if (n%2 == 0) {
    return p*p;            // recursion (n even)
  } else {
    return x*p*p;          // recursion (n odd)
  }
}
```

9.8   A recursive function that returns the integer binary logarithm of *n*:

```
int lg(int n) {
  if (n == 1) {
    return 0;              // basis
  }
  return 1 + lg(n/2);      // recursion
}
```

9.9   A recursive function that determines whether a string is a palindrome:

```
boolean isPalindrome(String s) {
  int len = s.length();
  if (len < 2) {
    return true;                                // basis
  } else if (s.charAt(0) != s.charAt(len-1))
    return false;                              // basis
  } else if (len == 2) {
    return true;
  } else {                                     // basis
    return isPalindrome(s.substring(1,len-1)); // recursion
  }
}
```

9.10 A recursive function that converts decimal to binary:

```
String binary(int n) {
  String s;
  if (n%2 == 0) {
    s = "0";
  } else {
    s = "1";
  }
  if (n < 2) {
    return s;                  // basis
  }
  return binary(n/2) + s;   // recursion
}
```

9.11 A recursive function that converts decimal to hexadecimal:

```
String hexadecimal(int n) {
  if (n < 16) {
    return Integer.toString(n%16)
  }
  return hexadecimal(n/16) + s;  // recursion
}
```

9.12 A recursive function that prints permutations:

```
void print(String str) {
  print("",str);
}

void print(String left, String right) {
  int n = right.length();
  if (n == 0) {
    return;
  } else if (n == 1)
    System.out.println(left+right);
    return;
  }
  StringBuilder buf = new StringBuilder(right);
  for (int i = 0; i < n; i++) {
    char temp = s.charAt(i);
    s.setCharAt(i, s.charAt(0));
    s.setCharAt(0, temp);
    print(left+temp, s.substring(1, n));
  }
}
```

9.13   Iterative implementation of the Fibonacci function:

```
int fib(int n) {
    if (n < 2) {
        return n;
    }
    int f0 = 0, f1 = 1, f = f0+f1;
    for (int i = 2; i < n; i++) {
        f0 = f1;
        f1 = f;
        f = f0 + f1;
    }
    return f;
}
```

9.14   The Ackermann function:

```
int ackermann(int m, int n) {
    if (m == 0) {
        return n + 1;                                        // basis
    } else if (n == 0) {
        return ackermann(m - 1, 1);                         // basis
    } else {
        return ackermann(m - 1, ackermann(m, n - 1));  // recursion
    }
}
```

9.15   Consider the relationship $c(8,3) = 56 = 35 + 21 = c(7,3) + c(7,2)$ from the expansion of $(x + 1)^8$:

$$(x + 1)^8 = (x + 1)(x + 1)^7$$
$$= (x + 1)(x^7 + 7x^6 + 21x^5 + 35x^4 + 35x^3 + 21x^2 + 7x + 1)$$
$$= x^8 + 7x^7 + 21x^6 + 35x^5 + 35x^4 + 21x^3 + 7x^2 + x$$
$$+ x^7 + 7x^6 + 21x^5 + 35x^4 + 35x^3 + 21x^2 + 7x + 1$$
$$= x^8 + 8x^7 + 28x^6 + 56x^5 + 70x^4 + 56x^3 + 28x^2 + 7x + 1$$

The coefficient $c(8,3)$ is for the x^5 term, which is $35x^5 + 21x^5 = 56x^5$. The sum $35x^5 + 21x^5$ came from $(x)(35x^4)$ and $(1)(21x^5)$. So those coefficients are $35 = c(7,3)$ and $21 = c(7,2)$.

The general proof is based upon the same argument: $c(n,k)$ is the coefficient of the term x^k in the expansion of $(x + 1)^n$. Since $(x + 1)^n = (x + 1)(x + 1)^{n-1}$, that term comes from the sum

$$(x)(c(n-1, k-1)\, x^{k-1}) + (1)(c(n-1, k)x^k) = (c(n-1, k-1) + c(n-1, k))x^k$$

Therefore $c(n, k) = c(n-1, k-1) + c(n-1, k)$.

9.16   Figure 9.7 shows the trace of the call gcd(616, 231):

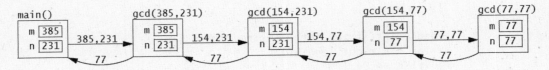

Figure 9.7 Tracing the Euclidean algorithm

9.17   Iterative implementation of the Euclidean algorithm:

```
int gcd(int m, int n) {
    while (m != n) {             // INVARIANT: gcd(m,n)
        if (m < n) {
            n -= m;
        } else {
            m -= n;
        }
    }
    return n;
}
```

9.18 Recursive implementation of the Euclidean algorithm using the remainder operator:

```
int gcd(int m, int n) {
   if (m == 0) {
     return n;               // basis
   } else if (n == 0) {
     return m;               // basis
   } else if (m < n) {
     return gcd(m, n%m);     // recursion
   } else {
     return gcd(m%n, n);     // recursion
   }
}
```

9.19 Iterative implementation of the Euclidean algorithm using the remainder operator:

```
int gcd(int m, int n) {
   while (n > 0) {      // INVARIANT: gcd(m,n)
     int r = m%n;
     m = n;
     n = r;
   }
   return m;
}
```

9.20 To prove that the recursive implementation of the Fibonacci function is correct, first verify the basis. The calls `fib(0)` and `fib(1)` return the correct values `0` and `1` because of the first line

```
if (n < 2) {
   return n;
}
```

Next, we assume that the function returns the correct value for all integers less than some $n > 1$. Then the second line

```
return fib(n-1) + fib(n-2);
```

will return the correct value because (by the inductive hypothesis) the calls `fib(n-1)` and `fib(n-2)` return the correct values for F_{n-1} and F_{n-2}, respectively, and $F_n = F_{n-1} + F_{n-2}$ by definition. Note that the basis here requires the verification of the first *two* steps in the sequence because the recurrence relation $F_n = F_{n-1} + F_{n-2}$ applies only for $n > 1$.

9.21 If $n = 1$, then the basis executes, returning `a[0]` which is the maximum element because it is the only element. If $n > 1$, then the function correctly computes the maximum `m` of the first $n-1$ elements (by the inductive hypothesis). If the condition (`a[n-1] > m`) is true, then that element `a[n-1]` is returned, and it is the largest because it is larger than `m`, which is larger than all the others. On the other hand, if the condition (`a[n-1] > m`) is false, then `m` is returned, and that is the largest because it is not smaller than `a[m-1]`, and it is the largest among all the others.

9.22 If $n = 1$, then the basis executes, returning `a[0]` which is the maximum element because it is the only element. If $n > 1$, then the function correctly computes the maxima `m1` and `m2` of the first and second halves of the array (by the inductive hypothesis). One of these two numbers is the correct maximum for the entire array. The larger is returned.

9.23 If $n = 1$, then the basis executes, returning `0`, which is the number of times n can be divided by 2. If $n > 1$, then the function correctly computes the number of times $n/2$ can be divided by 2 (by the inductive hypothesis). This is 1 less than the number of times n can be divided by 2, so the value returned, `1 + lg(n/2)`, is correct.

9.24 First, we prove the conjecture that the call `print(left, right)` will print $n!$ distinct strings, all having the same prefix string `left`, where $n = $ `right.length()`. If $n = 1$, the method prints `left+right` and returns; that is 1! (distinct) string. Assume that when `right.length()` $= n-1$, the call `print(left,right)` prints $(n-1)!$ distinct strings all having the same `left` prefix string. Then, when `right.length()` $= n$, the `for` loop makes n calls of the form `print(left+temp,ss)`, where temp is a distinct character and `ss = s.substring(1,n)`. Since the length of `s.substring(1,n)` is $n-1$, each of those calls will print $(n-1)!$ distinct strings all having the same `left+temp` prefix string.

Therefore, the loop will print $(n)(n-1)!$ distinct strings all having the same `left` prefix string. This proves the conjecture by mathematical induction. Now it follows from that conjecture that the call `print(str)` will print $n!$ distinct permutations of the characters in the string `str`, where n is its length. Since that is precisely the total number of permutations that the string has, it follows that the method is correct.

9.25 For the factorial function implemented in Example 9.2 on page 165, integer overflow occurs on the return type `long` with $n = 13$ on the author's computer. So the computable domain for this function is $0 \le n \le 12$.

9.26 For the `sum(b,n)` function implemented in Problem 9.2 on page 177 with `b` = 2, floating point overflow occurs on the return type `double` with $n = 1{,}023$ on the author's computer. So the computable domain for this function is $0 \le n \le 1{,}022$.

9.27 For the Fibonacci function implemented in Example 9.6 on page 167, the overhead from the recursive calls degrades the run-time performance noticeably after $n = 36$ on the author's computer. So the computable domain for this function is about $0 \le n \le 40$.

9.28 For the binomial coefficient function implemented in Example 9.7 on page 167, the overhead from the recursive calls degrades the run-time performance noticeably after $n = 25$ on the author's computer. So the computable domain for this function is about $0 \le n \le 30$.

9.29 The Towers of Hanoi program performs:
   a. 31 moves for 5 disks
   b. 63 moves for 6 disks
   c. $2^n - 1$ moves for n disks

9.30 To prove that the Towers of Hanoi program performs $2^n - 1$ disk moves for n disks, use mathematical induction. The basis is established in Example 9.15 on page 174. To move $n + 1$ disks, it takes $2^n - 1$ moves to move all but the last disk to peg B (by the inductive hypothesis). Then it takes 1 move to move the last disk to peg C, and $2^n - 1$ more moves to move the rest of the disks from peg B to peg C on top of that last disk. The total is $(2^n - 1) + 1 + (2^n - 1) = 2^{n+1} - 1$.

9.31 For the Ackermann function implemented in Problem 9.14 on page 178, exceptions are thrown for $m = 17$ when $n = 2$, for $m = 5$ when $n = 3$, for $m = 4$ when $n = 4$, and for $m = 3$ when $n = 5$. So the computable domain for this function is restricted to $0 \le m \le 16$ when $n = 2$, to $0 \le m \le 4$ when $n = 3$, to $0 \le m \le 3$ when $n = 4$, and to $0 \le m \le 2$ when $n = 5$.

9.32 The call tree for Example 9.15 on page 174 is:

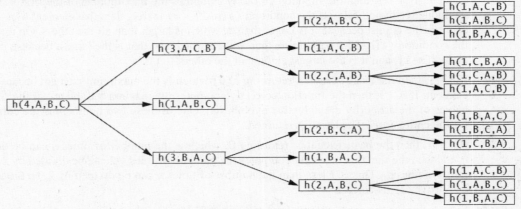

Figure 9.8 Call tree

9.33 These are more accurate recursive implementation of the sine and cosine functions:

```
public static double s(double x) {
   if (Math.abs(x) < 0.00005) {
      return x - x*x*x/6;     // basis
   }
```

```
            return 2*s(x/2)*c(x/2);  // recursion
          }

          public static double c(double x) {
            if (Math.abs(x) < 0.00005) {
              return 1.0 - x*x/2;        // basis
            }
            return 1 - 2*s(x/2)*s(x/2);  // recursion
          }
```

9.34 These are faster converging implementation of the sine and cosine functions:

```
          public static double s(double x) {
            if (-0.005 < x && x < 0.005) {
              return x - x*x*x/6 + x*x*x*x*x/120;     // basis
            }
            return 2*s(x/2)*c(x/2);  // recursion
          }

          public static double c(double x) {
            if (-0.005 < x && x < 0.005) {
              return 1.0 - x*x/2 + x*x*x*x*x/24;         // basis
            }
            return 1 - 2*s(x/2)*s(x/2);  // recursion
          }
```

9.35 These are mutually recursive implementations of the hyperbolic sine and cosine functions:

```
          public static double s(double x) {
            if (-0.005 < x && x < 0.005) {
              return x + x*x*x/6;     // basis
            }
            return 2*s(x/2)*c(x/2);  // recursion
          }

          public static double c(double x) {
            if (-0.005 < x && x < 0.005) {
              return 1.0 + x*x/2;         // basis
            }
            return 1 + 2*s(x/2)*s(x/2);  // recursion
          }
```

9.36 This is a recursive implementation of the tangent function:

```
          public static double t(double x) {
            if (Math.abs(x) < 0.5e-10) {
              return x + x*x/3 + x*x*x*x/5;  // basis
            }
            double tx2 = t(x/2);
            return 2*tx2/(1 - tx2*tx2);        // recursion
          }
```

9.37 This is a recursive evaluation of a polynomial function:

```
          public static double p(double[] a, double x) {
            // returns a[0] + a[1]*x + a[2]*x*x + ...
            return p(a, x, 0);
          }

          private static double p(double[] a, double x, int k) {
            // returns a[k] + a[k+1]*x + a[k+2]*x*x + ...
            if (k == a.length) {
              return 0.0;                   // basis
            }
            return a[k] + x*p(a, x, k+1);  // recursion
          }
```

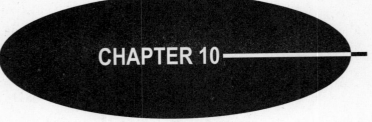

CHAPTER 10

Trees

A *tree* is a nonlinear data structure that models a hierarchical organization. The characteristic features are that each element may have several successors (called its "children") and every element except one (called the "root") has a unique predecessor (called its "parent"). Trees are common in computer science: Computer file systems are trees, the inheritance structure for Java classes is a tree, the run-time system of method invocations during the execution of a Java program is a tree, the classification of Java types is a tree, and the actual syntactical definition of the Java programming language itself forms a tree.

TREE DEFINITIONS

Here is the recursive definition of an (unordered) tree:

> **A *tree* is a pair (r, S), where r is a node and S is a set of disjoint trees, none of which contains r.**

The node r is called the *root* of the tree T, and the elements of the set S are called its *subtrees*. The set S, of course, may be empty. The restriction that none of the subtrees contains the root applies recursively: r cannot be in any subtree or in any subtree of any subtree.

Note that this definition specifies that the second component of a tree be a *set* of subtrees. So the order of the subtrees is irrelevant. Also note that a set may be empty, so $(r, \varnothing)$ qualifies as a tree. This is called a *singleton tree*. But the empty set itself does not qualify as an unordered tree.

EXAMPLE 10.1 Equal Unordered Trees

The two trees shown in Figure 10.1 are equal. The tree on the left has root **a** and two subtrees B and C, where B = (**b**, $\varnothing$), C = (**c**, {D}), and D is the subtree D = (**d**, $\varnothing$). The tree on the right has the same root **a** and the same set of subtrees {B, C} = {C, B}, so (**a**, {B, C}) = (**a**, {C, B}).

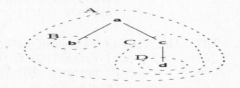

Figure 10.1 Equal trees

The elements of a tree are called its *nodes*. Technically, each node is an element of only one subtree, namely the tree of which it is the root. But indirectly, trees consist of nested subtrees, and each node is considered to be an element of every tree in which it is nested. So **a**, **b**, **c**, and **d** are all considered to be nodes of the tree A shown Figure 10.2. Similarly, **c** and **d** are both nodes of the tree C.

The *size* of a tree is the number of nodes it contains. So the tree A shown in Figure 10.2 has size 4, and C has size 2. A tree of size 1 is called a *singleton*. The trees B and D shown here are singletons.

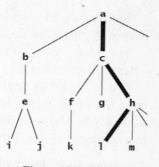

If $T = (x, S)$ is a tree, then x is the root of T and S is its set of subtrees $S = \{T_1, T_2, \ldots, T_n\}$. Each subtree T_j is itself a tree with its own root r_j. In this case, we call the node r the *parent* of each node r_j, and we call the r_j the *children* of r. In general, we say that two nodes are *adjacent* if one is the parent of the other.

A node with no children is called a *leaf*. A node with at least one child is called an *internal node*.

Figure 10.2 Subtrees

A *path* in a tree is a sequence of nodes $(x_0, x_1, x_2, \ldots, x_m)$ wherein the nodes of each pair with adjacent subscripts (x_{i-1}, x_i) are adjacent nodes. For example, (**a**, **b**, **c**, **d**) is a path in the tree shown above, but (**a**, **d**, **b**, **c**) is not. The *length* of a path is the number m of its adjacent pairs.

It follows from the definition that trees are *acyclic*, that is, no path can contain the same node more than once.

A *root path* for a node x_0 in a tree is a path $(x_0, x_1, x_2, \ldots, x_m)$ where x_m is the root of the tree. A root path for a leaf node is called a *leaf-to-root path*.

Theorem 10.1 Every node in a tree has a unique root path.
For a proof, see Problem 10.1 on page 194.

The *depth* of a node in a tree is the length of its root path. Of course, the depth of the root in any tree is 0. We also refer to the *depth* of a subtree in a tree, meaning the depth of its root.

A *level* in a tree is the set of all nodes at a given depth.

The *height* of a tree is the greatest depth among all of its nodes. By definition, the height of a singleton is 0, and the height of the empty tree is −1. For example, the tree A, shown in Figure 10.2, has height 2. Its subtree C has height 1, and its two subtrees B and D each have height 0.

A node y is said to be an *ancestor* of another node x if it is on x's root path. Note that the root of a tree is an ancestor of every other node in the tree.

A node x is said to be a *descendant* of another node y if y is an ancestor of x. For each node y in a tree, the set consisting of y and all its descendants form the *subtree* rooted at y. If S is a subtree of T, then we say that T is a *supertree* of S.

The *path length* of a tree is the sum of the lengths of all paths from its root. This is the same as the weighted sum, adding each level times the number of nodes on that level. The path length of the tree shown here is $1 \cdot 3 + 2 \cdot 4 + 3 \cdot 8 = 35$.

EXAMPLE 10.2 Properties of a Tree

The root of the tree shown in Figure 10.3 is node **a**. The six nodes **a**, **b**, **c**, **e**, **f**, and **h** are all internal nodes. The other nine nodes are leaves. The path (**1**, **h**, **c**, **a**) is a leaf-to-root path. Its length is 3. Node **b** has depth 1, and node **m** has depth 3. Level 2 consists of nodes **e**, **f**, **g**, and **h**. The height of the tree is 3. Nodes **a**, **c**, and **h** are all ancestors of node **1**. Node **k** is a descendant of node **c** but not of node **b**. The subtree rooted at **b** consists of nodes **b**, **e**, **i**, and **j**.

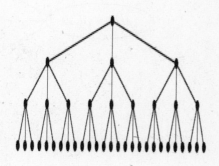

Figure 10.3 A leaf-to-root path

The *degree* of a node is the number of its children. In Example 10.2, **b** has degree 1, **d** has degree 0, and **h** has degree 5.

The *order* of a tree is the maximum degree among all of its nodes.

A tree is said to be *full* if all of its internal nodes have the same degree and all of its leaves are at the same level. The tree shown in Figure 10.4 is a full tree of degree 3. Note that it has a total of 40 nodes.

Figure 10.4 A full tree

Theorem 10.2 The full tree of order d and height h has $\dfrac{d^{h+1}-1}{d-1}$ nodes.
For a proof, see Problem 10.1 on page 194.

Corollary 10.1 The height of a full tree of order d and size n is $h = \log_d(nd - n + 1) - 1$.

Corollary 10.2 The number of nodes in any tree of height h is at most $\dfrac{d^{h+1}-1}{d-1}$ where d is the maximum degree among its nodes.

DECISION TREES

A *decision tree* is a tree diagram that summarizes all the different possible stages of a process that solves a problem by means of a sequence of decisions. Each internal node is labeled with a question, each arc is labeled with an answer to its question, and each leaf node is labeled with the solution to the problem.

EXAMPLE 10.3 Finding the Counterfeit Coin

Five coins that appear identical are to be tested to determine which one of them is counterfeit. The only feature that distinguishes the counterfeit coin is that it weighs less than the legitimate coins. The only available test is to weigh one subset of the coins against another. How should the subsets be chosen to find the counterfeit?

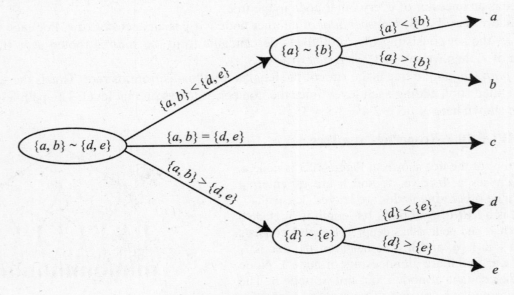

Figure 10.5 A decision tree

In the decision tree shown in Figure 10.5, the symbol $\sim$ means to compare the weights of the two operands. So, for example, $\{a, b\} \sim \{d, e\}$ means to weight coins a and b against coins d and e.

TRANSITION DIAGRAMS

A *transition diagram* is a tree or graph (see Chapter 15) whose internal nodes represent different states or situations that may occur during a multistage process. As in a decision tree, each leaf represents a different outcome from the process. Each branch is labeled with the conditional probability that the resulting child event will occur, given that the parent event has occurred.

EXAMPLE 10.4 The Game of Craps

The game of *craps* is a dice game played by two players, X and Y. First X tosses the pair of dice. If the sum of the dice is 7 or 11, X wins the game. If the sum is 2, 3, or 12, Y wins. Otherwise, the sum is designated as the "point," to be matched by another toss. So if neither player has won on the first toss, then the dice are tossed repeatedly until either the point comes up or a 7 comes up. If a 7 comes up first, Y wins. Otherwise, X wins when the point comes up.

The transition diagram shown in Figure 10.6 models the game of craps.

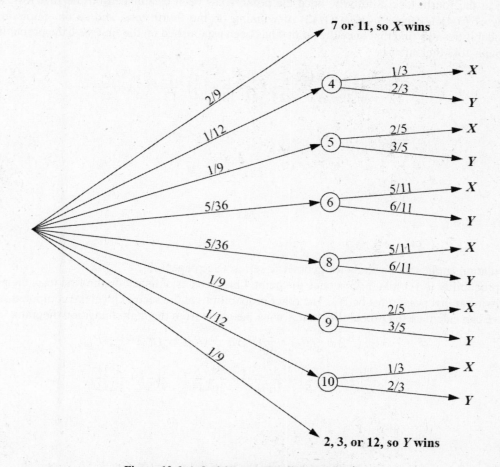

Figure 10.6 A decision tree for the game of craps

When a pair of dice is tossed, there are 36 possible outcomes (6 outcomes on the first die, and 6 outcomes on the second for each outcome on the first die). Of those 36 outcomes, 1 will produce a sum of 2 (1 + 1), 2 will produce a sum of 3 (1 + 2 or 2 + 1), and 1 will produce a sum of 12 (6 + 6). So there are a total of 4 chances out of 36 of the event "2, 3, or 12" happening. That's a probability of 4/36 = 1/9. Similarly, there are 6 ways that a sum of 7 will occur and 2 ways that a sum of 11 will occur, so the probability of the event "7 or 11" is 8/36 = 2/9. The other probabilities on the first level of the tree are computed similarly.

To see how the probabilities are computed for the second level of the tree, consider the case where the point is 4. If the next toss comes up 4, X wins. If it comes up 7, Y wins. Otherwise, that step is repeated. The transition diagram shown in Figure 10.7 summarizes those three possibilities. The probabilities 1/12, 1/6, and 3/4 are computed as shown in the transition diagram in Figure 10.7:

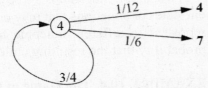

Figure 10.7 The game of craps

$$P(4) = 3/36 = 1/12$$
$$P(7) = 6/36 = 1/3$$
$$P(2,3,5,6,8,9,10,11, \text{ or } 12) = 27/36 = 3/4$$

So once the point 4 has been established on the first toss, X has a probability of 1/12 of winning on the second toss and a probability of 3/4 of getting to the third toss. So once the point 4 has been established on the first toss, X has a probability of (3/4)(1/12) of winning on the third toss and a probability of (3/4)(3/4) of getting to the fourth toss. Similarly, once the point 4 has been established on the first toss, X has a probability of (3/4)(1/12) + (3/4)(3/4)(1/12) of winning on the fourth toss, and so on. Summing these partial probabilities, we find that once the point 4 has been established on the first toss, the probability that X wins on *any* toss thereafter is

$$P_4 = \frac{1}{12} + \left(\frac{3}{4}\right)\frac{1}{12} + \left(\frac{3}{4}\right)^2\frac{1}{12} + \left(\frac{3}{4}\right)^3\frac{1}{12} + \left(\frac{3}{4}\right)^4\frac{1}{12} + \left(\frac{3}{4}\right)^5\frac{1}{12} + \cdots$$

$$= \frac{\dfrac{1}{12}}{1 - \dfrac{3}{4}}$$

$$= \frac{1/12}{1/4}$$

$$= \frac{1}{3}$$

This calculation applies the formula for geometric series. (See page 323.)

If the probability is 1/3 that X wins once the point 4 has been established on the first toss, the probability that Y wins at that point must be 2/3. The other probabilities at the second level are computed similarly.

Now we can calculate the probability that X wins the game from the main transition diagram:

$$P = \frac{2}{9} + \frac{1}{12}(P_4) + \frac{1}{9}(P_5) + \frac{5}{36}(P_6) + \frac{5}{36}(P_8) + \frac{1}{9}(P_9) + \frac{1}{12}(P_{10})$$

$$= \frac{2}{9} + \frac{1}{12}\left(\frac{1}{3}\right) + \frac{1}{9}\left(\frac{2}{5}\right) + \frac{5}{36}\left(\frac{5}{11}\right) + \frac{5}{36}\left(\frac{5}{11}\right) + \frac{1}{9}\left(\frac{2}{5}\right) + \frac{1}{12}\left(\frac{1}{3}\right)$$

$$= \frac{244}{495}$$

$$= 0.4929$$

So the probability that X wins is 49.29 percent, and the probability that Y wins is 50.71 percent.

A *stochastic process* is a process that can be analyzed by a transition diagram, that is, it can be decomposed into sequences of events whose conditional probabilities can be computed. The game of craps is actually an infinite stochastic process since there is no limit to the number of events that could occur. As with the analysis in Example 10.4, most infinite stochastic processes can be reformulated into an equivalent finite stochastic process that is amenable to (finite) computers.

Note that, unlike other tree models, decision trees and transition trees are usually drawn from left to right to suggest the time-dependent movement from one node to the next.

ORDERED TREES

Here is the recursive definition of an ordered tree:

An *ordered tree* is either the empty set or a pair $T = (r, S)$, where r is a node and S is a sequence of disjoint ordered trees, none of which contains r.

The node r is called the *root* of the tree T, and the elements of the sequence S are its *subtrees*. The sequence S of course may be empty, in which case T is a singleton. The restriction that none of the subtrees contains the root applies recursively: x cannot be in any subtree, or in any subtree of any subtree, and so on.

Note that this definition is the same as that for unordered trees except for the facts that the subtrees are in a sequence instead of a set and an ordered tree may be empty. Consequently, if two unordered trees have the same subsets, then they are equal; but as ordered trees, they won't be equal unless their equal subtrees are in the same order. Also subtrees of an ordered set may be empty.

EXAMPLE 10.5 Unequal Ordered Trees

The two trees shown in Figure 10.8 are not equal as ordered trees.

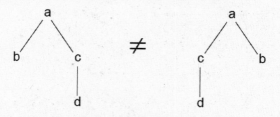

Figure 10.8 Unequal ordered trees

The ordered tree on the left has root node **a** and subtree sequence ((**b**, $\varnothing$), (**c**, (**d**, $\varnothing$))). The ordered tree on the right has root node **a** and subtree sequence ((**c**, (**d**, $\varnothing$)), (**b**, $\varnothing$)). These two subtree sequences have the same elements, but not in the same order. Thus the two ordered trees are not the same.

Strict adherence to the definition reveals a subtlety often missed, as illustrated by the next example.

EXAMPLE 10.6 Unequal Ordered Trees

The two trees $T_1 = ($**a**$, ($B, C$))$ and $T_2 = ($**a**$, ($B, $\varnothing$, C$))$ are not the same ordered trees, even though they would probably both be drawn the same, as shown in Figure 10.9.

Figure 10.9 A tree

All the terminology for unordered trees applies the same way to ordered trees. In addition, we can also refer to the *first child* and the *last child* of a node in an ordered tree. It is sometimes useful to think analogously of a human genealogical tree, where the children are ordered by age: oldest first and youngest last.

TRAVERSAL ALGORITHMS

A *traversal algorithm* is a method for processing a data structure that applies a given operation to each element of the structure. For example, if the operation is to print the contents of the element, then the traversal would print every element in the structure. The process of applying the operation to an element is called *visiting* the element. So executing the traversal algorithm causes each element in the structure to be visited. The order in which the elements are visited depends upon which traversal algorithm is used. There are three common algorithms for traversing a general tree.

The *level order traversal* algorithm visits the root, then visits each element on the first level, then visits each element on the second level, and so forth, each time visiting all the elements on one level before going down to the next level. If the tree is drawn in the usual manner with its root at the top and leaves near the bottom, then the level order pattern is the same left-to-right top-to-bottom pattern that you follow to read English text.

EXAMPLE 10.7 The Level Order Traversal

The level order traversal of the tree shown in Figure 10.10 would visit the nodes in the following order:
a, b, c, d, e, f, g, h, i, j, k, l, m.

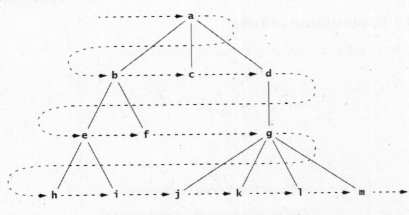

Figure 10.10 A level order traversal

Algorithm 10.1   The Level Order Traversal of an Ordered Tree

To traverse a nonempty ordered tree:
1. Initialize a queue.
2. Enqueue the root.
3. Repeat steps 4–7 until the queue is empty.
4. Dequeue node *x* from the queue.
5. Visit *x*.
6. Enqueue all the children of *x* in order.

The *preorder traversal* algorithm visits the root first and then does a preorder traversal recursively to each subtree in order.

EXAMPLE 10.8 The Preorder Traversal

The preorder traversal of the tree shown in Figure 10.11 would visit the nodes in this order: **a, b, e, h, i, f, c, d, g, j, k, l, m**.

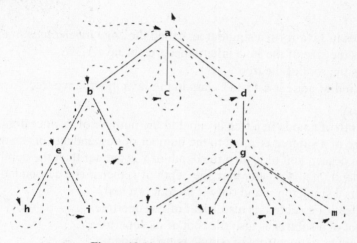

Figure 10.11 A preorder traversal

Note that the preorder traversal of a tree can be obtained by circumnavigating the tree, beginning at the root and visiting each node the first time it is encountered on the left.

Algorithm 10.2   The Preorder Traversal of an Ordered Tree
To traverse a nonempty ordered tree:
    1. Visit the root.
    2. Do a recursive preorder traversal of each subtree in order.

The *postorder traversal* algorithm does a postorder traversal recursively to each subtree before visiting the root.

EXAMPLE 10.9 The Postorder Traversal

The postorder traversal of the tree shown in Figure 10.12 would visit the nodes in the following order: **h, i, e, f, b, c, j, k, l, m, g, d, a**.

Algorithm 10.3   The Postorder Traversal of an Ordered Tree
To traverse a nonempty ordered tree:
    1. Do a recursive preorder traversal of each subtree in order.
    2. Visit the root.

Note that the level order and the preorder traversals always visit the root of each subtree first before visiting its other nodes. The postorder traversal always visits the root of each subtree last after visiting all of

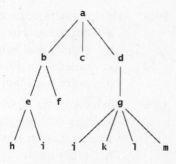

Figure 10.12 A tree

its other nodes. Also, the preorder traversal always visits the right-most node last, while the postorder traversal always visits the left-most node first.

The preorder and postorder traversals are recursive. They also can be implemented iteratively using a stack. The level order traversal is implemented iteratively using a queue.

Review Questions

10.1 All the classes in Java form a single tree, called the *Java inheritance tree*.
  a. What is the size of the Java inheritance tree in Java 1.3?
  b. What is the root of the tree?
  c. What kind of node is a `final` class in the Java inheritance tree?

10.2 True or false:
  a. The depth of a node in a tree is equal to the number of its ancestors.
  b. The size of a subtree is equal to the number of descendants of the root of the subtree.
  c. If x is a descendant of y, then the depth of x is greater than the depth of y.
  d. If the depth of x is greater than the depth of y, then x is a descendant of y.
  e. A tree is a singleton if and only if its root is a leaf.
  f. Every leaf of a subtree is also a leaf of its supertree.
  g. The root of a subtree is also the root of its supertree.
  h. The number of ancestors of a node equals its depth.
  i. If R is a subtree of S and S is a subtree of T, then R is a subtree of T.
  j. A node is a leaf if and only if it has degree 0.
  k. In any tree, the number of internal nodes must be less than the number of leaf nodes.
  l. A tree is full if and only if all of its leaves are at the same level.
  m. Every subtree of a full binary tree is full.
  n. Every subtree of a complete binary tree is complete.

10.3 For the tree shown in Figure 10.13, find:
  a. all ancestors of node F
  b. all descendants of node F
  c. all nodes in the subtree rooted at F
  d. all leaf nodes

10.4 For each of the five trees shown in Figure 10.14 on page 195, list the leaf nodes, the children of node C, the depth of node F, all the nodes at level 3, the height, and the order of the tree.

10.5 How many nodes are in the full tree of:
  a. order 3 and height 4?
  b. order 4 and height 3?
  c. order 10 and height 4?
  d. order 4 and height 10?

10.6 Give the order of visitation of the tree shown in Example 10.2 on page 187 using the:
  a. level order traversal
  b. preorder traversal
  c. postorder traversal

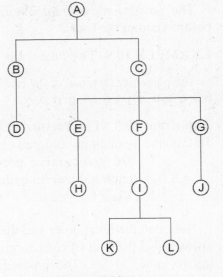

Figure 10.13 A tree

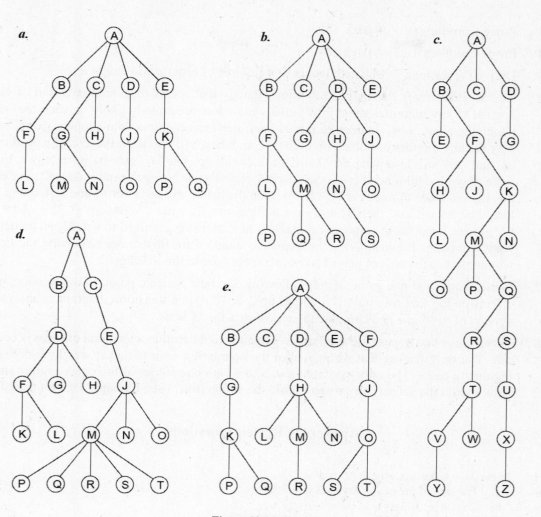

Figure 10.14 A tree

10.7 Which traversals always visit:
   a. the root first?
   b. the left-most node first?
   c. the root last?
   d. the right-most node last?

10.8 The level order traversal follows the pattern as reading a page of English text: left-to-right, row-by-row. Which traversal algorithm follows the pattern of reading vertical columns from left to right?

10.9 Which traversal algorithm is used in the call tree for the solution to Problem 9.32 on page 184?

Problems

10.1 Prove Theorem 10.1 on page 187.

10.2 Prove Theorem 10.2 on page 188.

10.3   Prove Corollary 10.1 on page 188.

10.4   Prove Corollary 10.2 on page 188.

10.5   Derive the formula for the path length of a full tree of order d and height h.

10.6   The *St. Petersburg Paradox* is a betting strategy that seems to guarantee a win. It can be applied to any binomial game in which a win or lose are equally likely on each trial and in which the amount bet on each trial may vary. For example, in a coin-flipping game, bettors may bet any number of dollars on each flip, and they will win what they bet if a head comes up, and they will lose what they bet if a tail comes up. The St. Petersburg strategy is to continue playing until a head comes up, and to double your bet each time it doesn't. For example, the sequence of tosses is {T, T, T, H}, then the bettor will have bet $1 and lost, then $2 and lost, then $4 and lost, then $8 and won, ending up with a net win of –$1 + –$2 + –$4 + $8 = $1. Since a head has to come up eventually, the bettor is guaranteed to win $1, no matter how many coin flips it takes. Draw the transition diagram for this strategy showing the bettor's winnings at each stage of play. Then explain the flaw in this strategy.

10.7   Some people play the game of craps allowing 3 to be a possible point. In this version, player Y wins on the first toss only if it comes up 2 or 12. Use a transition diagram to analyze this version of the game and compute the probability that X wins.

10.8   Seven coins that appear identical are to be tested to determine which one of them is counterfeit. The only feature that distinguishes the counterfeit coin is that it weighs less than the legitimate coins. The only available test is to weigh one subset of the coins against another. How should the subsets be chosen to find the counterfeit? (See Example 10.3 on page 188.)

Answers to Review Questions

10.1   In the *Java inheritance tree:*
   a.   The size of the tree in Java 1.3 is 1730.
   b.   The Object class is at the root of the tree.
   c.   A final class is a leaf node in the Java inheritance tree.

10.2   **a.**   True.
   b.   False: It's one more because the root of the subtree is in the subtree but is not a descendant of itself.
   c.   True
   d.   False
   e.   True
   f.   True
   g.   False
   h.   True
   i.   True
   j.   True
   k.   False
   l.   False
   m.   True
   n.   True

10.3   **a.**   The leaf nodes are L, M, N, H, O, P, Q; the children of node C are G and H; node F has depth 2; the nodes at 3 three are L, M, N, O, P, and Q; the height of the tree is 3; the order of the tree is 4.
   b.   The leaf nodes are C, E, G, O, P, Q, R, and S; node C has no children; node F has depth 2; the nodes at level 3 are L, M, N, and O; the height of the tree is 4; the order of the tree is 4.

    c. The leaf nodes are C, E, G, J, L, N, O, P, W, Y, and Z; node C has no children; node F has depth 2; the nodes at level 3 are H, J, and K; the height of the tree is 9; the order of the tree is 3.

    d. The leaf nodes are G, H, K, L, N, O, P, Q, R, S, and T; the only child node C has is node E; node F has depth 3; the nodes at level 3 are F, G, H, and J; the height of the tree is 5; the order is 5.

    e. The leaf nodes are D, E, L, N, P, Q, R, S, and T; node C has no children; node F has depth 1; the nodes at level 3 are K, L, M, N, and O; the height of the tree is 4; the order of the tree is 5.

10.4   **a.** The ancestors of F are C and A
        b. The descendants of F are I, K, and L.
        c. The nodes in the subtree rooted at F are F, I, K, and L.
        d. The leaf nodes are D, H, J, K, and L.

10.5   **a.** $(3^5 - 1)/2 = 121$ nodes
        b. $(4^4 - 1)/3 = 85$ nodes
        c. $(10^5 - 1)/9 = 11{,}111$ nodes
        d. $(4^{11} - 1)/3 = 1{,}398{,}101$ nodes

10.6   **a.** Level order: a, b, c, d, e, f, g, h, i, j, k, l, m, n, o.
        b. Preorder: a, b, e, i, j, c, f, k, g, h, l, m, n, o, d.
        c. Postorder: i, j, e, b, k, f, g, l, m, n, o, h, c, d, a.

10.7   **a.** The level order and the preorder traversals always visit the root first.
        b. The postorder traversal always visits the left-most node first.
        c. The postorder traversal always visits the root last.
        d. The preorder traversal always visits the right-most node last.

10.8   The preorder traversal follows the pattern of reading by column from left to right.

10.9   The preorder traversal is used in Problem 9.32 on page 184.

Solutions to Problems

10.1   Proof of Theorem 10.1 on page 187:

    If there were no path from a given node x to the root of the tree, then the definition of tree would be violated, because to be an element of the tree, x must be the root of some subtree. If there were more than one path from x back to the root, then x would be an element of more than one distinct subtree. That also violates the definition of tree, which requires subtrees to be disjoint.

10.2   Proof of Theorem 10.2 on page 188:

    If the tree is empty, then its height is $h = -1$ and the number of nodes $n = 0$. In that case, the formula is correct: $n = (d^{(h)+1} - 1)/(d-1) = (d^{(-1)+1} - 1)/(d-1) = (d^0 - 1)/(d-1) = (1-1)/(d-1) = 0$.

    If the tree is a singleton, then its height is $h = 0$ and the number of nodes $n = 1$. In that case, the formula is again correct: $n = (d^{(h)+1} - 1)/(d-1) = (d^{(0)+1} - 1)/(d-1) = (d-1)/(d-1) = 1$.

    Now assume that the formula is correct for any full tree of height $h-1$, where $h \geq 0$. Let T be the full tree of height h. Then by definition, T consists of a root node and a set of d subtrees. And since T is full, each of its d subtrees has height $h-1$. Therefore, by the inductive hypothesis, the number of nodes in each subtree is $n_S = (d^{(h-1)+1} - 1)/(d-1) = (d^h - 1)/(d-1)$. Thus, the total number of nodes in T is

$$n = 1 + (d)(n_S)$$

$$= 1 + d\left(\frac{d^h - 1}{d - 1}\right)$$

$$= \frac{d - 1}{d - 1} + \frac{d^{h+1} - d}{d - 1}$$

$$= \frac{d^{h+1} - 1}{d - 1}$$

Thus, by the Principle of Mathematical Induction (see page 321), the formula must be correct for all full trees of any height.

10.3   Proof of Corollary 10.1 on page 188:

This proof is purely algebraic:

$$n = \frac{d^{h+1} - 1}{d - 1}$$
$$n(d-1) = d^{h+1} - 1$$
$$d^{h+1} = n(d-1) + 1$$
$$= nd - n + 1$$
$$h + 1 = \log_d(nd - n + 1)$$
$$h = \log_d(nd - n + 1) - 1$$

10.4   Proof of Corollary 10.2 on page 188:

Let T be a tree of any order d and any height h. Then T can be embedded into the full tree of the same degree and height. That full tree has exactly $\dfrac{d^{h+1} - 1}{d - 1}$ nodes, so its subtree T has at most that many nodes.

10.5   The path length of a full tree of order d and height h is $\dfrac{d}{(d - 1)^2}[hd^{h+1} - (h+1)d + 1]$. For example, the path length of the full tree on Figure 10.4 on page 188 is 102.

10.6   The tree diagram analysis of the St. Petersburg Paradox is shown in Figure 10.15. The flaw in this strategy is that there is a distinct possibility (i.e., a positive probability) that enough tails could come up in a row to make the required bet exceed the bettor's stake. After n successive tails, the bettor must bet $\$2^n$. For example, if 20 tails come up in a row, the next bet will have to be more than a million dollars!

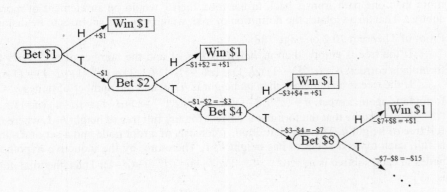

Figure 10.15 Analysis of the St. Petersburg Paradox

10.7   The decision tree for the version of craps where 3 can be a point is shown in Figure 10.16. The probability that X wins this version is 0.5068 or 50.68 percent.

10.8   The decision tree in Figure 10.17 shows all possible outcomes from the algorithm that solves the 7-coin problem.

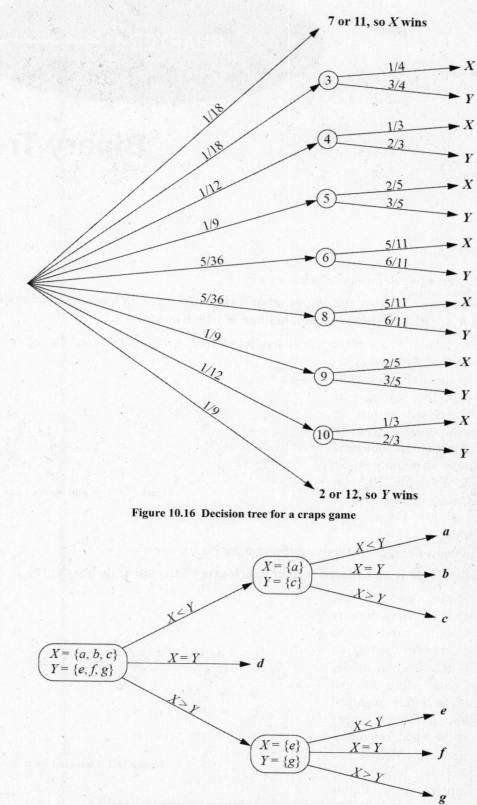

Figure 10.16 Decision tree for a craps game

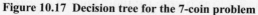

Figure 10.17 Decision tree for the 7-coin problem

CHAPTER 11

Binary Trees

DEFINITIONS

Here is the recursive definition of a binary tree:

> A *binary tree* is either the empty set or a triple $T = (x, L, R)$, where x is a node and L and R are disjoint binary trees, neither of which contains x.

The node x is called the *root* of the tree T, and the subtrees L and R are called the *left subtree* and the *right subtree* of T rooted at x.

Comparing this definition with the one on page 186, it is easy to see that a binary tree is just an ordered tree of order 2. But be aware that an empty left subtree is different from an empty right subtree. (See Example 10.5 on page 191.) Consequently, the two binary trees shown Figure 11.1 are not the same.

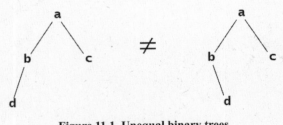

Figure 11.1 Unequal binary trees

Here is an equivalent, nonrecursive definition for binary trees:

> A *binary tree* is an ordered tree in which every internal node has degree 2.

In this simpler definition, the leaf nodes are regarded as dummy nodes whose only purpose is to define the structure of the tree. In applications, the internal nodes would hold data, while the leaf nodes would be either identical empty nodes, a single empty node, or just the null reference. This may seem inefficient and more complex, but it is usually easier to implement. In Figure 11.2, the dummy leaf nodes in the tree on the right are shown as asterisks.

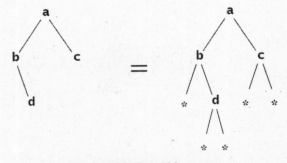

Figure 11.2 Equal binary trees

Except where noted, in this book we adhere to the first definition for binary trees. So some internal nodes may have only one child, either a left child or a right child.

The definitions of the terms *size*, *path*, *length* of a path, *depth* of a node, *level*, *height*, *interior* node, *ancestor*, *descendant*, *subtree*, and *supertree* are the same for binary trees as for general trees. (See page 186.)

EXAMPLE 11.1 Characteristics of a Binary Tree

Figure 11.3 shows a binary tree of size 10 and height 3. Node **a** is its root. The path from node **h** to node **b** has length 2. Node **b** is at level 1, and node **h** is at level 3. **b** is an ancestor of **h**, and **h** is a descendant of **b**. The part in the shaded region is a subtree of size 6 and height 2. Its root is node **b**.

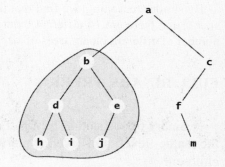

Figure 11.3 A binary tree

COUNTING BINARY TREES

EXAMPLE 11.2 All the Binary Trees of Size 3

There are five different binary trees of size $n = 3$, as shown in Figure 11.4.

Figure 11.4 The five different binary trees of size 3

Four have height 2, and the other one has height 1.

EXAMPLE 11.3 All the Binary Trees of Size 4

There are 14 different binary trees of size $n = 4$, as shown in Figure 11.5.

Figure 11.5 The 14 different binary trees of size 4

Ten have height 3, and the other four have height 2.

EXAMPLE 11.4 All the Binary Trees of Size 5

To find all the binary trees of size 5, apply the recursive definition for binary trees. If **t** is a binary tree of size 5, then it must consist of a root node together with two subtrees the sum of whose sizes equals 4. There are four possibilities: The left subtree contains either 4, 3, 2, 1, or 0 nodes.

First count all the binary trees of size 5 whose left subtree has size 4. From Example 11.3, we see that there are 14 different possibilities for that left subtree. But for each of those 14 choices, there are no other options because the right subtree must be empty. Therefore, there are 14 different binary trees of size 5 whose left subtree has size 4.

Next, count all the binary trees of size 5 whose left subtree has size 3. From Example 11.2, we see that there are five different possibilities for that left subtree. But for each of those five choices, there are no other options because the right subtree must be a singleton. Therefore, there are five different binary trees of size 5 whose left subtree has size 3.

Next, count all the binary trees of size 5 whose left subtree has size 2. There are only two different possibilities for that left subtree. But for each of those two choices, we have the same two different possibilities for the right subtree because it also must have size 2. Therefore, there are $2 \times 2 = 4$ different binary trees of size 5 whose left subtree has size 2.

By similar reasoning, we find that there are five different binary trees of size 5 whose left subtree has size 1, and there are 14 different binary trees of size 5 whose left subtree has size 0. Therefore, the total number of different binary trees of size 5 is $14 + 5 + 4 + 5 + 14 = 42$.

FULL BINARY TREES

A binary tree is said to be *full* if all its leaves are at the same level and every interior node has two children.

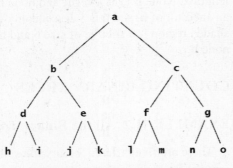

EXAMPLE 11.5 The Full Binary Tree of Height 3

The tree shown in Figure 11.6 is the full binary tree of height 3. Note that it has 15 nodes: 7 interior nodes and 8 leaves.

Figure 11.6 A full binary tree of height 3

Theorem 11.1 The full binary tree of height h has $l = 2^h$ leaves and $m = 2^h - 1$ internal nodes.

Proof: The full binary tree of height $h = 0$ is a single leaf node, so it has $n = 1$ node, which is a leaf. Therefore, since $2^h - 1 = 2^0 - 1 = 1 - 1 = 0$, and $2^h = 2^0 = 1$, the formulas are correct for the case where $h = 0$. More generally, let $h > 0$ and assume (the inductive hypothesis) that the formulas are true for all full binary trees of height less than h. Then consider a full binary tree of height h. Each of its subtrees has height $h - 1$, so we apply the formulas to them: $l_L = l_R = 2^{h-1}$ and $m_L = m_R = 2^{h-1} - 1$. (These are the number of leaves in the left subtree, the number of leaves in the right subtree, the number of internal nodes in the left subtree, and the number of internal nodes in the right subtree, respectively.) Then

$$l = l_L + l_R = 2^{h-1} + 2^{h-1} = 2 \cdot 2^{h-1} = 2^h$$

and

$$m = m_L + m_R + 1 = (2^{h-1} - 1) + (2^{h-1} - 1) + 1 = 2 \cdot 2^{h-1} - 1 = 2^l - 1$$

Therefore, by the (Second) Principle of Mathematical Induction, the formulas must be true for full binary trees of any height $h \geq 0$.

By simply adding the formulas for m and l, we obtain the first corollary.

Corollary 11.1 The full binary tree of height h has a total of $n = 2^{h+1} - 1$ nodes.

By solving the formula $n = 2^{h+1} - 1$ for h, we obtain this corollary:

Corollary 11.2 The full binary tree with n nodes has height $h = \lg(n+1) - 1$.

Note that the formula in Corollary 11.2 is correct even in the special case where $n = 0$: The *empty binary tree* has height $h = \lg(n+1) - 1 = \lg(0+1) - 1 = \lg(1) - 1 = 0 - 1 = -1$.

The next corollary applies Corollary 11.1 together with the fact that the full binary tree of height h has more nodes than any other binary tree of height h.

Corollary 11.3 In any binary tree of height h,
$$h + 1 \leq n \leq 2^{h+1} - 1 \text{ and } \lfloor \lg n \rfloor \leq h \leq n-1$$
where n is the number of its nodes.

IDENTITY, EQUALITY, AND ISOMORPHISM

In a computer, two objects are *identically equal* if they occupy the same space in memory, so they have the same address. In other words, there really only one object, but with two different names. That meaning of equality is reflected in Java by the equality operator. If x and y are references to objects, then the condition (x == y) will be true only if x and y both refer to the same object.

But the normal concept of equality in mathematics is that the two things have the same value. This distinction is handled in Java by the equals() method, defined in the Object class (see Chapter 4) and thus inherited by every class. As defined there, it has the same effect as the equals operator: x.equals(y) means x == y. But that equals() method is intended to be overridden in subclasses so that it will return true not only when the two objects are identically equal, but also when they are separate objects that are "the same" in whatever sense the class designer intends. For example, x.equals(y) could be defined to be true for distinct instances x and y of Point class if they have the same coordinates.

EXAMPLE 11.6 Testing Equality of Strings

```
 1      public class TestStringEquality {
 2        static public void main(String[] args) {
 3          String x = new String("ABCDE");
 4          String y = new String("ABCDE");
 5          System.out.println("x = " + x);
 6          System.out.println("y = " + y);
 7          System.out.println("(x == y) = " + (x == y));
 8          System.out.println("x.equals(y) = " + x.equals(y));
 9        }
10      }
```

The output is:
```
        x = ABCDE
        y = ABCDE
        (x == y) = false
        x.equals(y) = true
```

Here, the two objects x and y (or, more precisely, the two objects that are referenced by the reference variables x and y) are different objects, occupying different memory locations, so they are not identically equal: (x == y) evaluates to false at line 7. But they do both have the same contents, so they are mathematically equal, and x.equals(y) evaluates to true at line 8.

The distinction between identical equality and mathematical equality exists in Java only for reference variables (i.e., only for objects). For all variables of primitive types, the equality operator tests for mathematical equality.

Data structures have both content and structure. So it is possible for two data structures to have equal contents (i.e., have the same contents) but be organized differently. For example, two arrays could both contain the three numbers 22, 44, and 88, but in different orders.

EXAMPLE 11.7 Testing Equality of Arrays

```
1    public class TestArraysEquality {
2      public static void main(String[] args) {
3        int[] x = { 22, 44, 88 };
4        int[] y = { 88, 44, 22 };
5        ch02.ex02.DuplicatingArrays.print(x);
6        ch02.ex02.DuplicatingArrays.print(y);
7        System.out.println("Arrays.equals(x, y) = " + Arrays.equals(x, y));
8        Arrays.sort(x);
9        Arrays.sort(y);
10       ch02.ex02.DuplicatingArrays.print(x);
11       ch02.ex02.DuplicatingArrays.print(y);
12       System.out.println("Arrays.equals(x, y) = " + Arrays.equals(x, y));
13     }
14   }
```

The output it:
```
{22, 44, 88}
{88, 44, 22}
Arrays.equals(x, y) = false
{22, 44, 88}
{22, 44, 88}
Arrays.equals(x, y) = true
```
This shows that the java.util.Arrays.equal() method requires not only the same contents for arrays to be equal, but also in the same order, as would be expected.

Equality is a weaker relation than identity: Identical objects are always equal, but equal objects may not be identical; they could be distinct. Equality of data structures means the same structure and the same contents in the same order.

A weaker kind of reflexive relation is isomorphism. Two data structures are isomorphic if they have the same structure. This concept is used when the "data" part of the data structure is irrelevant.

Two arrays are isomorphic if they have the same length.

Two trees are isomorphic if one tree can be rearranged to match the other. More formally, T_1 is *isomorphic* to T_2 (sometimes written $T_1 \cong T_2$) if there is a one-to-one mapping (an *isomorphism*) between them that preserves parent-child relationship between all nodes.

EXAMPLE 11.8 Isomorphic Trees

As unordered trees, Tree 1 and Tree 2 in Figure 11.7 are isomorphic, but not equal.

However, Tree 3 is not isomorphic to either of the other two trees because it has only three leaves; the other two trees each have four leaves:Tthat's a different structure. That distinction leads fairly easily to a formal deduction that there is no isomorphism between Tree 1 and Tree 3.

As ordered trees, Tree 1 is not isomorphic to Tree 2 because their roots' left-most subtrees have different sizes. The left-most subtree in Tree 1 has three nodes, while that of Tree 2 has only two nodes. That distinction also leads fairly easily to a formal deduction that no isomorphism between Tree 1 and Tree 2 can exist.

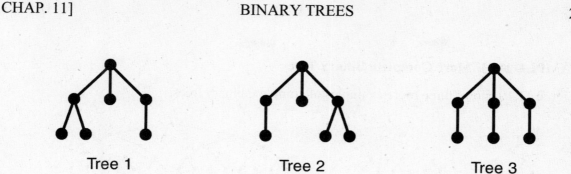

Figure 11.7 Isomorphic and nonisomorphic trees

Binary trees are ordered trees. The order of the two children at each node is part of the structure of the binary tree.

Binary trees are ordered trees. So any isomorphism between binary trees must preserve the order of each node's children.

EXAMPLE 11.9 Nonisomorphic Binary Trees

Figure 11.8 Nonisomorphic binary trees

In Figure 11.8, Binary Tree 1 is not isomorphic to Binary Tree 2, for the same reason that the ordered trees in Example 11.8 are not isomorphic: The subtrees don't all match, as ordered trees. In Tree 1, the root's right child has a left child; but in Tree 1, the root's right child has no (nonempty) left child.

COMPLETE BINARY TREES

A *complete binary tree* is either a full binary tree or one that is full except for a segment of missing leaves on the right side of the bottom level.

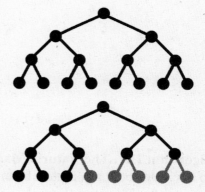

Figure 11.9 Complete binary trees

EXAMPLE 11.10 A Complete Binary Tree of Height 3

The tree shown in Figure 11.9 is complete. It is shown together with the full binary tree from which it was obtained by adding five leaves on the right at level 3.

Theorem 11.2 In a complete binary tree of height h,
$$h + 1 \le n \le 2^{h+1} - 1 \text{ and } h = \lfloor \lg n \rfloor$$
where n is the number of its nodes.

EXAMPLE 11.11 More Complete Binary Trees

Figure 11.10 shows three more examples of complete binary trees.

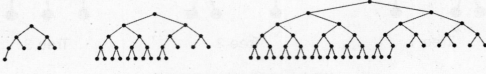

Figure 11.10 Complete binary trees

Complete binary trees are important because they have a simple and natural implementation using ordinary arrays. The *natural mapping* is actually defined for any binary tree: Assign the number 1 to the root; for any node, if i is its number, then assign $2i$ to its left child and $2i+1$ to its right child (if they exist). This assigns a unique positive integer to each node. Then simply store the element at node i in a[i], where a[] is an array.

Complete binary trees are important because of the simple way in which they can be stored in an array. This is achieved by assigning index numbers to the tree nodes by level, as shown in Figure 11.11. The beauty in this natural mapping is the simple way that it allows the array indexes of the children and parent of a node to be computed.

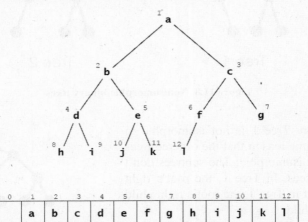

Figure 11.11 The natural mapping of a complete binary tree

Algorithm 11.1 The Natural Mapping of a Complete Binary Tree into an Array

To navigate about a complete binary tree stored by its natural mapping in an array:

1. The parent of the node stored at location i is stored at location $i/2$.
2. The left child of the node stored at location i is stored at location $2i$.
3. The right child of the node stored at location i is stored at location $2i + 1$.

For example, node **e** is stored at index $i = 5$ in the array; its parent node **b** is stored at index $i/2 = 5/2 = 2$, its left child node **j** is stored at location $2i = 2 \cdot 5 = 10$, and its right child node **k** is stored at index $2i + 1 = 2 \cdot 5 + 1 = 11$.

The use of the adjective "complete" should now be clear: The defining property for complete binary trees is precisely the condition that guarantees that the natural mapping will store the tree nodes "completely" in an array with no gaps.

EXAMPLE 11.12 An Incomplete Binary Tree

Figure 11.12 shows the incomplete binary tree from Example 11.1 on page 201. The natural mapping of its nodes into an array leaves some gaps, as shown in Figure 11.13.

Note: Some authors use the term "almost complete binary tree" for a complete binary tree and the term "complete binary tree" for a full binary tree.

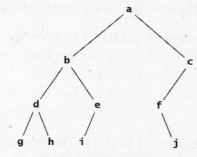

Figure 11.12 A binary tree

0	1	2	3	4	5	6	7	8	9	10	11	12	13
	a	b	c	d	e	f		g	h	i			j

Figure 11.13 The natural mapping of an incomplete binary tree

BINARY TREE TRAVERSAL ALGORITHMS

The three traversal algorithms that are used for general trees (see Chapter 10) apply to binary trees as well: the preorder traversal, the postorder traversal, and the level order traversal. In addition, binary trees support a fourth traversal algorithm: the inorder traversal. These four traversal algorithms are given next.

Algorithm 11.2 The Level Order Traversal of a Binary Tree
To traverse a nonempty binary tree:
1. Initialize a queue.
2. Enqueue the root.
3. Repeat steps 4–7 until the queue is empty.
4. Dequeue a node x from the queue.
5. Visit x.
6. Enqueue the left child of x if it exists.
7. Enqueue the right child of x if it exists.

EXAMPLE 11.13 The Level Order Traversal of a Binary Tree

Figure 11.14 on page 207 shows how the level order traversal looks on the full binary tree of height 3.

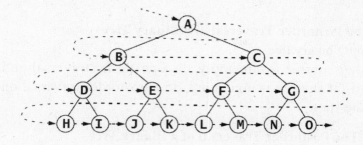

Figure 11.14 The level order traversal of a binary tree

The nodes are visited in the order A, B, C, D, E, F, G, H, I, J, K, L, M, N, O.

Algorithm 11.3   The Preorder Traversal of a Binary Tree

To traverse a nonempty binary tree:

1. Visit the root.
2. If the left subtree is nonempty, do a preorder traversal on it.
3. If the right subtree is nonempty, do a preorder traversal on it.

EXAMPLE 11.14   The Preorder Traversal of a Binary Tree

Figure 11.15 on page 208 shows the preorder traversal on the full binary tree of height 3.

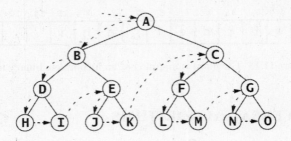

Figure 11.15   The preorder traversal of a binary tree

The nodes are visited in the order A, B, D, H, I, E, J, K, C, F, L, M, G, N, O.

Figure 11.16 shows how the preorder traversal of a binary tree can be obtained by circumnavigating the tree, beginning at the root and visiting each node the first time it is encountered on the left:

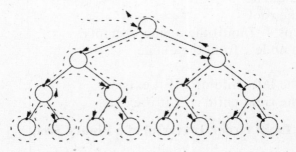

Figure 11.16   The preorder traversal of a binary tree

Algorithm 11.4   The Postorder Traversal of a Binary Tree

To traverse a nonempty binary tree:

1. If the left subtree is nonempty, do a postorder traversal on it.
2. If the right subtree is nonempty, do a postorder traversal on it.
3. Visit the root.

EXAMPLE 11.15   The Postorder Traversal of a Binary Tree

Figure 11.17 shows the postorder traversal looks on the full binary tree of height 3.

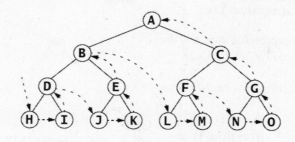

Figure 11.17 The postorder traversal of a binary tree

The nodes are visited in the order **H, I, D, J, K, E, B, L, M, F, N, O, G, C, A**.

The preorder traversal visits the root first and the postorder traversal visits the root last. This suggests a third alternative for binary trees: Visit the root in between the traversals of the two subtrees. That is called the *inorder traversal*.

Algorithm 11.5   The Inorder Traversal of a Binary Tree
To traverse a nonempty binary tree:
1.   If the left subtree is nonempty, do a preorder traversal on it.
2.   Visit the root.
3.   If the right subtree is nonempty, do a preorder traversal on it.

EXAMPLE 11.16 The Inorder Traversal of a Binary Tree

Figure 11.18 shows how the inorder traversal looks on the full binary tree of height 3.

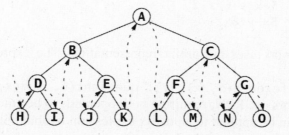

Figure 11.18 The inorder traversal of a binary tree

The nodes are visited in the order **H, D, I, B, J, E, K, A, L, F, M, C, N, G, O**.

EXPRESSION TREES

An *arithmetic expression* such as (5 - x)*y + 6/(x + z) is a combination of *arithmetic operators* (+, -, *, /, etc.), *operands* (5, x, y, 6, z, etc.), and parentheses to override the precedence of operations. Each expression can be represented by a unique binary tree whose structure is determined by the precedence of operations in the expression. Such a tree is called an *expression tree*.

EXAMPLE 11.17 An Expression Tree

Figure 11.19 shows the expression tree for the expression $(5 - x)*y + 6/(x + z)$.

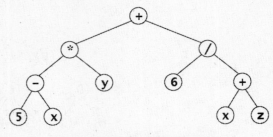

Here is a recursive algorithm for building an expression tree:

Algorithm 11.6 Build an Expression Tree
The expression tree for a given expression can be built recursively from the following rules:

Figure 11.19 An expression tree

1. The expression tree for a single operand is a single root node that contains it.
2. If E_1 and E_2 are expressions represented by expression trees T_1 and T_2, and if *op* is an operator, then the expression tree for the expression E_1 *op* E_2 is the tree with root node containing *op* and subtrees T_1 and T_2.

An expression has three representations, depending upon which traversal algorithm is used to traverse its tree. The preorder traversal produces the *prefix representation*, the inorder traversal produces the *infix representation*, and the postorder traversal produces the *postfix representation* of the expression. The postfix representation is also called *reverse Polish notation* or *RPN*. These are outlined on page 109.

EXAMPLE 11.18 The Three Representations of an Expression

The three representations for the expression in Example 11.17 are:

Prefix: +*-5xy/6+xz
Infix: 5-x*y+6/x+z
Postfix (RPN):   5x-y*6xz+/+

Ordinary function syntax uses the prefix representation. The expression in Example 11.17 could be evaluated as

    sum(product(difference(5, x), y), quotient(6, sum(x, z)))

Some scientific calculators use RPN, requiring both operands to be entered before the operator.
The next algorithm can be applied to a postfix expression to obtain its value.

Algorithm 11.7 Evaluating an Expression from Its Postfix Representation
To evaluate an expression represented in postfix, scan the representation from left to right:

1. Create a stack for operands.
2. Repeat steps 3–9 until the end of representation is reached.
3. Read the next token *t* from the representation.
4. If it is an operand, push its value onto the stack.
5. Otherwise, do steps 6–9:
6. Pop *a* from the stack.
7. Pop *b* from the stack.
8. Evaluate $c = a\ t\ b$.
9. Push *c* onto the stack.
10. Return the top element on the stack.

EXAMPLE 11.19 Evaluating an Expression from Its Postfix Representation

Figure 11.20 shows the evaluation of the expression in Example 11.18 using 2 for x, 3 for y, and 1 for z:

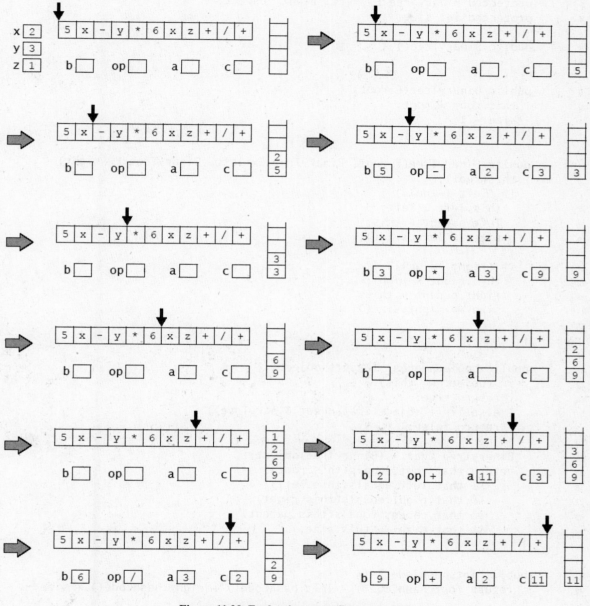

Figure 11.20 Evaluating a postfix expression

A `BinaryTree` CLASS

Here is a class for binary trees that directly implements the recursive definition. (See page 200.) By extending the `AbstractCollection` class, it remains consistent with the Java Collections Framework. (See Chapter 4.)

EXAMPLE 11.20 A BinaryTree Class

```
1    public class BinaryTree<E> extends AbstractCollection {
2      protected E root;
3      protected BinaryTree<E> left, right, parent;
4      protected int size;
5
6      public BinaryTree() {
7      }
8
9      public BinaryTree(E root) {
10       this.root = root;
11       size = 1;
12     }
13
14     public BinaryTree(E root, BinaryTree<E> left, BinaryTree<E> right) {
15       this(root);
16       if (left != null) {
17         this.left = left;
18         left.parent = this;
19         size += left.size();
20       }
21       if (right != null) {
22         this.right = right;
23         right.parent = this;
24         size += right.size();
25       }
26     }
27
28     public boolean equals(Object object) {
29       if (object == this) {
30         return true;
31       } else if (!(object instanceof BinaryTree)) {
32         return false;
33       }
34       BinaryTree that = (BinaryTree)object;
35       return that.root.equals(this.root)
36           && that.left.equals(this.left)
37           && that.right.equals(this.right)
38           && that.parent.equals(this.parent)
39           && that.size == this.size;
40     }
41
42     public int hashCode() {
43       return root.hashCode() + left.hashCode() + right.hashCode() + size;
44     }
45
46     public int size() {
47       return size;
48     }
49
50     public Iterator iterator() {
51       return new java.util.Iterator() { // anonymous inner class
52         private boolean rootDone;
53         private Iterator lIt, rIt;  // child iterators
```

```
54          public boolean hasNext() {
55            return !rootDone || lIt != null && lIt.hasNext()
56                             || rIt != null && rIt.hasNext();
57          }
58          public Object next() {
59            if (rootDone) {
60              if (lIt != null && lIt.hasNext()) {
61                return lIt.next();
62              }
63              if (rIt != null && rIt.hasNext()) {
64                return rIt.next();
65              }
66              return null;
67            }
68            if (left != null) {
69              lIt = left.iterator();
70            }
71            if (right != null) {
72              rIt = right.iterator();
73            }
74            rootDone = true;
75            return root;
76          }
77          public void remove() {
78            throw new UnsupportedOperationException();
79          }
80        };
81      }
82    }
```

The `java.util.AbstractCollection` class requires the four methods that are defined here: `equals()`, `hashCode()`, `iterator()`, and `size()`.[1]

The `iterator()` method overrides the empty version that is defined in the `AbstractCollection` class. Its job is to build an iterator object that can traverse its `BinaryTree` object. To do that, it creates its own anonymous inner `Iterator` class using the Java `return new` construct at line 47. The body of this anonymous class is defined between the braces that immediately follow the invocation of the constructor `Iterator()`. Note that this block must be followed by a semicolon because it is actually the end of the `return` statement. The complete construct looks like a method definition, but it is not. It really is a complete class definition embedded within a `return` statement.

To return an `Iterator` object, this anonymous class must implement the `Iterator` interface. (See page 77.) This requires definitions for the three methods

```
public boolean hasNext()  ...
public Object next()  ...
public void remove()  ...
```

This implementation is recursive. The `hasNext()` method invokes the `hasNext()` methods of iterators on the two subtrees, and the `next()` method invokes the `next()` methods of those two iterators, named `lIt` and `rIt`. The other local variable is a flag named `rootDone` that keeps track of whether the root object has been visited yet by the iterator.

The `hasNext()` method returns `true` unless all three parts of the tree have been visited: the root, the left subtree, and the right subtree. It does that by using the `lIt` and `rIt` iterators recursively.

---

1. Actually, the `equals()` and `hashCode()` methods are defined in the `Object` class and do not have to be overridden.

The next() method also uses the lIt and rIt iterators recursively. If the root has already been visited, then the iterator visits the next node in the left subtree if there are any, and otherwise visits the next node in the right subtree if there are any. If the root has not yet been visited, then this must be the first call to the iterator on that particular subtree, so it initializes the lIt and rIt iterators, sets the rootDone flag, and returns the root.

The remove() method is not implemented because there is no simple way to remove an internal node from a binary tree.

EXAMPLE 11.21 Testing the BinaryTree Class

```
1   public class TestBinaryTree {
2     static public void main(String[] args) {
3       BinaryTree<String> e = new BinaryTree<String>("E");
4       BinaryTree<String> g = new BinaryTree<String>("G");
5       BinaryTree<String> h = new BinaryTree<String>("H");
6       BinaryTree<String> i = new BinaryTree<String>("I");
7       BinaryTree<String> d = new BinaryTree<String>("D", null, g);
8       BinaryTree<String> f = new BinaryTree<String>("F", h, i);
9       BinaryTree<String> b = new BinaryTree<String>("B", d, e);
10      BinaryTree<String> c = new BinaryTree<String>("C", f, null);
11      BinaryTree<String> tree = new BinaryTree<String>("A", b, c);
12      System.out.printf("tree: %s", tree);
13    }
14  }
```

The output is:

```
tree: [A, B, D, G, E, C, F, H, I]
```

The program creates the binary tree shown in Figure 11.21 and then indirectly invokes its toString() method that it inherits from the AbstractCollections class.

Figure 11.21 shows two views of the same tree. The larger view shows all the details, representing each object reference with an arrow.

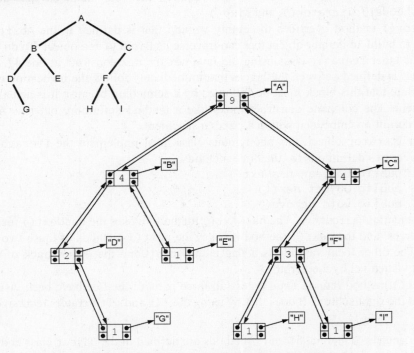

Figure 11.21 The binary tree constructed in Example 11.21

By extending the `AbstractCollection` class, the `BinaryTree` class automatically inherits these methods that are defined by using the `iterator()` and `size()` methods:

```
public boolean   isEmpty()
public boolean   contains(Object object)
public Object[]  toArray()
public Object[]  toArray(Object[] objects)
public String    toString()
public boolean   add(Object object)
public boolean   addAll(Collection collection)
public void      clear()
public boolean   containsAll(Collection collection)
public boolean   remove(Object object)
public boolean   removeAll(Collection collection)
public boolean   retainAll(Collection collection)
```

However, the mutating methods will throw an `UnsupportedOperationException` because they invoke other methods that are not implemented, namely the `add()` and the `Iterator.remove()` methods.

EXAMPLE 11.22 Testing the `contains()` Method on a Binary Tree

This example builds the same tree as the one in Example 11.21 and then tests the `contains()` method on it and its subtrees:

```
1    public class TestContains {
2    static public void main(String[] args) {
3      BinaryTree<String> e = new BinaryTree<String>("E");
4      BinaryTree<String> g = new BinaryTree<String>("G");
5      BinaryTree<String> h = new BinaryTree<String>("H");
6      BinaryTree<String> i = new BinaryTree<String>("I");
7      BinaryTree<String> d = new BinaryTree<String>("D", null, g);
8      BinaryTree<String> f = new BinaryTree<String>("F", h, i);
9      BinaryTree<String> b = new BinaryTree<String>("B", d, e);
10     BinaryTree<String> c = new BinaryTree<String>("C", f, null);
11     BinaryTree<String> a = new BinaryTree<String>("A", b, c);
12     System.out.printf("a: %s%n", a);
13     System.out.println("a.contains(\"H\") = " + a.contains("H"));
14     System.out.printf("b: %s%n", b);
15     System.out.println("b.contains(\"H\") = " + b.contains("H"));
16     System.out.printf("c: %s%n", c);
17     System.out.println("c.contains(\"H\") = " + c.contains("H"));
18    }
19   }
```

The output is:

```
a: [A, B, D, G, E, C, F, H, I]
a.contains("H") = true
b: [B, D, G, E]
b.contains("H") = false
c: [C, F, H, I]
c.contains("H") = true
```

The subtrees b and c are shown in Figure 11.22. The tree a contains the element H. The subtree b does not contain the element H. The subtree c does contain the element H.

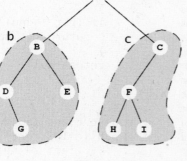

Figure 11.22

IMPLEMENTATIONS OF THE TRAVERSAL ALGORITHMS

The iterator that is returned by the `iterator()` method follows the preorder traversal algorithm (Algorithm 11.3 on page 208) to traverse the binary tree. The following modification of the `BinaryTree` class implements all four of the binary tree traversal algorithms.

EXAMPLE 11.23 Implementing the Four Traversal Algorithms

```
1   public class BinaryTree<E> extends AbstractCollection {
2     //  insert lines 2-49 from Example 11.20 on page 212
50    public Iterator iterator() {
51      return new PreOrder();
52    }
53
54    abstract public class BinaryTreeIterator implements Iterator {
55      protected boolean rootDone;
56      protected Iterator lIt, rIt;  // child iterators
57      public boolean hasNext() {
58        return !rootDone || lIt != null && lIt.hasNext()
59                          || rIt != null && rIt.hasNext();
60      }
61      abstract public Object next();
62      public void remove() {
63        throw new UnsupportedOperationException();
64      }
65    }
66
67    public class PreOrder extends BinaryTreeIterator {
68      public PreOrder() {
69        if (left != null) {
70          lIt = left.new PreOrder();
71        }
72        if (right != null) {
73          rIt = right.new PreOrder();
74        }
75      }
76      public Object next() {
77        if (!rootDone) {
78          rootDone = true;
79          return root;
80        }
81        if (lIt != null && lIt.hasNext()) {
82          return lIt.next();
83        }
84        if (rIt != null && rIt.hasNext()) {
85          return rIt.next();
86        }
87        return null;
88      }
89    }
90
91    public class InOrder extends BinaryTreeIterator {
92      public InOrder() {
93        if (left != null) {
94          lIt = left.new InOrder();
95        }
```

```
 96           if (right != null) {
 97             rIt = right.new InOrder();
 98           }
 99         }
100       public Object next() {
101         if (lIt != null && lIt.hasNext()) {
102           return lIt.next();
103         }
104         if (!rootDone) {
105           rootDone = true;
106           return root;
107         }
108         if (rIt != null && rIt.hasNext()) {
109           return rIt.next();
110         }
111         return null;
112       }
113     }
114
115     public class PostOrder extends BinaryTreeIterator {
116       public PostOrder() {
117         if (left != null) {
118           lIt = left.new PostOrder();
119         }
120         if (right != null) {
121           rIt = right.new PostOrder();
122         }
123       }
124       public Object next() {
125         if (lIt != null && lIt.hasNext()) {
126           return lIt.next();
127         }
128         if (rIt != null && rIt.hasNext()) {
129           return rIt.next();
130         }
131         if (!rootDone) {
132           rootDone = true;
133           return root;
134         }
135         return null;
136       }
137     }
138
139     public class LevelOrder extends BinaryTreeIterator {
140       Queue<BinaryTree<E>> queue = new ArrayDeque<BinaryTree<E>>();
141       public boolean hasNext() {
142         return (!rootDone || !queue.isEmpty());
143       }
144       public Object next() {
145         if (!rootDone) {
146           if (left != null) {
147             queue.add(left);
148           }
149           if (right != null) {
150             queue.add(right);
151           }
```

```
152          rootDone = true;
153          return root;
154        }
155        if (!queue.isEmpty()) {
156          BinaryTree<E> tree = queue.remove();
157          if (tree.left != null) {
158            queue.add(tree.left);
159          }
160          if (tree.right != null) {
161            queue.add(tree.right);
162          }
163          return tree.root;
164        }
165        return null;
166      }
167    }
168  }
```

At line 64 we define an abstract inner class named `BinaryTreeIterator`. This serves as a base class for all four of the concrete iterator classes. It declares the same three fields (`rootDone`, `rIt`, and `lIt`) as the anonymous iterator class defined previously.

The `hasNext()` and `remove()` methods are implemented (at lines 57 and 62) the same way the abstract `Iterator` class was done in the anonymous iterator class. But the `next()` method is declared `abstract` because each of the four traversal algorithms has a different implementation of it.

The `PreOrder` class defines the `lIt` and `rIt` iterators to be `PreOrder` iterators in its constructor to ensure that the recursive traversal follows the preorder traversal algorithm. That algorithm (Algorithm 11.3 on page 208) says to visit the root first, and then apply the same algorithm recursively to the left subtree and then to the right subtree. The three `if` statements do that at lies 77–86. The only differences between the `PreOrder`, `InOrder`, and `PostOrder` classes are their definitions of the recursive `rIt` and `lIt` iterators in the constructors and the order of those three `if` statements in the `next()` methods. For the `InOrder` class, the order visits the root between the two recursive traversals. For the `PostOrder` class, the order visits the root after the two recursive traversals. ("Pre" means before, "in" means between, and "post" means after.)

The `LevelOrder` traversal class is significantly different from the other three. Instead of being recursive, it uses a queue. (See Algorithm 11.5 on page 209.)

EXAMPLE 11.24 Testing the Traversal Algorithms

```
1   public class TestIterators {
2     public static void main(String[] args) {
3       BinaryTree<String> e = new BinaryTree<String>("E");
4       BinaryTree<String> g = new BinaryTree<String>("G");
5       BinaryTree<String> h = new BinaryTree<String>("H");
6       BinaryTree<String> i = new BinaryTree<String>("I");
7       BinaryTree<String> d = new BinaryTree<String>("D",null,g);
8       BinaryTree<String> f = new BinaryTree<String>("F",h,i);
9       BinaryTree<String> b = new BinaryTree<String>("B",d,e);
10      BinaryTree<String> c = new BinaryTree<String>("C",f,null);
11      BinaryTree<String> tree = new BinaryTree<String>("A",b,c);
12      System.out.println("tree = " + tree);
13      java.util.Iterator it;
14      System.out.print("PreOrder Traversal:   ");
15      for (it = tree.new PreOrder(); it.hasNext(); ) {
16        System.out.print(it.next() + " ");
17      }
18      System.out.print("\nInOrder Traversal:    ");
```

```
19        for (it = tree.new InOrder(); it.hasNext(); ) {
20          System.out.print(it.next() + " ");
21        }
22        System.out.print("\nPostOrder Traversal:  ");
23        for (it = tree.new PostOrder(); it.hasNext(); ) {
24          System.out.print(it.next() + " ");
25        }
26        System.out.print("\nLevelOrder Traversal: ");
27        for (it = tree.new LevelOrder(); it.hasNext(); ) {
28          System.out.print(it.next() + " ");
29        }
30        System.out.println();
31      }
32    }
```

The output is:

```
tree = [A, B, D, G, E, C, F, H, I]
PreOrder Traversal:   A B D G E C F H I
InOrder Traversal:    D G B E A H F I C
PostOrder Traversal:  G D E B H I F C A
LevelOrder Traversal: A B C D E F G H I
```

Each of the four iterators traverses the tree according to the algorithm that it implements.

FORESTS

A *forest* is a sequence of disjoint ordered trees.

EXAMPLE 11.25 A Forest

Figure 11.23 shows a forest that consists of three trees.

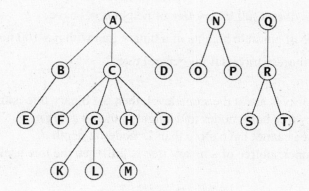

Figure 11.23 A forest

The following algorithm shows how a forest can be represented by a single binary tree.

Algorithm 11.8 The Natural Mapping of a Forest into a Binary Tree

1. Map the root of the first tree into the root of the binary tree.
2. If node X maps into X' and node Y is the first child of X, then map Y into the left child of X'.
3. If node X maps into X' and node Z is the sibling of X, then map Z into the right child of X'. The roots of the trees themselves are considered siblings.

EXAMPLE 11.26 Mapping a Forest into a Binary Tree

Figure 11.24 is the mapping of the forest shown in Example 11.25. For example, in the original forest, C has oldest child F and next sibling D. In the corresponding binary tree, C has left child F and right child D.

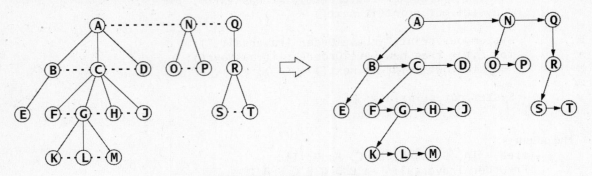

Figure 11.24 The natural mapping of a forest into a binary tree

Review Questions

11.1   How many leaf nodes does the full binary tree of height $h = 3$ have?

11.2   How many internal nodes does the full binary tree of height $h = 3$ have?

11.3   How many nodes does the full binary tree of height $h = 3$ have?

11.4   How many leaf nodes does a full binary tree of height $h = 9$ have?

11.5   How many internal nodes does a full binary tree of height $h = 9$ have?

11.6   How many nodes does a full binary tree of height $h = 9$ have?

11.7   What is the range of possible heights of a binary tree with $n = 100$ nodes?

11.8   Why is there no inorder traversal for general trees?

11.9   True or false:
    a. If all of its leaves are at the same level, then the binary tree is full.
    b. If the binary tree has n nodes and height h, then $h \geq \lfloor \lg n \rfloor$.
    c. A binary tree cannot have more than 2^d nodes at depth d.
    d. If every proper subtree of a binary tree is full, then the tree itself must also be full.

Problems

11.1   For each of the binary trees in Figure 11.25 on page 221, draw the equivalent version that satisfies the second definition, namely that every internal node has two children.

11.2   Give the order of visitation of the binary tree shown in Figure 11.26 using the specified traversal algorithm:
    a. the level order traversal
    b. the preorder traversal
    c. the inorder traversal
    d. the postorder traversal

a.

b.

c.

d.

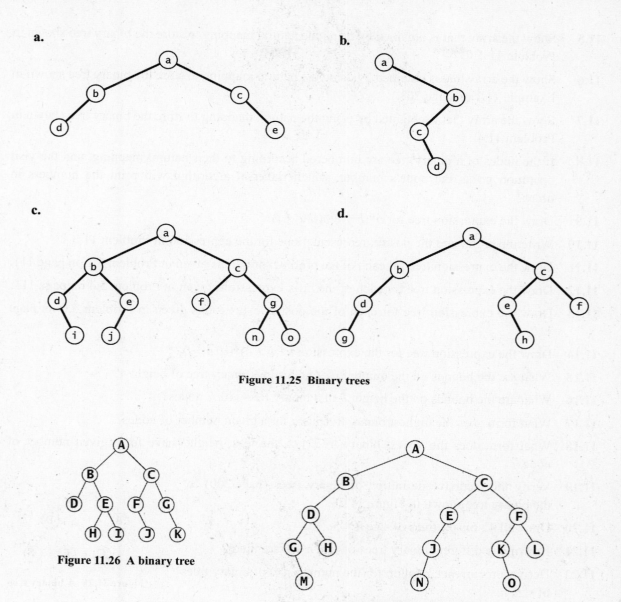

Figure 11.25 Binary trees

Figure 11.26 A binary tree

Figure 11.27 A binary tree

11.3   Give the order of visitation of the binary tree of size 10 shown in Example 11.1 on page 201
using:
    a. the level order traversal
    b. the preorder traversal
    c. the inorder traversal
    d. the postorder traversal

11.4   Give the order of visitation of the binary tree shown in Figure 11.27 using:
    a. the level order traversal
    b. the preorder traversal
    c. the inorder traversal
    d. the postorder traversal

11.5   Show the array that is obtained by using the natural mapping to store the binary tree shown in Problem 11.1.

11.6   Show the array that is obtained by using the natural mapping to store the binary tree shown in Example 11.1 on page 201.

11.7   Show the array that is obtained by using the natural mapping to store the binary tree shown in Problem 11.4.

11.8   If the nodes of a binary tree are numbered according to their natural mapping, and the visit operation prints the node's number, which traversal algorithm will print the numbers in order?

11.9   Draw the expression tree for $a*(b + c)*(d*e + f)$.

11.10 Write the prefix and the postfix representations for the expression in Problem 11.8.

11.11 Draw the expression tree for each of the prefix expressions given in Problem 5.2 on page 111.

11.12 Draw the expression tree for each of the infix expressions given in Problem 5.4 on page 111.

11.13 Draw the expression tree for each of the postfix expressions given in Problem 5.6 on page 111.

11.14 Draw the expression tree for the expression $a*(b + c)*(d*e + f)$.

11.15 What are the bounds on the number n of nodes in a binary tree of height 4?

11.16 What are the bounds on the height h of a binary tree with 7 nodes?

11.17 What form does the highest binary tree have for a given number of nodes?

11.18 What form does the lowest binary tree (i.e., the least height) have for a given number of nodes?

11.19 Verify the recursive definition of binary trees (page 200) for the binary tree shown in Figure 11.28.

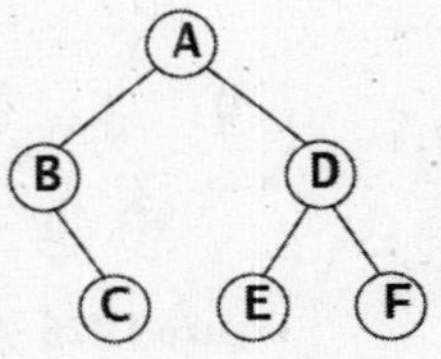

11.20 Draw all 42 binary trees of size $n = 5$.

11.21 How many different binary trees of size $n = 6$ are there?

11.22 Derive a recurrence relation for the number $f(n)$ of binary trees of size n.

Figure 11.28 A binary tree

11.23 Show that, for all $n \le 8$, the function $f(n)$ derived in Problem 11.22 produces the same sequence as the following explicit formula

$$f(n) = \frac{\binom{2n}{n}}{n + 1} = \frac{(2n)!}{n!(n + 1)!} \quad \frac{(2n)(2n - 1)(2n - 2) \cdots (2n + 3)(2n + 2)}{(n)(n - 1)(n - 2)(n - 3) \cdots (2)(1)}$$

For example,

$$f(4) = \frac{\binom{8}{4}}{5} = \frac{8!}{4!5!} = \frac{(8)(7)(6)}{(4)(3)(2)(1)} = \frac{(8)(7)}{4} = 14$$

11.24 Prove Corollary 11.3 on page 203.

11.25 Prove Theorem 11.2 on page 205.

11.26 Draw the forest that is represented by the binary tree shown in Figure 11.29.

11.27 Derive an explicit formula for the number $f(h)$ of complete binary trees of height h.

11.28 Derive an explicit formula for the number $f(h)$ of full binary trees of height h.

11.29 Implement the each of the following methods for the BinaryTree class:

    a.   `public int leaves();`
           `// returns the number of leaves in this tree`

    b.   `public int height();`
           `// returns the height of this tree`

    c.   `public int level(Object object);`
           `// returns -1 if the given object is not in this tree;`
           `// otherwise, returns its level in this tree;`

    d.   `public void reflect();`
           `// swaps the children of each node in this tree`

    e.   `public void defoliate();`
           `// removes all the leaves from this tree`

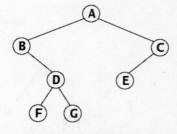

Figure 11.29 A binary tree

Answers to Review Questions

11.1 The full binary tree of height 3 has $l = 2^3 = 8$ leaves.

11.2 The full binary tree of height 3 has $m = 2^3 - 1 = 7$ internal nodes.

11.3 The full binary tree of height 3 has $n = 2^{3+1} - 1 = 2^4 - 1 = 16 - 1 = 15$ nodes.

11.4 The full binary tree of height 9 has $l = 2^9 = 512$ leaves.

11.5 The full binary tree of height 9 has $m = 2^9 - 1 = 512 - 1 = 511$ internal nodes.

11.6 The full binary tree of height 9 has $n = 2^{9+1} - 1 = 2^{10} - 1 = 1024 - 1 = 1023$ nodes.

11.7 By Corollary 11.3, in any binary tree: $\lfloor \lg n \rfloor \le h \le n-1$. Thus in a binary tree with 100 nodes $\lfloor \lg 100 \rfloor \le h \le 100-1 = 99$. Since $\lfloor \lg 100 \rfloor = \lfloor (\log 100)/(\log 2) \rfloor = \lfloor 6.6 \rfloor = 6$, it follows that the height must be between 6 and 99, inclusive: $6 \le h \le 99$.

11.8 The inorder traversal algorithm for binary trees recursively visits the root in between traversing the left and right subtrees. This presumes the existence of exactly two (possibly empty) subtrees at every (nonempty) node. In general trees, a node may have any number of subtrees, so there is no simple algorithmic way to generalize the inorder traversal.

11.9   **a.** True
       b. True
       c. True
       d. False

Solutions to Problems

11.1 The equivalent trees are shown in Figure 11.30.

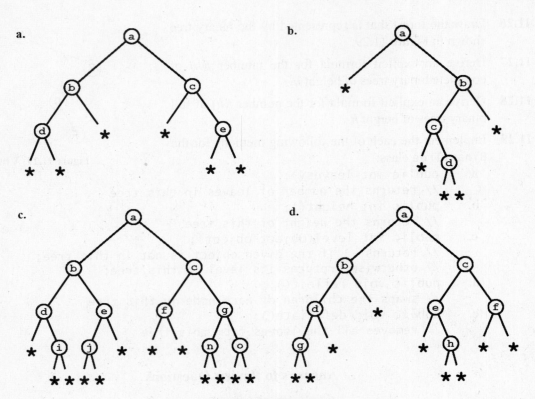

Figure 11.30 Binary trees

11.2   The order of visitation in the binary tree traversal:
    a. Level order: **A, B, C, D, E, F, G, H, I, J, K**
    b. Preorder: **A, B, D, E, H, I, C, F, J, G, K**
    c. Inorder: **D, B, H, E, I, A, F, J, C, G, K**
    d. Postorder: **D, H, I, E, B, J, F, K, G, C, A**

11.3   The order of visitation in the binary tree traversal:
    a. Level order traversal: **A, B, C, D, E, F, H, I, J, M**
    b. Preorder traversal: **A, B, D, H, I, E, J, C, F, M**
    c. Inorder traversal: **H, D, I, B, J, E, A, F, M, C**
    d. Postorder traversal: **H, I, D, J, E, B, M, F, C, A**

11.4   The order of visitation in the binary tree traversal:
    a. Level order traversal: **A, B, C, D, E, F, G, H, J, K, L, M, N, O**
    b. Preorder traversal: **A, B, D, G, M, H, C, E, J, N, F, K, O, L**
    c. Inorder traversal: **G, M, D, H, B, A, N, J, E, C, K, O, F, L**
    d. Postorder traversal: **M, G, H, D, B, N, J, E, O, K, L, F, C, A**

11.5   The natural mapping of the specified binary tree is shown in Figure 11.31.

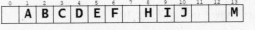

Figure 11.31 An array

11.6   The natural mapping of the specified binary tree is shown in Figure 11.32.

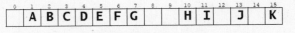

Figure 11.32 An array

11.7   The natural mapping of the specified binary tree is shown in Figure 11.33.

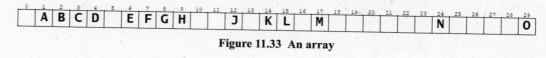

Figure 11.33 An array

11.8   The level order traversal will print the numbers from the natural mapping in order.

11.9   The expression tree for $a*(b + c)*(d*e + f)$ is shown in Figure 11.34.

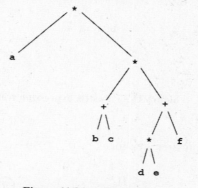

Figure 11.34 A binary tree

11.10 The prefix expression is $*a*+bc+*def$. The postfix expression is $*abc+de*f+**$.

11.11 Figure 11.35 shows the expression tree for each of the prefix expressions given in Problem 5.2 on page 111.

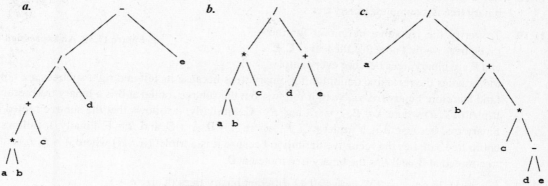

Figure 11.35 Prefix expression trees

11.12 Figure 11.36 shows the expression tree for each of the infix expressions given in Problem 5.4 on page 111.

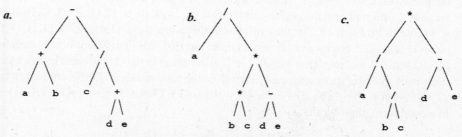

Figure 11.36 Infix expression trees

11.13 Figure 11.37 shows the expression tree for each of the postfix expressions given in Problem 5.6 on page 111.

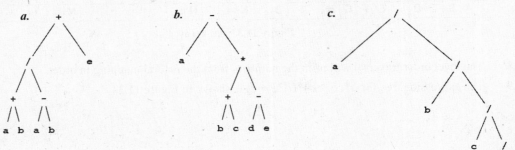

Figure 11.37 Postfix expression trees

11.14 Figure 11.38 shows the expression tree for $a*(b+c)*(d*e+f)$ is:

11.15 In a binary tree of height $h = 4$, $5 \le n \le 31$.

11.16 In a binary tree with $n = 7$ nodes, $2 \le h \le 6$.

11.17 For a given number of nodes, the highest binary tree is a linear sequence.

11.18 For a given number of nodes, the lowest binary tree is a complete binary tree.

11.19 To verify the recursive definition for the given tree, we first note that the leaves **C**, **E**, and **F** are binary trees because every single-

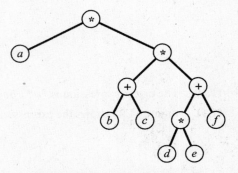

Figure 11.38 An expression tree

ton satisfies the recursive definition for binary trees because its left and right subtrees are both empty (and therefore binary trees). Next, it follows that the subtree rooted at **B** is a binary tree because it is a triplet (X,L,R) where $X = $ **B**, $L = \varnothing$, and $R = $ **C**. Similarly, it follows that the subtree rooted at **D** is a binary tree because it is a triplet (X,L,R) where $X = $ **D**, $L = $ **E**, and $R = $ **F**. Finally, it follows that the entire tree satisfies the recursive definition because it is a triplet (X,L,R) where $X = $ **A**, L is the binary tree rooted at **B**, and L is the binary tree rooted at **D**.

11.20 Figure 11.39 on page 227 shows all 42 different binary trees of size $n = 5$.

11.21 There are 132 different binary trees of size 6: $1 \cdot 42 + 1 \cdot 14 + 2 \cdot 5 + 5 \cdot 2 + 14 \cdot 1 + 42 \cdot 1 = 132$.

11.22 A nonempty binary tree consists of a root X, a left subtree L, and a right subtree R. Let n be the size of the binary tree, let $n_L = |L| = $ the size of L, and $n_R = |R| = $ the size of R. Then $n = 1 + n_L + n_R$. So there are only n different possible values for the pair (n_L, n_R): $(0, n-1)$, $(1, n-2)$, ..., $(n-1,0)$. For example, if $n = 6$ (as in Problem 11.21), the only possibilities are $(0,5)$, $(1,4)$, $(2,3)$, $(3,2)$, $(4,1)$, or $(5,0)$. In the $(0, n-1)$ case, L is empty and $|R| = n-1$; there are $f(0) \cdot f(n-1)$ different binary trees in that case. In the $(1, n-2)$ case, L is a singleton and $|R| = n-2$; there are $f(1) \cdot f(n-2)$ different binary trees in that case. The same principle applies to each case. Therefore the total number of different binary trees of size n is

$$f(n) = 1 \cdot f(n-1) + 1 \cdot f(n-2) + 2 \cdot f(n-3) + 5 \cdot f(n-4) + 14 \cdot f(n-5) + \cdots + f(i-1) \cdot f(n-i) + \cdots + f(n-1) \cdot 1$$

In closed form, the formula is

$$f(n) = \sum_{i=1}^{n} f(i-1) \cdot f(n-i)$$

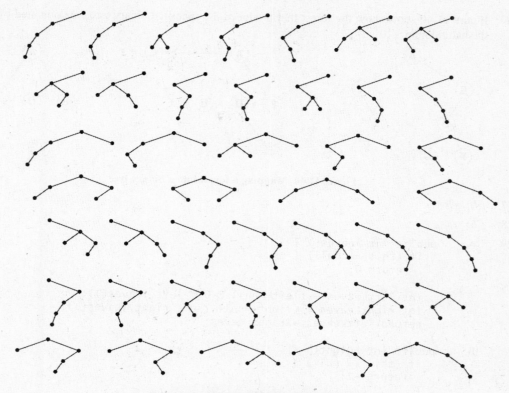

Figure 11.39 The 42 binary trees of size 5

11.23   These are called the *Catalan numbers*:

n	$\binom{2n}{n}$	$n+1$	$\dfrac{\binom{2n}{n}}{(n+1)}$	$\sum f(i-1) \cdot f(n-i)$
0	1	1	1	1
1	2	2	1	$1 \cdot 1 = 1$
2	6	3	2	$1 \cdot 1 + 1 \cdot 1 = 2$
3	20	4	5	$1 \cdot 2 + 1 \cdot 1 + 2 \cdot 1 = 5$
4	70	5	14	$1 \cdot 5 + 1 \cdot 2 + 2 \cdot 1 + 5 \cdot 1 = 14$
5	252	6	42	$1 \cdot 14 + 1 \cdot 5 + 2 \cdot 2 + 5 \cdot 1 + 14 \cdot 1 = 42$
6	924	7	132	$1 \cdot 42 + 1 \cdot 14 + 2 \cdot 5 + 5 \cdot 2 + 14 \cdot 1 + 42 \cdot 1 = 132$
7	3432	8	429	$1 \cdot 132 + 1 \cdot 42 + 2 \cdot 14 + 5 \cdot 5 + 14 \cdot 2 + 42 \cdot 1 + 132 \cdot 1 = 429$

Table 11.1 Catalan numbers

11.24   For a given height $h > 0$, the binary tree with the most nodes is the full binary tree. Corollary 11.1 on page 202 states that that number is $n = 2^{h+1} - 1$. Therefore, in any binary tree of height h, the number n of nodes must satisfy $n \leq 2^{h+1} - 1$. The binary tree with the fewest nodes for a given height h is the one in which every internal node has only one child; that linear tree has $n = h + 1$ nodes because every node except the single leaf has exactly one child. Therefore, in any binary tree of height h, the number n of nodes must satisfy $n \geq h + 1$. The second pair of inequalities follows from the first by solving for h.

11.25   Let T be any binary tree of height h and size n. Let T_1 be the smallest complete binary tree that contains T. Let h_1 be the height of T_1 and let n_1 be its size. Then $h = h_1$ and $n \leq n_1$. Then by Corollary 11.1 on page 202, $n \leq n_1 = 2^{h+1} - 1$. The required inequalities follow from this result.

11.26 Figure 11.40 shows how the forest that produced the specified binary tree was obtained by reversing the natural map.

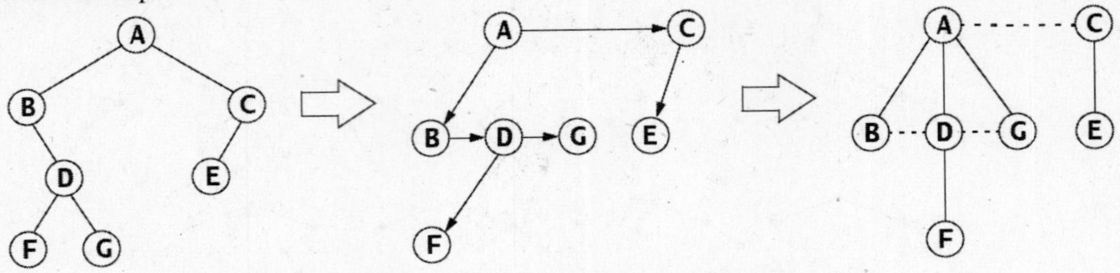

Figure 11.40 Mapping a forest into a binary tree

11.27 $f(h) = h + 1$

11.28 $f(h) = 1$

11.29   a.
```
public int leaves() {
    if (this == null) {
        return 0;
    }
    int leftLeaves = (left==null ? 0 : left.leaves());
    int rightLeaves = (right==null ? 0 : right.leaves());
    return leftLeaves + rightLeaves;
}
```
   b.
```
public int height() {
    if (this == null) {
        return -1;
    }
    int leftHeight = (left==null ? -1 : left.height());
    int rightHeight = (right==null ? -1 : right.height());
    return 1 + (leftHeight<rightHeight ? rightHeight : leftHeight);
}
```
   c.
```
public int level(Object object) {
    if (this == null) {
        return -1;
    } else if (object == root) {
        return 0;
    }
    int leftLevel = (left==null ? -1 : left.level(object));
    int rightLevel = (right==null ? -1 : right.level(object));
    if (leftLevel < 0 && rightLevel < 0) {
        return -1;
    }
    return 1 + (leftLevel<rightLevel ? rightLevel : leftLevel);
}
```
   d.
```
public void reflect() {
    if (this == null) {
        return;
    }
    if (left != null) {
        left.reflect();
    }
    if (right != null) {
        right.reflect();
    }
    BinaryTree temp=left;
    left = right;
    right = temp;
}
```

e.
```
        public void defoliate() {
          if (this == null) {
            return;
          } else if (left == null && right == null) {
            root = null;
            return;
          }
          if (left != null && left.left==null && left.right==null) {
            left = null;
          } else {
            left.defoliate();
          }
          if (right != null && right.left==null && right.right==null)
            right = null;
          } else {
            right.defoliate();
          }
        }
```

Search Trees

Tree structures are used to store data because their organization renders more efficient access to the data. A *search tree* is a tree that maintains its data in some sorted order.

MULTIWAY SEARCH TREES

Here is the recursive definition of a multiway search tree:

> A *multiway search tree of order m* is either the empty set or a pair (k, S), where the first component is a sequence $k = (k_1, k_2, \ldots, k_{n-1})$ of $n-1$ keys and the second component is a sequence $S = (S_0, S_1, S_2, \ldots, S_{n-1})$ of n multiway search trees of order m, with $2 \le n \le m$, and $s_0 \le k_1 \le s_1 \le \ldots \le k_{n-1} \le s_{n-1}$ for each $s_i \in S_i$.

This is similar to the recursive definition of a general tree on page 186. A multiway search tree of order m can be regarded as a tree of order m in which the elements are sequences of keys with the ordering property described above.

EXAMPLE 12.1 A Five-Way Search Tree

Here is an m-way search tree with $m = 5$. It has three internal nodes of degree 5 (each containing four keys), three internal nodes of degree 4 (each containing three keys), four internal nodes of degree 3 (each containing two keys), and one internal node of degree 2 (containing one key).

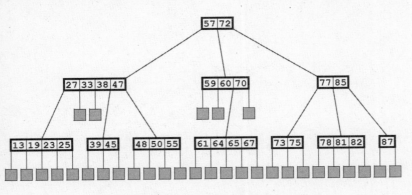

Figure 12.1 A five-way search tree

230

The root node has two keys and three children. All four keys in the first child are less than $k_1 = 57$. All three keys in the second child are between $k_1 = 57$ and $k_2 = 72$. Both keys in the third child are greater than $k_2 = 72$. In fact, all thirteen keys in the first subtree are less than 57, all seven keys in the second subtree are between 57 and 72, and all eight keys in the third subtree are greater than 72.

An m-way search tree is called a search tree because it serves as a multilevel index for searching large lists. To search for a key value, begin at the root and proceed down the tree until the key is found or a leaf is reached. At each node, perform a binary search for the key. It it is not found in that node, the search will stop between two adjacent key values (with $k_0 = -\infty$ and $k_n = \infty$). In that case, follow the link that is between those two keys to the next node. If we reach a leaf, then we know that the key is not in the tree.

For example, to search for key value 66, start at the root of the tree and then follow the middle link (because $57 \leq 66 < 72$) down to the middle three-key node. Then follow its third link (because $60 \leq 66 < 70$) down to the bottom four-key node. Then follow its third link (because $65 \leq 66 < 67$) down to that leaf node. Then conclude that the key 66 is not in the tree.

To insert a key into an m-way search tree, first apply the search algorithm. If the search ends at a leaf node, then the two bracketing keys of its parent node locate the correct position for the new key. So insert it in that internal node between those two bracketing keys. If that insertion gives the node m keys (thereby exceeding the limit of $m-1$ keys per node), then split the node into two nodes after moving its middle key up to its parent node. If that move gives the parent node m keys, repeat the splitting process. This process can iterate all the way back up to the root, if necessary. Splitting the root produces a new root, thereby increasing the height of the tree by one level.

EXAMPLE 12.2 Inserting into a Five-Way Tree

To insert 66 into the search tree of Example 12.1, first perform the search, as described above. This leads to the leaf node marked with an X in Figure 12.2:

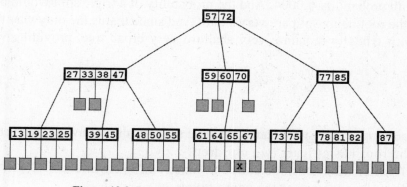

Figure 12.2 Inserting 66 into a five-way search tree

Insert the new key 66 in that last parent node between the bracketing keys 65 and 67 as shown in Figure 12.3 on page 232.

Now that node contains five keys, which violates the four-key limit for a five-way tree. So the node gets split, shifting its middle key 65 up to its parent node as shown in Figure 12.4 on page 232.

Node splitting occurs relatively infrequently, especially if m is large. For example, if $m = 50$, then on average only 2 percent of the nodes would be full, so a bottom-level split would be

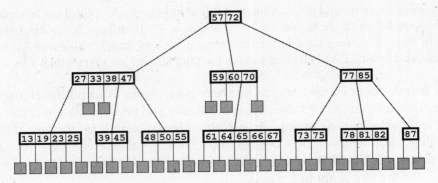

Figure 12.3 Inserting 66 into a five-way search tree

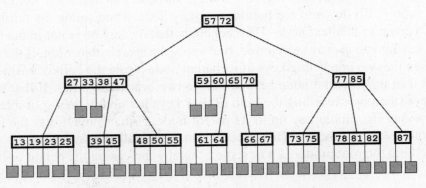

Figure 12.4 Inserting 66 into a five-way search tree

required for only about 2 percent of the insertions. Furthermore, a second-from-bottom-level split (i.e., a double split) would be required for only about 2 percent of 2 percent of the insertions, that is, with probability 0.0004. And the probability of a triple split would be 0.000008. So the chances of the root being split are very small. And since that is the only way that the tree can grow vertically, it tends to remain a very shallow, very broad tree, providing very fast search time.

B-TREES

A *B-tree of order m* is an *m*-way search tree that satisfies the following extra conditions:

1. The root has at least two children.
2. All other internal nodes have at least $\lceil m/2 \rceil$ children.
3. All leaf nodes are at the same level.

These conditions make the tree more balanced (and thus more efficient), and they simplify the insertion and deletion algorithms.

B-trees are used as indexes for large data sets stored on disk. In a relational database, data are organized in separate sequences of records called tables. Each table could be stored as a sequential data file in which the records are numbered like the elements of an array. Or the database system might access the records directly by their disk addresses. Either way, each record is directly accessible on disk via some addressing scheme. So once we have the record's disk address, we can access it immediately (i.e., with a single disk read). So the "key" that is stored in the B-tree is actually a key/address pair containing the record's actual key value (e.g., a U.S. Social Security number for personnel records, or an ISBN for books) together with its disk address. In the outline that follows, only the key value is shown, the accompanying disk address being understood to accompany it.

EXAMPLE 12.3 A B-Tree

Figure 12.5 shows a B-tree of order 5. Each of its internal nodes has 3, 4, or 5 children, and all the leaves are at level 3.

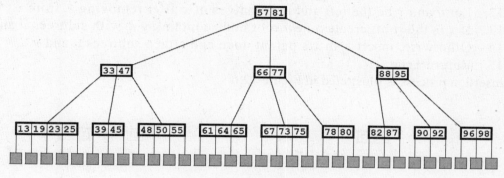

Figure 12.5 A B-tree of order 5

Algorithm 12.1 Searching in a B-Tree

To find a record with key k using a B-tree index of order m:

1. If the tree is empty, return `null`.
2. Let x be the root.
3. Repeat steps 4–6 until x is a leaf node.
4. Apply the binary search (page 31) to node x for the key k_i, where $k_{i-1} < k \le k_i$ (regarding $k_0 = -\infty$ and $k_m = \infty$).
5. If $k_i = k$, retrieve the record from disk and return it.
6. Let x be the root of subtree S_i.

Return `null`.

Note how similar this process is to looking up a topic in the index of a book. Each page of the index is labeled with a word or letter that represents the topics listed on that page. The page labels are analogous to the keys in the internal nodes of the search tree. The actual page number listed next to the topic in the book's index is analogous to the disk address of file name that leads you to the actual data. The last step of the search process is searching through that page in the book, or through that file on the disk. This analogy is closer if the book's index itself had an index. Each internal level of the multiway tree corresponds to another index level.

Algorithm 12.2 Inserting into a B-Tree

To insert a record with key k using a B-tree index of order m:

1. If the tree is empty, create a root node with two dummy leaves, insert k there, and return `true` (indicating that the insertion was successful).
2. Let x be the root.
3. Repeat steps 4–6 until x is a leaf node.
4. Apply the binary search to node x for the key k_i, where $k_{i-1} < k \le k_i$ (regarding $k_0 = -\infty$ and $k_m = \infty$).

5. If $k_i = k$, return `false` (indicating that the insertion was unsuccessful because a record with key k already exists, and keys should be unique).
6. Let x be the root of subtree S_i.
7. Add the record to disk.
8. Insert k (with the record's disk address) into x between k_{i-1} and k_i.
9. Add a dummy leaf node to x.
10. If degree(x) = m, repeat steps 11–13 until degree(x) < m.
11. Let k_j be the middle key in node x.
12. Let u and v be the left and right halves of x after removing k_j from x.
13. If x is the root, create a new root node containing k_j with subtrees u and v.
14. Otherwise, insert k_j in x's parent node and attach subtrees u and v.
15. Return `true`.

This insertion process is illustrated in Figure 12.6.

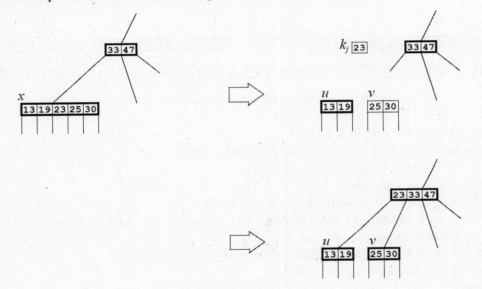

Figure 12.6 Inserting into a B-tree

The deletion algorithm for B-trees is similar to the insertion algorithm.

All three algorithms run in time proportional to the height of the tree. From Corollary 10.1 on page 188 it follows that that height is proportional to $\log_m n$. From Theorem A.2 on page 320, it follows that that is proportional to $\lg n$. Thus we have:

Theorem 12.1 In a B-tree, searching, inserting, and deleting all run in $O(\lg n)$ time.

BINARY SEARCH TREES

A *binary search tree* is a binary tree whose elements include a *key field* of some ordinal type and which has this property: If k is the key value at any node, then $k \geq x$ for every key x in the node's left subtree and $k \leq y$ for

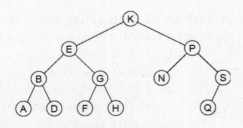

Figure 12.7 A binary search tree

every key *y* in the node's right subtree. This property, called the *BST property*, guarantees that an inorder traversal of the binary search tree will produce the elements in increasing order.

The BST property is applied for each insertion into the tree:

Algorithm 12.3 Inserting into a binary search Tree

To insert an element with key value *k* into a binary search tree:

1. If the tree is empty, insert the new element at the root. Then return.
2. Let *p* locate the root.
3. If *k* is less than the key stored at *p* and if the node at *p* has no left child, insert the new element as the left child of *p*. Then return.
4. If *k* is less than the key stored at *p* and if the node at *p* has a left child, let *p* locate that left child of *p*. Then go back to step 3.
5. If the node at *p* has no right child, insert the new element as the right child of *p*. Then return.
6. Let *p* locate the right child of *p*. Then go back to step 3.

EXAMPLE 12.4 Inserting into a Binary Search Tree

Apply Algorithm 12.3 to insert an element with key M into the binary search tree shown in Figure 12.7.

Step 1 starts the iterator *p* at the root K. Since M is greater than K (i.e., it follows it lexicographically) and node K has a right child, the algorithm proceeds to step 6, resetting the iterator *p* to node P, and then goes back to step 3. Next, since M is less than P (i.e., it precedes it lexicographically) and node P has a left child, the algorithm proceeds to step 4, resetting the iterator *p* to node N, and then goes back to step 3. Next, since M is also less than N but node N has no left child, the algorithm proceeds to step 5, inserts the new element as the left child of node N, and then returns.

This is illustrated in Figure 12.8.

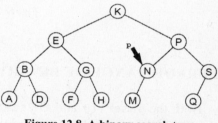

Figure 12.8 A binary search tree

EXAMPLE 12.5 Building a Binary Search Tree

Figure 12.9 on page 236 shows the binary search tree that is built by inserting the input sequence 44, 22, 77, 55, 99, 88, 33.

If a binary search tree is balanced, it allows for very efficient searching. As with the binary search, it takes $O(\lg n)$ steps to find an element in a balanced binary search tree. But without further restrictions, a binary search tree may grow to be very unbalanced. The worst case is when the elements are inserted in sorted order. In that case the tree degrades to a linear list, thereby making the search algorithm an $O(n)$ sequential search.

EXAMPLE 12.6 An Unbalanced Binary Search Tree

This is the same input data as in Example 12.5, but in a different order: 99, 22, 88, 33, 77, 55, 44. The resulting binary search tree is shown in Figure 12.10 on page 236.

This shows that the same input in different order produces a different tree. But more important, it shows that it is not unlikely for the binary search tree to be linear, or nearly linear.

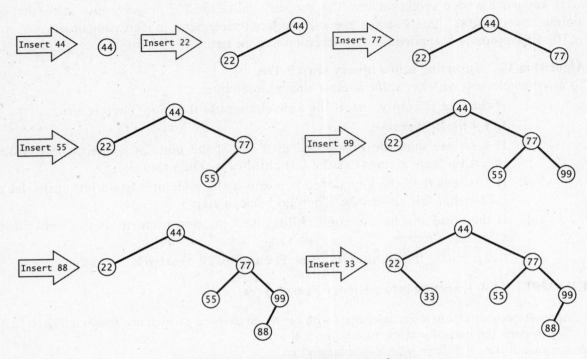

Figure 12.9 Inserting into a binary search tree

PERFORMANCE OF BINARY SEARCH TREES

Both the insert() and the search() functions begin at the root of the tree and proceed down toward the leaves, making one comparison at each level of the tree. Therefore the time required to execute either algorithm is proportional to $h + 1$, where h is the height of the tree. The search() function may terminate before reaching a leaf, but $h + 1$ is still an upper bound on the number of comparisons that it can make.

Theorem 12.2 In a binary search tree of size n, the insert() and the search() functions each require $O(\lg n)$ comparisons in the best case.

In the best case, the binary tree is completely balanced and nearly full, so by Corollary 11.2 on page 202, $h = \lg(n+1) - 1 = O(\lg n)$.

Theorem 12.3 In a binary search tree of size n, the insert() and the search() functions each require $O(n)$ comparisons in the worst case.

In the worst case the tree is linear, so $h + 1 = n = O(n)$.

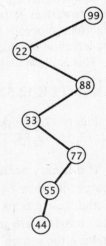

Figure 12.10 A BST

Theorem 12.4 In a binary search tree of size n, the insert() and the search() functions each require $O(2 \ln n) \approx O(1.39 \lg n)$ comparisons in the average case.

The proof of this result is beyond the scope of this outline.

AVL TREES

The imbalance problem illustrated in Example 12.6 can be avoided by imposing balance constraints on the nodes of the binary search tree.

Define the *balance number* at any node of a tree to be the difference between the height of its left subtree and the height of its right subtree. An *AVL tree* is a binary search tree where the balance number at each node is either -1, 0, or 1. The name comes from the two inventors of this method: G.M. Adel'son-Velskii and Y.M. Landis.

The tree in Figure 12.12 is not an AVL tree because it is imbalanced at node C. Its balance number there is 2, which is outside the allowable range. It is also imbalanced at node G. The tree in Figure 12.11 is an AVL tree: Every balance number is either -1, 0 or 1.

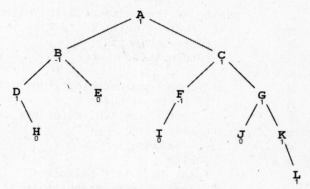

Figure 12.11 An AVL tree

EXAMPLE 12.7 An AVLTree CLASS

This class for AVL trees extends the BinaryTree class defined in Example 11.20 on page 212:

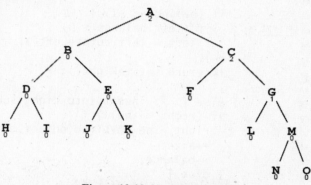

Figure 12.12 Not an AVL tree

```
1    public class AVLTree extends BinaryTree {
2        protected AVLTree left, right;
3        protected int balance;
4        protected java.util.Comparator comp;
5
6        public AVLTree(java.util.Comparator comp){
7            this.comp = comp;
8        }
9
10       public AVLTree(Object root, java.util.Comparator comp) {
11           this.root = root;
12           this.comp = comp;
13       }
14
15       public boolean add(Object object) {
16         AVLTree temp = attach(object);
17         if (temp != this) {
18           left = temp.left;
19           right = temp.right;
20           balance = temp.balance;
21         }
22         return true;
23       }
24
```

```
25   public AVLTree attach(Object object) {
26     if (root == null) {  // tree is empty
27       root = object;
28       return this;
29     }
30     if (comp.compare(object,root) < 0) {  // insert into left subtree
31       if (left == null) {
32         left = new AVLTree(object,comp);
33         ++size;
34         --balance;
35       } else {
36         int lb = left.balance;
37         left = left.attach(object);
38         if (left.balance != lb && left.balance != 0) {
39           --balance;
40         }
41       }
42       if (balance < -1) {
43         if (left.balance > 0) {
44           left = left.rotateLeft();
45         }
46         return rotateRight();
47       }
48     } else {  // insert into right subtree
49       if (right == null) {
50         right = new AVLTree(object,comp);
51         ++size;
52         ++balance;
53       } else {
54         int rb = right.balance;
55         right = right.attach(object);
56         if (right.balance != rb && right.balance != 0) {
57           ++balance;
58         }
59       }
60       if (balance > 1)  {
61         if (right.balance < 0) {
62           right = right.rotateRight();
63         }
64         return rotateLeft();
65       }
66     }
67     return this;
68   }
69
70   private AVLTree rotateRight()  // see Problem 12.5 on page 240
71
72   private AVLTree rotateLeft() {
73     AVLTree x = this, y = right, z = y.left;
74     x.right = z;
75     y.left = x;
76     int xb = x.balance, yb = y.balance;
77     if (yb < 1) {
78       --x.balance;
79       y.balance = ( xb>0 ? yb-1 : xb+yb-2 );
```

```
80            } else if (yb < xb) {
81                x.balance -= yb+1;  --y.balance;
82            } else {
83                y.balance = xb-2;
84            }
85            return y;
86        }
87    }
```

EXAMPLE 12.8 Building an AVL Tree

Insertions of G, M, T, D, and P into an empty AVL tree are shown in Figure 12.13.

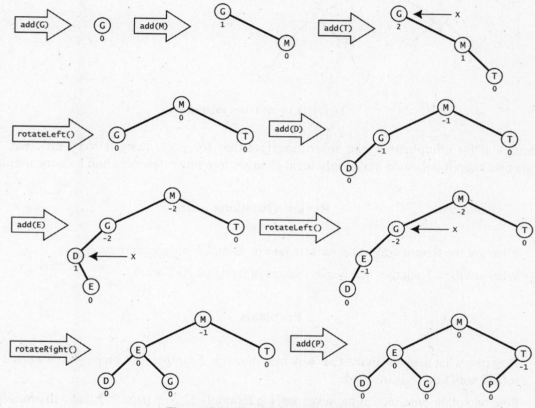

Figure 12.13 Inserting into an AVL tree

The first rotation occurs with the insertion of T. That increases the balance at the root to 2, which violates the AVL constraint. The left rotation about the root x makes M become the parent of its prior parent G.

The next rotation occurs after E in inserted. The right rotation at its parent D straightens out the dogleg G — D — E but leaves the balance at G at −2. That requires a second rotation in the opposite direction. Double rotations like this are required when the imbalance is at the top of a dogleg.

Note how efficient the rotations are. By making only local changes to references and balance numbers, they restore the tree to nearly perfect balance.

Figure 12.14 on page 240 shows a later insertion into the same AVL tree, inserting W after U, V, and Z have been inserted.

This illustrates a double rotation where a nontrivial subtree gets shifted. The subtree containing U is shifted from parent V to parent T. Note that the BST property is maintained.

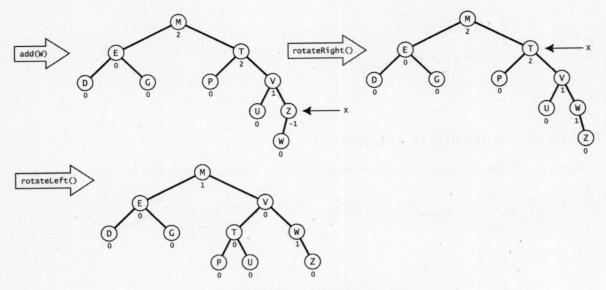

Figure 12.14 AVL tree rotations

Although a bit complicated, the insertion algorithm for AVL trees is very efficient. The rotations that keep it balanced make only local changes to a few references and balance numbers.

Review Questions

12.1   What are the advantages and disadvantages of using a binary search tree?

12.2   What are the advantages and disadvantages of using an AVL tree?

Problems

12.1   Describe what happens in the five-way tree shown in Example 12.1 on page 230 when a new record with key 16 is inserted.

12.2   Find two other orderings of the seven keys in Example 12.5 on page 235 that will produce the same binary search tree.

12.3   Describe a method for sorting arrays of objects using a binary search tree. Then determine the complexity of the algorithm.

12.4   Determine which of the binary trees shown in Figure 12.15 on page 241 is a binary search tree.

12.5   Write the `rotateRight()` method for the `AVLTree` class.

12.6   Prove that every subtree of a binary search tree is also a binary search tree.

12.7   Prove that every subtree of an AVL tree is also an AVL tree.

12.8   Here are the U.S. Postal Service abbreviations of the first 10 states, in the order that they ratified the U.S. Constitution: DE, PA, NJ, GA, CT, MA, MD, SC, NH, VA. Show the AVL tree after the insertion of each of these strings.

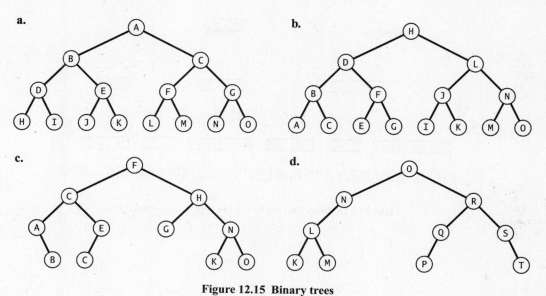

Figure 12.15 Binary trees

Answers to Review Questions

12.1   The disadvantage of a binary search tree is that it may become very unbalanced, in which case search-ing degenerates into an $O(n)$ algorithm. The advantage is the efficiency that a binary tree provides for insertions and deletions.

12.2   The advantage of an AVL tree is that it is always balanced, guaranteeing the $O(\lg n)$ speed of the binary search algorithm. The disadvantages the complex rotations used by the insertion and removal algo-rithms needed to maintain the tree's balance.

Solutions to Problems

12.1   To insert a new record with key 16 into the tree shown in Figure 12.16, the initial search would lead to the first leaf node. Since that is a five-way search tree, that first leaf node has overflowed, causing it to be split into two leaf nodes and moving its middle key 19 up to its parent node, as shown in Figure 12.17. But now that parent node has overflowed. So it also gets split, moving its middle key up to its parent node, as shown in Figure 12.18.

12.2   Two other ordering of the seven keys in Example 12.5 on page 235 that will produce the same BST:

    a.   44, 22, 33, 77, 55, 99, 88

    b.   44, 22, 77, 33, 55, 99, 88

12.3   An array of objects could be sorted by inserting their objects into a binary search tree and then using an inorder traversal to copy them back into the array. The BST property guarantees that the inorder tra-versal will visit the elements in order.

       If an AVL tree is used, then each insertion runs in $O(\lg n)$ time, so building the tree with n elements will require $O(n \lg n)$ time. The subsequent inorder traversal also has $O(n \lg n)$ complexity, so the entire algorithm sorts the array in $O(n \lg n)$ time.

12.4   All except **a** are binary search trees.

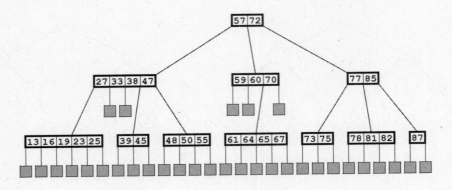

Figure 12.16 Inserting the key 16 in a five-way search tree

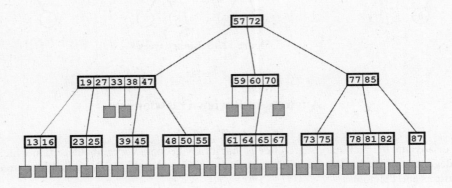

Figure 12.17 Inserting the key 16 in a five-way search tree

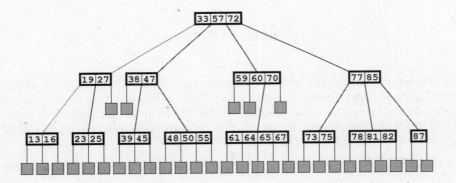

Figure 12.18 Inserting the key 16 in a five-way search tree

12.5

```
private AVLTree rotateRight() {
   AVLTree x = this, y = left, z = y.left;
   x.left = z;
   y.left = x;
   int xb = x.balance;
   int yb = y.balance;
```

```
        if (yb > 1) {
          ++x.balance;
          y.balance = ( xb<0 ? yb+1 : xb+yb+2 );
        } else if (yb > xb) {
          x.balance += yb-1;
          ++y.balance;
        } else {
          y.balance = xb+2;
        }
        return y;
    }
```

12.6   Theorem. Every subtree of a binary search tree is a binary search tree.

Proof: Let T be a binary search tree, and let S be a subtree of T. Let x be any element in S, and let L and R be the left and right subtrees of x in S. Then, since S is a subtree of T, x is also an element of T, and L and R are the left and right subtrees of x in T. Therefore, $y \leq x \leq z$ for every $y \in L$ and every $z \in R$ because T has the BST property. Thus, S also has the BST property.

12.7   Theorem. Every subtree of an AVL tree is an AVL tree.

Proof: The proof that every subtree of a binary search tree is a binary search tree is given in Problem 12.6. If a S is a subtree of an AVL tree T, then every node is S is also in T. Therefore, the balance number at every node in S is −1, 0, or 1.

**12.8   **The solution is shown in Figure 12.19.

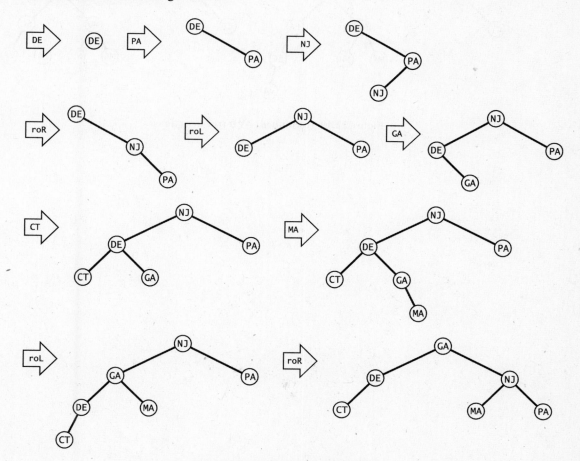

Figure 12.19 AVL tree insertions

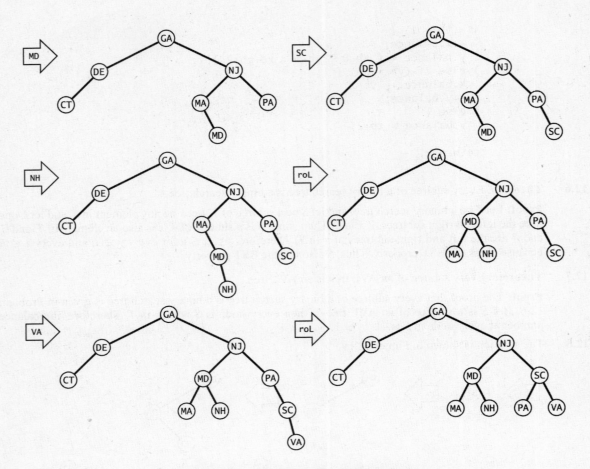

Figure 12.19 (continued) AVL tree insertions

CHAPTER 13

Heaps and Priority Queues

HEAPS

A *heap* is a complete binary tree whose elements have keys that satisfy the following *heap property*: the keys along any path from root to leaf are descending (i.e., nonincreasing).

EXAMPLE 13.1 A Heap

Figure 13.1 shows a heap. Note that the keys along each of its root-to-leaf paths are descending:

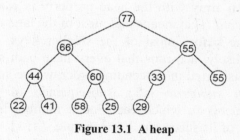

$77 \geq 66 \geq 44 \geq 22$;
$77 \geq 66 \geq 44 \geq 41$;
$77 \geq 66 \geq 60 \geq 58$;
$77 \geq 66 \geq 60 \geq 25$;
$77 \geq 55 \geq 33 \geq 29$;
$77 \geq 55 \geq 55$.

Figure 13.1 A heap

Heaps could represent family descendant trees because the heap property means that every parent is older than its children.

Heaps are used to implement priority queues (page 247) and to the heap sort algorithm (page 266).

THE NATURAL MAPPING

Every complete binary tree has a natural mapping into an array. (See Algorithm 11.1 on page 206.) The mapping is obtained from a level-order traversal of the tree. In the resulting array, the parent of the element at index i is at index $i/2$, and the children are at indexes $2i$ and $2i+1$.

EXAMPLE 13.2 Storing a Heap in an Array

The heap shown in Figure 13.1 maps into the array shown Figure 13.2.

For example, element 60 is at index $i = 5$, its parent is element 66 at index $i/2 = 2$, and its children are elements 58 and 25 at indexes $2i = 10$ and $2i + 1 = 11$.

0	1	2	3	4	5	6	7	8	9	10	11	12
	77	66	55	44	60	33	55	22	41	58	25	29

Figure 13.2 Array storage of a heap

The natural mapping between a complete binary tree and an array is a two-way correspondence. To map the array elements back into a complete binary tree, simply number the tree nodes consecutively in a level-order traversal beginning with number 1 at the root. Then copy the array element at index *i* into the tree node numbered *i*. The locations for those indexes are shown in Figure 13.3. If the resulting tree has the heap property, then we also say that the array has the *heap property*.

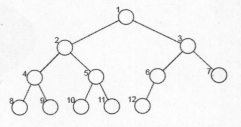

Figure 13.3 Array indexes in a heap

EXAMPLE 13.3 Determining Whether an Array Has the Heap Property

To determine whether this array has the heap property, we first map it into a binary tree, and then check each root-to-leaf path.

The root-to-leaf path {88, 66, 44, 51} shown in Figure 13.4 is *not* descending because 44 < 51. Hence, the tree does not have the heap property. Therefore, the array does not have the heap property.

An array with the heap property is *partially ordered*. That means that most of the larger keys come before most of the smaller keys. More precisely, it means that every heap-path subarray is sorted in descending order, where a *heap-path subarray* is a subsequence of array elements in which each index number is half that of its successor. For example, {a[1], a[2], a[5], a[11], a[22], a[45], a[90], a[180]}

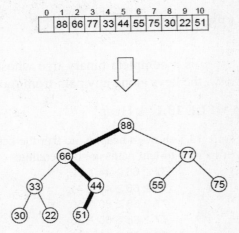

Figure 13.4 Checking the heap property

would be a heap-path subarray of an array a[] of 200 elements. The heap sort algorithm (Algorithm 14.8 on page 266) exploits this fact to obtain a fast and efficient method for sorting arrays.

INSERTION INTO A HEAP

Elements are inserted into a heap next to its right-most leaf at the bottom level. Then the heap property is restored by percolating the new element up the tree until it is no longer "older" (i.e., its key is greater) than its parent. On each iteration, the child is swapped with its parent.

EXAMPLE 13.4 Inserting into a Heap

Figure 13.5 on page 247 shows how the key 75 would be inserted into the heap shown in Figure 13.4. The element 75 is added to the tree as a new last leaf. Then it is swapped with its parent element 44 because 75 > 44. Then it is swapped with its parent element 66 because 75 > 66. Now the heap property has been restored because the new element 75 is less than its parent and greater than its children.

Note that the insertion affects only the nodes along a single root-to-leaf path.

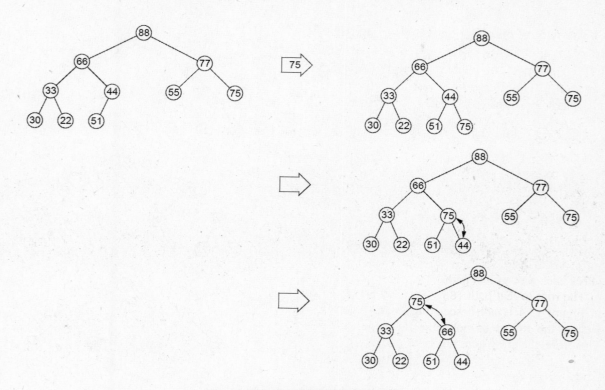

Figure 13.5 Inserting 75 into a heap

REMOVAL FROM A HEAP

The heap removal algorithm always removes the root element from the tree. This is done by moving the last leaf element into the root element and then restoring the heap property by percolating the new root element down the tree until it is no longer "younger" (i.e., its key is less) than its children. On each iteration, the parent is swapped with the older of its two children.

EXAMPLE 13.5 Removing from a Heap

Figure 13.6 shows how the root element (key 88) would be removed from a heap.

The last leaf (key 44) is removed and copied into the root, replacing the previous root (key 88), which is removed. Then, to restore the heap property, the element 44 is swapped with the larger of its two children (77). That step is repeated until the element 44 is no longer smaller than any of its children. In this case, the result is that 44 ends up as a leaf again.

Note that the removal affects only the nodes along a single root-to-leaf path. That gives us this result from Corollary 11.2 on page 202:

Theorem 13.1 Insertions into and removals from a heap run in $O(\lg n)$ time.

PRIORITY QUEUES

A *stack* is a LIFO container: The last one in comes out first. A *queue* is a "FIFO container: The first one in comes out first. A *priority queue* is a "BIFO container": The best one in comes

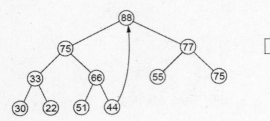
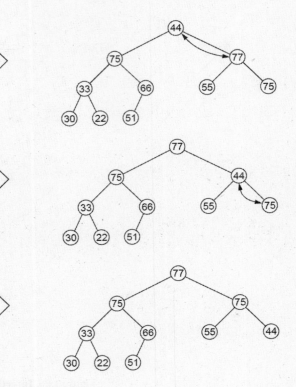

Figure 13.6 Deleting 88 from a heap

out first. That means that each element is assigned a priority number, and the element with the highest priority comes out first.

Priority queues are widely used in computer systems. For example, if a printer is shared by several computers on a local area network, the print jobs that are queued to it would normally be held temporarily in a priority queue wherein smaller jobs are given higher priority over larger jobs.

Priority queues are usually implemented as heaps since the heap data structure always keeps the element with the largest key at the root and its insertion and removal operations are so efficient. According to Theorem 13.1, those operations are guaranteed to run in in $O(\lg n)$ time.

THE JCF `PriorityQueue` CLASS

The Java Collections Framework includes a `PriorityQueue` class. As Figure 4.1 on page 70 shows, that class extends the `AbstractQueue` and `AbstractList` classes, implementing the `Queue` and `List` interfaces.

EXAMPLE 13.6 The `java.util.PriorityQueue` Class

```
1   public class TestingPriorityQueues {
2     public static void main(String[] args) {
3       PriorityQueue<String> pq = new PriorityQueue<String>();
4       pq.add("FR");
5       pq.add("DE");
6       pq.add("GB");
```

```
7          pq.add("IT");
8          pq.add("ES");
9          while (!pq.isEmpty()) {
10           System.out.printf("%s  ", pq.remove());
11         }
12       }
13     }
```

The output is:

```
DE  ES  FR  GB  IT
```

The collection pq is a priority queue, so its elements are removed according to their priorities. The element type for this queue is String, which has its own natural ordering: alphabetical order. So regardless of the order in which they are inserted, they are removed in alphabetical order.

If the element type has no natural ordering, then PriorityQueue instances will apply the compareTo() method to determine priorities among the elements.

EXAMPLE 13.7 Using Elements that Explicitly Implement the Comparable Interface

```
1     public class TestingPriorityQueues {
2       public static void main(String[] args) {
3         PriorityQueue<Student> pq = new PriorityQueue<Student>();
4         pq.add(new Student("Ann",44));
5         pq.add(new Student("Bob",99));
6         pq.add(new Student("Cal",33));
7         pq.add(new Student("Don",66));
8         while (!pq.isEmpty()) {
9           System.out.printf("%s  ", pq.remove());
10        }
11      }
12    }
13
14    class Student implements Comparable{
15      private String name;
16      private int credits;
17
18      public Student(String name, int credits) {
19        this.name = name;
20        this.credits = credits;
21      }
22
23      public int compareTo(Object object) {
24        if (object == this) {
25          return 0;
26        } else if (!(object instanceof Student)) {
27          throw new IllegalArgumentException("comparing apples and oranges!");
28        }
29        Student that = (Student)object;
30        return this.credits - that.credits;
31      }
32      public String toString() {
33        return String.format("%s(%d)", name, credits);
34      }
35    }
```

The output is:

```
Cal(33)  Ann(44)  Don(66)  Bob(99)
```

The priority queue pq defined at line 3 stores instances of the Student class that is defined at line 14. That class is declared to implement the Comparable interface, which obliges it to define a compareTo() method. That method, defined at line 23, uses the credits field of the Student objects to compare them. Students with more credits have higher priority.

The print loop at line 8 is the same as the one in Example 13.6: It applies the priority queue's remove() method to remove and print the elements according to their ascending priority levels, independently of their insertion order (except for equal priorities).

Review Questions

13.1   What are the two main applications of heaps?

13.2   How efficient are insertions into and removals from a heap?

13.3   Why is a priority queue called a BIFO container?

13.4   What is the difference between a queue and a priority queue?

13.5   Why are heaps used to implement priority queues?

13.6   In the natural mapping of a binary tree into an array a[], why do we start at a[1] instead of at a[0]?

13.7   If it takes an average of 3ms to remove an element from a priority queue with 1,000 elements, how long would you expect it to take to remove an element from a priority queue with 1,000,000 elements?

13.8   Suppose a method is devised to sort an array by storing its element in a priority queue and then removing them back into the array. What is the run time for such an algorithm?

Problems

13.1   Determine which of the binary trees in Figure 13.7 is a heap.

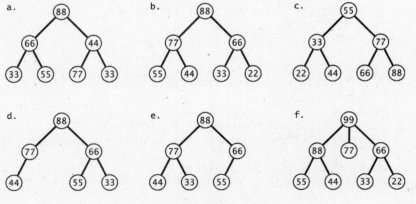

Figure 13.7 Binary trees

13.2   Determine which of the arrays in Figure 13.8 on page 251 has the heap property.

13.3   Show the heap after inserting each of these keys in this order: 44, 66, 33, 88, 77, 77, 22.

13.4   Show the array obtained from the natural map of each of the heaps obtained in Problem 13.3.

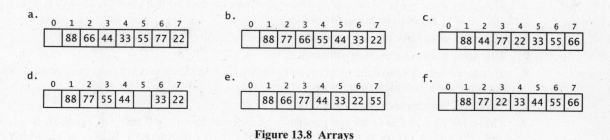

Figure 13.8 Arrays

13.5 Write and test this method
```
boolean isHeap(int[] a)
// returns true if and only if the specified array
// has the heap property
```

13.6 Prove that every subtree of a heap is a heap.

13.7 Show the heap after inserting each of these keys in this order: 50, 95, 70, 30, 90, 25, 35, 80, 60, 40, 20, 10, 75, 45, 35.

Answers to Review Questions

13.1 Heaps are used to implement priority queues and the heap sort. (See page 266.)

13.2 Insertions into and removals from a heap are very efficient; they run in $O(\lg n)$.

13.3 A priority queue is a "best-in-first-out" container, that is, the element with the highest priority comes out first.

13.4 Elements are removed from a queue in the same order in which they are inserted: first-in-first-out. Elements in a priority queue must have an ordinal key field which determines the priority order in which they are to be removed.

13.5 Heaps are used to implement priority queues because they allow $O(\lg n)$ insertions and removals. This is because both the add() and the remove() methods are implemented by traversing a root-to-leaf path through the heap. Such paths are no longer than the height of the tree which is at most $\lg n$.

13.6 The natural mapping starts at a[1] instead of a[0] to facilitate navigation up and down the heap tree. By numbering the root 1 and continuing sequentially with a level order traversal, the number of the parent of any node numbered k will be $k/2$, and the numbers of its child nodes will be $2k$ and $2k+1$.

13.7 If it takes an average of 3ms to remove an element from a priority queue with 1,000 elements, then it should take about 6ms to remove an element from a priority queue with 1,000,000 elements.

13.8 The run time for a method that uses a priority queue to sort an array would be $O(2n \lg n)$ because it will make n insertions and n removals, each running in $O(\lg n)$ time.

Solutions to Problems

13.1　**a.** This is not a heap because the root-to-leaf path {88, 44, 77} is not descending (44 < 77).
b. This is a heap.
c. This is not a heap because the root-to-leaf path {55, 33, 44} is not descending (33 < 44) and the root-to-leaf path {55, 77, 88} is not descending (55 < 77 < 88).
d. This is not a heap because the binary tree is not complete.
e. This is a heap.
f. This is not a heap because the tree is not binary.

13.2   **a.** This array does not have the heap property because the root-to-leaf path {a[1], a[3], a[6]} = {88, 44, 77} is not descending (44 < 77).

        b. This array does have the heap property.

        c. This array does have the heap property.

        d. This array does not have the heap property because its data elements are not contiguous: It does not represent a complete binary tree.

        e. This array does have the heap property.

        f. This array does not have the heap property because the root-to-leaf path {a[1], a[3], a[6]} = {88, 22, 55} is not descending (22 < 55) and the root-to-leaf path {a[1], a[3], a[7]} = {88, 22, 66} is not descending (22 < 66).

13.3   Figure 13.9 shows a trace of the insertion of the keys 44, 66, 33, 88, 77, 55, 22 into a heap.

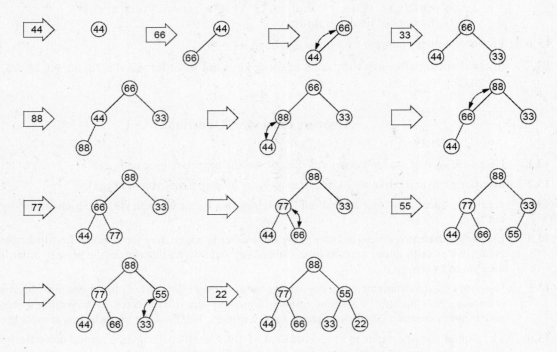

Figure 13.9 Trace of insertions into a heap

13.4   Figure 13.10 on page 253 shows the arrays for the heaps in Problem 13.3.

13.5
```
boolean isHeap(int[] a) {
    // returns true if and only if the specified array
    // has the heap property
    int n = a.length;
    for (int i = n/2; i < n; i++) {
      for (int j = i; j > 1; j /=2) {
        if (a[j/2] < a[j]) {
          return false;
        }
      }
    }
    return true;
}
```

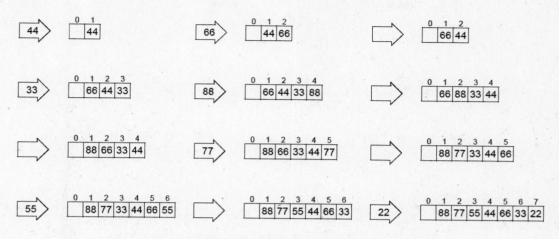

Figure 13.10 Trace of heap insertions into an array

13.6   Theorem. Every subtree of a heap is also a heap.

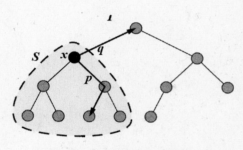

Figure 13.11 Subtree of a heap

Proof: Let T be a heap, and let S be a subtree of T. (See Figure 13.11.) By definition, T is a complete binary tree with the heap property. Thus, by the theorem in the solution, S is also a complete binary tree. Let x be the root of S, and let p be any root-to-leaf path in S. Then x is an element of T since S is a subtree of T, and there is a unique path q in T from x to the root of T. Also, p is a path in T that connects x to a leaf of T since S is a subtree of T. Let q^{-1} represent the reverse of the path q, and let $q^{-1}p$ represent the concatenation of q^{-1} with p in T. Then $q^{-1}p$ is a root-to-leaf path in T. Hence the elements along $q^{-1}p$ must be descending because T has the heap property. Therefore the elements along p are descending. Thus S also has the heap property.

13.7   Figure 13.12 shows a trace of the insertion of the keys 50, 95, 70, 30, 90, 25, 35, 80, 60, 40, 20, 10, 75, 45, 35 into a heap.

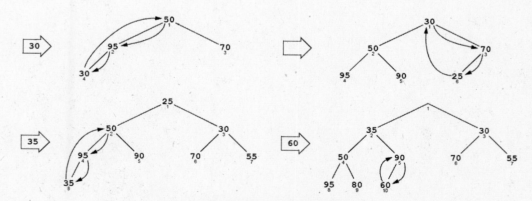

Figure 13.12 Insertion into a heap

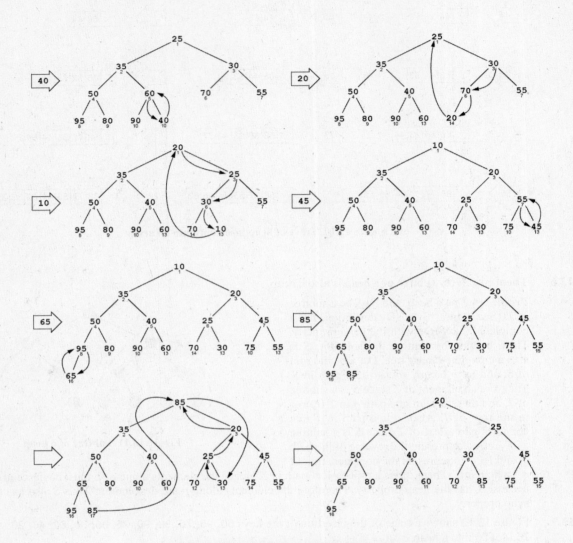

Figure 13.12 (continued) Insertion into a heap

CHAPTER 14

Sorting

We saw in Chapter 2 that searching through an array is far more efficient if its elements are sorted first. That fact is obvious to anyone who has ever looked up a number in a phone book or a word in a dictionary. This chapter outlines nine of the most common algorithms for sorting a linear data structure such as an array or a list.

CODE PRELIMINARIES

All of the sorting algorithms are implemented in this chapter using the same Java signature

```
public static void sort(int[] a)
```

for sorting an array of integers. This can easily be modified to sort an array of any other primitive type or an array of objects that implement the `Comparable` interface.

The pseudocode and the Java code include preconditions, postconditions, and loop invariants. These are used to prove that the algorithms are correct and to analyze their complexity.

In the pseudocode we use the notation $s = \{s_0, s_1, \ldots, s_{n-1}\}$ for a sequence of n elements. The notation $\{s_p \ldots s_{q-1}\}$ denotes the subsequence $\{s_p, s_{p+1}, \ldots, s_{q-1}\}$ of elements from s_p to s_{q-1}. In Java code comments, we represent the subsequence by `s[p..q)`. For example, $\{s_3 \ldots s_7\}$ and `s[3..8)` would both denote the subsequence $\{s_3, s_4, s_5, s_6, s_7\}$.

Unless otherwise noted, "sorted" will always mean that the elements of the sequence are in ascending order: $s_0 \le s_1 \le s_2 \le \cdots \le s_{n-1}$.

All the exchange sorts use this `swap()` method:

EXAMPLE 14.1 A `swap()` Method for Arrays

```
1    private static void swap(int[] a, int i, int j) {
2      // PRECONDITIONS: 0 <= i < a.length; 0 <= j < a.length;
3      // POSTCONDITION: a[i] and a[j] are interchanged;
4      if (i == j) {
5        return;
6      }
7      int temp=a[j];
8      a[j] = a[i];
9      a[i] = temp;
10   }
```

This method simply swaps the *i*th and *j*th elements of the array.

Note the use of preconditions and postconditions, included as comments at lines 2 and 3 of Example 14.1. A *precondition* is a condition that is assumed to be true before the method is invoked. A *postcondition* is a condition that is guaranteed to be true after the method has been invoked, provided that the preconditions were true. Preconditions and postconditions define the *contract* for a method: the "consumer guarantee" that defines the method. They can be used to prove, logically, that the method will always "work" as expected. (For example, see Theorem 14.10 on page 262.)

All the array examples use this `print()` method:

EXAMPLE 14.2　A `print()` Method for Arrays

```
1      private static void print(int[] a) {
2        for (int ai : a) {
3          System.out.printf("%s ", ai);
4        }
5        System.out.println();
6      }
```

Note the use of Java's enhanced `for` loop construct at line 2. The variable `ai` represents array elements `a[i]` as the index `i` traverses its entire range from 0 to `a.length − 1`.

THE JAVA `Arrays.sort()` METHOD

The standard Java class library defines a `sort()` method in the `java.util.Arrays` class. It actually includes twenty overloaded versions of the method: four for arrays of objects, two for arrays of each primitive type except `boolean`, and two for generic types. (See page 95.)

The signatures for the two `sort()` methods for arrays of `int`s are

```
      public static void sort(int[] a)
      public static void sort(int[] a, int p, int q)
```

The first of these sorts the entire array. The second sorts the subarray `a[p..q]`.

EXAMPLE 14.3　Using the `Arrays.sort()` Method

```
1      public static void main(String[] args) {
2        int[] a = { 77, 44, 99, 66, 33, 55, 88, 22 };
3        print(a);
4        java.util.Arrays.sort(a);
5        print(a);
6      }
```

The output is:

```
      77 44 99 66 33 55 88 22
      22 33 44 55 66 77 88 99
```

For arrays of elements of a primitive type, the `Arrays.sort()` method implements the quick sort. (See Algorithm 14.6 on page 263.). For arrays of elements of a reference type, it implements the merge sort. (See Algorithm 14.5 on page 261.)

THE BUBBLE SORT

The *bubble sort* makes $n-1$ passes through a sequence of n elements. Each pass moves through the array from left to right, comparing adjacent elements and swapping each pair that is out of order. This gradually moves the larger elements to the right. It is called the bubble sort because if the elements are visualized in a vertical column, then each pass appears to "bubble up" the next largest element by bouncing it off smaller elements, much like the rising bubbles in a carbonated beverage.

Algorithm 14.1 The Bubble Sort

(Precondition: $s = \{s_0 \ldots s_{n-1}\}$ is a sequence of n ordinal values.)

(Postcondition: The entire sequence s is sorted.)

1. Do steps 2–4 for $i = n - 1$ down to 1.
2. Do step 3 for $j = 0$ up to $i-1$.
3. If the two consecutive elements s_j and s_{j+1}, are out of order, swap them.
4. (Invariants: The subsequence $\{s_i \ldots s_{n-1}\}$ is sorted, and $s_i = \max\{s_0 \ldots s_i\}$.)

EXAMPLE 14.4 The Bubble Sort

```
1    public static void sort(int[] a) {
2    // POSTCONDITION: a[0] <= a[1] <= ... <= a[a.length-1];
3      for (int i = a.length-1; i > 0; i--) {   // step 1
4        for (int j = 0; j < i; j++) {          // step 2
5          if (a[j] > a[j+1]) {
6            swap(a, j, j+1);                    // step 3
7          }
8        }
9        // INVARIANTS: a[i] <= a[i+1] <= ... <= a[a.length-1];
10       //             a[j] <= a[i] for all j < i;
11     }
```

Theorem 14.1 The Bubble Sort is correct.

See the solution to Problem 14.14 on page 276 for a proof of this theorem.

Theorem 14.2 The Bubble Sort runs in $O(n^2)$ time.

See the solution to Problem 14.15 on page 276 for a proof of this theorem.

THE SELECTION SORT

The *selection sort* is similar to the bubble sort. It makes the $n-1$ passes through a sequence of n elements, each time moving the largest of the remaining unsorted elements into its correct position. But it is more efficient than the bubble sort because it doesn't move any elements in the process of finding the largest. It makes only one swap on each pass after it has found the largest. It is called the selection sort because on each pass it selects the largest of the remaining unsorted elements and puts it in its correct position.

Algorithm 14.2 The Selection Sort

(Precondition: $s = \{s_0 \ldots s_{n-1}\}$ is a sequence of n ordinal values.)

(Postcondition: The entire sequence s is sorted.)

1. Do steps 2–4 for $i = n - 1$ down to 1.
2. Locate the index m of the largest element among $\{s_0 \ldots s_i\}$.
3. Swap s_i and s_m.
4. (Invariants: the subsequence $\{s_i \ldots s_{n-1}\}$ is sorted, and $s_i = \max\{s_0 \ldots s_i\}$.)

EXAMPLE 14.5 The Selection Sort

```
1    public static void sort(int[] a) {
2      // POSTCONDITION: a[0] <= a[1] <= ... <= a[a.length-1];
3      for (int i = a.length-1; i > 0; i--) {         // step 1
4        int m = 0;                                    // step 2
5        for (int j = 1; j <= i; j++) {
6          if (a[j] > a[m]) {
7            m = j;
8          }
9        }
10       // INVARIANT: a[m] >= a[j] for all j <= i;
11       swap(a, i, m);                                // step 3
12       // INVARIANTS: a[j] <= a[i] for all j <= i;
13       //             a[i] <= a[i+1] <= ... <= a[a.length-1];
14     }
15   }
```

Theorem 14.3 The selection sort is correct.

See the solution to Problem 14.19 on page 276 for a proof of this theorem.

Theorem 14.4 The selection sort runs in $O(n^2)$ time.

See the solution to Problem 14.20 on page 276 for a proof of this theorem.

Note that even though the bubble sort and the selection sort have the same complexity function, the latter runs quite a bit faster. That fact is suggested by the two traces: The bubble sort made 18 swaps while the selection sort made only 7. The selection sort has the advantage of swapping elements that are far apart, so it makes one swap where the bubble sort could require several. (See Exercise 11.8.)

THE INSERTION SORT

Like the two previous algorithms, the *insertion sort* makes $n - 1$ passes through a sequence of n elements. On each pass it inserts the next element into the subarray on its left, thereby leaving that subarray sorted. When the last element is "inserted" this way, the entire array is sorted.

Algorithm 14.3 The Insertion Sort

(Precondition: $s = \{s_0 \ldots s_{n-1}\}$ is a sequence of n ordinal values.)
(Postcondition: The entire sequence s is sorted.)

1. Do steps 2–4 for $i = 1$ up to $n - 1$.
2. Hold the element s_i in a temporary space.
3. Locate the least index j for which $s_j >= s_i$.
4. Shift the subsequence $\{s_j \ldots s_{i-1}\}$ up one position to $\{s_{j+1} \ldots s_i\}$.
5. Copy the held value of s_i into s_j.
6. (Invariant: the subsequence $\{s_0..s_i\}$ is sorted.)

EXAMPLE 14.6 The Insertion Sort

```
1    public static void sort(int[] a) {
2      // POSTCONDITION: a[0] <= a[1] <= ... <= a[a.length-1];
```

```
3      for (int i = 1; i < a.length; i++) {      // step 1
4        int ai = a[i], j;                        // step 2
5        for (j = i; j > 0 && a[j-1] > ai; j--) { // step 3
6          a[j] = a[j-1];                         // step 4
7        }
8        a[j] = ai;                               // step 5
9        // INVARIANT: a[0] <= a[1] <= ... <= a[i];
10     }
11   }
```

Theorem 14.5 The insertion sort is correct.
See the solution to Problem 14.23 on page 277 for a proof of this theorem.

Theorem 14.6 The insertion sort runs in $O(n^2)$ time.
See the solution to Problem 14.24 on page 277 for a proof of this theorem.

Theorem 14.7 The insertion sort runs in $O(n)$ time on a sorted sequence.
See the solution to Problem 14.25 on page 283 for a proof of this theorem.

THE SHELL SORT

Theorem 14.7 suggests that if the sequence is nearly sorted, then the insertion sort will run nearly in $O(n)$ time. That is true. The *shell sort* exploits that fact to obtain an algorithm that in general runs in better than $O(n^{1.5})$ time. It applies the insertion sort repeatedly to skip subsequences such as $\{s_0, s_3, s_6, s_9, \ldots, s_{n-2}\}$ and $\{s_1, s_4, s_7, s_{10}, \ldots, s_{n-1}\}$. These are two of the three skip-3-subsequences.

Algorithm 14.4 The Shell Sort
(Precondition: $s = \{s_0 \ldots s_{n-1}\}$ is a sequence of n ordinal values.)
(Postcondition: The entire sequence s is sorted.)
  1. Set $d = 1$.
  2. Repeat step 3 until $9d > n$.
  3. Set $d = 3d + 1$.
  4. Do steps 5–6 until $d = 0$.
  5. Apply the insertion sort to each of the d skip-d-subsequences of s.
  6. Set $d = d/3$.

Suppose that s has $n = 200$ elements. Then the loop at step 2 would iterate three times, increasing d from 1 to $d = 4$, 13, and 40.

The first iteration of the loop at step 4 would apply the insertion sort to each of the 40 skip-40-subsequences $\{s_0, s_{40}, s_{80}, s_{120}, s_{160}\}$, $\{s_1, s_{41}, s_{81}, s_{121}, s_{161}\}$, $\{s_2, s_{42}, s_{82}, s_{122}, s_{162}\}, \ldots, \{s_{39}, s_{79}, s_{119}, s_{159}, s_{199}\}$. Then step 6 would reduce d to 13, and then the second iteration of the loop at step 4 would apply the insertion sort to each of the thirteen skip-13-subsequences $\{s_0, s_{13}, s_{26}, s_{39}, s_{52}, s_{65}, \ldots, s_{194}\}$, $\{s_1, s_{14}, s_{27}, s_{40}, s_{53}, s_{66}, \ldots, s_{195}\}, \ldots, \{s_{12}, s_{25}, s_{38}, s_{51}, s_{64}, s_{77}, \ldots, s_{193}\}$. Then step 6 would reduce d to 4, and the third iteration of the loop at step 4 would apply the insertion sort to each of the four skip-4-subsequences $\{s_0, s_4, s_8, s_{12}, \ldots, s_{196}\}$, $\{s_1, s_5, s_9, s_{13}, \ldots, s_{197}\}$, $\{s_2, s_6, s_{10}, s_{14}, \ldots, s_{198}\}$, and $\{s_3, s_7, s_{11}, s_{15}, \ldots, s_{199}\}$. Then step 6 would reduce d to 1, and, and the fourth iteration of the loop at step 4 would apply the insertion sort to the entire sequence. This entire process would apply the insertion sort 58 times: 40 times to subsequences of size $n_1 = 5$, 13 times to subsequences of size $n_2 = 15$, 4 times to subsequences of size $n_3 = 50$, and once to the entire sequence of size $n_4 = n = 200$.

At first glance, the repeated use of the insertion sort within the shell sort would seem to take longer than simply applying the insertion sort directly just once to the entire sequence. Indeed, a direct calculation of the total number of comparisons, using the complexity function n^2, yields

$$40(n_1^2) + 13(n_2^2) + 4(n_3^2) + 1(n_4^2) = 40(5^2) + 13(15^2) + 4(50^2) + 1(200^2) = 53,925$$

which is quite a bit worse than the single

$$n^2 = 200^2 = 40,000$$

But after the first iteration of step 4, the subsequent subsequences are nearly sorted. So the actual number of comparisons needed there is closer to n. Thus, the actual number of comparisons is more like

$$40(n_1^2) + 13(n_2) + 4(n_3) + 1(n_4) = 40(5^2) + 13(15) + 4(50) + 1(200) = 1,595$$

which is quite a bit better than 40,000.

Theorem 14.8 The shell sort runs in $O(n^{1.5})$ time.

Note that, for $n = 200$, $n^{1.5} = 200^{1.5} = 2,829$, which is a lot better than $n^2 = 200^2 = 40,000$.

EXAMPLE 14.7 The Shell Sort

```
1    public static void sort(int[] a) {
2        // POSTCONDITION: a[0] <= a[1] <= ... <= a[a.length-1];
3        int d = 1, j, n = a.length;          // step 1
4        while (9*d < n) {                     // step 2
5            d = 3*d + 1;                      // step 3
6        }
7        while (d > 0) {                       // step 4
8            for (int i = d; i < n; i++) {     // step 5
9                int ai = a[i];
10               j = i;
11               while (j >= d && a[j-d] > ai) {
12                   a[j] = a[j-d];
13                   j -= d;
14               }
15               a[j] = ai;
16           }
17           d /= 3;                           // step 6
18       }
19   }
```

THE MERGE SORT

The *merge sort* applies the divide-and-conquer strategy to sort a sequence. First it subdivides the sequence into subsequences of singletons. Then it successively merges the subsequences pairwise until a single sequence is re-formed. Each merge preserves order, so each merged subsequence is sorted. When the final merge is finished, the complete sequence is sorted.

Although it can be implemented iteratively, the merge sort is naturally recursive: Split the sequence in two, sort each half, and then merge them back together preserving their order. The basis occurs when the subsequence contains only a single element.

Algorithm 14.5 The Merge Sort

(Precondition: $s = \{s_p \ldots s_{q-1}\}$ is a sequence of $q - p$ ordinal values.)

(Postcondition: The entire sequence s is sorted.)

1. If $q - p > 1$, do steps 2–5.
2. Split s into two subsequences, $a = \{s_p \ldots s_{m-1}\}$ and $b = \{s_m \ldots s_{q-1}\}$, where $m = (q - p)/2$.
3. Sort a.
4. Sort b.
5. Merge a and b back into s, preserving order.

EXAMPLE 14.8 The Merge Sort

```
1   public static void sort(int[] a) {
2     // POSTCONDITION: a[0] <= a[1] <= ... <= a[a.length-1];
3     sort(a, 0, a.length);
4   }
5
6   private static void sort(int[] a, int p, int m, int q) {
7     // PRECONDITIONS: 0 <= p <= q <= a.length;
8     // POSTCONDITION: a[p..q) is sorted;
9     if (q - p < 2) {      // step 1
10       return;
11    }
12    int m = (p + q)/2;    // step 2
13    sort(a, p, m);        // step 3
14    sort(a, m, q);        // step 4
15    merge(a, p, m, q);    // step 5
16  }
17
18  private static void merge(int[] a, int p, int m, int q) {
19    // PRECONDITIONS: 0 <= p <= m < q <= a.length;
20    //                a[p..m) is sorted;
21    //                a[m..q) is sorted;
22    // POSTCONDITION: a[p..q) is sorted;
23    if (a[m-1] <= a[m]) {
24      return;
25    }
26    int i = p, j = m, k = 0;
27    int[] tmp = new int[q-p];
28    while (i < m && j < q) {
29      // INVARIANT: tmp[0..k) is sorted
30      tmp[k++] = ( a[i]<=a[j] ? a[i++] : a[j++] );
31    }
32    System.arraycopy(a, i, a, p+k, m-i);
33    System.arraycopy(tmp, 0, a, p, k);
34  }
```

The main `sort()` method sorts the entire array by invoking the overloaded `sort()` method with parameters for the starting index k and the length n of the subarray. That three-parameter method sorts the subarray by sorting its left half and its right half separately and then merging them.

The `merge()` method merges the two halves a[p..m] and a[m..q] into a temporary array, where m is the middle index m = p + n/2. The `while` loop copies one element on each iteration; it copies the smaller of the two elements a[i] and a[j]. The post increment operator automatically advances the index of the copied element. When all the elements of one half have been copied, the `while` loop stops and then all the elements are copied back into a[].

Theorem 14.9 The merge sort runs in $O(n \lg n)$ time.

In general, the merge sort works by repeatedly dividing the array in half until the pieces are singletons, and then it merges the pieces pairwise until a single piece remains. This is illustrated by the diagram in Figure 14.1. The number of iterations in the first part equals the number of times n can be halved: that is, $\lg n - 1$. In terms of the number and sizes of the pieces, the second part of the process reverses the first. So the second part also has $\lg n - 1$ steps. So the entire algorithm has $O(\lg n)$ steps. Each step compares all n elements. So the total number of comparisons is $O(n \lg n)$.

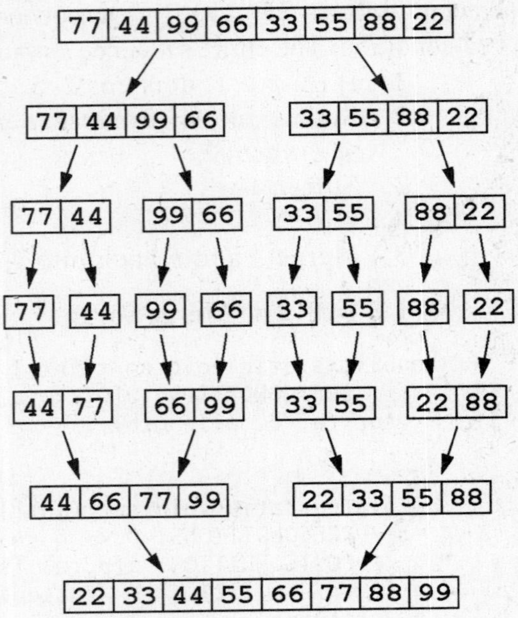

Figure 14.1 The merge sort

Theorem 14.10 The merge sort is correct.

The proof follows from the preconditions and postconditions given in the code. In the main `sort()` method, the array is already sorted if its length is 0 or 1. Otherwise, the postcondition of the three-parameter `sort()` method guarantees that the array will be sorted after that method returns because the entire array is passed to it. That postcondition is the same as the postcondition of the `merge()` method, which is invoked last, so it remains to verify that the `merge()` method's postcondition will be true.

The `merge()` method's postcondition follows from its loop invariant, because when that loop has finished, the `tmp[]` array is sorted and that is copied back into `a[]` in the same order. So it remains to verify the loop invariant for all `k < q - p`.

Suppose the invariant is false for some k, that is, `tmp[0..k)` is not sorted. Then there must be some x and y in `tmp[0..k)`, where x was copied into `tmp[]` before y but x > y. We may assume without loss of generality that x was copied from the left half of `a[]` and y from the right half, as shown in Figure 14.2. Thus, x = a[r] and y = a[s] for some indexes r and s such

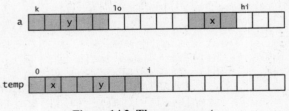

Figure 14.2 The merge sort

that $p \le r < i$ and $m \le s < j$. Now the two halves of `a[]` are each already separately sorted. Then for every element z in `a[m..s]`, $z \le a[s]$. But a[s] = y < x. Therefore, every element z in `a[m..s]` must have been copied into `tmp[]` before x was, because this assignment

        tmp[k++] = (a[i]<=a[j] ? a[i++] : a[j++]);

always copies the smaller element first. But that means that a[s] was copied into `tmp[]` before x. But a[s] = y, which was assumed to have been copied into `tmp[]` after x. This contradiction proves that the invariant must be true.

By using the *divide-and-conquer* strategy, the merge sort obtains an $O(n \lg n)$ run time, a significant improvement over the $O(n^2)$ times spent by the previous sorting algorithms. The strategy is

1. Split the sequence into two subsequences.
2. Sort each subsequence separately.
3. Merge the two subsequences back together.

The merge sort does the first step in the simplest balanced way possible: It splits the sequence at its middle. If the first step is done in other ways, we obtain different sorting algorithms. The divide-and-conquer strategy is also used in the binary search (page 31).

The simplest unbalanced way to split the sequence is to put all but the last element in the first subsequence, leaving only the last element in the second subsequence. This produces the recursive version of the insertion sort. (See Problem 14.22 on page 277.)

Another unbalanced way to split the sequence is to put the largest element alone in the second subsequence, leaving all the other elements in the first subsequence. This produces the recursive version of the selection sort. (See Problem 14.18 on page 276.) Not that this makes the merge step 3 trivial: Merely append the largest element to the end of the first subsequence.

A fourth way to split the sequence is to partition it so that every element in the first subsequence is less than every the element in the second subsequence. This condition of course is true in the previous case that led to the recursive selection sort. However, if we can obtain this property together with having the two subsequences the same size, then we obtain a new $O(n \lg n)$ algorithm, called the quick sort.

THE QUICK SORT

The quick sort is like the merge sort: It is recursive, it requires an auxiliary function with several loops, and it runs in $O(n \lg n)$ time. But in most cases it is quicker than the merge sort.

The quick sort works by partitioning the array into two pieces separated by a single element x that is greater than or equal to every element in the left piece and less than or equal to every element in the right piece. This guarantees that the single element x, called the *pivot* element, is in its correct position. Then the algorithm proceeds, applying the same method to the two pieces separately. This is naturally recursive and very quick.

Algorithm 14.6 The Quick Sort
(Precondition: $s = \{s_p \ldots s_{q-1}\}$ is a sequence of $q - p$ ordinal values.)
(Postcondition: The entire sequence s is sorted.)

1. If $q - p > 1$, do steps 2–5.
2. Apply Algorithm 14.7 to s, obtaining the pivot index m.
3. (Invariant: the pivot element s_m is in its correct sorted position.)
4. Apply the quick sort to $\{s_0, s_1, \ldots, s_{m-1}\}$.
5. Apply the quick sort to $\{s_{m+1}, s_{i+2}, \ldots, s_{n-1}\}$.

Algorithm 14.7 Partition
(Precondition: $s = \{s_p \ldots s_{q-1}\}$ is a sequence of $q - p$ ordinal values.)
(Postcondition: Return m, where $p \leq m < q$ and $s_i \leq s_m \leq s_j$ for $p \leq i \leq m \leq j < q$.)

1. Set $x = s_p$ (the *pivot* element).
2. Set $i = p$ and $j = q$.

3. Repeat steps 4–7 while $i < j$.
4. Decrement j until either $s_j < x$ or $j = i$.
5. If $j > i$, copy s_j into s_i.
6. Increment i until either $s_i > x$ or $i = j$.
7. If $j > i$, copy s_j into s_i.
8. Copy x into s_j.

EXAMPLE 14.9 The Quick Sort

```
1   public static void sort(int[] a) {
2     // POSTCONDITION: a[0] <= a[1] <= ... <= a[a.length-1];
3     sort(a, 0, a.length);
4   }
5
6   private static void sort(int[] a, int p, int q) {
7     //  PRECONDITION: 0 <= p <= q <= a.length
8     // POSTCONDITION: a[p..q] is sorted;
9     if (q - p < 2) {
10      return;
11    }
12    int m = partition(a, p, q);  // step 2
13    sort(a, p, m);               // step 4
14    sort(a, m+1, q);             // step 5
15  }
16
17  private static int partition(int[] a, int p, int q) {
18    // RETURNS: index m of pivot element a[m];
19    // POSTCONDITION: a[i] <= a[m] <= a[j] for p <= i <= m <= j < q;
20    int pivot = a[p], i = p, j = q;       // steps 1-2
21    while (i < j) {                       // step 3
22      while (i < j && a[--j] >= pivot) ;  // step 4
23      if (i < j) {
24        a[i] = a[j];                      // step 5
25      }
26      while (i < j && a[++i] <= pivot) ;  // step 6
27      if (i < j) {
28        a[j] = a[i];                      // step 7
29      }
30    }
31    a[j] = pivot;                         // step 8
32    return j;
33  }
```

Note the *empty loop* at line 22 and line 26. All the action is managed within the loop condition, so no statements are in its body.

Algorithm 14.7 selects the pivot element to be the last element in the sequence. The algorithm works just as well if it is selected to be the first element or the middle element. Slightly better performance is obtained by selecting the median of those three elements.

The Java Arrays.sort() method implements the quick sort, selecting the pivot as the median of the three elements $\{s_0, s_{n/2}, s_{n-1}\}$ when $n \le 40$, and the median of 9 equally spaced elements when $n > 40$. It also switches to the insertion sort (Algorithm 14.3 on page 258) when $n < 7$.

Theorem 14.11 The quick sort runs in $O(n \lg n)$ time in the best case.

The best case is when the sequence values are uniformly randomly distributed so that each call to the quick partition algorithm will result in balanced split of the sequence. In that case, each recursive call to the quick sort algorithm divides the sequence into two subsequences of nearly equal length. As with the binary search and the merge sort (Algorithm 14.5 on page 261), this repeated subdivision takes $\lg n$ steps to get down to size 1 subsequences, as illustrated in the diagram in Figure 14.2 on page 262. So there are $O(\lg n)$ calls made to the quick partition algorithm which runs in $O(n)$ time, so the total running time for the quick sort algorithm is $O(n \lg n)$.

Theorem 14.12 The quick sort runs in $O(n^2)$ time in the worst case.

The worst case is when the sequence is already sorted (or sorted in reverse order). In that case, the quick partition algorithm will always select the last element (or the first element, if the sequence is sorted in reverse order), resulting in the most unbalanced split possible: One piece has $n{-}2$ elements, and the other piece has 1 element. Repeated division of this type will occur $O(n)$ times before both pieces get down to size 1. So there are $O(n)$ calls made to the quick partition algorithm which runs in $O(n)$ time, so the total running time for the quick sort algorithm is $O(n^2)$.

Note that in the worst case, the quick sort reverts to the selection sort (Algorithm 14.2 on page 257) because each call to quick partition amounts to selecting the largest element from the subsequence passed to it. So actually, Theorem 14.12 is a corollary to Theorem 14.4 on page 258.

Theorem 14.13 The quick sort runs in $O(n \lg n)$ time in the average case.

The proof of this fact is beyond the scope of this outline.

Theorem 14.14 The quick sort is correct.

The invariant inside the `while` loop proof claims that all the elements to the left of `a[i]` are less than or equal to the `pivot` element and that all the elements to the right of `a[j]` are greater than or equal to the `pivot`. This is true because every element to the left of `a[i]` that is greater than the `pivot` was swapped with some element to the right of `a[j]` that is less than the `pivot`, and conversely (every element to the right of `a[j]` that is less than the `pivot` was swapped with some element to the left of `a[i]` that is greater than the `pivot`. When that loop terminates, `j` $\leq$ `i`, so at that point all the elements that are greater than the `pivot` have been moved to the right of `a[i]`, and all the elements that are less than the `pivot` have been moved to the left of `a[i]`. This is the invariant in step 7 of the quick partition algorithm. So after the swap in step 8, all the elements that are greater than the `a[i]` are to the right of `a[i]`, and all the elements that are less than the `a[i]` are to the left of `a[i]`. This is the invariant in step 7 of the quick partition algorithm, which is the same as the invariant in step 3 of the quick sort algorithm. So then sorting the left segment and the right segment independently will render the entire sequence sorted.

THE HEAP SORT

A heap is by definition partially sorted, because each linear string from root to leaf is sorted. (See Chapter 13.) This leads to an efficient general sorting algorithm called the *heap sort*. As with all sorting algorithms, it applies to an array (or `vector`). But the underlying heap structure (a binary tree) that the array represents is used to define this algorithm.

Like the merge sort and the quick sort, the heap sort uses an auxiliary function that is called from the `sort()` function. And also like the merge sort and the quick sort, the heap sort has complexity function $O(n \lg n)$. But unlike the merge sort and the quick sort, the heap sort is not recursive.

The heap sort essentially loads n elements into a heap and then unloads them. By Theorem 13.1 on page 247, each element takes $O(\lg n)$ time to load and $O(\lg n)$ time to unload, so the entire process on n element runs in $O(n \lg n)$ time.

Algorithm 14.8 The Heap Sort

(Precondition: $s = \{s_0 \ldots s_{n-1}\}$ is a sequence of n ordinal values.)
(Postcondition: The entire sequence s is sorted.)

1. Do steps 2–3 for $i = n/2 - 1$ down to 0.
2. Apply the heapify algorithm to the subsequence $\{s_i \ldots s_{n-1}\}$.
3. (Invariant: every root-to-leaf path in s is nonincreasing.)
4. Do steps 5–7 for $i = n - 1$ down to 1.
5. Swap s_i with s_0.
6. (Invariant: The subsequence $\{s_i \ldots s_{n-1}\}$ is sorted.)
7. Apply the heapify algorithm to the subsequence $\{s_0 \ldots s_{i-1}\}$.

Algorithm 14.9 The Heapify

(Preconditions: $ss = \{s_i \ldots s_{j-1}\}$ is a subsequence of $j-i$ ordinal values, and both subsequences $\{s_{i+1} \ldots s_{j-1}\}$ and $\{s_{i+2} \ldots s_{j-1}\}$ have the heap property.)
(Postcondition: ss itself has the heap property.)

1. Let $t = s_{2i+1}$.
2. Let $s_k = \max\{s_{2i+1}, s_{2i+2}\}$, so $k = 2i+1$ or $2i+2$, the index of the larger child.
3. If $t < s_k$, do steps 4–6.
4. Set $s_i = s_k$.
5. Set $i = k$.
6. If $i < n/2$ and $s_i < \max\{s_{2i+1}, s_{2i+2}\}$, repeat steps 1–4.
7. Set $s_k = t$.

There are two aspects to these algorithms that distinguish them from the methods outlined in Chapter 12. The heaps here are in the reverse order, so each root-to-leaf path is descending. And these algorithms use 0-based indexing. The reverse order guarantees that heapify will always leave the largest element at the root of the subsequence. Using 0-base indexing instead of 1-based indexing renders the `sort()` method consistent with all the other `sort()` methods at the expense of making the code a little more complicated.

EXAMPLE 14.10 The Heap Sort

```
34     public static void sort(int[] a) {
35        // POSTCONDITION: a[0] <= a[1] <= ... <= a[a.length-1];
36        int n = a.length;
37        for (int i = n/2 - 1; i >= 0; i--) {      // step 1
38           heapify(a, i, n);                      // step 2
39        }
```

```
40        for (int i = n - 1; i > 0; i--) {        // step 4
41          swap(a, 0, i);                          // step 5
42          heapify(a, 0, i);                       // step 7
43        }
44      }
45
46      private static void heapify(int[] a, int i, int j) {
47        int ai = a[i];                            // step 1
48        while (2*i+1 < j) {
49          int k = 2*i + 1;
50          if (k + 1 < j && a[k+1] > a[k]) {
51            ++k;  // a[k] is the larger child
52          }
53          if (ai >= a[k]) {
54            break;                                // step 3
55          }
56          a[i] = a[k];                            // step 4
57          i = k;                                  // step 5
58        }
59        a[i] = ai;                                // step 7
60      }
```

The sort() function first converts the array so that its underlying complete binary tree is transformed into a heap. This is done by applying the heapify() function to each nontrivial subtree. The nontrivial subtrees (i.e., those having more than one element) are the subtrees that are rooted above the leaf level. In the array, the leaves are stored at positions a[n/2] through a[n]. So the first for loop in the sort() function applies the heapify() function to elements a[n/2-1] back through a[0] (which is the root of the underlying tree). The result is an array whose corresponding tree has the heap property, illustrated in Figure 14.3.

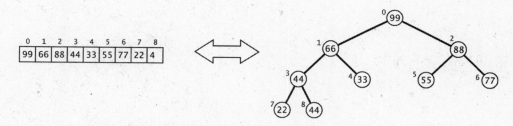

Figure 14.3 The natural mapping for the heap sort

Now the main (second) for loop progresses through n-1 iterations. Each iteration does two things: it swaps the root element with element a[i], and then it applies the heapify() function to the subtree of elements a[0..i]. That subtree consists of the part of the array that is still unsorted. Before the swap() executes on each iteration, the subarray a[0..i] has the heap property, so a[i] is the largest element in that subarray. That means that the swap() puts element a[i] in its correct position.

The first seven iterations of the main for loop have the effect shown by the seven pictures in Figure 14.4 on page 268. The array (and its corresponding imaginary binary tree) is partitioned into two parts: The first part is the subarray a[0..i) that has the heap property, and the second part is the remaining a[i..n) whose elements are in their correct positions. The second part is shaded in each of the seven pictures in Figure 14.4 on page 268. Each iteration of the main for loop decrements the size of the first part and increments the size of the second part. So when the loop has finished, the first part is empty and the second (sorted) part constitutes the entire array. This analysis verifies the following theorem.

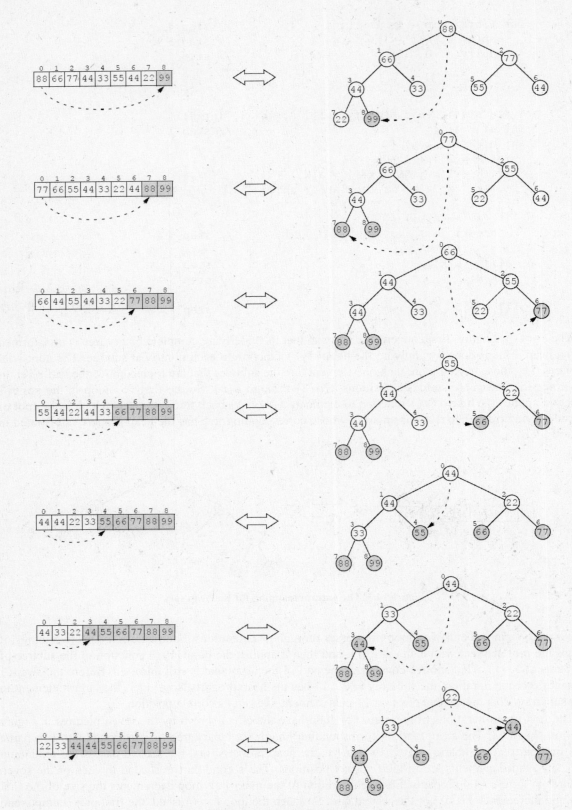

Figure 14.4 Tracing the heap sort

Theorem 14.15 The heap sort is correct.

See Problem 14.31 on page 277.

Theorem 14.16 The heap sort runs in $O(n \lg n)$ time.

Each call to the `heapify()` function takes at most $\lg n$ steps because it iterates only along a path from the current element down to a leaf. The longest such path for a complete binary tree of n elements is $\lg n$. The `heapify()` function is called $n/2$ times in the first `for` loop and $n-1$ times in the second `for` loop. That comes to less than $(3n/2) \lg n$, which is proportional to $n \lg n$.

If we regard a sorting algorithm as a stream process wherein elements stream into an array in random order and then stream out in sorted order, then the heap sort can be regarded as an efficient mean between the extremes of the selection sort and the insertion sort. The selection sort does all its sorting during the removal stage of the process, having stored the elements in the unsorted order in which they arrived. The insertion sort does all its sorting during the insertion stage of the process so that the elements can stream out of the array in the sorted order in which they were stored. But the heap sort does a partial sorting by inserting the elements into a heap and then finishes the sorting as the elements are removed from the heap. The payoff from this mean between the extremes is greater efficiency: $O(n \lg n)$ instead of $O(n^2)$.

THE SPEED LIMIT FOR COMPARISON SORTS

Theorem 14.17 No sorting algorithm that rearranges the array by comparing its elements can have a worst-case complexity function better than $O(n \lg n)$.

Consider the decision tree that covers all possible outcomes of the algorithm on an array of size n. Since the algorithm rearranges the array by comparing its elements, each node in the decision tree represents a condition of the form (`a[i] < a[j]`). Each such condition has two possible outcomes (`true` or `false`), so the decision tree is a binary tree. And since the tree must cover all possible arrangements, it must have at least $n!$ leaves. Therefore, by Corollary 11.3 on page 203, the height of the decision tree must be at least $\lg(n!)$. In the worst case, the number of comparisons that the algorithm makes is the same as the height of the decision tree. Therefore, the algorithm's worst-case complexity function must be $O(\lg(n!))$.

Now by Stirling's Formula (outlined on page 325),

$$n! \approx \sqrt{2n\pi}\left(\frac{n}{e}\right)^n$$

so

$$\log(n!) \approx \log\left(\sqrt{2n\pi}\left(\frac{n}{e}\right)^n\right) \approx \log(n^n) = n \log n$$

(Here, "log" means the binary logarithm $\log_2$.) Therefore, the algorithm's worst-case complexity function must be $O(n \log n)$.

Theorem 14.17 applies only to comparison sorts. A *comparison sort* is an algorithm that sorts elements by comparing their values and then changes their relative positions according to the outcomes of those comparisons. All the sorting algorithms outlined previously are comparison sorts. In contrast, the following sorting algorithms are not comparisons sorts.

THE RADIX SORT

The radix sort assumes that the sequence's element type is a lexicographic array of constant size, that is, either a character string type or an integer type. Let r be the array element's *radix* (e.g., $r = 26$ for ASCII character strings, $r = 10$ for decimal integers, $r = 2$ for bit strings), and let w be the constant width of the lexicographic array. For example, for U.S. Social Security numbers, $d = 10$ and $w = 9$.

EXAMPLE 14.11 Sorting Books by Their ISBNs

Every book published since the 1970s has been assigned a unique international standard book number (ISBN). These are usually printed at the bottom of the back cover of the book. For example, the ISBN for this book is 0071476989. (ISBNs are usually hyphenated, like this: 0-07-147698-9, to distinguish the four separate fields that make up the code.) The last digit is a check digit, computed from the other nine digits. Since it can be any of the 10 numeric digits or the letter X, we have that the radix $r = 11$, while the number of digits $d = 10$.

Algorithm 14.10 The Radix Sort

(Precondition: $s = \{s_0 \ldots s_{n-1}\}$ is a sequence of n integers or character strings with radix r and width w.)

(Postcondition: The sequence s is sorted numerically or lexicographically.)

1. Repeat step 2 for $d = 0$ up to $w - 1$.
2. Apply a stable sorting algorithm to the sequence s, sorting only on digit number d.

A sorting algorithm is said to be *stable* if it preserves the relative order of elements with equal keys. For example, the insertion sort is stable, but the heap sort is not.

EXAMPLE 14.12 Sorting ISBNs with the radix sort

Figure 14.5 shows a sequence of 12 ISBNs and the first four iterations of the radix sort applied to it.

```
0070308373        0071353461        0071342109        0071342109
0071353461        0070308373        8838650527        007052713X
0071342109        0071353453        0830636528        0071361286
0071353453        0070308683        007052713X        0070308373
0070308683        8838650454        0071353453        0071353453
0071361286        9742080585        8838650454        8838650454
007052713X        0071361286        0071353461        0071353461
0830636528        8838650527        0070308373        0830628479
0830628479        0830636528        0830628479        8838650527
8838650527        0830628479        0070308683        0830636528
8838650454        0071342109        9742080585        9742080585
9742080585        007052713X        0071361286        0070308683
```

Figure 14.5 Tracing the radix sort

Note how the stability is needed to conserve the work done by previous iterations. For example, after the first iteration, **8838650527** precedes **0830636528** because **7 < 8**. Both of these keys have the same value 2 in their second least significant digit (digit number $d = 1$). So on the second iteration, which sorts only on digit number 1, these two keys evaluate as being equal. But they should retain their previous relative order because **27 < 28**. Stability guarantees that they do.

The columns that have been processed are shaded. So after the third iteration, the right-most 3-digit subsequences are sorted: **109 < 13X < 373 < 453**. (Note that **X** stands for the value 10. So **13X** numerically means $130 + 10 = 140$.)

EXAMPLE 14.13 The Radix Sort

This method assumes that the constants RADIX has WIDTH have been defined. For example, for arrays of ints:

```
1     public static void sort(int[] a) {
2       // POSTCONDITION: a[0] <= a[1] <= ... <= a[a.length-1];
3       for (int d = 0; d < WIDTH; d++) {  // step 1
4         sort(a, d);                       // step 2
5       }
6     }
7
8     private static void sort(int[] a, int d) {
9       // POSTCONDITION: a[] is sorted stably on digit d;
10      int n = a.length;
11      int[] c = new int[RADIX];
12      for (int ai : a) {
13        ++c[digit(d,ai)];   // tally the values in a[]
14      }
15      for (int j = 1; j < RADIX; j++) {
16        c[j] += c[j-1];    // c[j] == num elts in a[] that are <= j
17      }
18      int[] tmp = new int[n];
19      for (int i = n - 1; i >= 0; i--) {
20        tmp[--c[digit(d, a[i])]] = a[i];
21      }
22      for (int i = 0; i < n; i++)
23      a[i] = tmp[i];
24    }
25
26    private static int digit(int d, int x) {
27      // returns digit number d of integer x
28      // e.g., digit(2, 1234567890) returns 8;
29      return x/(int)Math.pow(10,d)%RADIX;
30    }
```

The secondary sorting method at line 8 is called a *counting sort* or *tally sort*.

Theorem 14.18 The radix sort runs in $O(n)$ time.

The algorithm has WIDTH iterations and processes all n elements on each iteration three times. Thus, the running time is proportional to WIDTH*n and is a constant.

Although $O(n)$ is theoretically better than $O(n \lg n)$, the radix sort is rarely faster than the $O(n \lg n)$ sorting algorithms (merge sort, quick sort, and heap sort). That is because it has a lot of overhead extracting digits and copying arrays.

THE BUCKET SORT

The *bucket sort* is another distribution sort. It distributes the elements into "buckets" according to some coarse grain criterion and then applies another sorting algorithm to each bucket. It is similar to the quick sort in that all the elements in bucket i are greater than or equal to all the elements in bucket $i-1$ and less than or equal to all the elements in bucket $i+1$. Whereas quick sort partitions the sequence into two buckets, the bucket sort partitions the sequence into n buckets.

Algorithm 14.11 The Bucket Sort

(Precondition: $s = \{s_0 \ldots s_{n-1}\}$ is a sequence of n ordinal values with known minimum value min and maximum value max.)

(Postcondition: the sequence s is sorted.)

1. Initialize an array of n buckets (collections).
2. Repeat step 3 for each s_i in the sequence.
3. Insert s_i into bucket j, where $j = \lfloor rn \rfloor$, $r = (s_i - \text{min})/(\text{max} + 1 - \text{min})$.
4. Sort each bucket.
5. Repeat step 6 for j from 0 to $n-1$.
6. Add the elements of bucket j sequentially back into s.

EXAMPLE 14.14 Sorting U.S. Social Security Numbers with the Bucket Sort.

Suppose you have 1000 nine-digit identification numbers. Set up 1000 arrays of type `int` and then distribute the numbers using the formula $j = \lfloor rn \rfloor$, $r = (s_i - \text{min})/(\text{max} + 1 - \text{min}) = (s_i - 0)/(10^9 + 1 - 0) \cong s_i/10^9$. So, for example, the identification number 666666666 would be inserted into bucket number j where $j = \lfloor rn \rfloor = \lfloor (666666666/10^9)(10^3) \rfloor = \lfloor 666.666666 \rfloor = 666$. Similarly, identification number 123456789 would be inserted into bucket number 123, and identification number 666543210 would be inserted into bucket 666. (See Figure 14.6.)

Then each bucket would be sorted. Note that the number of elements in each bucket will average 1, so the choice of sorting algorithm will not affect the running time.

Finally, the elements are copied back into s, starting with bucket number 0.

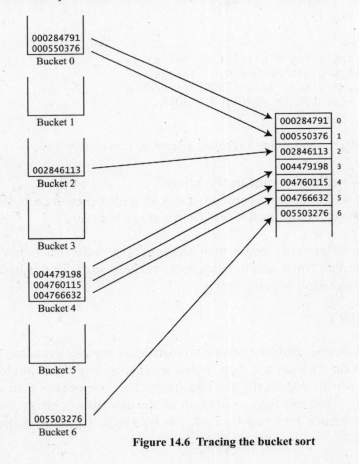

Figure 14.6 Tracing the bucket sort

EXAMPLE 14.15 The Bucket Sort

```
1      public static void sort(int[] a) {
2        // POSTCONDITION: a[0] <= a[1] <= ... <= a[a.length-1];
3        int min = min(a);
4        int max = max(a);
5        int n = a.length;
6        Bucket[] bucket = new Bucket[n];              // step 1
7        for (int j=0; j<n; j++) {
8          bucket[j] = new Bucket();
9        }
10       for (int i=0; i<n; i++) {                     // step 2
11         int j = n*(a[i] - min)/(max + 1 - min);
12         bucket[j].add(a[i]);                        // step 3
13       }
14       int i=0;
15       for (int j=0; j<n; j++) {
16         Bucket bj=bucket[j];
17         bj.sort();                                  // step 4
18         for (int k=0; k<bj.size(); k++) {           // step 5
19           a[i++] = bj.get(k);
20         }
21       }
22     }
23
24     private static int min(int[] a) {
25       int min = a[0];
26       for (int ai: a) {
27         if (ai < min) {
28           min = ai;
29         }
30       }
31       return min;
32     }
33
34     private static int max(int[] a) {
35       int max = a[0];
36       for (int ai: a) {
37         if (ai > max) {
38           max = ai;
39         }
40       }
41       return max;
42     }
```

This program requires the implementation of this interface:

```
              public interface Bucket {
                public void add(int x);   // appends x to end of bucket
                public int get(int k);    // returns element k from bucket
                public int size();        // returns the number of elements
              }
```

For example:

```
43     private static class Bucket extends java.util.ArrayList<Integer> {
44       void sort() {
45         java.util.Arrays.sort(this.toArray());
46       }
47     }
```

Theorem 14.19 The bucket sort runs in $O(n)$ time.

The algorithm has three parallel loops, each iterating n times. The last loop has an inner loop, but it averages only one iteration. The `minimum()` and `maximum()` methods also require n steps each. Hence the number of steps executed is proportional to $5n$.

Like the radix sort, the $O(n)$ bucket sort is in practice much slower than the $O(n \lg n)$ sorting algorithms because of the substantial overhead costs.

Review Questions

14.1 Why is the bubble sort so slow?

14.2 The bubble sort makes $n(n-1)/2$ comparisons to sort n elements. How does it follow that its complexity function is $O(n^2)$?

14.3 Why are the $O(n)$ sorting algorithms (radix sort and bucket sort) slower than the $O(n \lg n)$ sorting algorithms (merge sort, quick sort, and heap sort)?

14.4 The merge sort applies the general method, known as *divide and conquer*, to sort an array. It divides the array into pieces and applies itself recursively to each piece. What other sorting algorithm(s) use this method?

14.5 Which sorting algorithms work as well on linked lists as on arrays?

14.6 Which sorting algorithms have a different worst case complexity than their average case?

14.7 Which sorting algorithms have a different best case complexity than their average case?

14.8 Why is the nonrecursive version of a recursive sorting algorithm usually more efficient?

14.9 How is the quick sort like the merge sort?

14.10 Under what circumstances would the merge sort be preferred over the other two $O(n \lg n)$ sorting algorithms?

14.11 Under what circumstances is the quick sort like the selection sort?

14.12 Under what circumstances would the quick sort be preferred over the other two $O(n \lg n)$ sorting algorithms?

14.13 How is the heap sort similar to the selection sort and the insertion sort?

14.14 Which algorithm does the Java API use to implement its `java.util.Arrays.sort()` methods?

14.15 A sorting algorithm is said to be *stable* if it preserves the order of equal elements. Which of the sorting algorithms are not stable?

14.16 Which of the nine sorting algorithms outlined in this chapter require extra array space?

14.17 Which of the nine sorting algorithms outlined in this chapter would work best on an external file of records?

14.18 The merge sort is *parallelizable*. This means that parts of it can be performed simultaneously, independent of each other, provided that the computer has multiple processors that can run in parallel. This works for the merge sort because several different parts of the array can be subdivided or merged independently of other parts. Which of the other sorting algorithms described in this chapter are parallelizable?

14.19 Imagine a Web site that has a Java applet for each sorting algorithm that shows how the algorithm works by displaying an animation of a test run on an array a[] of 256 random numbers in the range 0.0 to 1.0. The animation shows on each iteration of the algorithm's main loop a two-dimensional plot of 256 points (x, y), one for each element in the array, where $x = $ i+1 and $y = $ a[i]. Each plot in Figure 14.7 shows the progress halfway through the sort for one of the following six algorithms:

>   selection sort
>   insertion sort
>   merge sort
>   quick sort
>   heap sort
>   radix sort

Match each plot with the sorting algorithm that produced it:

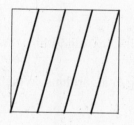
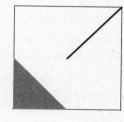

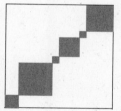
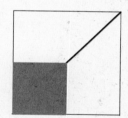
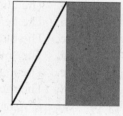

Figure 14.7 Sorting algorithms in motion

Problems

14.1 If an $O(n^2)$ algorithm (e.g., the bubble sort, the selection sort, or the insertion sort) takes 3.1 milliseconds to run on an array of 200 elements, how long would you expect it to take to run on a similar array of:

    a. 400 elements?

    b. 40,000 elements?

14.2 If an $O(n \lg n)$ algorithm (e.g., the merge sort, the quick sort, or the heap sort) takes 3.1 milliseconds to run on an array of 200 elements, how long would you expect it to take to run on a similar array of 40,000 elements?

14.3 The insertion sort runs in linear time on an array that is already sorted. How does it do on an array that is sorted in reverse order?

14.4   How does the bubble sort perform on:
    a.   An array that is already sorted?
    b.   An array that is sorted in reverse order?

14.5   How does the selection sort perform on:
    a.   An array that is already sorted?
    b.   An array that is sorted in reverse order?

14.6   How does the merge sort perform on:
    a.   An array that is already sorted?
    b.   An array that is sorted in reverse order?

14.7   How does the quick sort perform on:
    a.   An array that is already sorted?
    b.   An array that is sorted in reverse order?

14.8   How does the heap sort perform on:
    a.   An array that is already sorted?
    b.   An array that is sorted in reverse order?

14.9   The bubble sort, the selection sort, and the insertion sort are all $O(n^2)$ algorithms. Which is the fastest and which is the slowest among them?

14.10   The merge sort, the quick sort, and the heap sort are all $O(n \lg n)$ algorithms. Which is the fastest and which is the slowest among them?

14.11   Trace by hand the sorting of this array
```
      int a[] = { 44, 88, 55, 99, 66, 33, 22, 88, 77 }
```
by each of the following algorithms:
    a.   The quick sort
    b.   The heap sort
    c.   The bubble sort
    d.   The selection sort
    e.   The insertion sort
    f.   The merge sort

14.12   Modify the bubble sort so that it sorts the array in descending order.

14.13   Modify the bubble sort so that it is "smart" enough to terminate as soon as the array is sorted.

14.14   Prove Theorem 14.1 on page 257.

14.15   Prove Theorem 14.2 on page 257.

14.16   The shaker sort is the same as the bubble sort except that it alternates "bubbling" up and down the array. Implement the shaker sort, and determine whether it is more efficient than the straight insertion sort.

14.17   Modify the selection sort (Algorithm 14.2 on page 257) so that it uses the smallest element of $\{s_i \ldots s_{n-1}\}$ in step 2.

14.18   Rewrite the selection sort recursively.

14.19   Prove Theorem 14.3 on page 258.

14.20   Prove Theorem 14.4 on page 258.

14.21   Modify the insertion sort so that it sorts the array indirectly. This requires a separate *index array* whose values are the indexes of the actual data elements. The indirect sort rearranges the index array, leaving the data array unchanged.

14.22　Rewrite the insertion sort recursively.

14.23　Prove Theorem 14.5 on page 259.

14.24　Prove Theorem 14.6 on page 259.

14.25　Prove Theorem 14.7 on page 259.

14.26　Modify the quick sort so that it selects its pivot as the last element instead of the first element of the subsequence.

14.27　Modify the quick sort so that it selects its pivot as the median of the first, middle, and last elements.

14.28　Modify the quick sort so that it reverts to the insertion sort when the array size is below 8.

14.29　Since the heap sort runs in $O(n \lg n)$ time, why isn't it always preferred over the quick sort, which runs in $O(n^2)$ in the worst case?

14.30　Since the heap sort runs in $O(n \lg n)$ time and requires no extra array space, why isn't it always preferred over the merge sort, which requires duplicate array space?

14.31　Prove Theorem 14.15 on page 269.

14.32　Here is the Las Vegas sort, as applied to sorting a deck of cards:
1. Randomly shuffle the cards.
2. If the deck is not sorted, repeat step 1.
Derive the complexity function for this sorting algorithm.

Answers to Review Questions

14.1　The bubble sort is so slow because it operates only locally. Each element moves only one position at a time. For example, the element 99 in Example 14.3 on page 256 is moved by six separate calls to the `swap()` function to be put into its correct position at `a[8]`.

14.2　The run time is nearly proportional to the number of comparisons made. That number is $n(n-1)/2$. For every positive integer n, $n(n-1)/2 < n^2$, so $n(n-1)/2 = O(n^2)$. Thus, $O(n^2)$ is the complexity function.

14.3　The $O(n)$ sorting algorithms (radix sort and bucket sort) are slower than the $O(n \lg n)$ sorting algorithms (merge sort, quick sort, and heap sort) because, although their running time is proportional to n, the constant of proportionality is large because of large overhead. For both the radix sort and the bucket sort, each iteration requires copying all the elements into a list of queues or arrays and then copying them back.

14.4　The merge sort, quick sort, and bucket sort all use the divide-and-conquer strategy.

14.5　The bubble sort, selection sort, insertion sort, merge sort, and quick sort work as well on linked lists as on arrays.

14.6　The quick sort and bucket sort are significantly slower in the worst case.

14.7　The insertion sort, shell sort, and radix sort are significantly faster in the best case.

14.8　Recursion carries the overhead of many recursive method invocations.

14.9　The quick sort implements the divide-and-conquer strategy: first it performs its $O(\lg n)$ partitioning of the sequence, and then it recursively sorts each of the two pieces independently. The merge sort implements the divide-and-conquer strategy but in the reverse order: It makes its two recursive calls first before performing its $O(\lg n)$ merge. Both algorithms do $O(n)$ amount of work $O(\lg n)$ times thus obtaining $O(n \lg n)$ complexity.

14.10　The merge sort is best for sorting linked lists and external files.

14.11　The quick sort reverts to the selection sort in the worst case, when the sequence is already sorted.

14.12 The quick sort is best for sorting large arrays of primitive types.

14.13 The selection sort can be seen as a sort-on-output process: Insert the elements into an array as they are given, and then repeatedly select out the next largest element. The insertion sort can be seen as a sort-on-input process: Repeatedly insert each element into its correct ordered position in an array, and then remove them in their array order. So the selection sort inserts the elements into the array in $O(n)$ time and removes them in $O(n^2)$, while the insertion sort inserts the elements into the array in $O(n^2)$ time and removes them in $O(n)$. Both result in an $O(n^2)$ algorithm.

The heap sort can be seen as a partial-sort-on-input-and-partial-sort-on-output process: Insert the elements into an array maintaining the (partially sorted) heap property, and then repeatedly select the first (which is the smallest) element and restore the heap property. Both the insertion process and the removal process have the same $O(n \lg n)$ running time, resulting in a total $O(n \lg n)$ running time.

14.14 The Java API uses the merge sort to implement its `Arrays.sort()` methods for arrays of objects, and it uses the quick sort to implement its `Arrays.sort()` methods for arrays of primitive types.

14.15 The shell sort, quick sort, and heap sort are unstable.

14.16 The merge sort, radix sort, and bucket sort require extra array storage.

14.17 The bubble sort, selection sort, insertion sort, merge sort, and quick sort work as well on external files of records.

14.18 The shell sort, merge sort, quick sort, and bucket sort all would run significantly faster on a parallel computer.

14.19 Matching the algorithms with their graphical output is shown in Figure 14.8.

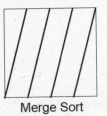

Merge Sort

Heap Sort

Radix Sort

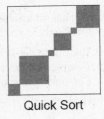

Quick Sort

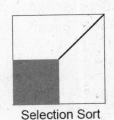

Selection Sort

Insertion Sort

Figure 14.8 Sorting algorithms in motion

Solutions to Problems

14.1 The $O(n^2)$ algorithm should take:
  a. 12.4 milliseconds (4 times as long) to run on the 400-element array.
  b. 124 seconds (40,000 times as long) to run on the 40,000-element array. That's about 2 minutes. This answer can be computed algebraically as follows. The running time t is proportional to n^2, so there is some constant c for which $t = c \cdot n^2$. If it takes $t = 3.1$ milliseconds to sort $n = 200$ elements, then (3.1 milliseconds) $= c \cdot (200 \text{ elements})^2$, so $c = (3.1 \text{ milliseconds})/(200 \text{ elements})^2 = 0.0000775$ milliseconds/element^2. Then, for $n = 40,000$, $t = c \cdot n^2 = (0.0000775 \text{ milliseconds}/\text{element}^2) \cdot (40,000 \text{ elements})^2 = 124,000$ milliseconds $= 124$ seconds.

14.2 The $O(n \lg n)$ algorithm should take 1.24 seconds (400 times as long) to run on the 40,000-element array. This answer can be computed algebraically. The running time t is proportional to $n \lg n$, so there is some constant c for which $t = c \cdot n \lg n$. If it takes $t = 3.1$ milliseconds to sort $n = 200$ elements, then $(3.1) = c \cdot (200) \lg(200)$, so $c = (3.1 \text{ milliseconds})/(200 \cdot \lg(200)) = 0.0155/\lg(200)$. Then, for $n = 40{,}000$, $t = c \cdot n \lg n = (0.0155/\lg(200))(40{,}000 \cdot \lg(40{,}000)) = 620 \cdot (\lg(40{,}000)/\lg(200))$. Now $40{,}000 = 200^2$, so $\lg(40{,}000) = \lg(200^2) = 2 \cdot \lg 200$. Thus, $\lg(40{,}000)/\lg(200) = 2$, so $t = 620 \cdot 2$ milliseconds $= 1240$ milliseconds $= 1.24$ s.

14.3 The insertion sort has its worst performance on an array that is sorted in reverse order, because each new element inserted requires all of the elements on its left to be shifted one position to the right.

14.4 The bubble sort, as implemented in Algorithm 14.1 on page 257, is *insensitive to input*. That means that it will execute the same number $n(n-1)/2$ of comparisons regardless of the original order of the elements in the array. So it doesn't matter whether the array is already sorted or whether it is sorted in reverse order; it is still very slow.

14.5 The selection sort is also insensitive to input: It takes about the same amount of time to sort arrays of the same size, regardless of their initial order.

14.6 The merge sort is also insensitive to input: It takes about the same amount of time to sort arrays of the same size, regardless of their initial order.

14.7 The quick sort is quite sensitive to input. As implemented in Algorithm 14.6 on page 263, the quick sort will degrade into an $O(n^2)$ algorithm in the special cases where the array is initially sorted in either order. That is because the pivot element will always be an extreme value within its subarray, so the partitioning splits the subarray very unevenly, thereby requiring n steps instead of $\lg n$.

14.8 The heap sort is a little sensitive to input, but not much. The `heapify()` function may require fewer than $\lg n$ iterations.

14.9 The bubble sort is slower than the selection sort, and the insertion sort (in most cases) is a little faster.

14.10 The merge sort is slower than the heap sort, and the quick sort (in most cases) is faster.

14.11 **a.** Trace of the quick sort:

a[0]	a[1]	a[2]	a[3]	a[4]	a[5]	a[6]	a[7]	a[8]
44	88	55	99	66	33	22	88	77
22	33	44			55	88		
			77					99
			55		77			

b. Trace of the heap sort:

a[0]	a[1]	a[2]	a[3]	a[4]	a[5]	a[6]	a[7]	a[8]
44	88	55	99	66	33	22	88	77
	99		88					
99	44							
	88						44	
77								99
88			77					
44							88	
88	77		44					
22						88		
77	66			22				
33					77			
66	44		33					
22				66				
55		22						
33			55					
44	22							
33		44						
22	33							

c. Trace of the bubble sort:

a[0]	a[1]	a[2]	a[3]	a[4]	a[5]	a[6]	a[7]	a[8]
44	88	55	99	66	33	22	88	77
	55	88						
			66	99				
				33	99			
					22	99		
						88	99	
							77	99
		66	88					
			33	88				
				22	88			
						77	88	
					77	88		
			33	66				
				22	66			
		33	55					
			22	55				
33	44							
	22	44						
22	33							

d. Trace of the selection sort:

a[0]	a[1]	a[2]	a[3]	a[4]	a[5]	a[6]	a[7]	a[8]
44	88	55	99	66	33	22	88	77
22						44		
	33				88			
		44				55		
			55			99		
					77			88
						88		99

e. Trace of the insertion sort:

a[0]	a[1]	a[2]	a[3]	a[4]	a[5]	a[6]	a[7]	a[8]
44	88	55	99	66	33	22	88	77
	55	88						
		66	88	99				
33	44	55	66	88	99			
22	33	44	55	66	88	99		
						88	99	
					77	88	88	99

f. Trace of the merge sort:

a[0]	a[1]	a[2]	a[3]	a[4]	a[5]	a[6]	a[7]	a[8]
44	88	55	99	66	33	22	88	77
44	55	77	99					
				33	66			
							77	88
				22	33	66	77	88
22	33	44	55	66	77	88	88	99

14.12
```
public static void sort(int[] a) {
  for (int i = a.length-1; i > 0; i--) {
    for (int j = 0; j < i; j++) {
      if (a[j] > a[j+1]) {
        swap(a, j, j+1);
      }
    }
  }
}
```

14.13
```
public static void sort(int[] a) {
  boolean sorted=false;
  int i = a.length-1;
  while (i > 0 && !sorted) {
    for (int j = 0; j < i; j++) {
      sorted = true;
      if (a[j] > a[j+1]) {
        swap(a, j, j+1);
        sorted = false;
      }
    }
    --i;
  }
}
```

14.14 The loop invariant can be used to prove that the bubble sort does indeed sort the array. After the first iteration of the main i loop, the largest element must have moved to the last position. Wherever it began, it had to be moved step by step all the way to the right, because on each comparison the larger element is moved right. For the same reason, the second largest element must have been moved to the second-from-last position in the second iteration of the main i loop. So the two largest elements are in the correct locations. This reasoning verifies that the loop invariant is true at the end of every iteration of the main i loop. But then, after the last iteration, the n-1 largest elements must be in their correct locations. That forces the nth largest (i.e., the smallest) element also to be in its correct location, so the array must be sorted.

14.15 The complexity function $O(n^2)$ means that, for large values of n, the number of loop iterations tends to be proportional to n^2. That means that, if one large array is twice the size of another, it should take about four times as long to sort. The inner j loop iterates $n-1$ times on the first iteration of the outside i loop, $n-2$ times on the second iteration of the i loop, $n-3$ times on the third iteration of the i loop, and so on. For example, when $n = 7$, there are six comparisons made on the first iteration of the i loop, five comparisons made on the second iteration of the i loop, four comparisons made on the third iteration of the i loop, and so forth, so the total number of comparisons is $6 + 5 + 4 + 3 + 2 + 1 = 21$. In general, the total number of comparisons will be $(n-1) + (n-2) + (n-3) + \cdots + 3 + 2 + 1$. This sum is $n(n-1)/2$. (See Theorem A.7 on page 323.) For large values of n, that expression is nearly $n^2/2$ which is proportional to n^2.

14.16
```
public static void sort(int[] a) {
  boolean sorted=false;
  for (int i = a.length; i > 0; i -= 2) {
    for (int j = 1; j < i; j++) {
      if (a[j-1] > a[j]) {
        swap(a,j-1,j);
      }
    }
    for (int j = i-2; j > 0; j--) {
      if (a[j-1] > a[j]) {
        swap(a, j-1, j);
      }
    }
  }
}
```

14.17
```
public static void sort(int[] a) {
   for (int i = 0; i < a.length-1; i++) {
      int j=i;
      for (int k = i+1; k < a.length; k++) {
         if (a[k] < a[j]) {
            j = k;
         }
      }
      swap(a, i, j);
   }
}
```

14.18
```
public static void sort(int[] a) {
   sort(a, a.length);
}

private static void sort(int[] a, int n) {
   if (n < 2) {
      return;
   }
   int j = 0;
   for (int k = 1; k < n; k++) {
      if (a[k] > a[j]) {
         j = k;
      }
   }
   swap(a, n-1, j);
   sort(a, n-1);
}
```

14.19   The last loop invariant proves correctness. So, like the proof for the bubble sort, we need only verify the loop invariants.

On the first iteration of the main loop (step 1), a[i] is the last element in the array, so the index k of the inner loop runs through every element after a[0]. The value of the index j begins at 0 and then changes each time k finds a larger element. Since j is always reset to the index of the larger element, a[j] will be the largest element of the array when the inner loop finishes. This verifies the first loop invariant. On each successive iteration of the outer loop, the index k runs through the remaining unsorted segment of the array, so for the same reason, a[j] will be the largest element of that remaining segment when the inner loop finishes. This verifies that the first loop invariant is true on every iteration of the outer loop.

Since swap(a,i,j) simply interchanges a[i] with a[j], the second loop invariant follows from the first.

The third loop invariant follows from the second and by mathematical induction. During the first iteration of the main loop, the inner loop finds a[j] to be the largest element in the array. The swap(a,i,j) puts that largest element in the last location a[i], so a[i] must be >= all the a[j]. Prior to the ith iteration of the main loop, we have by the inductive hypothesis that the subarray a[i+1..n] is sorted and all the values in the subarray a[0..i] are smaller than a[i+1]. Then after the ith iteration, a[i] is one of those smaller elements, so a[i] ≤ a[i+1] ≤ . . . ≤ a[n-1].

14.20   Again, the proof is essentially the same as that for the corresponding theorem for the bubble sort. On the first iteration of the outer i loop, the inner j loop iterates $n-1$ times. On the second, it iterates $n-2$ times. This progression continues, for a total of $(n-1) + (n-2) + \cdots + 2 + 1 = n(n-1)/2$.

14.21
```
public static void sort(int[] a, int[] ndx) {
   for (int i = 1; i < a.length; i++) {
      int ndxi = ndx[i], j;
      for (j = i; j > 0 && a[ndx[j-1]] > a[ndxi]; j--) {
         ndx[j] = ndx[j-1];
      }
      ndx[j] = ndxi;
   }
}
```

14.22
```
       public static void sort(int[] a) {
         sort(a, a.length);
       }

       public static void sort(int[] a, int n) {
         if (n < 2) {
           return;
         }
         sort(a, n-1);
         int temp = a[n-1], j;
         for (j = n-1; j > 0 && a[j-1] > temp; j--) {
           a[j] = a[j-1];
         }
         a[j] = temp;
       }
```

14.23 On the first iteration of the main loop, a[1] is compared with a[0] and interchanged if necessary. So a[0] ≤ a[1] after the first iteration. If we assume that the loop invariant is true prior to some kth iteration, then it must also be true after that iteration because during it a[k] is inserted between the elements that are less than or equal to it and those that are greater. It follows by mathematical induction that the loop invariant is true for all k.

14.24 The proof is similar to that for the corresponding theorems for the bubble sort and the selection sort. On the first iteration of the outer i loop, the inner j loop iterates once. On the second, it iterates once or twice, depending upon whether a[1] > a[2]. On the third iteration, the inner j loop iterates at most three times, again depending upon how many of the elements on the left of a[3] are greater than a[3]. This pattern continues, so that on the kth iteration of the outer loop, the inner loop iterates at most k times. Thus the maximum total number of iterations is $1 + 2 + \cdots + (n-1) = n(n-1)/2$.

14.25 In this case, the inner loop will iterate only once for each iteration of the outer loop. So the total number of iterations of the inner loop is: $1 + 1 + 1 + \cdots + 1 + 1 = n - 1$.

14.26 For the quick sort pivoting on the last element, the only changes needed are in the partition() method:
```
           private static int partition(int[] a, int p, int q) {
             int pivot = a[q-1], i = p-1, j = q-1;
             while (i < j) {
               while (i < j && a[++i] <= pivot) ;  // empty loop
               if (i < j) {
                 a[j] = a[i];
               }
               while (j > i && a[--j] >= pivot) ;  // empty loop
               if (j > i) {
                 a[i] = a[j];
               }
             }
             a[j] = pivot;
             return j;
           }
```

14.27 For the quick sort pivoting on median of three elements, the only changes needed are in the partition() method:
```
           private static int partition(int[] a, int p, int q) {
             int m = (p + q)/2;
             m = indexOfMedian(a, p, m, q-1);
             swap(a, p, m);
             // The rest is the same as lines 20-32 in Example 14.9 on page 264
           }
```

This requires a method for locating the index of three array elements:

```
private static int indexOfMedian(int[] a, int i, int j, int k) {
    // Returns the index of the median of {a[i], a[j], a[k]}
    if (a[i] <= a[j] && a[j] <= a[k]) return j;
    if (a[i] <= a[k] && a[k] <= a[j]) return k;
    if (a[j] <= a[i] && a[i] <= a[k]) return i;
    if (a[j] <= a[k] && a[k] <= a[i]) return k;
    if (a[k] <= a[i] && a[i] <= a[j]) return i;
    return j;
}
```

14.28 For the quick sort with reversion to the insertion sort on arrays of size < 8, the only changes needed are in the sort() method:

```
private static void sort(int[] a, int p, int q) {
    if (q - p < 2) {
        return;
    }
    if (q - p < 8) {
        insertionSort(a, p, q);
        return;
    }
    int m = partition(a, p, q);
    sort(a, p, m);        // steps 2 & 3
    sort(a, m+1, q);      // step 4
}
```

This requires a generalization of the insertion sort:

```
public static void insertionSort(int[] a, int p, int q) {
    for (int i = p+1; i < q; i++) {
        int ai = a[i], j;
        for (j = i; j > 0 && a[j-1] > ai; j--) {
            a[j] = a[j-1];
        }
        a[j] = ai;
    }
}
```

14.29 The heap sort is not always preferred over the quick sort because it is slower in the average case.

14.30 The heap sort is not always preferred over the merge sort because it is not stable.

14.31 The postcondition of heapify (Algorithm 14.9 on page 266) establishes the loop invariant in step 3. That guarantees that the root s_0 is the maximum element of the subsequence. Step 5 inserts that maximum at the end of the subsequence. So when the loop at step 4 is finished, the sequence will be sorted. The heapify algorithm restores the heap property to the complete segment ss by applying the heapifyDown() method from its root.

14.32 The Las Vegas sort has complexity $O(n^n)$.

There are $n!$ different permutations of a deck of n cards. Shuffling them is equivalent to selecting one permutation at random. Only one of the $n!$ permutations leaves the cards in order. So the expected number of random shuffles required before the correct one occurs is $n!/2$. Then each permutation takes $n-1$ comparisons to see if it is the correct one. So the total complexity is $O(n\,n!/2)$. By Stirling's Formula (page 325), $O(n\,n!/2) = O(n!) = O(2^n)$.

CHAPTER 15

Graphs

A *graph* is a nonlinear structure. Like linear data structures (lists), it can be implemented with either an indexed or a linked backing data structure.

SIMPLE GRAPHS

A (*simple*) *graph* is a pair $G = (V, E)$, where V and E are finite sets and every element of E is a two-element subset of V (i.e., an unordered pair of distinct elements of V). The elements of V are called *vertices* (or *nodes*), and the elements of E are called *edges* (or *arcs*). If $e \in E$, then $e = \{a, b\}$ for some $a, b \in V$. In this case, we can denote e more simply as $e = ab = ba$. We say that the edge e *connects* the two vertices a and b, that e is *incident with* a and b, that a and b are *incident upon* e, that a and b are the *terminal points* or *end points* of the edge e, and that a and b are *adjacent*.

The *size* of a graph is the number of elements in its vertex set.

EXAMPLE 15.1 A Simple Graph

Figure 15.1 shows a simple graph (V, E) of size 4. Its vertex set is $V = \{a, b, c, d\}$, and its edge set is $E = \{ab, ac, ad, bd, cd\}$. This graph has four vertices and five edges.

Figure 15.1 A graph

Note that by definition an edge is a set with exactly two elements. This prevents the possibility of a loop being an edge because a loop involves only one vertex. So the definition of simple graphs excludes the possibility of loops.

Also note that since E is a set, an edge cannot be listed more than once. (Sets do not allow repeated members.) So the definition of simple graphs excludes the possibility of multiple edges.

In general, graphs may include loops and multiple edges; simple graphs do not.

GRAPH TERMINOLOGY

If $G = (V, E)$ is a graph and $G' = (V', E')$ where $V' \subseteq V$ and $E' \subseteq E$, then G' is called a *subgraph* of G. If $V' = V$, then G' is called a *spanning subgraph* of G.

Every graph is a spanning subgraph of itself.

EXAMPLE 15.2 Subgraphs

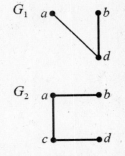

The graph $G_1 = (V_1, E_1)$ in Figure 15.2 with vertex set $V_1 = \{a, b, d\}$ and edge set $E_1 = \{ad, bd\}$ is a nonspanning subgraph of the graph in Example 15.1. This subgraph has size 3.

The graph $G_2 = (V_2, E_2)$ in Figure 15.2 with vertex set $V_2 = \{a, b, c, d\}$ and edge set $E_2 = \{ab, ac, cd\}$ is a spanning subgraph of the graph in Example 15.1. This subgraph has size 4.

Figure 15.2 Subgraphs

The *degree* (or *valence*) of a vertex is the number of edges that are incident upon it. For example, in the graph in Figure 15.1 on page 285, vertex a has degree 3 and vertex b has degree 2. But in the subgraph G_1 in Figure 15.2, vertices a and b both have degree 1.

An *isolated point* is a vertex of degree 0.

Theorem 15.1 The sum of the degrees of the vertices of a graph with m edges is $2m$.

Each edge contributes 1 to the degree of each of the two vertices that determine it. So the total contribution if m edges is $2m$.

A *complete graph* is a simple graph in which every pair of vertices is connected by an edge. For a given number n of vertices, there is only one complete graph of that size, so we refer to the complete graph on a given vertex set.

EXAMPLE 15.3 The Complete Graph on a Set of Four Vertices

Figure 15.3 shows the complete graph on the set $V = \{a, b, c, d\}$. Its edge set E is $E = \{ab, ac, ad, bc, bd, cd\}$.

Note that the graphs in the previous examples are subgraphs of this one.

Figure 15.3 A complete

Theorem 15.2 The number of edges in the complete graph on n vertices is $n(n-1)/2$.

There are n vertices, and each of them could be adjacent to $n-1$ other vertices. So there are $n(n-1)$ ordered pairs of vertices. Therefore, there are $n(n-1)/2$ unordered pairs because each unordered pair could be ordered in two ways. For example, the unordered pair $\{a, b\}$ can be ordered as either (a, b) or (b, a).

For example, the number of edges in the complete graph on the four-vertex set in Example 15.3 is $n(n-1)/2 = 4(4-1)/2 = 6$.

Corollary 15.1 The number of edges in any graph on n vertices is $m \leq n(n-1)/2$.

PATHS AND CYCLES

A *walk from vertex a to vertex b* in a graph is a sequence of edges $(a_0a_1, a_1a_2, \ldots, a_{k-1}a_k)$ where $a_0 = a$ and $a_k = b$, that is, a sequence of edges $(e_1, e_2, \ldots, e_k)$ where if edge e_i connects some vertex to vertex a_i then the next edge e_{i+1} connects that vertex a_i to some other vertex, thereby forming a chain of connected vertices from a to b. The *length* of a walk is the number k of edges that form the walk.

Although a walk is a sequence of edges, it naturally induces a sequence of adjacent vertices which the edges connect. So we may denote the walk $(a_0a_1, a_1a_2, \ldots, a_{k-1}a_k)$ more simply by $a_0a_1a_2 \ldots a_{k-1}a_k$ as long as each pair (a_{i-1}, a_i) is a valid edge in the graph.

If $p = a_0a_1a_2 \ldots a_{k-1}a_k$ is a walk in a graph, then we refer to p as a walk *from a_0 to a_k* (or *from a_k to a_0*), and we say that p *connects* a_0 to a_k and that a_0 and a_k are *connected* by p. We also refer to a_0 and a_k as the *terminal points* or the *end points* of the walk.

A *path* is a walk whose vertices are all distinct.

EXAMPLE 15.4 Graph Paths

In the graph in Figure 15.4, *abcfde* is a path of length 5. It is, more formally, the path (*ab, bc, cf, fd, de*).

The walk *abefdbc* of length 6 is not a path because vertex *b* appears twice. The walk *abefa* of length 4 is also not a path.

The sequence *abf* is not a walk because *bf* is not an edge. And the sequence *abb* is not a walk because *bb* is not an edge.

Finally, *aba* is a walk of length 2, and *ab* is a walk of length 1.

A graph is said to be *connected* if every pair of its vertices are connected by some path. A graph that is not connected is called *disconnected*.

All the graphs in the previous examples are connected.

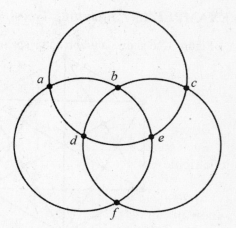

Figure 15.4 Paths in graphs

EXAMPLE 15.5 A Disconnected Graph

Figure 15.5 shows a graph of size 12 that is not connected.

A *connected component* of a graph is a subgraph that is maximally connected, that is, a connected subgraph with the property that any larger subgraph that contains it is disconnected.

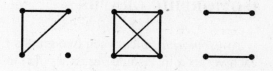

Figure 15.5 A disconnected graph

The graph in Example 15.5 has five connected components, of sizes 3, 1, 4, 2, and 2.

Theorem 15.3 Every graph is a union of a unique set of connected components.

A walk is *closed* if its two end points are the same vertex. A *cycle* is a closed walk of length at least 3 whose interior vertices are all distinct.

EXAMPLE 15.6 Graph Cycles

In the graph shown in Figure 15.4:
- The walk *abefa* is a cycle.
- The walk *abedbcfa* is not a cycle because it is not a path: It has the duplicate internal vertex *b*.
- The path *abef* is not a cycle because it is not closed.
- And the walk *aba* is not a cycle because its length is only 2.

A graph is said to be *acyclic* if it contains no cycles.

Among the graphs shown above, only the ones in Figure 15.2 on page 286 are acyclic.

An acyclic graph is also called a *free forest*, and a connected acyclic graph is also called a *free tree*. Note that a tree is the same as a free tree in which one node has been designated as the root. So in the context of graph theory, a tree is called a *rooted tree*, which is defined to be a connected acyclic graph with one distinguished node.

A *spanning tree* of a graph is a connected acyclic spanning subgraph.

EXAMPLE 15.7 Spanning Trees

Figure 15.6 shows a graph and a spanning tree for it.

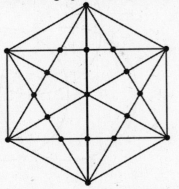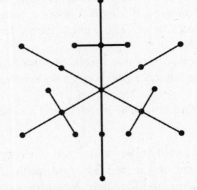

Figure 15.6 The graph on the right is a spanning tree of the graph on the left

ISOMORPHIC GRAPHS

An *isomorphism* between two graphs $G = (V, E)$ and $G' = (V', E')$ is a function f that assigns to each vertex x in V some vertex $y = f(x)$ in V' so that the following three conditions are satisfied:

1. f is *one-to-one*: Each x in V gets assigned a different $y = f(x)$ in V'.
2. f is *onto*: Every y in V' gets assigned to some x in V.
3. f *preserves adjacency*: If $\{x_1, x_2\}$ is an edge in E, then $\{f(x_1), f(x_2)\}$ is an edge in E'.

Two graphs are said to be *isomorphic* if there is an isomorphism from one to the other. The word *isomorphic* means "same form." When applied to graphs, it means that they have the same topological structure. Graphically, two graphs are isomorphic if one can be twisted around to the same shape as the other without breaking any of the edge connections.

EXAMPLE 15.8 Isomorphic Graphs

The two graphs in Figure 15.7 on page 289 are isomorphic. The isomorphism is indicated by the corresponding vertex labels.

It can be verified that if vertex x_1 is adjacent to vertex x_2 in one graph, then the corresponding vertices are adjacent in the other graph. For example, vertex a is adjacent to vertices b, d, e, and f (but not c, g, or h) in both graphs.

To prove that two graphs are isomorphic (by definition), it is necessary to find an isomorphism between them. This is equivalent to labeling both graphs with the same set of labels so that adjacency applies equally to both labelings. Finding such an isomorphism by chance is unlikely

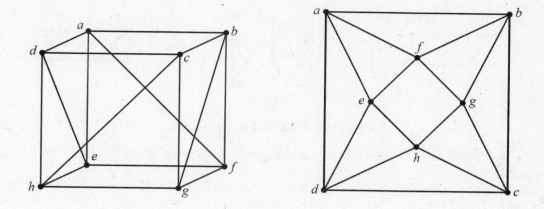

Figure 15.7 Isomorphic graphs

because there are *n*! different possibilities. For example, there are 8! = 40,320 different possible ways to assign the 8 labels to the 8 vertices of each graph in Example 15.8. The following algorithm is more efficient:

1. Arbitrarily label the vertices of one graph. (Assume here that the positive integers are used for labels.)
2. Find a vertex on the second graph that has the same degree as vertex 1 on the first graph, and number that vertex 1 also.
3. Label the vertices that are adjacent to the new vertex 1 with the same numbers that correspond to the vertices that are adjacent to the other vertex 1.
4. Repeat step 3 for each of the other newly labeled vertices.

If at some point in the process, step 3 is not possible, then backtrack and try a different labeling. If no amount of backtracking seems to help, try proving that the two graphs are not isomorphic.

To prove that two graphs are not isomorphic (by definition) would require showing that every one of the possible *n*! different labellings fails to preserve adjacency. That is impractical. The following theorem makes it much easier to prove that two graphs are not isomorphic.

Theorem 15.4 Isomorphism Tests for Graphs

All of the following conditions are necessary for two graphs to be isomorphic:
1. They must have the same number of vertices.
2. They must have the same number of edges.
3. They must have the same number of connected components.
4. They must have the same number of vertices of each degree.
5. They must have the same number of cycles of each length.

EXAMPLE 15.9 Proving that Two Graphs Are Not Isomorphic

Figure 15.8 shows three graphs, to be compared with the two isomorphic graphs in Figure 15.7. Each of these graphs has eight vertices, so each could be isomorphic to those two graphs.

Graph G_1 is not isomorphic to those two graphs because it has only 14 edges. The graphs in Figure 15.7 each have 16 edges. Condition 2 of Theorem 15.4 says that isomorphic graphs must have the same number of edges.

Graph G_2 does have 16 edges. But it is not isomorphic to the two graphs in Figure 15.7 because it has two connected components. Each of the two graphs in Figure 15.7 has only one connected component.

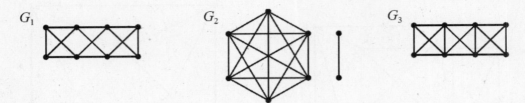

Figure 15.8 Possibly isomorphic graphs

Condition 3 of Theorem 15.5 says that isomorphic graphs must have the same number of connected components.

Graph G_3 has 16 edges and only one connected component. But it is still not isomorphic to the two graphs in Figure 15.7 because it has some vertices of degree 3 (and some of degree 5). All the vertices of the two graphs in Figure 15.7 have degree 4. Condition 4 of Theorem 15.5 says that isomorphic graphs must have the same number of vertices of each degree.

Note that in Example 15.9 we really only have to compare each graph with one of the two graphs in Figure 15.7 on page 289, not both of them.

Theorem 15.5 Graph Isomorphism Is an Equivalence Relation
The isomorphism relation among graphs satisfies the three properties of an equivalence relation:
1. Every graph is isomorphic to itself.
2. If G_1 is isomorphic to G_2 then G_2 is isomorphic to G_1.
3. If G_1 is isomorphic to G_2 and G_2 is isomorphic to G_3, then G_1 is isomorphic to G_3.

THE ADJACENCY MATRIX FOR A GRAPH

An *adjacency matrix* for a graph (V, E) is a two-dimensional boolean array
        `boolean[][] a;`
obtained by ordering the vertices $V = \{v_0, v_1, ..., v_{n-1}\}$ and then assigning `true` to `a[i][j]` if and only if vertex v_i is adjacent to vertex v_j.

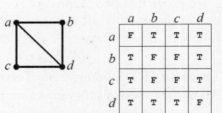

Figure 15.9 An adjacency matrix

EXAMPLE 15.10 An Adjacency Matrix

Figure 15.9 shows the adjacency matrix for the graph in Figure 15.1 on page 285.

Note the following facts about adjacency matrices:
1. The matrix is *symmetric*, that is, `a[i][j] == a[j][i]` will be true for all i and j
2. The number of `true` entries is twice the number of edges.
3. Different orderings of the vertex set V will result in different adjacency matrices for the same graph.

Adjacency matrices are often expressed with 0s and 1s instead of `true`s and `false`s. In that form, the adjacency matrix for Figure 15.1 would be the one shown in Figure 15.10 on page 291.

THE INCIDENCE MATRIX FOR A GRAPH

An *incidence matrix* for a graph (V, E) is a two-dimensional array

```
int[][] a;
```

obtained by ordering the vertices $V = \{v_0, v_1, \ldots, v_{n-1}\}$ and the edges $E = \{e_0, e_1, \ldots, e_{m-1}\}$ and then assigning 1 to a[i][j] if vertex v_i is incident upon edge e_j and 0 otherwise.

EXAMPLE 15.11 An Incidence Matrix

Figure 15.11 shows the incidence matrix for the graph in Figure 15.1 on page 285. The first row indicates that vertex a is incident upon edges 1, 2, and 3; the second row indicates that vertex b is incident upon edges 1 and 4, and so forth.

Note that for simple graphs, no matter how many vertices and edges they have, there will always be exactly two 1s in each column of any incidence matrix. Why? (See Review Question 15.9 on page 305.)

THE ADJACENCY LIST FOR A GRAPH

An *adjacency list* (or *adjacency structure*) for a graph (V, E) is a list that contains one element for each vertex in the graph and in which each vertex list element contains a list of the vertices that are adjacent to its vertex. The secondary list for each vertex is called its *edge list*.

EXAMPLE 15.12 An Adjacency List

Figure 15.12 shows the adjacency list for the graph in Figure 15.1 on page 285.

The edge list for vertex a has three elements, one for each of the three edges that are incident with a; the edge list for vertex b has two elements, one for each of the two edges that are incident with b; and so on.

Note that each edge list element corresponds to a unique 1 entry in the graph's corresponding incidence matrix. For example, the three elements in the edge list for vertex a correspond to the three 1s in the first row (the row for vertex a) in the incidence matrix in Figure 15.11.

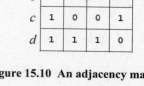

Figure 15.10 An adjacency matrix

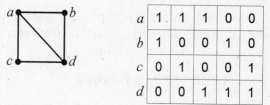

Figure 15.11 A graph and its incidence matrix

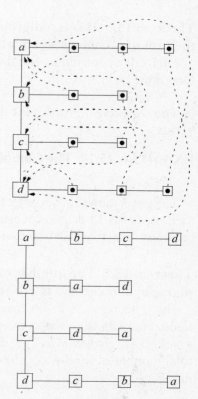

Figure 15.12 An adjacency list

Also note that the edge lists are not ordered, that is, their order is irrelevant.

DIGRAPHS

A *digraph* (or *directed graph*) is a pair $G = (V, E)$ where V is a finite set and E is a set of ordered pairs of elements of V. As with (undirected) graphs, the elements of V are called *vertices* (or *nodes*) and the elements of E are called *edges* (or *arcs*). If $e \in E$, then $e = (a, b)$ for some a, $b \in V$. In this case, we can denote e more simply as $e = ab$. We say that the edge e *emanates from* (or is *incident from*) vertex a and *terminates at* (or is *incident to*) vertex b. The *outdegree* of a vertex is the number of edges that emanate from it. The *indegree* of a vertex is the number of edges that terminate at it.

Note that, unlike the graph definition, the digraph definition naturally allows an edge to terminate at the same vertex from which it emanates. Such an edge is called a *loop*. A *simple digraph* is a digraph that has no loops.

EXAMPLE 15.13 A Digraph

Figure 15.13 shows a digraph with vertex set $V = \{a, b, c, d\}$ and edge set $E = \{ab, ad, bd, ca, dc\}$.

Vertex a has outdegree 2 and indegree 1. Vertices b and c each have outdegree 1 and indegree 1. Vertex d has outdegree 1 and indegree 2.

Figure 15.13 A digraph

Theorem 15.6 If G is a digraph with m edges, then the sum of all outdegrees equals m and the sum of all indegrees equals m.

Each edge contributes 1 to the total of all outdegrees and 1 to the total of all indegrees. So each total must be m.

The *complete digraph* a the digraph that has a (directed) edge from every vertex to every other vertex.

EXAMPLE 15.14 The Complete Digraph on Six Vertices

The graph shown in Figure 15.14 is the complete digraph on six vertices. It has 15 double-directed edges, so the total number of (one-way) edges is 30, which is $n(n-1) = 6(6-1) = 6(5) = 30$.

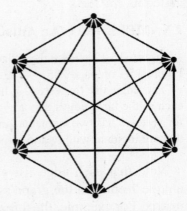

Theorem 15.7 The number of edges in the complete digraph on n vertices is $n(n-1)$.

By Theorem 15.2 on page 286, there are $n(n-1)/2$ undirected edges on the corresponding complete undirected graph. That makes $n(n-1)/2$ double-directed edges, so the total number of (one-way) directed edges must be twice that number.

Figure 15.14 A complete digraph

Corollary 15.2 The number of edges in any digraph on n vertices is $m \leq n(n-1)$.

Every digraph has an *embedded graph*, obtained by converting each directed edge into an undirected edge and then removing duplicate edges and loops. Mathematically, this amounts to converting each ordered pair (x, y) of vertices in E into the set $\{x, y\}$ and then removing all sets of size one (i.e., singletons).

EXAMPLE 15.15 The Embedded Graph of a Digraph

The embedded graph of the digraph in Figure 15.13 is the graph shown in Figure 15.15.

An *adjacency matrix* for a digraph (V, E) is a two-dimensional boolean array

        boolean[][] a;

Figure 15.15 An embedded graph

obtained by ordering the vertices $V = \{v_0, v_1, \ldots, v_{n-1}\}$ and then assigning true to a[i][j] if and only if there exists an edge emanating from vertex v_i and terminating at vertex v_j.

EXAMPLE 15.16 An Adjacency Matrix for a Digraph

Figure 15.16 shows the adjacency matrix for the graph in Figure 15.13 on page 292.

Note that the number of true entries in an adjacency matrix for a digraph is equal to the number of edges. Also, as with undirected graphs, different orderings of the vertex set V will result in different adjacency matrices for the same digraph.

	a	b	c	d
a	F	T	F	T
b	F	F	F	T
c	T	F	F	F
d	F	F	T	F

Figure 15.16 An adjacent matrix

An *incidence matrix* for a digraph (V, E) is a two-dimensional integer array

        int[][] a;

obtained by ordering the vertices $V = \{v_0, v_1, \ldots, v_{n-1}\}$ and the edges $E = \{e_0, e_1, \ldots, e_{m-1}\}$ and then assigning 1 to a[i][j] and −1 to a[j][i] if there exists an edge emanating from vertex v_i and terminating at vertex v_j, and assigning 0 everywhere else.

EXAMPLE 15.17 An Incidence Matrix for a Digraph

Figure 15.17 shows an incidence matrix for the digraph in Figure 15.13 on page 292.

The first row indicates that two edges emanate from vertex a and one edge terminates there.

The last 1 is in the row for vertex d and the last column. The only other nonzero entry in that column is the -1 in the row for vertex c, meaning that this edge emanates from vertex d and terminates at vertex c.

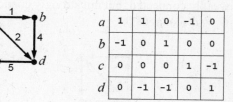

a	1	1	0	-1	0
b	-1	0	1	0	0
c	0	0	0	1	-1
d	0	-1	-1	0	1

Figure 15.17 An incidence matrix

An *adjacency list* for a digraph (V, E) is a list that contains one element for each vertex in the graph and in which each vertex list element contains a list of the edges that emanate from that vertex. This is the same as the adjacency list for a graph, except that the links are not duplicated unless there are edges going both ways between a pair of vertices.

EXAMPLE 15.18 An Adjacency List for a Digraph

Figure 15.18 shows the adjacency list for the digraph in Figure 15.13 on page 292. The edge list for vertex *a* has two elements, one for each of the two edges that emanate from *a*: *ab* and *ad*.

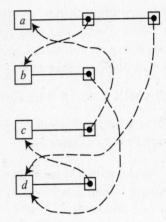

Figure 15.18 An adjacency list

PATHS IN A DIGRAPH

A *walk from vertex a to vertex b* in a digraph is a sequence of edges $(a_0a_1, a_1a_2, \ldots, a_{k-1}a_k)$ where $a_0 = a$ and $a_k = b$. As with undirected paths in an undirected graphs, directed paths are usually abbreviated by their vertex string: $p = a_0a_1a_2 \ldots a_{k-1}a_k$. Either way, we say that the path *emanates from* (or *starts at*) vertex *a* and *terminates at* (or *ends at*) vertex *b*.

A walk is *closed* if it terminates at the same vertex from which it emanates. A *path* is a walk with all distinct vertices. A *cycle* is a closed walk with all interval vertices distinct.

EXAMPLE 15.19 Directed Paths

In the digraph of Figure 15.13, *adcabdc* is a walk of length 6 which is not closed. The walk *abdcacda* is closed, but it is not a cycle because *d* (and *c*) are repeated internal vertices. The walk *dcab* is a path, which is not closed. The walk *cabdc* is a cycle of length 4, and the walk *dcad* is a cycle of length 3.

Note that different cycles may traverse the same vertices. For example, *adca* and *cadc* are different cycles in the digraph in Figure 15.13.

A digraph is *strongly connected* if there is a path between every pair of vertices. A digraph is *weakly connected* if its embedded graph is connected. A digraph that is not weakly connected is said to be *disconnected*.

EXAMPLE 15.20 Strongly Connected and Weakly Connected Digraphs

In Figure 15.19, digraph G_1 is strongly connected (and therefore also weakly connected). Digraph G_2 is weakly connected, but not strongly connected because there is no path that terminates at vertex *x*. Digraph G_3 is disconnected.

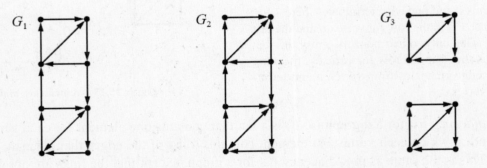

Figure 15.19 Strongly connected and weakly connected components

WEIGHTED DIGRAPHS AND GRAPHS

A *weighted digraph* is a pair (V, w) where V is a finite set of vertices and w is a function that assigns to each pair (x, y) of vertices either a positive integer or ∞ (infinity). The function w is called the *weight function*, and its value $w(x, y)$ can be interpreted as the cost (or time or distance) for moving directly from x to y. The value $w(x, y) = \infty$ indicates that there is no edge from x to y.

A *weighted graph* is a weighted digraph (V, w) whose weight function w is symmetric, that is, $w(y,x) = w(x,y)$ for all $x,y \in V$. Just as every digraph has an embedded graph, every weighted digraph has an *embedded weighted graph* (V, w) and an embedded (unweighted) digraph. The weight function for the embedded weighted graph can be defined as $w'(x, y) = \min\{w(x,y), w(y,x)\}$, where w is the weight function of the weighted digraph. The vertex set for the embedded digraph can be defined as $E = \{(x,y) : w(x,y) < \infty\}$.

The properties described above for digraphs and graphs apply to weighted digraphs and weighted graphs. In addition there are some extended properties that depend upon the underlying weight function in the obvious manner. For example, the *weighted path length* is the sum of the weights of the edges along the path. And the *shortest distance* from x to y would be the minimum weighted path length among all the paths from x to y.

EXAMPLE 15.21 A Weighted Digraph and Its Embedded Structures

Figure 15.20 shows a weighted digraph together with its embedded weighted graph, its embedded digraph, and its embedded graph. The weights are shown on the edges.

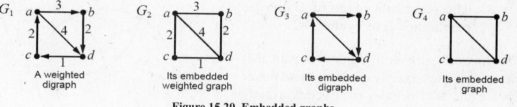

Figure 15.20 Embedded graphs

In graph G_1 the weighted path length of the path *cabd* is $|cabd| = 2 + 3 + 2 = 7$, and the shortest distance from c to d is 6 (along the path *cad*). But in graph G_2 that shortest distance is 1 (along the path *cd*).

Note that graph G_3 is the same as that in Example 15.13 on page 292, and graph G_4 is the same as that in Example 15.1 on page 285.

Figure 15.21 shows the adjacency matrix, the incidence matrix, and the adjacency list for graph G_1.

EULER PATHS AND HAMILTONIAN CYCLES

An *euler path* in a graph is a walk that includes each edge exactly once. An *euler cycle* is a closed walk that includes each edge exactly once. An *eulerian graph* is a graph that has an euler cycle.

Note that euler paths and cycles need not have distinct vertices, so they are not strict paths.

EXAMPLE 15.22 Euler Paths and Cycles

In the graph in Figure 15.22, the closed walk *acedabefdbcfa* is an euler cycle. So this is an eulerian graph. Note that every vertex in this graph has degree 4, and its 12 edges are partitioned into three circles. As the Theorem 15.8 reports, each of these two properties will always guarantee that the graph is eulerian.

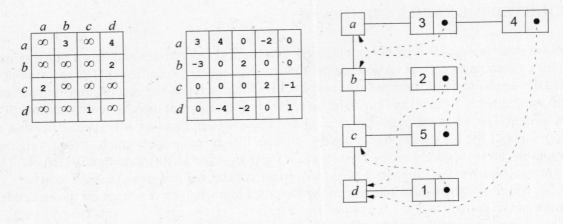

Figure 15.21 Adjacency matrix, incidence matrix, and adjacency list

Theorem 15.8 Eulerian Graphs

If G is a connected graph, then the following conditions are equivalent:

1. G is eulerian.
2. The degree of each vertex is even.
3. The set of all edges of G can be partitioned into cycles.

A *hamiltonian path* in a graph is a path that includes each vertex exactly once. A *hamiltonian cycle* is a cycle that includes each vertex exactly once. A *hamiltonian graph* is a graph that has a hamiltonian cycle.

Unfortunately, there is no simple characterization like Theorem 15.8 for hamiltonian graphs. In fact, the problem of finding such a simple characterization is one of the big unsolved problems in computer science.

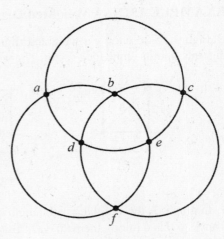

Figure 15.22 An eulerian graph

EXAMPLE 15.23 Hamiltonian Graphs

In Figure 15.23, the graph on the left is hamiltonian. The graph on the right is not; it has a hamiltonian path, but no hamiltonian cycle.

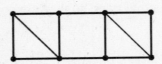
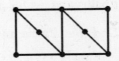

Figure 15.23 A graph with a hamiltonian cycle, and one with without one

DIJKSTRA'S ALGORITHM

Dijkstra's algorithm finds the shortest path from one vertex v_0 to each other vertex in a digraph. When it has finished, the length of the shortest distance from v_0 to v is stored in the vertex v, and the shortest path from v_0 to v is recorded in the back pointers of v and the other vertices along that path. (See Example 15.24.) The algorithm uses a priority queue, initializing it with all the vertices and then dequeueing one vertex on each iteration.

Algorithm 15.1 Dijkstra's Shortest Paths Algorithm

(Precondition: $G = (V,w)$ is a weighted graph with initial vertex v_0.)
(Postcondition: Each vertex v in V stores the shortest distance from v_0 to v and a back reference to the preceding vertex along that shortest path.)

1.   Initialize the distance field to 0 for v_0 and to ∞ for each of the other vertices.
2.   Enqueue all the vertices into a priority queue Q with highest priority being the lowest distance field value.
3.   Repeat steps 4–10 until Q is empty.
4.   (Invariant: The distance and back reference fields of every vertex that is not in Q are correct.)
5.   Dequeue the highest priority vertex into x.
6.   Do steps 7–10 for each vertex y that is adjacent to x and in the priority queue.
7.   Let s be the sum of the x's distance field plus the weight of the edge from x to y.
8.   If s is less than y's distance field, do steps 9–10; otherwise go back to Step 3.
9.   Assign s to y's distance field.
10. Assign x to y's back reference field.

EXAMPLE 15.24 Tracing Dijkstra's Algorithm

This is a trace of Algorithm 15.1 on a graph with eight vertices. On each iteration, the vertices that are still in the priority queue are shaded, and vertex x is labeled. The distance fields for each vertex are shown adjacent to the vertex, and the back pointers are drawn as arrows.

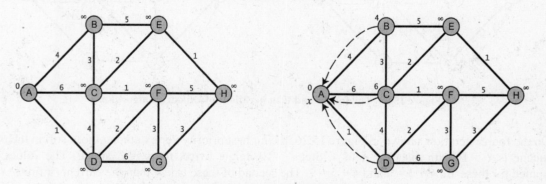

Figure 15.24 The first iteration of Dijkstra's algorithm

The first two iterations are shown in Figure 15.24. On the first iteration, the highest priority vertex is $x = A$ because its distance field is 0 and all the others are infinity. Steps 7–10 iterate three times, once for each of A's neighbors y = B, C, and D. The values of s computed for these are $0 + 4 = 4$, $0 + 6 = 6$, and $0 + 1 = 1$. Each of these is less than the current (infinite) value of the corresponding distance field, so all three of those values are assigned, and the back pointers for all three neighbors are set to point to A.

On the second iteration, the highest priority vertex among those still in the priority queue is x = D with distance field 1. Steps 7–10 iterate three times again, once for each of D's unvisited neighbors: y = B, F, and G. The values of s computed for these are $1 + 4 = 5$, $1 + 2 = 3$, and $1 + 6 = 7$, respectively. Each of these is less than the current value of the corresponding distance field, so all of those values are assigned and the back pointers are set to D. Note how this changes the distance field and pointer in vertex C.

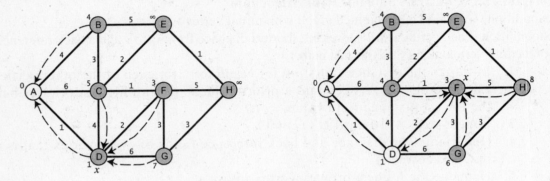

Figure 15.25 The second and third iterations of Dijkstra's algorithm

The next two iterations are shown in Figure 15.25. On the third iteration, the highest priority vertex among those still in the priority queue is x = F with distance field 3. Steps 7–10 iterate three times again, once for each of F's unvisited neighbors y = C, G, and H. The values of s computed for these are $3 + 1 = 4$, $3 + 3 = 6$, and $3 + 5 = 8$. Each of these is less than the current value, so all of them are assigned and the back pointers are set to F. Note how this changes the distance field and pointer in vertex C again.

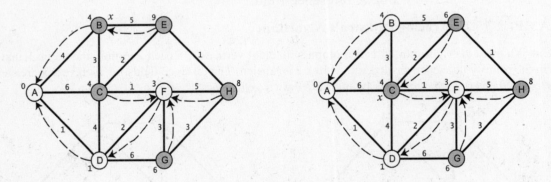

Figure 15.26 The fourth and fifth iterations of Dijkstra's algorithm

On the fourth iteration, shown in Figure 15.26, the highest priority vertex among those still in the priority queue is x = B with distance field 4. Steps 7–10 iterate twice, for y = C and E. The values of s computed for these are $4 + 3 = 7$ and $4 + 5 = 9$. The second of these is less than the current (infinite) value at E, so its distance field assigned the value 9 and its back pointer is set to B. But the s value 7 is not less than the current distance field for C, so its fields do not change.

The algorithm progresses through its remaining iterations, shown in Figure 15.27, for x = C, E, G, and finally H the same way.

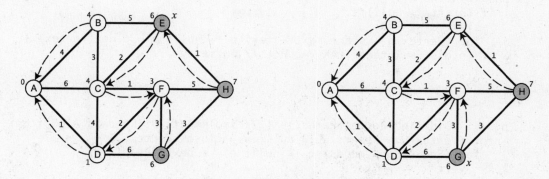

Figure 15.27 The sixth and seventh iterations of Dijkstra's algorithm

The final result is shown in Figure 15.28. It shows, for example, that the shortest path from A to E is ADFCE with length 6.

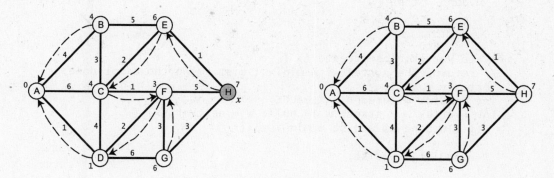

Figure 15.28 The last two iterations of Dijkstra's algorithm

EXAMPLE 15.25 An Implementation of Dijkstra's Algorithm

Here is a Java implementation of Algorithm 15.1. It defines a Network class whose instances represent weighted digraphs.

```
1    public class Network {
2      Vertex start;
3
4      private class Vertex {
5        Object object;
6        Edge edges;
7        Vertex nextVertex;
8        boolean done;
9        int dist;
10       Vertex back;
11     }
12
13     private class Edge {
14       Vertex to;
15       int weight;
16       Edge nextEdge;
17     }
18
```

```
19    public Network() {
20      if (start != null) {
21        start.dist = 0;
22        for (Vertex p = start.nextVertex; p != null; p = p.nextVertex) {
23          p.dist = Integer.MAX_VALUE;   // infinity
24        }
25      }
26    }
27
28    public void findShortestPaths()  { // implements Dijkstra's Algorithm:
29      for (Vertex v = start; v != null; v = closestVertex()) {
30        for (Edge e = v.edges; e != null; e = e.nextEdge) {
31          Vertex w = e.to;
32          if (!w.done && v.dist+e.weight < w.dist) {
33            w.dist = v.dist+e.weight;
34            w.back = v;
35          }
36        }
37        v.done = true;
38      }
39    }
40
41    private Vertex closestVertex() {
42      // returns the vertex with minimal dist among those not done:
43      Vertex v = null;
44      int minDist = Integer.MAX_VALUE;
45      for (Vertex w = start; w != null; w = nextVertex) {
46        if (!w.done && w.dist < minDist) {
47          v = w;
48          minDist = w.dist;
49        }
50      }
51      return v;
52    }
53  }
```

In this implementation, we have used a simple search method `closestVertex()` instead of a priority queue. This is less efficient, running in $O(n)$ time instead of the $O(\lg n)$ time that a priority queue would use.

GRAPH TRAVERSAL ALGORITHMS

The paths produced by Dijkstra's algorithm produce a *minimal spanning tree* for the graph. That is a spanning tree whose total weighted length is minimal for the graph; that is, no other spanning tree has a smaller total length. The spanning tree is formed in a breadth-first manner, by considering the vertices that are adjacent to the current vertex on each iteration. This is one of two general ways to traverse a graph.

The *breadth-first search* algorithm is essentially the same as Dijkstra's algorithm without regard to the distance fields.

Algorithm 15.2 The Breadth-First Search (BFS) Algorithm

(Preconditions: $G = (V,E)$ is a graph or digraph with initial vertex v_0; each vertex has a boolean visited field initialized to false; T is an empty set of edges; L is an empty list of vertices.)
(Postcondition: L lists the vertices in BFS order, and T is a BFS spanning tree for G.)

1. Initialize an empty queue Q for temporary storage of vertices.
2. Enqueue v_0 into Q.
3. Repeat steps 4–6 while Q is not empty.
4. Dequeue Q into x.
5. Add x to L.
6. Do step 7 for each vertex y that is adjacent to x.
7. If y has not been visited, do steps 8–9.
8. Add the edge xy to T.
9. Enqueue y into Q.

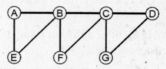

EXAMPLE 15.26 Tracing the BFS Algorithm

Table 15.1 shows a trace of Algorithm 15.2 on the graph shown in Figure 15.29. The start vertex is $v_0 = $ A.

Figure 15.29 Tracing the BFS

Q	x	L	y	T
A	A	A	B	AB
B			E	AB, AE
B, E	B		C	AB, AE, BC
E, C		A, B	F	AB, AE, BC, BF
E, C, F	E	A, B, E		
C, F	C	A, B, E, C	D	AB, AE, BC, BF, CD
F, D			G	AB, AE, BC, BF, CD, CG
F, D, G	F	A, B, E, C, F		
D, G	D	A, B, E, C, F, D		
G	G	A, B, E, C, F, D, G		

Table 15.1 Trace of Algorithm 15.2

The resulting BFS order of visitation is returned in the list $L = $ (A, B, E, C, F, D, G), and the resulting BFS spanning tree (Figure 15.30) is returned in the set $T = $ {AB, AE, BC, BF, CD, CD}.

The *depth-first search* algorithm uses a stack instead of a queue.

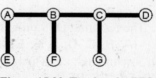

Figure 15.30 Tracing the BFS

Algorithm 15.3 The Depth-First Search (DFS) Algorithm

(Preconditions: $G = (V, E)$ is a graph or digraph with initial vertex v_0; each vertex has a boolean visited field initialized to false; T is an empty set of edges; L is an empty list of vertices.)
(Postcondition: L lists the vertices in DFS order, and T is a DFS spanning tree for G.)

1. Initialize an empty stack S for temporary storage of vertices.
2. Add v_0 to L.
3. Push v_0 onto S.
4. Mark v_0 visited.
5. Repeat steps 6–8 while S is not empty.
6. Let x be the top element on S.
7. If x has any adjacent unvisited vertices, do steps 9–13.
8. Otherwise, pop the stack S and go back to step 5.

    9.   Let y be an unvisited vertex that is adjacent to x.

  10.   Add the edge xy to T.

  11.   Add y to L.

  12.   Push y onto S.

  13.   Mark y visited.

EXAMPLE 15.27 Tracing the DFS Algorithm

Table 15.2 shows a trace of Algorithm 15.3 on the same graph (Figure 15.29) as in Example 15.26. The start vertex is $v_0 = $ A.

L	S	x	y	T
A	A	A	B	AB
A, B	A, B	B	C	AB, BC
A, B, C	A, B, C	C	D	AB, BC, CD
A, B, C, D	A, B, C, D	D	G	AB, BC, CD, DG
A, B, C, D, G	A, B, C, D, G	G		
	A, B, C, D	D		
	A, B, C	C	F	AB, BC, CD, DG, CF
A, B, C, D, G, F	A, B, C, F	F		
	A, B, C	C		
	A, B	B	E	AB, BC, CD, DG, CF, BE
A, B, C, D, G, F, E	A, B, E	E		
	A, B	B		
	A	A		

Table 15.2 Trace of Algorithm 15.3

The resulting DFS order of visitation is returned in the list $L = $ (A, B, C, D, G, F, E). Figure 15.31 shows the resulting DFS spanning tree, which is returned in the set $T = $ {AB, BC, CD, DG, CF, BE}.

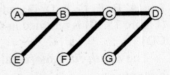

Figure 15.31 Tracing the DFS

Since the depth-first traversal uses a stack, it has a natural recursive version:

Algorithm 15.4 The Recursive Depth-First Search (DFS) Algorithm

(Preconditions: $G = (V,E)$ is a graph or digraph with initial vertex x; each vertex has a boolean visited field initialized to false; T is a global set of edges; L is a global list of vertices.)

(Postcondition: L lists the vertices in DFS order, and T is a DFS spanning tree for G.)

    1.   Mark x visited.

    2.   Add x to L.

    3.   Repeat steps 4–5 for each unvisited vertex y that is adjacent to x.

    4.   Add the edge xy to T.

    5.   Apply the DFS algorithm to the subgraph with initial vertex y.

EXAMPLE 15.28 Tracing the Recursive DFS Algorithm

Table 15.3 shows a trace of Algorithm 15.4 on the same graph as in Example 15.26 (Figure 15.29 on page 301). The start vertex v_0 = A.

The result, of course, is the same as that in Example 15.27. The only real difference is that the explicit

L	x	y	T
A	A	B	AB
A, B	B	C	AB, BC
A, B, C	C	D	AB, BC, CD
A, B, C, D	D	G	AB, BC, CD, DG
A, B, C, D, G	G		
	D		
	C	F	AB, BC, CD, DG, CF
A, B, C, D, G, F	F		
	C		
	B	E	AB, BC, CD, DG, CF, BE
A, B, C, D, G, F, E	E		
	B		
	A		

Table 15.3 Trace of Algorithm 15.4

stack S has been replaced by the system stack that keeps track of the recursive calls.

EXAMPLE 15.29 Implementing the Graph Traversal Algorithms

Here is a Java implementation of the two traversal algorithms for the Network class introduced in Example 15.25 on page 299:

```java
1    public class Network {
2      Vertex start;
3
4      private class Vertex {
5        Object object;
6        Edge edges;
7        Vertex nextVertex;
8        boolean visited;
9      }
10
11     private class Edge {
12       Vertex to;
13       int weight;
14       Edge nextEdge;
15     }
16
17     public static void visit(Vertex x) {
18       System.out.println(x.object);
19     }
20
```

```
21    public void breadthFirstSearch() {
22      if (start == null) {
23        return;
24      }
25      Vector queue = new Vector();
26      visit(start);
27      start.visited = true;
28      queue.addElement(start);
29      while (!queue.isEmpty()) {
30        Vertex v = queue.firstElement();
31        queue.removeElementAt(0);
32        for (Edge e = v.edges; e != null; e = e.nextEdge) {
33          Vertex w = e.to;
34          if (!w.visited) {
35            visit(w);
36            w.visited = true;
37            queue.addElement(w);
38          }
39        }
40      }
41    }
42
43    public void depthFirstSearch() {
44      if (start != null) {
45        depthFirstSearch(start);
46      }
47    }
48
49    public void depthFirstSearch(Vertex x) {
50      visit(x);
51      x.visited = true;
52      for (Edge e = x.edges; e != null; e = e.nextEdge) {
53        Vertex w = e.to;
54        if (!w.visited) {
55          depthFirstSearch(w);
56        }
57      }
58    }
59  }
```

This uses the recursive version of the depth-first search. That requires the depthFirstSearch() method with zero parameters to start the recursive depthFirstSearch() method.

Review Questions

15.1   What is the difference between a graph and a simple graph?

15.2   In an undirected graph, can an edge itself be a path?

15.3   What is the difference between connected vertices and adjacent vertices?

15.4   Using only the definition of graph isomorphism, is it easier to prove that two graphs are isomorphic or to prove that two graphs are not isomorphic? Why?

15.5   Are the five conditions in Theorem 15.4 on page 289 sufficient for two graphs to be isomorphic?

15.6   Why is it that the natural definition of a simple graph prohibits loops while the natural definition of a digraph allows them?

15.7   True or false:
   a. If a graph has n vertices and $n(n-1)/2$ edges, then it must be a complete graph.
   b. The length of a path must be less than the size of the graph.
   c. The length of a cycle must equal the number of distinct vertices it has.
   d. If the incidence matrix for a graph has n rows and $n(n-1)/2$ columns, then the graph must be a complete graph.
   e. In an incidence matrix for a digraph, the sum of the entries in each row equals the indegree for that vertex.
   f. The sum of all the entries in an incidence matrix for a graph is $2|E|$.
   g. The sum of all the entries in an incidence matrix for a digraph is always 0.

15.8   A graph (V, E) is called *dense* if $|E| = \Theta(|V|^2)$, and it is called *sparse* if $|E| = O(|V|)$.
   a. Which of the three representations (adjacency matrix, incidence matrix, or adjacency list) would be best for a dense graph?
   b. Which representation would be best for a sparse graph?

15.9   Why is it that, in the incidence matrix of a simple graph, there are always exactly two 1s in each column?

Problems

15.1   Find each of the following properties for the graph shown in Figure 15.32:
   a. Its size n
   b. Its vertex set V
   c. Its edge set E
   d. The degree $d(x)$ of each vertex x
   e. A path of length 3
   f. A path of length 5
   g. A cycle of length 4
   h. A spanning tree
   i. Its adjacency matrix
   j. Its incidence matrix
   k. Its adjacency list

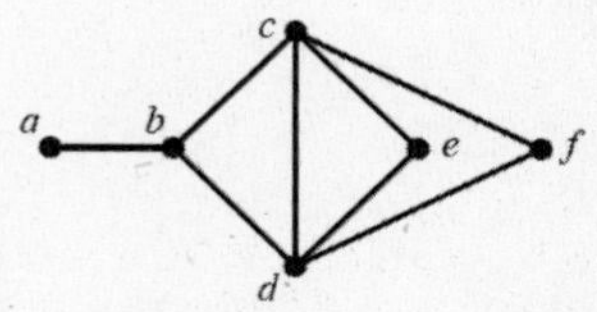

Figure 15.32 A graph

15.2   Find each of the following properties for the digraph shown in Figure 15.33:
   a. Its size n
   b. Its vertex set V
   c. Its edge set E
   d. The indegree $id(x)$ of each vertex x
   e. The outdegree $od(x)$ of each vertex x
   f. A path of length 3
   g. A path of length 5
   h. A cycle of length 4

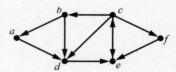

Figure 15.33 A digraph

    i. Its adjacency matrix

    j. Its incidence matrix

    k. Its adjacency list

15.3   Draw the complete graph on n vertices for $n = 2, 3, 4, 5,$ and 6.

15.4   Determine whether the graph G_1 in Figure 15.34 is either eulerian or hamiltonian.

15.5   Determine whether the graph G_2 in Figure 15.34 is either eulerian or hamiltonian.

G_1 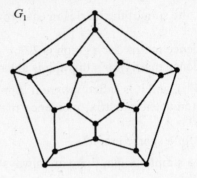 G_2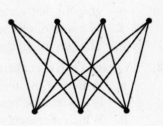

Figure 15.34 Two graphs

15.6   Figure 15.35 shows 12 subgraphs of the graph in Figure 15.6 on page 288. Determine whether each of these is connected, acyclic, and/or spanning.

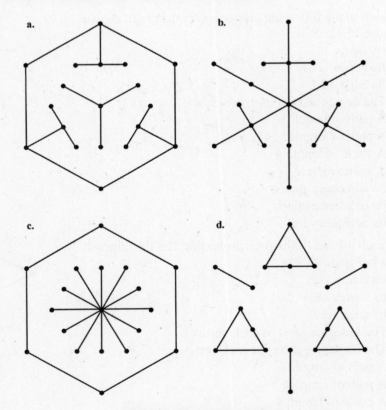

Figure 15.35 Twelve graphs

e.

f.

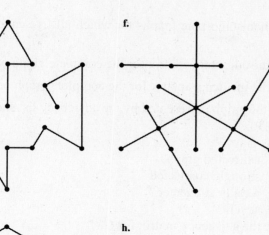

g.

h.

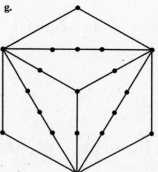

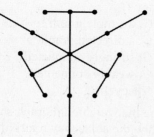

i.

j.

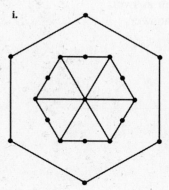

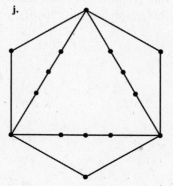

k.

l.

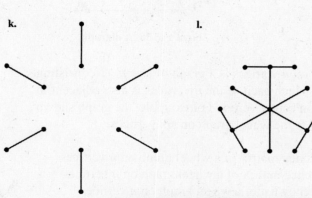

Figure 15.35 (continued) Twelve graphs

15.7   Find two nonisomorphic graphs for which all five conditions of Theorem 15.4 on page 289 are true.

15.8   Describe the adjacency matrix for the complete graph on n vertices.

15.9   Describe the incidence matrix for the complete graph on n vertices.

15.10   Let G_1 be the graph represented by the adjacency list shown in Figure 15.36:

    a. Draw G_1.
    b. Is G_1 a directed graph?
    c. Is G_1 strongly connected?
    d. Is G_1 weakly connected?
    e. Is G_1 acyclic?
    f. Give the adjacency matrix for G_1.

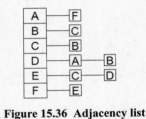

Figure 15.36 Adjacency list

15.11   Let G_1 be the graph whose adjacency matrix is shown in Figure 15.37:

    a. Draw G_1.
    b. Is G_1 a simple graph?
    c. Is G_1 a directed graph?
    d. Is G_1 strongly connected?
    e. Is G_1 weakly connected?
    f. Is G_1 acyclic?

$$\begin{bmatrix} 0 & 1 & 0 & 1 & 0 \\ 1 & 0 & 1 & 0 & 1 \\ 0 & 1 & 0 & 1 & 0 \\ 1 & 1 & 1 & 0 & 1 \\ 0 & 1 & 1 & 0 & 1 \end{bmatrix}$$

Figure 15.37 A matrix

15.12   Let G_2 be the weighted digraph shown in Figure 15.38:

    a. Draw the adjacency matrix for this graph.
    b. Draw the adjacency list for this graph.
    c. Is this graph connected? Justify your answer.
    d. Is this graph acyclic? Justify your answer.

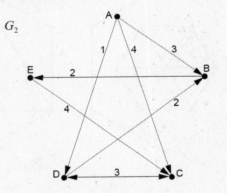

Figure 15.38 A digraph

15.13   A *wheel graph* on n vertices is a graph of size $n+1$ consisting of a n-cycle in which each of the n vertices is also adjacent to a single common center vertex. For example, the graph shown in Figure 15.39 is the wheel graph on six vertices. Describe:

    a. The adjacency matrix of a wheel graph on n vertices
    b. The incidence matrix of a wheel graph on n vertices
    c. The adjacency list of a wheel graph on n vertices

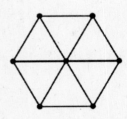

Figure 15.39 A graph

15.14 Let G_1 and G_2 be the graphs shown in Figure 15.40:

    a. Determine whether G_1 and G_2 are isomorphic. Justify your conclusion.

    b. Either find an euler cycle for G_2 or explain why it has none.

    c. Either find a hamiltonian cycle for G_2 or explain why it has none.

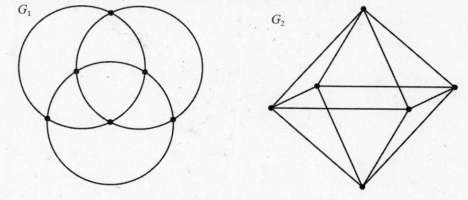

Figure 15.40 Two graphs

15.15 Trace Dijkstra's algorithm (Algorithm 15.1 on page 297) on the graph in Figure 15.41, showing the shortest path and its distance from node A to every other node.

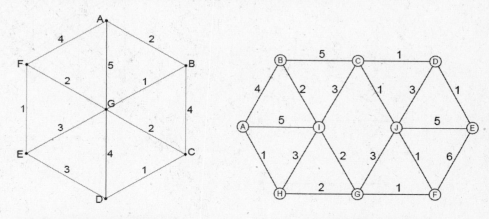

Figure 15.41 A weighted graph   **Figure 15.42 A weighted graph**

15.16 Trace Dijkstra's algorithm on the graph in Figure 15.42, showing the shortest path and its distance from node A to every other node.

15.17 There are four standard algorithms for traversing binary trees: the preorder traversal, the inorder traversal, the postorder traversal. and the level-order traversal. If a binary tree is regarded as a connected acyclic graph, which tree traversal results from a:

    a. Depth-first search

    b. Breadth-first search

15.18 Determine which of the graphs in Figure 15.43 on page 310 are isomorphic. Note that all seven graphs have size 10.

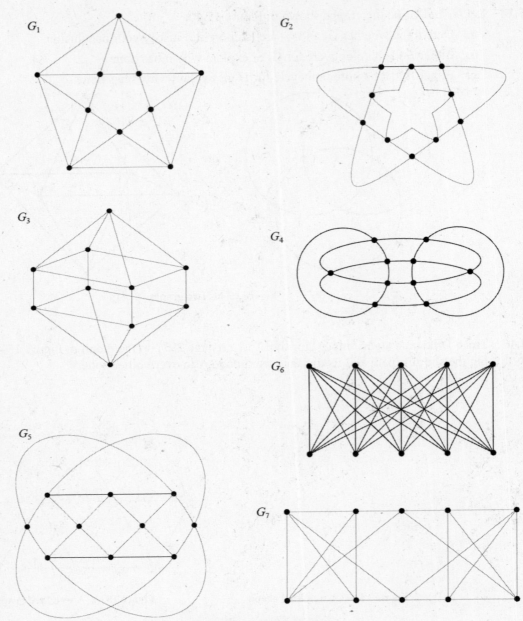

Figure 15.43 Seven graphs

15.19 For the weighted digraph G_1 shown in Figure 15.44 on page 311.
   a. Draw the adjacency matrix.
   b. Draw the adjacency list.

15.20 Perform the indicated traversal algorithm on the graph shown in Figure 15.45 on page 311. Give the order of the vertices visited and show the resulting spanning tree:
   a. Trace the breadth-first search starting at node A.
   b. Trace the depth-first search of the graph, starting at node A and printing the label of each node when it is visited.

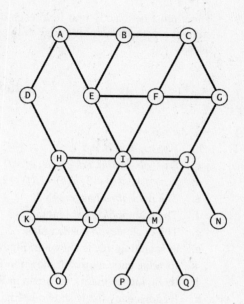

Figure 15.44 A digraph　　　　　　　　　　　**Figure 15.45 A graph**

Answers to Review Questions

15.1　A graph is simple if it has no loops or repeated edges.

15.2　No: In an undirected graph, an edge cannot be a path because an edge is a set of two elements (i.e., an unordered pair) while a path is a sequence (i.e., an ordered list of vertices).

15.3　Two vertices are connected if there is a path from one to the other. Two vertices are adjacent if they form an edge.

15.4　Using only the definition of graph isomorphism, it is easier to prove that two graphs are isomorphic because it only requires finding an isomorphism and verifying that it is one. Proving from the definition that two graphs are not isomorphic would require verifying that every one of the $n!$ one-to-one functions is not an isomorphism.

15.5　No: The five conditions of are not sufficient for two graphs to be isomorphic. It is possible for all five conditions to be true for two nonisomorphic graphs. (See Problem 15.7.)

15.6　The reason that the natural definition of a graph prohibits loops is that an edge in a graph is a two-element set, and that requires the two elements to be different. In the natural definition of a digraph, an edge is an ordered pair, and that allows both components to be the same.

15.7　　**a.**　True

　　　　　　b.　True

　　　　　　c.　True

　　　　　　d.　True

　　　　　　e.　False

　　　　　　f.　True

　　　　　　g.　True

15.8　The adjacency matrix is best for a dense graph because it is compact and provides fast direct access. The adjacency list is best for a sparse graph because it allows easy insertion and deletion of edges.

15.9 There must be exactly two 1s in each column of an incidence matrix of a simple graph because each column represents a unique edge of the graph, and each edge is incident upon exactly two distinct vertices.

Solutions to Problems

15.1   **a.** $n = 6$.

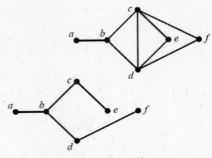

   b. $V = \{a, b, c, d, e, f\}$.

   c. $E = \{ab, bc, bd, cd, ce, de, cf, df\}$.

   d. $d(a) = 1$, $d(b) = 3$, $d(e) = d(f) = 2$, $d(c) = d(d) = 4$.

   e. The path *abcd* has length 3.

   f. The path *abcfde* has length 5.

   g. The cycle *bcedb* has length 4.

   h. A spanning tree is shown in Figure 15.46.

   i. Its adjacency matrix is shown in Figure 15.47.

   j. Its incidence matrix is shown in Figure 15.47.

   k. Its adjacency list is shown in Figure 15.47.

Figure 15.46 Spanning tree

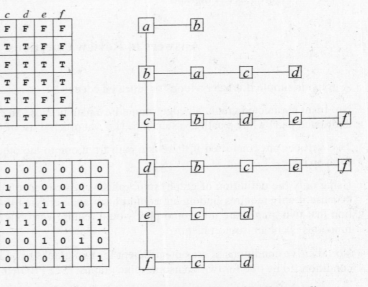

Figure 15.47 Adjacency matrix, incidence matrix, and adjacency list

15.2   **a.** $n = 6$.

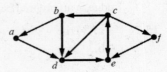

   b. $V = \{a, b, c, d, e, f\}$.

   c. $E = \{ad, ba, bd, cb, cd, ce, cf, de, ec, fe\}$.

   d. $id(a) = id(b) = id(c) = id(f) = 1$, $id(d) = id(e) = 3$.

   e. $od(a) = od(d) = od(e) = od(f) = 1$, $od(b) = 2$, $od(c) = 4$.

   f. The path *adec* has length 3.

   g. The path *fecbad* has length 5.

   h. The cycle *adcba* has length 4.

   i. A spanning tree is shown in Figure 15.48.

   j. Its adjacency matrix is shown in Figure 15.49.

   k. Its incidence matrix is shown in Figure 15.49.

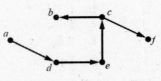

Figure 15.48 Spanning tree

l. its adjacency list is shown in Figure 15.49.

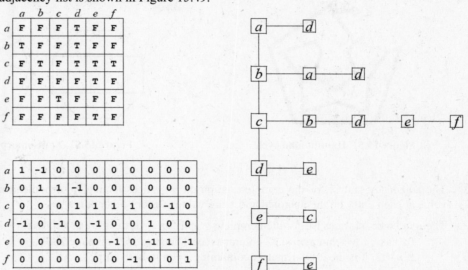

	a	b	c	d	e	f
a	F	F	F	T	F	F
b	T	F	F	T	F	F
c	F	T	F	T	T	T
d	F	F	F	F	T	F
e	F	F	T	F	F	F
f	F	F	F	F	T	F

a	1	-1	0	0	0	0	0	0	0	0
b	0	1	1	-1	0	0	0	0	0	0
c	0	0	0	1	1	1	1	0	-1	0
d	-1	0	-1	0	-1	0	0	1	0	0
e	0	0	0	0	0	-1	0	-1	1	-1
f	0	0	0	0	0	0	-1	0	0	1

Figure 15.49 Adjacency matrix, incidence matrix, and adjacency list

15.3　　The complete graphs are shown in Figure 15.50:

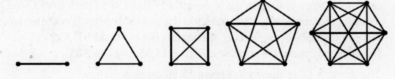

Figure 15.50 Complete graphs

15.4　　The graph G_1 cannot be eulerian because it has odd degree vertices. But the hamiltonian cycle shown in Figure 15.51 on page 314 verifies that it is hamiltonian.

15.5　　The graph G_2 is neither eulerian nor hamiltonian.

15.6　　**a.** Disconnected, cyclic, and spanning.

　　　　　b. Disconnected, acyclic, and spanning.

　　　　　c. Disconnected, cyclic, and spanning.

　　　　　d. Disconnected, cyclic, and not spanning.

　　　　　e. Connected, acyclic, and spanning.

　　　　　f. Connected, acyclic, and spanning.

　　　　　g. Connected, cyclic, and spanning.

　　　　　h. Connected, acyclic, and not spanning.

　　　　　i. Disconnected, cyclic, and spanning.

　　　　　j. Connected, cyclic, and not spanning.

　　　　　k. Disconnected, acyclic, and not spanning.

　　　　　l. Connected, acyclic, and not spanning.

15.7　　The two graphs shown in Figure 15.52 on page 314 are not isomorphic because the one on the left has a 4-cycle containing two vertices of degree 2 and the one on the right does not. Yet, all five conditions of Theorem 15.4 on page 289 are satisfied.

Figure 15.51 Hamiltonian cycle

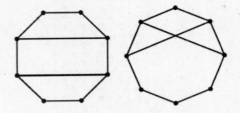

Figure 15.52 Nonisomorphic graphs

15.8   The adjacency matrix for the complete graph on n vertices is an n-by-n boolean matrix with `false` value at each entry on the diagonal and `true` value at every other entry.

15.9   The incidence matrices M_n for the complete graphs on n vertices are as follows:

Its has n rows and $n(n-1)/2$ columns (see Theorem 15.2 on page 286).

If $n = 2$, it is the 2-by-1 matrix containing `true` in both entries.

If $n > 2$, it is the matrix A concatenated horizontally with the matrix obtained from M_{n-1} by placing one row of all `false` values on top of it.

The four matrices are shown in Figure 15.53.

15.10   **a.**   The digraph is shown in Figure 15.54.

   b.   Yes, this is a digraph: It has at least one one-way edge.

   c.   No, the digraph is not strongly connected: There is no path from C to D.

   d.   Yes, the digraph is weakly connected: Its embedded (undirected) graph is connected.

   e.   No, the digraph is not acyclic: It contains the cycle AFEDA.

   f.   Its adjacency matrix is shown in Figure 15.55 on page 315.

15.11   **a.**   The digraph G_1 is shown in Figure 15.56 on page 315.

   b.   Yes it is a digraph: Its adjacency matrix is not symmetric.

   c.   No, this is not a simple digraph because it has a loop.

   d.   Yes, this digraph is strongly connected.

   e.   Yes, this digraph is weakly connected.

   f.   No, the digraph is not acyclic: It contains the cycle ADB.

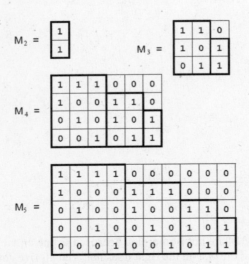

Figure 15.53 Incidence matrices

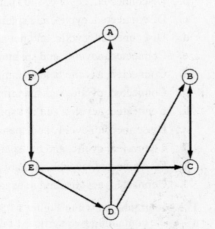

Figure 15.54 Digraph

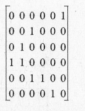

Figure 15.55 Incidence matrix

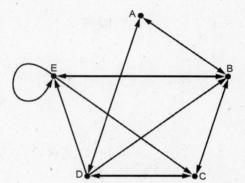

Figure 15.56 Digraph

15.12 **a.** The adjacency matrix is shown in Figure 15.57.
b. The adjacency list is shown in Figure 15.57.
c. The graph is not connected because there is no path from B to A.
d. The graph is not acyclic because it contains the cycle BECDB.

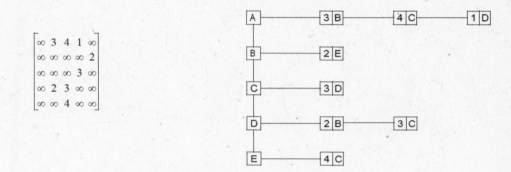

Figure 15.57 Adjacency matrix and adjacency list

15.13 **a.** The adjacency matrix for a wheel graph looks like matrix A shown in Figure 15.58 on page 316.
b. The incidence matrix for a wheel graph looks like matrix B shown in Figure 15.58 (for the case $n = 4$). In general, it will have n 1s followed by n 0s on the first row. Below that will lie the identity matrix (all 1s on the diagonal and 0s elsewhere) followed by the square matrix with 1s on the diagonal and the subdiagonal. Compare this with the recursive solution to Problem 15.9 on page 308.
c. The adjacency list for a wheel graph looks like the list shown in Figure 15.58 on page 316. The edge list for the first vertex (the central vertex) has n edge nodes, one for every other vertex. Every other edge list has three edge nodes: one pointing to the central vertex (labeled a in Figure 15.58) and one to each of its neighbors.

15.14 **a.** The two graphs are isomorphic. The bijection is defined by the vertex labels shown in Figure 15.59 on page 316.
b. An euler cycle for G_2 is ABCDEBFCADFEA.
c. A hamiltonian cycle for G_2 is ABCDFEA.

15.15 The trace of Dijkstra's algorithm is shown in Figure 15.60 on page 316.

15.16 The trace of Dijkstra's algorithm is shown in Figure 15.61 on page 316.

15.17 **a.** If the depth-first search is applied to a tree, it does a preorder traversal.
b. If the breadth-first search is applied to a tree, it does a level-order traversal.

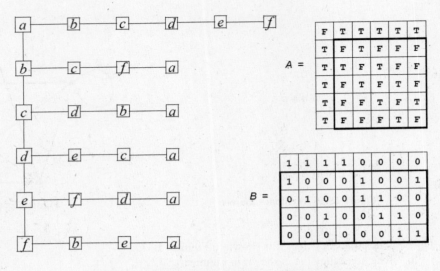

Figure 15.58 Adjacency matrix and adjacency list

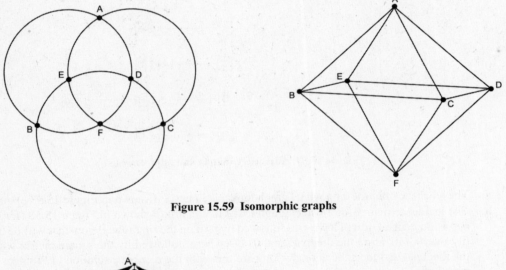

Figure 15.59 Isomorphic graphs

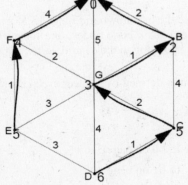

Figure 15.60 Dijkstra's algorithm

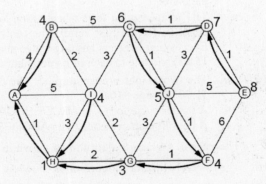

Figure 15.61 Dijkstra's algorithm

15.18 The seven graphs are labeled in Figure 15.62. Among them:

G_1 is isomorphic to G_2 : The isomorphism is shown by the vertex labels *a–j*.

G_3 is isomorphic to G_4 : The isomorphism is shown by the vertex labels *p–y*.

G_6 cannot be isomorphic to any of the other graphs because it has 25 edges and all the others have 20.

G_3 (and thus also G_4) cannot be isomorphic to any of the other graphs because it has a pyramid of four adjacent 3-cycles (*pqr*, *prs*, *pst*, and *ptq*) and none of the other graphs (except G_6) does.

G_6 cannot be isomorphic to any of the other graphs because it has a chain of three adjacent 4-cycles (*ABCD*, *CEFG*, and *FHIJ*) and none of the other graphs (except G_6) does.

Similarly, G_7 cannot be isomorphic to any of the other graphs because it has a chain of four adjacent 3-cycles (*PQS*, *QSR*, *SRT*, and *RTU*) and none of the other graphs (except G_6) does.

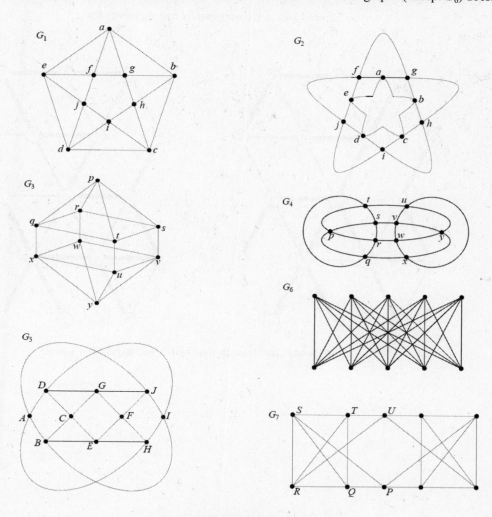

Figure 15.62 Graph isomorphisms

15.19 The adjacency matrix and the adjacency list are shown in Figure 15.63 on page 318.

15.20 **a.** The breadth-first search visits ABDECHFIGKLJMONPQ; its spanning tree is shown on the left in Figure 15.64 on page 318.

b. The depth-first search visits ABCFEIHDKLMJGNPQO; its spanning tree is shown on the right in Figure 15.64 on page 318.

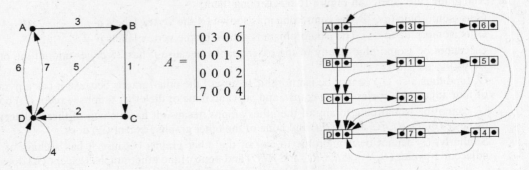

Figure 15.63 Adjacency matrix and adjacency list

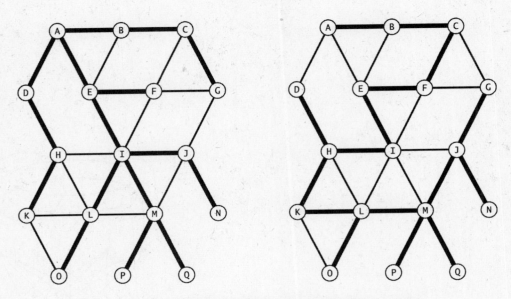

Figure 15.64 Breadth-first search and depth-first search

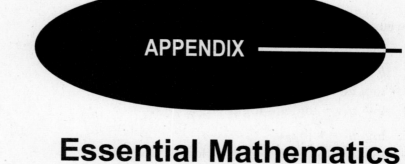

APPENDIX

Essential Mathematics

This appendix summarizes mathematical topics used in the study of data structures.

THE FLOOR AND CEILING FUNCTIONS

The floor and ceiling functions return the two nearest integers of a given real number. The *floor* of x, denoted by $\lfloor x \rfloor$, is the greatest integer that is not greater than x. The *ceiling* of x, denoted by $\lceil x \rceil$, is the smallest integer that is not smaller than x.

Here are the main properties of these two functions. (The symbol $\mathbb{Z}$ stands for the set of all integers.)

Theorem A.1 Properties of the Floor and Ceiling Functions

1. $\lfloor x \rfloor = \max\{m \in \mathbb{Z} \mid m \le x\}$, and $\lceil x \rceil = \min\{n \in \mathbb{Z} \mid n \ge x\}$.
2. $\lfloor x \rfloor \le x < \lfloor x \rfloor + 1$, and $\lceil x \rceil - 1 < x \le \lceil x \rceil$.
3. $x - 1 < \lfloor x \rfloor \le x \le \lceil x \rceil < x + 1$.
4. If $n \in \mathbb{Z}$ and $n \le x < n + 1$, then $n = \lfloor x \rfloor$. If $n \in \mathbb{Z}$ and $n - 1 < x < n$, then $n = \lceil x \rceil$.
5. If $x \in \mathbb{Z}$, then $\lfloor x \rfloor = x = \lceil x \rceil$.
6. If $x \notin \mathbb{Z}$, then $\lfloor x \rfloor < x < \lceil x \rceil$.
7. $\lfloor x \rfloor = -\lceil -x \rceil$ and $\lceil -x \rceil = -\lfloor x \rfloor$.
8. $\lfloor x + 1 \rfloor = \lfloor x \rfloor + 1$ and $\lceil x + 1 \rceil = \lceil x \rceil + 1$.

LOGARITHMS

The *logarithm with base b* of a positive number x is the exponent y on b for which $b^y = x$. For example, the logarithm of 1000 base 10 is 3 because $10^3 = 1000$. This is written $\log_{10} 1000 = 3$.

The logarithm with base 2 is called the *binary logarithm* and is written $\lg x = \log_2 x$. For example, $\lg 8 = 3$.

As a mathematical function, the logarithm is the inverse of the exponential function with the same base:

$$y = \log_b x \iff b^y = x$$

For example, $3 = \lg 8$ because $2^3 = 8$.

Theorem A.2 Laws of Logarithms

1. $\log_b(b^y) = y$
2. $b^{\log_b x} = x$
3. $\log_b uv = \log_b u + \log_b v$
4. $\log_b u/v = \log_b u - \log_b v$
5. $\log_b u^v = v \log_b u$
6. $\log_b x = (\log_c x)/(\log_c b) = (\log_b c)(\log_c x)$
7. For a positive integer n, $\lceil \lg(n+1) \rceil = \lfloor \lg n \rfloor + 1$.

EXAMPLE A.1 Applying the Laws of Logarithms

$\log_2 256 = \log_2(2^8) = 8$

$\log_2 1000 = (\log_{10} 1000)/(\log_{10} 2) = 3/0.30103 = 9.966$

$\log_2 1{,}000{,}000{,}000{,}000 = \log_2 1000^4 = 4(\log_2 1000) = 4(9.966) = 39.86$

$(\ln n)/(\lg n) = (\log_e n)/(\log_2 n) = \log_e 2 = \ln 2 = 0.693147$, for any $n > 1$

ASYMPTOTIC COMPLEXITY CLASSES

In computer science, algorithms are classified by their complexity functions. These are functions that describe an algorithm's running time relative to the size of the problem. For example, the Bubble Sort belongs to the complexity class $\Theta(n^2)$. This means that if the Bubble Sort takes T milliseconds to sort an array of n elements, then it will take about $4T$ milliseconds to sort an array of $2n$ elements because $(2n)^2 = 4n^2$.

The symbol $\Theta()$ is one of five symbols used to describe complexity functions. They all can be defined in terms of the ratios of $f(n)$ and $g(n)$, where $f(n)$ is the algorithm's timing function and $g(n)$ is a characterizing function such as $\lg n$ or n^2. For a given function $g(n)$, the five asymptotic complexity classes are

$O(g(n)) = \{ f(n) \in S \mid f(n)/g(n)$ is bounded $\}$

$\Omega(g(n)) = \{ f(n) \in S \mid g(n)/f(n)$ is bounded $\}$

$\Theta(g(n)) = \{ f(n) \in S \mid f(n)/g(n)$ is bounded and $g(n)/f(n)$ is bounded $\}$

$o(g(n)) = \{ f(n) \in S \mid f(n)/g(n) \to 0$ as $n \to \infty \}$

$\omega(g(n)) = \{ f(n) \in S \mid g(n)/f(n) \to 0$ as $n \to \infty \}$

These definitions assume that $f(n)$ and $g(n)$ that are positive ascending functions.

As sets of functions,

$o(g) \subseteq O(g)$

$\omega(g) \subseteq \Omega(g)$

$\Theta(g) = O(g) \cap \Omega(g)$

EXAMPLE A.2 Asymptotic Growth Classes

For every $k > 0$, $n^k = o(2^n)$, because $n^k/2^n \to 0$.

For every $k > 0$, $(\lg n)^k = o(n)$, because $(\lg n)^k/n \to 0$.

For every base $b > 1$, $\log_b n = \Theta(\lg n)$, because $\log_b n/\lg n = \log_b 2$.

The factorial numbers $n! = \omega(2^n)$, because $2^n/n! \to 0$.

The five complexity classes can be imprecisely described by these phrases:

$f(n) = o(g(n))$ means that $f(n)$ grows more slowly than $g(n)$.
$f(n) = O(g(n))$ means that $f(n)$ grows more slowly or at the same rate as $g(n)$.
$f(n) = \Theta(g(n))$ means that $f(n)$ grows at the same rate $g(n)$.
$f(n) = \Omega(g(n))$ means that $f(n)$ grows faster or at the same rate as $g(n)$.
$f(n) = \omega(g(n))$ means that $f(n)$ grows faster than $g(n)$.

EXAMPLE A.3 Asymptotic Growth Classes

$250 \lg n = o(n)$, because $250 \lg n$ grows more slowly than n.
$0.086\, n \lg n = \omega(n)$, because $0.086\, n \lg n$ grows faster than n.

Keep in mind that these functions $f(n)$, $g(n)$, and so on, are usually used to describe how long it takes to run an algorithm. So if $f(n)$ grows "more slowly" than $g(n)$, then the algorithm with complexity $f(n)$ is generally faster than the algorithm with complexity $g(n)$. Less time is better.

THE FIRST PRINCIPLE OF MATHEMATICAL INDUCTION

The First Principle of Mathematical Induction, also called "weak induction," is often used to prove formulas about positive integers.

Theorem A.3 The First Principle of Mathematical Induction

If $\{P_1, P_2, P_3, \dots\}$ is a sequence of statements such that:
- P_1 is true.
- Each statement P_n can be deduced from its predecessor P_{n-1}.

Then all of the statements $P_1, P_2, P_3, \dots$ are true.

EXAMPLE A.4 Weak Induction

Suppose we want to prove that the inequality $2^n \le (n+1)!$ is true for every $n \ge 1$. Then the sequence of statements is

P_1:　　$2^1 \le 2!$
P_2:　　$2^2 \le 3!$
P_3:　　$2^3 \le 4!$
etc.

The first few statements can be verified explicitly:

$2^1 = 2 \le 2 = 2!$
$2^2 = 4 \le 6 = 3!$
$2^3 = 8 \le 24 = 4!$

In particular, P_1 is true, satisfying the first of the two requirements for weak induction. This is called the *base of the induction*.

To verify the second requirement, we have to show that each statement P_n can be deduced from its predecessor P_{n-1}. So we examine the two general statements P_{n-1} and P_n, and look for a connection:

P_{n-1}:　　$2^{n-1} \le n!$
P_n:　　　$2^n \le (n+1)!$

To derive P_n from P_{n-1}, we note that $2^n = (2)(2^{n-1})$ and $(n+1)! = (n+1)(n!)$. Thus, if we assume that P_{n-1} is true, then we have $2^n = (2)(2^{n-1}) \le (2)(n!) \le (n+1)(n!) = (n+1)!$, because $n+1 > 2$.

Verifying the second requirement of mathematical induction is called the *inductive step*.

THE SECOND PRINCIPLE OF MATHEMATICAL INDUCTION

The Second Principle of Mathematical Induction, also called "strong induction," is nearly the same as the first principle. The only difference is in the inductive step.

Theorem A.4 The Second Principle of Mathematical Induction

If $\{P_1, P_2, P_3, \dots\}$ is a sequence of statements such that:
- P_1 is true.
- Each statement P_n can be deduced from its predecessors $\{P_1, P_2, P_3, \dots, P_{n-1}\}$.

Then all of the statements $P_1, P_2, P_3, \dots$ are true.

So to verify the inductive step with strong induction, we may assume that all $n-1$ statements $P_1, P_2, P_3, \dots, P_{n-1}$ are true.

EXAMPLE A.5 Strong Induction

Prove that the Fibonacci numbers 0, 1, 1, 2, 3, 5, 8, 13, 21, . . . are asymptotically exponential. More precisely, we prove that $F_n = O(2^n)$, where the Fibonacci numbers F_n are defined as $F_0 = 0$, $F_1 = 1$, and $F_n = F_{n-1} + F_{n-2}$. So our sequence of statements is

$$P_1: \qquad F_1 \le 2^1$$
$$P_2: \qquad F_2 \le 2^2$$
$$P_3: \qquad F_3 \le 2^3$$
etc.

These first few are true because of the following relationships:

$$P_1: \qquad F_1 = 1 \le 2$$
$$P_2: \qquad F_2 = 2 \le 4$$
$$P_3: \qquad F_3 = 3 \le 8$$

For the inductive step, we assume that $n-1$ statements $P_1, P_2, P_3, \dots, P_{n-1}$ are true and compare them with the nth statement P_n:

$$P_1: \qquad F_1 \le 2^1$$
$$P_2: \qquad F_2 \le 2^2$$
$$P_3: \qquad F_3 \le 2^3$$
$$\vdots \qquad \vdots$$
$$P_{n-2}: \qquad F_{n-2} \le 2^{n-2}$$
$$P_{n-1}: \qquad F_{n-1} \le 2^{n-1}$$
$$P_n: \qquad F_n \le 2^n$$

Comparing the nth statement with the two that precede it, we see that

$$F_n = F_{n-1} + F_{n-2}$$
$$2^n = (2)(2^{n-1}) = 2^{n-1} + 2^{n-1} > 2^{n-1} + 2^{n-2}$$

So we can derive P_n from P_{n-1} and P_{n-2} like this:

$$F_n = F_{n-1} + F_{n-2} \le 2^{n-1} + 2^{n-2} < 2^n$$

This proves that all the statements are true (i.e., $F_n \le 2^n$ for all n).

GEOMETRIC SERIES

A *series* is a sequence of possibly infinitely many terms whose sum is to be determined. A *geometric series* is a series in which each term is the same multiple of its predecessor. For example, $20 + 60 + 180 + 540 + 1620 + 4860 + \cdots$ is a geometric series because each term is 3 times the size of its predecessor. The multiplier 3 is called the *common ratio* of the series.

Theorem A.5 Sum of a Finite Geometric Series

If $r \neq 1$, then

$$a + ar + ar^2 + ar^3 + \cdots + ar^{n-1} = \frac{a(1 - r^n)}{1 - r}$$

Here, a is the first term in the series, r is the common ratio, and n is the number of terms in the series.

EXAMPLE A.6 Finite Geometric Series

For the sum $20 + 60 + 180 + 540 + 1620 + 4860$, the three parameters are $a = 20$, $r = 3$, and $n = 6$. So the sum is

$$\frac{a(1 - r^n)}{1 - r} = \frac{20(1 - 3^6)}{1 - 3} = \frac{20(1 - 729)}{-2} = \frac{20(-729)}{-2} = 7280$$

Theorem A.6 Sum of an Infinite Geometric Series

If $-1 < r < 1$, then

$$a + ar + ar^2 + ar^3 + \cdots = \frac{a}{1 - r}$$

EXAMPLE A.7 Infinite Geometric Series

For the sum $0.42 + 0.0042 + 0.000042 + 0.00000042 + 0.0000000042 + \cdots$, the three parameters are $a = 0.42$ and $r = 0.01$. So the infinite sum is

$$\frac{a}{1 - r} = \frac{0.42}{1 - 0.01} = \frac{0.42}{0.99} = \frac{42}{99} = \frac{14}{33}$$

Note that $14/33 = 0.4242424242 \cdots$. This repeating decimal is obviously the same as the infinite sum $0.42 + 0.0042 + 0.000042 + 0.00000042 + 0.0000000042 + \cdots$.

OTHER SUMMATION FORMULAS

Theorem A.7 Sum of the First n Positive Integers

$$1 + 2 + 3 + \cdots + n = \frac{n(n + 1)}{2}$$

Note that the parameter n equals the number of terms in the sum.

EXAMPLE A.8 Summing Positive Integers

The sum of the first 10 integers is $1 + 2 + 3 + 4 + 5 + 6 + 7 + 8 + 9 + 10 = 10(10+1)/2 = 55$.

Theorem A.8 Sum of the First n Squares

$$1^2 + 2^2 + 3^2 + \cdots + n^2 = \frac{n(n+1)(2n+1)}{6}$$

The expression on the right appears to be a fraction. But it will always turn out to be an integer because it equals a sum of integers.

EXAMPLE A.9 Summing Squares

The sum of the first six squares is $1^2 + 2^2 + 3^2 + 4^2 + 5^2 + 6^2 = 6(7)(13)/6 = 546/6 = 91$.

HARMONIC NUMBERS

The *harmonic series* is the series of reciprocals:

$$\sum_{k=1}^{\infty} \frac{1}{k} = 1 + \frac{1}{2} + \frac{1}{3} + \frac{1}{4} + \frac{1}{5} + \cdots$$

It is not hard to see that this series diverges. That is, its partial sums increase without bound.

The partial sums of the harmonic series are called the *harmonic numbers* and are denoted by H_n:

$$H_n = \sum_{k=1}^{n} \frac{1}{k} = 1 + \frac{1}{2} + \frac{1}{3} + \frac{1}{4} + \frac{1}{5} + \cdots + \frac{1}{n}$$

The first three harmonic numbers are

n	H_n
1	1.000000
2	1.500000
3	1.833333
4	2.083333
5	2.283333
6	2.450000
7	2.592857
8	2.717857
9	2.828968
10	2.928968

Table A.1 Harmonic numbers

$$H_1 = \sum_{k=1}^{1} \frac{1}{k} = 1$$

$$H_2 = \sum_{k=1}^{2} \frac{1}{k} = 1 + \frac{1}{2} = \frac{3}{2}$$

$$H_3 = \sum_{k=1}^{3} \frac{1}{k} = 1 + \frac{1}{2} + \frac{1}{3} = \frac{5}{6}$$

Although the harmonic numbers increase without bound, it is not obvious how fast they increase. Table A.1 suggests that they increase very slowly.

The fact is that the harmonic numbers increase logarithmically: $H_n = \Theta(\lg n)$. This means that they increase at about the same rate as logarithmic numbers. More precisely, it means that both ratios $H_n / \lg n$ and $\lg n / H_n$ are bounded.

STIRLING'S FORMULA

The *factorial numbers* frequently appear in the analysis of algorithms. They are defined by:

$$n! = \prod_{k=1}^{n} k = (1)(2)(3)(4) \cdots (n)$$

The first ten factorials are shown in Table A.2.

n	$n!$
0	1
1	1
2	2
3	6
4	24
5	120
6	720
7	5040
8	40,320
9	362,880

Table A.2 Factorial numbers

Unlike the harmonic sequence, the factorial sequence grows exponentially. This is reflected by *Stirling's formula*:

$$n! = \sqrt{2n\pi}\left(\frac{n}{e}\right)^n e^{\theta/12n}, \text{ where } 0 < \theta < 1$$

The value of the variable θ depends upon n, but in any case it is bounded between 0 and 1. Thus, for large n, the exponent $\theta/12n$ will be very close to 0, making the factor $e^{\theta/12n}$ very close to 1. Consequently, Stirling's formula is often expressed in this simpler approximate form:

$$n! \approx \sqrt{2n\pi}\left(\frac{n}{e}\right)^n$$

The factorial numbers grow exponentially: $n! = \Omega(2^n)$. This fact follows from Stirling's formula.

Another important consequence of Stirling's formula is that $\lg(n!)$ is asymptotically equivalent to $n\lg n$: $\lg(n!) = \Theta(n\lg n)$.

FIBONACCI NUMBERS

The *Fibonacci numbers* also frequently appear in the analysis of algorithms. They are defined by:

$$F_n = \begin{cases} 0, \text{ if } n = 0 \\ 1, \text{ if } n = 1 \\ F_{n-1} + F_{n-2}, \text{ if } n > 1 \end{cases}$$

The first 13 Fibonacci numbers are shown in Table A.3.

Like the factorial sequence, the Fibonacci sequence grows exponentially, as is verified by *De Moivre's formula*:

$$F_n = \frac{\phi^n - \psi^n}{\sqrt{5}}, \text{ where } \phi = \frac{1+\sqrt{5}}{2}, \text{ and } \psi = \frac{1-\sqrt{5}}{2}$$

Thus, $F_n = \Theta(\phi^n)$. Here, $\phi = 1.618034$ and $\psi = -0.618034$. These two constants are the *golden mean* and its *conjugate*.

n	F_n
0	0
1	1
2	1
3	2
4	3
5	5
6	8
7	13
8	21
9	34
10	55
11	89
12	144

Table A.3 Fibonacci numbers

Review Questions

A.1 A function $f()$ is called *idempotent* if $f(f(x)) = f(x)$ for all x in the domain of $f()$. Explain why the floor and ceiling functions are idempotent.

A.2 What is a logarithm?

A.3 What is the difference between weak induction and strong induction?

A.4 How can you decide when to use strong induction?

A.5 What is Euler's constant?

A.6 What makes Stirling's formula useful?

Problems

A.1   Prove Theorem A.1 on page 319.

A.2   Prove Theorem A.2 on page 320.

A.3   True or false:
  a. $f = o(g) \Leftrightarrow g = \omega(f)$
  b. $f = O(g) \Leftrightarrow g = \Omega(f)$
  c. $f = \Theta(g) \Leftrightarrow g = \Theta(f)$
  d. $f = O(g) \Rightarrow f = \Theta(g)$
  e. $f = \Theta(g) \Rightarrow f = \Omega(g)$
  f. $f = \Theta(h) \wedge g = \Theta(h) \Rightarrow f + g = \Theta(h)$
  g. $f = \Theta(h) \wedge g = \Theta(h) \Rightarrow fg = \Theta(h)$
  h. $n^2 = O(n \lg n)$
  i. $n^2 = \Theta(n \lg n)$
  j. $n^2 = \Omega(n \lg n)$
  k. $\lg n = \omega(n)$
  l. $\lg n = o(n)$

A.4   Prove Theorem A.5 on page 323.

A.5   Prove Theorem A.6 on page 323.

A.6   Prove Theorem A.7 on page 323.

A.7   Run a program that tests De Moivre's formula on page 325 by comparing the values obtained from it with those obtained from the recursive definition of the Fibonacci numbers.

Answers to Review Questions

A.1   The floor and ceiling functions are idempotent because they return integer values, and according to Theorem A.1 on page 319, the floor or ceiling of an integer is itself.

A.2   A *logarithm* is an exponent. It is the exponent on the given base that produces the given value.

A.3   The First Principle of Mathematical Induction ("weak" induction) allows the inductive hypothesis that assumes that the proposition $P(n)$ is true for some single value of n. The Second Principle of Mathematical Induction ("strong" induction) allows the inductive hypothesis that assumes that all the propositions $P(k)$ are true for all k less than or equal to some value of n.

A.4   Use weak induction (the first principle) when the proposition $P(n)$ can be directly related to its predecessor $P(n–1)$. Use strong induction (the second principle) when the proposition $P(n)$ depends upon $P(k)$ for $k < n–1$.

A.5   *Euler's constant* is the limit of the difference $(1 + 1/2 + 1/3 + \ldots + 1/n) - \ln n$. Its value is approximately 0.5772.

A.6   Stirling's formula is a useful method for approximating $n!$ for large n (e.g., $n > 20$).

Solutions to Problems

A.1   Proof of Theorem A.1 on page 319:
  a.   The relationships $\lfloor x \rfloor = \max\{m \in \mathbf{Z} \mid m \le x\}$, and $\lceil x \rceil = \min\{n \in \mathbf{Z} \mid n \ge x\}$ are merely restatements of the definitions of $\lfloor x \rfloor$ and $\lceil x \rceil$.

b. Let $m = \lfloor x \rfloor$ and $n = \lceil x \rceil$. Then by definition, $m \le x < m + 1$ and $n - 1 < x \le n$. Then $x - 1 < m$ and $n < x + 1$. Thus $x - 1 < m \le x \le n < x + 1$.

c. The inequalities $x - 1 < \lfloor x \rfloor \le x \le \lceil x \rceil < x + 1$ merely summarize those in **b** above.

d. Let $n \in \mathbf{Z}$ such that $n \le x < n + 1$, and let $A = \{m \in \mathbf{Z} \mid m \le x\}$. Then $n \in A$ and $\lfloor x \rfloor = \max A$, so $n \le \lfloor x \rfloor$. Now if $n < \lfloor x \rfloor$, then $n + 1 \le \lfloor x \rfloor$ (since both n and $\lfloor x \rfloor$ are integers). But $n + 1 \le \lfloor x \rfloor$, by hypothesis. Therefore, $n = \lfloor x \rfloor$. The proof of the second part is analogous.

e. Assume that $x \in \mathbf{Z}$ (i.e., x is an integer). Then let $n = x$ in **d** above: $x \le x < x + 1$ so $x = \lfloor x \rfloor$, and $x - 1 < x \le x$ so $x = \lceil x \rceil$.

f. Assume that $x \notin \mathbf{Z}$ (i.e., x is not an integer). Let $u = x - \lfloor x \rfloor$ and $v = \lceil x \rceil - x$. Then, by **c**, $u \ge 0$ and $v \ge 0$. Also by **c**, $x - 1 < \lfloor x \rfloor = x - u$ and $v + x = \lceil x \rceil < x + 1$, so $u < 1$ and $v < 1$. Thus $0 \le u < 1$ and $0 \le v < 1$. But u and v cannot be integers because if either were, then so would x because $x = \lfloor x \rfloor + u = \lceil x \rceil - v$. Therefore, $0 < u < 1$ and $0 < v < 1$, so $x = \lfloor x \rfloor + u > \lfloor x \rfloor$ and $x = \lceil x \rceil - v < \lceil x \rceil$.

g. Let $n = -\lfloor -x \rfloor$. Then $(-n) = \lfloor (-x) \rfloor$ so by **c**, $(-x) - 1 < (-n) \le (-x)$, so $x \le n < x + 1$, so $x \le n$ and $n - 1 < x$, so $n - 1 < x \le n$. Thus by **d**, $n = \lceil x \rceil$. Thus $-\lfloor -x \rfloor = \lceil x \rceil$, so $\lfloor -x \rfloor = -\lceil x \rceil$. The second identity follows from the first by replacing x with $-x$.

h. Let $n = \lfloor x + 1 \rfloor$. Then by **c**, $(x + 1) - 1 < n \le (x + 1)$, so $x - 1 < n - 1 \le x$ and $x = (x + 1) - 1 < n$. Thus, $n - 1 \le x < n$; that is, $(n - 1) \le x < (n - 1) + 1$. Thus by **d**, $(n - 1) = \lfloor -x \rfloor$, so $\lfloor x + 1 \rfloor = n = \lfloor x \rfloor + 1$. The proof of the second identity is similar.

A.2 Proof of Theorem A.2 on page 320:

a. Let $x = b^y$. Then by definition, $\log_b(b^y) = \log_b(x) = y$.

b. Let $y = \log_b x$. Then by definition, $b^{\log_b x} = b^y = x$.

c. Let $y = \log_b u$ and $z = \log_b v$. Then by definition, $u = b^y$ and $v = b^z$, so $uv = (b^y)(b^z) = b^{y+z}$, so $\log_b(uv) = y + z = \log_b u + \log_b v$.

d. By Law **c** above, $\log_b v + \log_b u/v = \log_b(v \, u/v) = \log_b u$, so $\log_b u/v = \log_b u + \log_b u$.

e. Let $y = \log_b u$. Then by definition, $u = b^y$, so $u^v = (b^y)^v = b^{vy}$. Then by definition, $\log_b(u^v) = vy = v \log_b u$.

f. Let $y = \log_b x$. Then by definition, $x = b^y$, so $\log_c x = \log_c(b^y) = y \log_c b$, by Law **e** above. Thus $\log_b x = y = (\log_c x)/(\log_c b)$.

A.3
a. True
b. True
c. True
d. False
e. True
f. True
g. False
h. False
i. False
j. True
k. False
l. True

A.4 Proof of Theorem A.5 on page 323:

Let $S = a + ar + ar^2 + ar^3 + \cdots + ar^{n-1}$. Then $rS = ar + ar^2 + ar^3 + ar^4 + \cdots + ar^n$, so $S - rS = a - ar^n$, $(1 - r)S = a(1 - r^n)$, and thus $S = a(1 - r^n)/(1 - r)$.

A.5 Proof of Theorem A.6 on page 323:

If $-1 < r < 1$, then as n increases without bound, r^n shrinks down to zero. Let $r^n = 0$ in the formula in Theorem A.5.

A.6 Proof of Theorem A.7 on page 323:

Let $S = 1 + 2 + 3 + \cdots + n$. Then $S = n + \cdots + 3 + 2 + 1$ also. Add these two equations, summing the $2n$ terms on the right pairwise: $(1 + n)$, $(2 + (n-1))$, etc. There are n pairs, and each pair has the same sum of $n + 1$. So the total sum on the right is $n(n + 1)$. Then, since the sum on the left is $2S$, the correct value of S must be $n(n + 1)/2$.

A.7   Program to test the De Moivre's formula for Fibonacci numbers:

```
public class Fibonacci {
  public static void main(String[] args) {
    final double SQRT5 = Math.sqrt(5.0);
    final double PHI = (1 + SQRT5)/2;
    final double PSI = (1 - SQRT5)/2;
    long f0, f1 = 0, f2 = 1;
    for (int n = 2; n < 32; n++)  {
      f0 = f1;
      f1 = f2;
      f2 = f1 + f0;
      double fn = (Math.pow(PHI, n) - Math.pow(PSI, n))/SQRT5;
      System.out.print("%4d%12.2", f2, fn);
    }
  }
}
```

INDEX